THE POLITICS OF BEI

THE POLITICS OF BEING

The Political Thought of Martin Heidegger

RICHARD WOLIN

Columbia University Press   *New York*

Columbia University Press
Publishers Since 1893
New York   Chichester, West Sussex
cup.columbia.edu

ISBN 978-0-231-17932-4 (cloth : alk. paper)—ISBN 978-0-231-17933-1
(pbk. : alk. paper)—ISBN 978-0-231-54302-6 (e-book)
Library of Congress Control Number: 2016933812

Columbia University Press books are printed on permanent and durable
acid-free paper.

Printed in the United States of America
c 10 9 8 7 6 5 4 3 2 1
p 10 9 8 7 6 5 4 3 2 1

Cover designer: Rebecca Lown
Cover image: Giorgio de Chirico, the Great Metaphysician: 1917. Oil on
canvas, Philip L. Goodwin Collection.

For Melissa

Ma femme à la chevelure de feu de bois
Aux pensées d'éclairs de chaleur
Ma femme aux épaules de champagne
Ma femme aux yeux de savane

André Breton, "L'Union Libre"

CONTENTS

Contents

It is possible that a Philosopher might be guilty of a compromise with political authority in an apparently inconsequential manner; he himself might be aware of this. But what he might not be aware of is the possibility that this apparent compromise with authority is grounded in the deepest deficiency . . . of his own doctrine. If therefore a philosopher should "conform" [with authority], his disciples will have to explain in an internal and essential fashion what he himself was aware of in a merely external way.

Karl Marx, *Contribution to a Critique of Hegel's* Philosophy of Right

PREFACE TO THE 2016 EDITION

The Politics of Epistemology: Heidegger's Black Notebooks in Real Time

> The National Socialist Revolution is bringing about the total transformation of our German Dasein. . . . The choice that the German people must now make is . . . the strongest expression of the new German reality embodied in the National Socialist State. Our will to national [*völkisch*] self-responsibility desires that each people find and preserve the greatness and truth of its destiny [*Bestimmung*] . . . Let not propositions and "ideas" be the rules of your Being [*Sein*]. The Führer is the future German Reality and its law. Heil Hitler!
> —Martin Heidegger, *Freibürger Studentenzeitung*, November 3, 1933

> The rebirth of philosophy and its future will not come to pass at anytime or anyplace through the efforts of World Reason [*Weltvernunft*]; it will only be realized through a *Volk*: as we believe, through the Germans.
> —Martin Heidegger, *The Fundamental Concepts of Metaphysics*

I

The spring 2014 publication of Martin Heidegger's *Black Notebooks* confirms many of the fundamental arguments and claims I set forth during the 1990s in the first edition of *The Politics of Being* and subsequent works.[1] To my great satisfaction, upon its initial publication some twenty-five years ago, *The Politics of Being* was rapidly translated into five languages (French, German, Portuguese, Chinese, and Japanese) and has continued to serve as a touchstone for the recurrent debates about the fraught connection between politics and philosophy in Heidegger's work.[2]

My argument was and remains the following: from its earliest beginnings, Heidegger's thought was *"always already" ideological*—which, by the same token, does not mean or imply that "ideology is all there was and is." (I will return to this point shortly.) Thus from Heidegger's very first lecture courses at the University of Freiburg as well as his earliest publications (e.g., the articles he published in his early twenties for the Catholic journal *Der Akademiker*), Heidegger was an impassioned advocate of the values of German "particularism." (However, this aspect of his work, which is striking and undeniable in the original German, has been intentionally neutralized or extruded in many English translations of his work.)

When all is said and done, there is nothing especially shocking or revolutionary about this claim. It is well known that Heidegger set great store by considerations of temporality (*Zeitlichkeit*) and historicity (*Geschichtlichkeit*). In fact, one of his central ripostes to the tradition of Western metaphysics was that its main currents had banished temporality from consideration. Nor did Heidegger ever try to conceal the fact that, during the early 1920s, the temporal or "ontic" spur to his own philosophizing had been the experiences of his "Generation"—colloquially known as the "War Youth Generation" (*Kriegsjugendgeneration*)—an age cohort whose worldview had been permanently forged amid the combat experience of World War I.[3] The War Youth Generation with which Heidegger identified so profoundly venerated the so-called "ideas of 1914" and vaunted the values of German particularism.[4] Of course, Hitler was also a member of this generation, and in the *Black Notebooks* and elsewhere, Heidegger exalted the fact that the German Führer and he were born in the same year, 1889.[5] So greatly did Heidegger esteem the existential value of the concept of "Generation" that he would accord it a prominent role in his *Meisterstück* of 1927, *Being and Time*.[6]

Consequently, henceforth, any fair-minded evaluation of Heidegger's work and legacy must take into account both questions of "first philosophy" as well as considerations of *Weltanschauung* (worldview).[7] Heidegger's intellectual testament is not a case of "either/or" but one of "both/and": legitimate philosophical themes as well as markedly ideological elements both come into play. Needless to say, the interpretive challenge involved in attempting to sort out these two facets of Heidegger's voluminous and demanding oeuvre (his *Collected Works* is projected to run to 102 volumes upon completion) is immense—unmasterable, perhaps, in view of the ways that these two dimensions of his thought are so profoundly and inextricably interwoven.

Certainly, by trying to mask his early cultural and political allegiances—he staunchly opposed all attempts to interpret his work biographically—Heidegger compounded the difficulties for researchers seeking to discern the qualities or nuances of his thought that bear affinities with what Karl Marx once labeled the "German ideology." Critical scholarship has been further hampered by the fact that Heidegger rejected the idea of a "critical edition" of his work, that is, an annotated edition that would have made clear the genesis of his manuscripts as well as, crucially, their textual variations. Instead, Heidegger stubbornly insisted on an edition *aus letzter Hand*, meaning that his texts should be published as found in his estate at the time of his death, without an accompanying editorial apparatus.[8] Consequently, it has become extremely difficult for well-meaning scholars to ascertain the textual history of Heidegger's manuscripts. As recent research has shown, Heidegger frequently returned to earlier texts to revise them; moreover, in many cases, he actively sought to conceal the later alterations and emendations—a practice that poses insuperable obstacles for the task of reconstructing his *Denkweg*, or path of thought.[9] In the *Black Notebooks*, for example, one regularly encounters passages that "signpost" or anticipate later entries, a practice that raises the question: how often did Heidegger return to these texts to edit or revise earlier entries or passages?[10]

In March 2015, the publisher of Heidegger's *Gesamtausgabe*, Vittorio Klostermann, went so far as to issue a desperate plea to the editors of earlier volumes to come forward with information about passages that have been omitted.[11] The occasion for Klostermann's bizarre request was the admission that an unseemly, anti-Semitic passage from Heidegger's 1938 lecture course, *History of Being (Geschichte des Seins)*, alleging world Jewry's "planetary criminality" (*planetarische Verbrechertum*), had been mysteriously excised.[12]

According to Peter Trawny, the editor of the volume and director of the Heidegger Institute at the University of Wuppertal, the passage was removed at the suggestion of Friedrich-Wilhelm von Herrmann, a Heidegger student and longtime editor of the philosopher's literary estate. This avowal raises questions concerning what, if any, other compromising or unsightly passages have been omitted from the *Gesamtausgabe*. Here, there are few grounds for optimism or confidence—especially considering that, in another lecture course from the 1930s, *Hölderlins Hymne Germanien und der Rhein*, Heidegger's employment of a standard abbreviation for "National Socialism," "N. Soz.," was disingenuously and misleadingly (and somewhat laughably) transcribed as "natural science"![13]

II

The *Black Notebooks'* publication has been a headline-grabbing event that has preoccupied the feuilleton sections of major European dailies for nearly two years. As such, it offers an unparalleled opportunity for a forthright reckoning with the ideological deformations of Heidegger's thought.[14]

By "ideological deformations" I mean the philosopher's hypertrophic allegiance to central aspects of the German intellectual *Sonderweg*, or "special path." The German *Sonderweg* developed in the aftermath of the French victory under Napoleon at the battle of Jena (1806), which put an end to the (largely mythological) Holy Roman Empire of the German Nation and gave rise to the so-called Stein-Hardenberg Reforms and the German Confederation (1815). *Sonderweg* ideology entailed a visceral hostility to the "ideas of 1789"—liberalism, individualism, constitutionalism, and *droits de l'homme*—and a correlative elevation of the values of German particularism: above all, an uncritical glorification of the Volk idea as an approach to questions of national identity far superior to the lifeless platitudes and abstractions of Western "universalism."

Heidegger's loyalties and indebtedness to the *Sonderweg* ethos are apparent from his earliest writings. Already in *Being and Time*, Heidegger had linked the notions of "fate" (*Geschick*), "decisiveness" (*Entschlossenheit*), "struggle" (*Kampf*), and "destiny" (*Schicksal*)—all of which were keywords in the discourse of 1920s German radical conservatism—with the concept of "Generation."

On first view, Generation may seem an unlikely inclusion in a scholarly treatise on existential ontology. Nevertheless, Heidegger is adamant in his insistence on Generation's centrality for understanding the meaning of "authenticity" (*Eigentlichkeit*). As Heidegger declaims in paragraph 74 of *Being and Time*, "Our fates have already been guided in advance, in our Being with one another in the same world in our resoluteness for definite possibilities. Only in communication and struggle [*Kampf*] does the power of destiny [*das Geschick*] become free. *Dasein's fateful destiny in and with its 'Generation' goes to make up the full authentic historicizing of Dasein.*"[15]

In this quote, the "historical" or "factical" derivation of "Generation" is unambiguous: it serves to exalt ontologically the experiences of the War Youth Generation (*Kriegsjugendgeneration*) with which Heidegger identified so profoundly. The experiences of this "community of the trenches" (*Grabenschutzgemeinschaft*) would also become a touchstone for Germany's far-right literati during the 1920s.

The war youth generation was born between 1880 and 1900. Thus Heidegger's birth year, 1889, represents the mean. One can justifiably speak of the "generation of 1914" as a pan-European phenomenon. But in Germany, this concept entailed deep-seated anti-Western, illiberal ideological valences. Thus, as we have seen, the generation of 1914 embraced a standpoint that exalted the ends of German particularism and advocated markedly *völkisch* views.

So profoundly did Heidegger identify with the experiences of the War Youth Generation that, in 1933–34, he falsified a biographical submission to the *Deutsches Führer Lexicon*—in essence, a Nazi *Who's Who*—by claiming that, during the Great War, he had been posted at Verdun. This was the site of one of the war's deadliest battles: over a four-month stretch in 1916, German and French commanders had each sacrificed 200,000 men and, despite the immense human cost, had almost nothing to show for their losses. Heidegger thereby implied that he had seen action as a soldier on the front lines (*Frontkämpfer*).[16]

Unsurprisingly, Heidegger acolytes, who remain wedded to narrowly exegetical, text-immanent readings of Heidegger's work and who, consequently, seek to keep historical considerations at bay, prefer to ignore the well-nigh overwhelming evidence concerning the "historicity," or historical determinacy, of the Master's thought. Writing during the 1930s, the philosopher and Heidegger-intimate Karl Löwith seemed to provide the definitive answer to these questions by pointing out:

> Given [Heidegger's] significant attachment . . . to the climate and intellectual habitus of National Socialism, it would be inappropriate to criticize or exonerate his political decision in isolation from the very principles of Heidegger's philosophy itself. It is not Heidegger, who, in opting for Hitler, "misunderstood himself"; instead, those who cannot understand why he acted this way fail to understand him. A Swiss lecturer regretted that Heidegger consented to compromise himself with everyday life, as if a philosophy that explains Being from the standpoint of time

and the everyday would not stand in relation to daily affairs. The possibility of a Heideggerian political philosophy was not born as the result of a regrettable miscue, but from the very conception of *Existenz* that simultaneously combats and absorbs the *Zeitgeist*.[17]

III

The mentality of eliminationist anti-Semitism that suffuses the *Black Notebooks*, which has been the target of unsparing and widespread criticism, had also been anticipated by Heidegger's earliest writings.

In his very first lecture courses at the University of Freiburg, Heidegger already demonstrated a profound attraction to the discourse of *Vernunftkritik* (the "critique of reason"), an orientation that went hand in hand with the temptations of vitalism or *Lebensphilosophie*—a philosophical current with which Heidegger was also highly enamored. At the time, Heidegger announced that his goal as a philosopher was to gain access to "life in and for itself" or, as he termed it, "pre-social, living substance" (*"vorweltliche Lebens-etwas"*).[18] In *Toward a Definition of Philosophy* (1919), one finds a preliminary—yet, for this reason, no less extreme—adumbration of the variety of radical *Vernunftkritik* that would resurface in his later writings. As Heidegger asserts: "decomposition means *destruction*"; "all theoretical comportment [is] *devitalizing* [*Entlebendes*]"; "all attempts to objectify are *devitalizing*."[19]

The problem with *Vernunftkritik* as a paradigm or worldview is that it does not seek to mollify or redress reason's biases and excesses, however one might choose to define them. It is uninterested in providing a mere "course correction" for a Western civilization that, to its detriment, has become too enamored of the world-transformative potentials of instrumental reason. Instead, in the spirit of counterenlightenment, *Vernunftkritik* holds reason exclusively accountable for a vast and vexatious array of incurable social ills. Its tone, therefore, is often apocalyptic. When all is said and done, reason and intellection are perceived as antagonists of "life" (*Leben*) in its lived immediacy. As such, they are held responsible for a rash and inexorable process of civilizational decline. In the words of one of Heidegger's influential contemporaries:

Concepts kill Being and falsify Waking-Being. Long ago in the springtime of language history . . . this machination was without importance for life. But now, from a being that occasionally thought, man has become a thinking being, and it is the ideal of every thought system to subject life, once and for all to the domination of the intellect. This is achieved in theory by according validity only to the known and branding the actual [*Wirklichkeit*] as a sham and a delusion. It is achieved in practice by forcing the voices of the blood to be silent in the presence of universal ethical principles.

Abstract maxims of life are acceptable only as figures of speech: trite maxims of daily use underneath which . . . life [*Leben*] flows onward. *Race, in the end, is stronger than language.*[20]

Moreover, the proximity of *Lebensphilosophie* to anti-Semitism is an irrefutable Durkheimian social fact. Thus Jews were frequently caricatured as being hyper-intellectual social parvenus. Already in 1916, Heidegger vociferously lamented the excessive "Jewification [*Verjudung*] of our [German] culture and universities."[21] Here, his use of "*Verjudung*" leaves no doubt about his proximity to the standpoint of the German Extreme Right.

As I have already suggested, the interpretive key to deciphering the ideological valences of Heidegger's thought was furnished by the Master himself in *Being and Time*, especially in those passages where Heidegger develops the concept of historicity. Thus in *Being and Time*, Division II, Heidegger asserts that when Dasein exists authentically, with knowledge of its "fate" (*Geschick*) and in an essential relation with other Daseins, the path is cleared for a Volk to engage in "historicity" (*Geschichtlichkeit*)—Heidegger's euphemism for authentic historical existence.

Already in 1927, Heidegger viewed the German Volk as an authentic carrier and embodiment of historicity in ways that other nations were not. By the early 1920s, this conviction had become one of the central pillars of German "antidemocratic thought."[22] Going back to the early nineteenth century, the ideology of German particularism held that the German Volk possessed a distinct eschatological-historical mission—that is, a unique capacity to redeem humanity from the decadence-cum-barbarism of Western civilization.[23]

It is at this point that the link between the role that the Volk idea plays in *Being and Time* as a quintessential determinant of historicity and its reappearance as a central figure in the *Black Notebooks* emerges with undeniable clarity. As Heidegger proclaims, "The metaphysics of Dasein must deepen itself in a manner consistent with its inner structures and extend to the metapolitics 'of' the historical Volk."[24] And in a lecture course, from the same period, he redefines "philosophy" as "the constant questioning struggle [*Kampf*] concerning the essence and Being of beings. This questioning is itself historical, that is, it is the encouragement, struggle, and celebration of a Volk for the sake of the hardness and clarity of its destiny."[25]

During his rectorship (1933–34), Heidegger devoted a number of seminars and lecture courses to explicating the Volk idea. He viewed this task as essential, both for "fundamental ontology" (as he commonly referred to his philosophical project) as well as for Germany's political self-understanding during the tenuous initial months of the Nazi dictatorship, when so much was at stake.

The *Black Notebooks* reveal that, although Heidegger had a number of specific policy disagreements with the regime—foreseeably, his criticisms became more numerous after his rectorship foundered in 1934—he remained perennially loyal to what he described, in 1935, as "the inner truth and greatness" of National Socialism.[26]

In a lecture course "On the Essence of Truth," Heidegger asserts—astoundingly—that the search for truth is integrally related to "the fundamental possibilities of primeval Germanic tribalism [*des urgermanischen Stammeswesens*] for the sake of according these possibilities predominance [*Herrschaft*]."[27] The more one peruses Heidegger's lectures, seminars, and treatises from the 1930s, the more it is undeniable that, in the philosopher's own mind, the "question of Being" was inextricably tied to the themes pertaining to German destiny and German historicity. In Heidegger's view, the German Volk—its genocidal wartime depredations notwithstanding—represented the "saving power" (*das Rettende*) that, 150 years earlier, came to the fore in Friedrich Hölderlin's poetry. Thus, Heidegger remarks during the early 1940s, as the Battle of Stalingrad raged: "the planet is in flames, the earth is coming apart; but the saving power, if it is to be found, *will only come from the Germans*."[28] Similarly, one of the *Black Notebooks'* guiding threads is

Heidegger's myopic allegiance to the virtues of German "exceptionalism," expressed in a manner wholly consistent with his dogged insistence on the redemptory mission of *Germanentum* (Germanness).

By the same token, this steadfast *völkisch* enthusiasm rendered Heidegger oblivious to the transgressions and misdeeds that were inseparable from National Socialism's ruthless struggle for European hegemony. Hence, the perverse double standard with which he operates. Thus in the *Black Notebooks*, Heidegger observes that reports of Soviet atrocities have been especially gruesome. Conversely, when it comes to the transgressions of the *Wehrmacht* and the *Einsatzgruppen* (the mobile SS killing units that were responsible for the atrocities and mass shootings on the Eastern Front), he remains silent. Heidegger justifies Nazi Germany's brutal treatment of conquered Slavic lands, such as Serbia and Poland, claiming that, were France and England to triumph, they would do the same to Germany.

Equally alarming is the fact that Heidegger's understanding of European political culture and traditions rarely rises above the level of caricature and cliché. He suggests that, from the perspective of the "history of Being," a combined French and English triumph would be catastrophic, since it would retard Being's emergence as "Event" (*Ereignis*). In virtually the same breath, Heidegger expresses the fear that a victorious France would inflict its "ahistoricality" (*Geschichtslosigkeit*)—not to mention its inferior metaphysics!—on Germany. England would do the same, turning all that it touched into a "giant business concern" (*Riesengeschäft*).[29]

For all of these reasons, Heidegger viewed a German victory in the war as an historico-ontological imperative. Since Germany's geopolitical opponents—England, France, and the United States—were representatives of an ontologically inferior *Weltanschauung* (he explicates the nature of this inferiority on countless occasions and in numerous passages), at stake in a German triumph was the *Seinsfrage* or "question of Being" itself. In sum, a German triumph alone would make the world *safe for Being*. Only a German victory would ensure what Heidegger disturbingly refers to as the "transition toward reflection" (*Übergang zur Besinnung*).

However, in keeping with his antipathy to Idealism, Heidegger deprives "reflection" of its most valuable trait: the subject's capacity for self-consciousness and self-awareness, the capacity that facilitates the emergence of human consciousness from its blind integration with nature, and which thereby allows it to become self-determining or autonomous rather than remaining a plaything of fate. In the *Phenomenology of Spirit*, Hegel eloquently expresses this thought, remarking that, "With self-consciousness, we have therefore entered the native realm of truth. . . . Self-consciousness is the reflection out of the being of the world of sense and perception, and is essentially the return from otherness. . . . It is in self-consciousness, in the notion of spirit, that consciousness first finds its turning point, where it leaves behind it the colorful show of the sensuous here and now and the night like void of the supersensible beyond and steps out into the spiritual daylight of the present."[30]

Heidegger's ceaseless polemics against the Cartesian "I think" (and transcendental subjectivity more generally) are also part and parcel of a calculated ideological crusade against the Western ideals of selfhood.[31]

It is at this point that Heidegger's proximity to National Socialism risks metastasizing into an outright betrayal of philosophy. After all, since the days of Socrates, the capacity for "reflection"—that is, the ability of the mind to form so-called second-order concepts—is what differentiates philosophy from the entrapments of cultural conformity, from the blind allegiances of mere habit or convention. When viewed in this light, "reflection" (*Besinnung*) constitutes the very fundament of philosophy's capacity for refusal or negation. As such, it goes to the heart of philosophy's distinctive emancipatory function, which since Socrates's day has been integrally tied to its ability to oppose the reigning consensus in the name of considerations of principle—that is, in the name of norms of a higher order. When thought remains true to its innate capacities for critical vigilance, it stands as the inveterate foe of conventional morality and blind adaptation. Thus in the *Black Notebooks*, Heidegger expressly betrays philosophy's emancipatory raison d'être by associating "reflection" (*Besinnung*) with the trappings and characteristics of National Socialist domination (*Herrschaft*).

IV

In practically every instance, pulling the strings behind the scenes of world politics, Heidegger finds the ignominious practices of "world Jewry." In this way, he remains faithful to the precepts of eliminationist anti-Semitism that formed the core of the National Socialist worldview.

In this respect, Heidegger's discourse displays an obsessional quality that verges on paranoia. As he observes at one point, whereas "since time immemorial, the Jews, relying on their express talents for calculation, have 'lived' according to the principle of race, they now seek to defend themselves against that same principle's unrestricted application." Here, the "application" of race to which Heidegger refers is National Socialist racial legislation: above all, the 1935 Nuremburg laws that finalized the terms of German-Jewish de-emancipation.[32] Moreover, in this passage, Heidegger takes pains to place the word "live" in quotation marks, thereby indicating that the Jews as a people lack the capacity for "authentic historicity." This is yet another way of saying that they are devoid of ontological worth. Thus, in Heidegger's view, the Jews as a race—in stark contrast with the Germans—display an inauthentic mode of "temporality" (*Zeitlichkeit*). They lack a "destiny" (*Schicksal*) as well as the capacity for "authentic decision" (*Entschlossenheit*)—a point that, in the *Black Notebooks*, Heidegger returns to on several occasions. By the same token, in the social Darwinist universe that Heidegger inhabits, it goes without saying that peoples like the Jews who lack the capacity for authentic historicity (*Geschichtlichkeit*) have essentially forfeited their right to exist.

Heidegger repeatedly expresses the view that international Jewry is responsible for secretly orchestrating a world-historical process of deracination—the German word he uses is *Entrassung*—which abets and encourages the alienation of the world's peoples from their "rootedness-in-soil." The term that Heidegger employs to connote "existential rootedness" is *Bodenständigkeit*, an epithet that, in the *völkisch* tradition, possesses indelible and profound racial connotations and traits. *Bodenständigkeit* is linked to the *Blut und Boden* ideology of the *Kaiserreich* or Second Empire (commonly satirized by its opponents as *Blu-Bo*), but following the Great War, its tonality changed qualitatively, in keeping with German conservatism's rightward ideological shift. Hence in the 1920s many German conservatives became—in a phrase coined by radical conservative stalwart, Edgar Jung—"conservative revolutionaries." Having realized the wisdom of the Italian writer Giuseppi Lampedusa's insight that "for things to remain the same, everything must change," the German right began to pursue a

Flucht nach vorne; in other words, it went on the offensive. Henceforth, the discourse of radical anti-Semitism that had been somewhat of a fringe phenomenon gained momentum among a wide coterie of influential right-wing publicists and political figures.

The fear of diminishing *Bodenständigkeit* had been a recurrent leitmotif in Heidegger's work going back to the Weimar years, attaining prominence in his writings well in advance of the Nazi *Machtergreifung*. It surfaced prominently in Heidegger's 1925 Kassel lectures on the *Concept of Time*, a crucial way station in the development of his concept of historicity.[33] As Heidegger laments in an address he gave that same year, "Life today gravitates entirely toward the metropolis. The human beings that determine life there are uprooted human beings [entwurzelte Menschen]. The rootlessness [Bodenlosigkeit] of contemporary life is the ground of the advancing decay [Verfall]. All renewal and innovation would remain hopeless, if one does not again manage to restore the leading forces back from out of the native soil [aus heimatlichem Boden]."[34]

In a manner that is both uncanny and disturbing, at a certain point Heidegger's critique of "Cartesianism," or the "philosophy of the subject," and his denigration of "world Jewry" coalesce. As Heidegger declaims in "On the Essence of Truth": "Not only is this purported new beginning of modern philosophy with Descartes a sham; in truth, it is the beginning of a further decline [*Verfall*] of philosophy. Instead of bringing philosophy back to itself, that is, to its basis and roots [*Boden*], Descartes removes it even further from fundamental questioning."[35] The convergence between "first philosophy" and "worldview" occurs insofar as the discourse of the German ideology that Heidegger embraces typecasts Jews as the leading carriers of modernity. According to this perspective, what Descartes initiated epistemologically, the Jews put into practice sociologically and politically. Consequently, the momentous transition from *Gemeinschaft* to *Gesellschaft*—a persistent trope in turn-of-the-century Central European *Kulturkritik*—is simultaneously a story of the "triumph of Judaism over Germany."[36] According to the "politics of Being," the struggle against world Jewry's disintegrative sociohistorical influence goes hand in hand with the struggle against the "philosophy of the subject."

In the *Black Notebooks* the idea of *Bodenlosigkeit*, a lack of ontological rootedness, underlies Heidegger's racial castigation of world Jewry. Heidegger accuses the Jews of being "worldless"—an apparently innocuous charge, perhaps, until one delves into the philosophical particulars subtending this indictment. In the existential ontology of *Being and Time,* the capacity to "have a world" constitutes the crux of what it means to be human. In opposition to the traditional Western paradigm that understands man qua "animal rationale" or "thinking substance," Heidegger reconceives epistemology in terms of "Being-in-the-world" (*In-der-Welt-Sein*). This represents the essential difference between "fundamental ontology" and competing, "modern" attempts to resolve the riddles of *Erkenntnistheorie,* or theory of knowledge. Since in the existential analytic of *Being and Time* the capacity to have a world becomes an indispensable hallmark of authentic Selfhood, beings or peoples that are divested of this capacity suffer from a deep-seated and irremediable ontological deficiency. In essence, they are inhuman. As Heidegger explains: "Man is not simply regarded as part of the world within which he appears and which he makes up in part. Man also stands over against the world. This standing over against is a '*having*' of world as that in which man moves, with which he engages, which he both masters and serves, and to which he is exposed. Thus man is, first, a part of the world, and second, as this part, he is at once master and servant of the world."[37]

By describing world Jewry as "worldless," Heidegger makes a point of ascribing to Jews an ontological shortcoming that they share with inferior forms of organic and inorganic life: plants, stones, and animals. The upshot of this rather crude normative scheme in which the capacity to have a "world" plays a determinative role is that Jews as a people are devoid of a raison d'être. Insofar as they are "worldless," they are incapable of authenticity as well as historicity. In sum, they have no compelling ontological reason to be.

Heidegger would take this manner of ontological-historical discrimination a step further by distinguishing between "historical" and "unhistorical" peoples. It is in this vein that, in his 1934 lectures on *Logic as the Essence of Language* he observes that "negroes," like "nature," have no history.[38]

In Heidegger's view, world Jewry as a race stands for deracination (*Entrassung*) simpliciter. For this reason, the Jewish contribution to world history is essentially negative: as inveterate cultural interlopers devoid of "roots," Jews are corrosive elements that serve to accelerate a world historical process of civilizational decline (*Verfall, Untergang*). All of these rationales furnish justifications for world Jewry's annihilation (*Vernichtung*).[39]

Such pejorative characterizations of Jews harmonize with another one of Heidegger's standard, cliché-ridden inculpations of world Jewry: the allegation that Jews have somehow taken the lead in the degenerative process of *Machenschaft* ("machination").

In Heidegger's view, *Machenschaft* indicates Western civilization's obsessive preoccupation with the ends of technological world mastery. Heidegger contends that these developments threaten to reduce Being in its totality to mere stuff of domination or "standing reserve" (*der Bestand*). As Heidegger comments: "One of the stealthiest forms of Gigantism and perhaps the most ancient . . . [is] the fast-paced history of calculation, pushiness and intermixing whereby [world] Jewry's worldlessness is established."[40]

Thus in the *Black Notebooks* one of Heidegger's central arguments is that world Jewry is the prime mover behind the two most serious manifestations of European cultural dissolution: deracination (*Entrassung*) and machination (*Machenschaft*). In Heidegger's view, National Socialism, by virtue of its "inner truth and greatness,"[41] represented the only viable counterweight to this precipitous trajectory of decline. In all of these respects, Heidegger's hyperbolic anti-Judaism coincided with the "redemptive anti-Semitism" that constituted National Socialism's ideological core. As a worldview or belief system, "redemptive anti-Semitism" held that the intractable problems of political modernity would be magically resolved were one only to eliminate the Jews as a people.[42]

To attribute to Jews—who were, of course, mercilessly persecuted at the time—fantastic and mysterious powers, to maintain that they are, in truth, the "string-pullers" (*Drahtzieher*) who secretly controlled world politics behind the scenes, is the quintessence of anti-Semitism as a worldview or belief system. As the preceding examples make clear, Heidegger embraced this standpoint without reservation. Moreover, he contended that National Socialism's anti-Semitic measures and practices— measures and practices that, very shortly, would metamorphose into full-blown annihilation (*Vernichtung*)—were eminently justified. Given world Jewry's satanic preeminence, in Heidegger's view the persecution of the Jews amounted to a case of self-defense. In this respect, as we have seen, his perception of Jewish influence meshed seamlessly with the delusional Judeophobia characteristic of National Socialist race theory. When in 1936 Heidegger, inspired by Ernst Jünger's doctrine of "total mobilization," observes matter-of-factly that "It would be important to enquire into the basis of [world] Jewry's unique predisposition toward planetary criminality [*planetarisches Verbrechertum*]," he not only confirms this supposition but adds fuel to the flames.[43]

Heidegger's attribution of "planetary criminality" to world Jewry singles out the Jews' leading role, qua "carriers of modernity," in fomenting and abetting a process of advanced cultural disintegration. As Heidegger expresses this view in "Overcoming Metaphysics," it entails "the collapse of the world," "the devastation of the earth," and the "unconditional objectification of everything present."[44] As we have seen, to attribute fantastic powers and influence to Jews, in stark contrast with their real-world powerlessness, constitutes one of the classic tropes of the anti-Semitic mentality.[45]

One finds further evidence of Heidegger's delusional anti-Semitism—"delusional," insofar as a group that was totally deprived of political power was deemed to be omnipotent—in Karl Jaspers's *Philosophical Autobiography*. There, Jaspers recounts a conversation with Heidegger in which the topic of the Jewish Question arose. At one point, Jaspers belittled *The Protocols of the Elders of Zion* as anti-Semitic drivel. Heidegger adamantly disagreed, insisting that, "There really is a dangerous international alliance of Jews."[46]

With Heidegger's hypertrophic fears about world Jewry, deracination, and Western decline, the affinities between his philosophy and the German idiom of *völkisch* particularism emerge with compelling and undeniable clarity. Thus in its Heideggerian iteration, fundamental ontology is inexorably entwined with the discourse of the German *Sonderweg*.[47] Moreover, many of Heidegger's political observations and claims are the rhetorical equivalent of a declaration of war.

How far would Heidegger carry such professions of rhetorical violence? In the *Black Notebooks*, he glorifies "National Socialism [as] a barbaric principle. Therein," he continues, "lies its essence and its capacity for greatness." He argues that "the danger . . . is not [National Socialism] itself, but instead that it will be rendered innocuous via homilies about the True, the Good, and the Beautiful."[48]

In Heidegger's 1934 lecture course "On the Essence of Truth," we find another disturbing avowal.

Writing at a critical moment in the political evolution of the National Socialist behemoth, as Hitler sought to consolidate his grip on power, Heidegger proffers his own account of how to define the "enemy." He also pauses to reflect on the measures that must be taken to ensure that the threat the enemy poses for the *Volksgemeinschaft* is permanently and definitively eradicated:

> The enemy is one who poses an essential threat to the existence of the Volk and its members. The enemy is not necessarily the outside enemy, and the outside enemy is not necessarily the most dangerous. It may even appear that there is not an enemy at all. The root requirement is then to find the enemy, to bring him to light or even to create him, in order that there may be that standing up to the enemy, and that existence not become apathetic. The enemy may have grafted himself onto the innermost root of the existence of a Volk, and oppose the latter's ownmost essence, acting contrary to it. All the keener and harsher and more difficult is then the struggle, for only a very small part of the struggle consists in mutual blows; it is often much harder and more exhausting to seek out the enemy as such, and to lead him to reveal himself, to avoid nurturing illusions about him, to remain ready to attack, to cultivate and increase constant preparedness and to initiate the attack on a long-term basis, *with the goal of total extermination.*[49]

Needless to say, far from being an innocent gesture, to exalt the value of "total extermination" (*völlige Vernichtung*) in the context of the Nazi dictatorship—even though the latter was, technically speaking, still in its infancy—testifies to the uncompromising radicalism of Heidegger's National Socialist convictions. The *Black Notebooks* abound with additional evidence thereof.

Clearly, the "enemy" to whom Heidegger refers in this passage— as he meticulously explains, not necessarily the "outside enemy," but instead, a more dangerous and insidious one, insofar as he has "grafted himself onto the innermost root of the existence of a Volk"—is Germany's assimilated Jews. It is this internal or domestic enemy that, in Heidegger's view, poses a special risk since, as a foreign body, it threatens to contaminate the "ownmost essence" of the Volk and, thereby, obstruct the Volk's ontological-historical appointment with destiny, as specified by Heidegger's doctrine of *Seinsgeschick*, or the "destining of Being."

Only recently has it come to light that, in Heidegger's 1936 lecture course, *Geschichte des Seyns* (*The History of Being*), a key passage that sheds important light on Heidegger's anti-Semitism has been omitted.[50] As one can see, Heidegger's anti-Semitic convictions were not always couched in euphemism or indirect language. As a loyal Party member and as someone who regularly closed his correspondence with the so-called "Deutscher Grüss" ("Heil Hitler!"), he was by no means averse to "naming names."

V

In the fateful year of 1933, Heidegger became "Rektor-Führer"— his official title, in keeping with the reorganization of German cultural and political life in accordance with the precepts of *Gleichschaltung* (the elimination of political opposition) and the *Führerprinzip*—of Freiburg University. The motto cited at the outset of this foreword concerning the Führer's status as "the future German Reality and its Law" was a statement that Heidegger made in conjunction with a plebiscite called by the Nazi leadership to ratify, after the fact, Germany's withdrawal from the League of Nations. Germany's exit under the auspices of the Nazi dictatorship effectively torpedoed what hopes for international peace still existed following Hitler's accession to power ten months earlier. At the time, Berlin had been engaged in heated negotiations with the leading European powers in Switzerland in order to reach an agreement on the terms of German rearmament. With Nazi Germany's abrupt departure from the League, these peace talks became moot. Indeed, since Japan had summarily withdrawn from the League earlier in the year, its existence as an organ of international peace had been effectively destroyed.

In the poem "September 1, 1939," W. H. Auden aptly referred to the 1930s as a "low dishonest decade."[51] The sequence of events that shook Germany in 1933, beginning with the Nazi seizure of power on January 30, signifies the onset of the European catastrophe. Thus Heidegger's misstep was not a minor error in judgment but rather—given the bellicose and genocidal nature of the regime he was supporting—one of vast proportions. To compound the problem, Heidegger did not demonstrate the least bit of regret after the war. Instead, as we have seen, eight years after the Third Reich's collapse, he demonstratively reaffirmed his belief in National Socialism's "inner truth and greatness." To the very end, Heidegger remained wedded to the ethnocentric delusion that Germany, among all peoples, possessed a messianic capacity to redeem Western civilization from a fate of rash and interminable decline (*Untergang*).

In Heidegger's conception of philosophy, the threadbare solace that metaphysics has to offer merely exposed the intellectual bankruptcy and delusions of mediocre spirits. Little wonder that he held the majority of his philosophical contemporaries in such paltry esteem. Concerning the philosopher Richard Kroner, author of the classic study *Von Kant zu Hegel*, who held appointments in Dresden and Kiel before being quite literally hounded from the podium by the National Socialist Student Association in 1934 because of his Jewish background, Heidegger observes: "I have never encountered such a miserable human being—now he lets himself be pitied like an old woman—the only act of charity that one might still show him would be to deprive him of the *venia legendi* [right to teach] this very day."[52] In Heidegger's view, inferior types like these jeopardized the realization of Germany's destiny, its ontological-historical mandate (*Auftrag*); abetted the West's "abandonment by Being" (*Seinsverlassenheit*); and prevented accession to the realm of "another Beginning" (*anderer Anfang*). Such mediocrities could never measure up to the luminosity and sublimity of the figures that Heidegger glorifies and celebrates as *die Schaffenden*: the "Great Creators," like Heidegger himself.[53]

In the *Black Notebooks*, Heidegger rails incessantly against these inferior spirits. At several points, his speculative-ontological musings devolve into torrents of splenetic invective. He brusquely disqualifies psychoanalysis insofar as it was founded by "the Jew, Freud."[54] He displays a visceral antipathy to *Historie*—that is, to history writing and to historians more generally—which he wishes to supplant with his own conception of "historicity" (*Geschichtlichkeit*). His unbridled contempt for all rivals, real or imagined, highlights his political and intellectual isolation during the 1930s.

With the foundering of his rectorship in spring 1934, Heidegger and the National Socialist movement temporarily parted ways. For this reason, especially during the years 1934–39—that is, from the failure of his rectorship to the outbreak of the Second World War—the *Black Notebooks* are suffused with acrimony and ressentiment. Given their status as a philosophical sketchbook not slated for publication until decades after the philosopher's death, Heidegger could vent his political frustrations and misgivings without inhibition, seizing the opportunity to denounce the party hacks and other contemporaries who, Heidegger believed, had conspired to short-circuit Germany's national awakening (*Nationaler Aufbruch*), as the Nazi movement was known among enthusiasts.

VI

The rationalizations that have arisen recently in defense of Heidegger's more egregious rhetorical excesses and political transgressions are troubling. Many of the apologias one finds are inordinately crude; by attempting to downplay Heidegger's misdeeds, they end up exonerating his actions.

For example, in an attempt to minimize the severity and extent of Heidegger's anti-Semitism, his disciples have argued that, going back to the Enlightenment era, one finds a long history of anti-Semitic pronouncements among German philosophers—thereby suggesting that, since in the *longue durée* of German intellectual history (*Geistesgeschichte*) Heidegger is merely one offender among many, one ought to view his transgressions with greater sympathy and compassion.[55]

But this seems like a rather transparent attempt to exonerate Heidegger by lamely claiming safety in numbers. Moreover, to argue in this manner abstracts from the important discursive and political transformations of European anti-Semitism: the twisted road from religiously based, traditional anti-Judaism to modern, eliminationist anti-Semitism grounded in the imperatives of race. As the *Black Notebooks* reveal, one of the factors that differentiates Heidegger's anti-Semitism from that of precursors like Kant, Hegel, or Marx was the *systematic* rather than *episodic* character of his racism. After all, Heidegger's anti-Judaism harmonized with that of the genocidal regime in which he enthusiastically participated. By seeking "to lead the leader" (*den Führer führen*)—that is, in seeking to play "philosopher king" to Hitler's Dionysius (the Syracusan tyrant who almost cost Plato his life)—Heidegger showed himself to be a National Socialist zealot, *plus royaliste que le roi*. In consequence of his actions in support of the regime, Heidegger was censured by a favorably disposed Freiberg University denazification commission and deprived of his *venia legendi*, or right to teach, for a period of five years (1945–50).[56]

In a similar vein, Heidegger's publisher, Vittorio Klostermann, has recently sought to mitigate the accusations of anti-Semitism by suggesting that, upon closer examination, Heidegger possessed no special animosity toward Jews. Instead, Klostermann asserts, with what one can only describe as breathtaking insensitivity, that Heidegger discriminated equitably against *all* races and nationalities whose values were opposed to those of the *Volksgemeinschaft*. In support of this claim, Klostermann furnishes us with a detailed list: "Jews, Christians, Bolsheviks, Americans," and, last but not least, "National Socialists [*sic*]." Heidegger excoriated all of the aforementioned groups, insofar as all were, in his view, "so many varieties of the Oblivion of Being."[57]

To place Heidegger's lifelong, philosophically grounded antipathy to Jews on the same footing as his rather unsystematic and piecemeal criticisms of the Third Reich is a macabre equivalence. Moreover, coming from the publisher of Heidegger's *Black Notebooks*, this argument intersects with a broader revisionist agenda that seeks to relativize Heidegger's anti-Semitism by blurring or diluting its annihilationist gist. One cannot help but wonder on what grounds Klostermann can include National Socialism on this list of enemies in light of the fact that Heidegger was a dues-paying member of the NSDAP until the regime's final collapse or *Zusammenbruch* in May 1945. In view of Heidegger's fervent professions of faith in the National Socialist cause in the *Black Notebooks* and related texts from the 1930s, Klostermann's public declaration of such transparently apologetic insinuations and claims suggests ignorance, maliciousness, or both.[58] Common sense indicates that there is a qualitative distinction between Heidegger's tirades against world Jewry during the 1930s and 1940s—outbursts that occurred while he was a member in good standing of the NSDAP—and his occasional criticisms of these other groups—none of which, in contrast with the Jews, was targeted for extermination (*Ausrottung*).

One disturbing aspect of such rationalizations, or efforts to relativize Heidegger's National Socialist commitments, is that, in their obedience to Heidegger's teachings, his supporters embrace positions that prove inimical to the values of spirit, reflexivity, and autonomy. Such craven servility to a chosen intellectual master merely internalizes the logic of discipleship that Heidegger himself so carefully cultivated. Thus when all is said and done, those who have sought so energetically to absolve Heidegger in the face of an ever-growing store of countervailing evidence have ended up, *nolens volens,* whitewashing the political dossier of a former Nazi.

In an insightful essay originally published in *Partisan Review* in 1946, Hannah Arendt recognized the intractable ethical problems posed by Heidegger's antipathy to the Kantian ethos of moral autonomy. It was in this vein that, in the article in question, Arendt suggested that the existential ontology that Heidegger developed in *Being and Time* promoted what she characterized as a retrograde "functionalism." As Arendt observes appositely,

> What Heidegger calls . . . Dasein dispenses with all those human characteristics that Kant provisionally defined as freedom, human decency, and reason, that arise from human spontaneity. . . . [Thus] behind Heidegger's ontological approach lies a functionalism not unlike Hobbes's realism. If man consists in the fact that *he is,* he is no more than his modes of Being or function in the world. . . . Heidegger's functionalism says man would function even better in a preordained world because he would then be "freed" of all spontaneity.[59]

By radically rejecting the quintessential Enlightenment maxim formulated by Kant, *Sapere aude!*—"Dare to be wise!"—Heidegger's philosophy promotes a mentality of heteronomy or dependency.[60] One would be dishonest, moreover, were one to deny that this orientation was related to Heidegger's partisanship for National Socialism, whose success was predicated in part on the *Untertan* or "subject" mentality that had been cultivated during the Second Empire (*Kaiserreich*). Thus from the standpoint of intellectual history, Heidegger's critique of the "subject" and "subjectivity" is simultaneously a critique of the Western conception of selfhood and, more seriously, of a self-serving caricatural version thereof.[61]

A critique of subjectivity whose goal is to deliver the self over to nameless and mysterious higher powers, as occurs with Heidegger's later doctrine of "the history of Being," is a retrograde development, insofar as it is pointedly at odds with modern norms of emancipation.[62] When in 1933 Heidegger proclaims, "Let not propositions and 'ideas' be the rules of your Being. The Führer is the future German Reality and its law," one perceives how the precepts of fundamental ontology mesh seamlessly with Germany's so-called Brown Revolution.

Ironically, the critique of Heidegger as an enemy of autonomy and a champion of human dependency is one of the few points on which Arendt and Theodor Adorno would ultimately agree. As Adorno observes in his pathbreaking essay "Education after Auschwitz," only by cultivating the values of autonomy (*Mündigkeit*) can one guard against future instances of genocide and mass persecution—although even then, of course, there are no guarantees. In Adorno's words: "Every debate about the ideals of education is trivial and inconsequential compared to this single ideal: *never again Auschwitz*. . . . The single genuine power standing against the principle of Auschwitz is autonomy: . . . the power of reflection, of self-determination, of not playing along."[63]

It was for similar reasons that Karl Jaspers, Heidegger's *campagnon de route* during the 1920s, remarked in a letter written to a Freiburg University denazification committee that the influence of Heidegger's philosophy on the post-1945 generation of German university students would "in its pedagogical effects be a disaster."[64] Jaspers correctly surmised that Heidegger's portentous brand of "Being-mysticism" (*Seinsmystik*), instead of contributing to an understanding of the German catastrophe, would instead lead only to the obfuscation of its underlying causes, rooted as they were in the *longue durée* of German history.[65]

When all is said and done, the answer to the intellectual puzzles and conundrums that have arisen in connection with the theme of "Heidegger and National Socialism" is, certainly, *not* to consign his work to an imaginary rubbish heap of philosophers whose work is no longer worth reading. Solutions that tend in this direction only end up suppressing argument and debate, and thereby circumvent difficult questions rather than confronting them head-on. The proper course to pursue is to exercise historically informed, critical vigilance in our encounters with Heidegger's texts, in order that we, his heirs, avoid duplicating his—at times, quite grave—errors, transgressions, and miscues.

Coda

Given the *Black Notebooks'* salience in recent Heidegger literature, in addition to the wide array of animated public discussions that their publication has provoked, it may be instructive to review some of the main interpretive strategies that have been employed by Heidegger's followers—approaches that have sought to minimize or, in certain cases, to conjure away the *Black Notebooks'* disturbing ideological freightedness.[66]

By "ideological freightedness" I am referring not merely to Heidegger's explicit decision in 1933 to cast his lot with Germany's "National Revolution," but to those aspects of his thought that more generally reflect his commitment to the worldview of "German particularism"—the infamous *Sonderweg*. As I have already suggested, herein lies one of the central and all-pervasive dilemmas with Heidegger's work when viewed as a totality. It is imperative to formulate the problem from this broader historical perspective, since this is the only way to appreciate the important elements of cultural-political continuity between Heidegger's existential ontology of the 1920s and his nefarious political commitments of the 1930s.

This approach also helps to expose the retrograde intentions underlying one of the main "strategies of containment" adopted by Heidegger's champions since the *Black Notebooks'* appearance two years ago: the implausible attempt to confine his enthusiasm for National Socialism to the years 1933–34—that is, to his Freiburg University rectorship.

This strategy is unsustainable on several grounds. For example, in a *Black Notebooks* entry from 1939, Heidegger asserts that his enthusiasm for National Socialism as a harbinger of "another beginning" dates from 1930—the year of the Party's major electoral breakthrough.[67] In addition, Heidegger's correspondence with his brother Fritz reveals that, as early as 1931, he was convinced that Hitler was the figure who possessed the combination of will and vision needed to lead Germany out of its contemporary political impasse. On this basis, he recommended that Fritz undertake a reading of *Mein Kampf*—as Heidegger himself had already done—and join the NSDAP.[68]

These letters also help to clarify the *völkisch* orientation that was endemic to Heidegger's thought at the time—a standpoint that was inseparable from the basic tenets of "racial thinking" and an exaltation of the salvific mission of *Germanentum* (Germannness). They also help to account for Heidegger's aversion to half-measures (*Halbheiten*), and, correspondingly, to his self-understanding as a philosophical and political radical. Lastly, Heidegger's lecture courses and seminars from the 1930s make it indubitably clear that he viewed fundamental ontology as the philosophical corollary to the revolutionary tendencies of *völkisch* movements like National Socialism.

In the *History of Sexuality*, Michel Foucault invokes the trope of an "incitement to discourse" to characterize the hypertrophic outpouring of discussions of sexuality that emerged during the nineteenth century—a logorrheic compulsion that undermines the "repressive hypothesis," which alleged that frank talk about sexuality had been stifled during this same period.

Surveying the vast spate of apologetic Heidegger literature that has amassed in recent months, a literature that has often been conceived with the express aim of diminishing the perceived severity of Heidegger's vigorous pro-Nazi loyalties, the appropriateness of Foucault's epithet leaps to mind. Moreover, there is something perverse about this discursive compulsion on the part of Heidegger's defenders and acolytes, insofar as texts that are suffused with the verbiage of "exterminatory anti-Semitism"—the *Black Notebooks*—are being utilized as a springboard to provide the otherwise staid and insular world of Heidegger scholarship with a much needed shot in the arm. It is as though Heidegger's supporters, in their rush to rescue the Master's reputation, were trampling over the corpses and gravesites of Nazism's victims anew. In this respect, the concerns of academic corporatism have triumphed over an honest reckoning with the misdeeds of the German past.

Yet, as Heidegger student Herbert Marcuse aptly reminded his mentor in the course of their epistolary exchange of the late 1940s, there are "reasonable" transgressions that a philosopher may commit, and then there are misdeeds of another register that permanently cross the line. By placing his philosophy in the service of an inherently genocidal regime that, as Marcuse went on to argue, was the negation of the ideals on which Western civilization had been predicated, Heidegger betrayed the vocation of philosophy itself—in the eyes of Marcuse, an unpardonable offense. Witnessing the frenzied attempts of Heidegger's devotees to rescue the standing of their badly damaged imago, at times, one is uncertain whether to laugh or to cry. In a now familiar syndrome, the parochialism of self-interested, academic guild-politics trumps considerations of substance. And thus among Heidegger's champions, it is more important to keep the Master's ship afloat at all costs than it is to render Nazism's victims their due.

One of the more transparent and pathetic strategies of damage control that has emerged in the wake of the *Black Notebooks'* publication is the contention that, given the nature of the current historical crisis, we need Heidegger more than ever. Often, this gambit is accompanied by nebulous claims concerning the Holocaust that are leveraged as part of a strategy of moral suasion, thereby seeking to reverse the terms on Heidegger's accusers. Ultimately, once the fog has cleared, we are presumptively and summarily informed that we need Heidegger—someone who was both a true believer and an active participant in a regime that was responsible for Auschwitz and kindred mass atrocities—in order to "think the Holocaust." It was the late Pierre Bourdieu who, with admirable concision, delivered the *coup de grace* to all such transparent apologetics, declaring: "When I hear people say that Heidegger alone makes it possible for us to think the Holocaust—but perhaps I am insufficiently postmodern—I think I must be dreaming!"[69]

Bourdieu's caveat notwithstanding, this is the interpretive strategy that Donatella Di Cesare pursues in "Being and the Jew: Heidegger's Metaphysical Anti-Semitism," her contribution to *Heidegger, die Juden—noch einmal*, published in fall 2015 by *Gesamtausgabe* editor Vittorio Klostermann.[70] Since, according to Di Cesare, Heidegger's anti-Semitism was grounded in Western "metaphysics" (what she means by this assertion is never really clarified), she contends that it represented an instance of self-betrayal on Heidegger's part, insofar as, at heart, Heidegger was a trenchant critic of metaphysics.

Hence, according to Di Cesare, when viewed philosophically, Heidegger's anti-Semitism represents little more than an unfortunate lapsus: a misguided and regrettable slackening of the philosopher's characteristic antimetaphysical vigilance. When all is said and done, Heidegger's anti-Semitic utterances may be discounted, because in such instances, Heidegger was being untrue to himself. In other words, these are cases in which Heidegger was not really being Heidegger.

However, such conclusions are unsustainable and misleading on a number of counts. For one, Heidegger's views concerning the viability of "metaphysics" fluctuated over time. At times, he was quite favorably disposed toward the paradigm of metaphysics. Otherwise he would not have written texts with titles like "What is Metaphysics?" (1929) and *Introduction to Metaphysics* (1935). As late as 1940, in his lectures on "Nietzsche [and] European Nihilism," Heidegger (crassly) praised Germany's blitzkrieg victory over France as a "metaphysical act." As he observes, "From the viewpoint of bourgeois culture and intellectuality one might view the total 'motorization' of the Wehrmacht from the ground up as an example of boundless 'technicism' and 'materialism.' In truth, this is a *metaphysical act* which certainly surpasses in depth something like the abolition of 'philosophy.'"[71] Heidegger's later doctrine of the history of Being never dispenses with the eminently metaphysical notion of "essence" (*Wesen*). Moreover, this reliance adversely affects his phenomenological capacity to appreciate the intrinsic nature of "things themselves" (here, one will recall Husserl's original phenomenological summons: "Zu den Sachen!"— "To the things!"), the manner in which beings show or manifest themselves. This shortcoming influences the later Heidegger's critique of technology in debilitating ways: above all, in a lack of empirical cogency that reveals itself in simplistic generalizations about the reduction of all Being to "standing reserve" (*Bestand*). All of these examples demonstrate that, Di Cesare's caveats and pleas notwithstanding, when it served his purposes, Heidegger continued to invoke metaphysics in a highly positive sense.

In addition, Di Cesare's contention that Heidegger's anti-Semitism was in some mysterious, unspecified fashion metaphysically conditioned is erroneous. Such claims seem to derive from a strategic maneuver that aims to immunize the later, purportedly "postmetaphysical" Heidegger from criticism. However, as I have sought to demonstrate, Heidegger's anti-Semitism was a natural outgrowth of his cultural-political attachment to the ethos of Germanocentrism. Hence, in point of fact, as a corollary to his advocacy of German particularism, Heidegger's anti-Semitism, had virtually nothing to do with metaphysics. It would be more accurate to say that Heidegger's anti-Semitism derived from his having rejected the standpoint of the "Universal," which, historically has been a natural ally or concomitant of metaphysical thinking.[72]

Foreseeably, once Di Cesare has gone through the motions of criticizing Heidegger—for the most part, a sideshow, an exercise in Kabuki philosophy—she can return to endorsing his philosophical standpoint in good conscience and with redoubled enthusiasm. Having left the question of Heidegger's Nazism permanently behind, we can breathe a welcome sigh of relief and re-pose the *Seinsfrage* or question of Being. Di Cesare predictably concludes that, given the perils and catastrophes of twentieth-century history, today we need Heidegger more than ever. In her final paragraph, Di Cesare shamelessly seeks to elevate a thinker who characterized the Holocaust as an act of "Jewish self-annihilation" (*jüdische Selbstvernichtung*) to the status of the philosopher of the Shoah. As she informs us, "After the *Black Notebooks*, Auschwitz appears more closely connected with [the Heideggerian trope of] the oblivion of being. . . . [Heidegger] has provided those concepts that today allow a reflection on the Shoah: from *enframing*, *Gestell*, to technology, from the banality of evil to the 'fabrication of corpses.'"[73]

Yet if Di Cesare truly cared about investigating the historical causes of the Shoah, she would realize that, ultimately, Heideggerian *Seinsvergessenheit* (the oblivion of Being) falls rather far down the list. Heidegger employed this nebulous abstraction—in truth, a pseudo-explanation that obscures much more than it clarifies—in order to absolve his fellow Germans of responsibility for these ghastly deeds: as a convenient way of avoiding what Karl Jaspers termed *Die Schuldfrage*, or *The Question of German Guilt*.[74] As Jürgen Habermas has observed in "Work and Weltanschauung: the Heidegger Controversy from a German Perspective": "With the help of an operation that we might call 'abstraction via essentialization,' the history of Being is disconnected from political and historical events. . . . Under the leveling gaze of the philosopher of Being even the extermination of the Jews seems merely an event equivalent to many others." Thus as Heidegger, making a series of macabre equivalences, explains in his 1949 Bremen lectures on technology, "Farming is now a motorized food industry, in essence the same as the fabrication of corpses in gas chambers and extermination camps, the same as the blockade and starving of the peasantry, the same as the fabrication of the hydrogen bomb."[75] This claim is merely another illustration of the way that Heidegger's later thought preempts all questions of human volition and responsibility in favor of the pseudo-causality of the "destiny of Being" (*Seinsgeschick*).

Ultimately, the moral ambiguities involved in suggesting that we rely on a philosopher who, as the *Black Notebooks* reveal, was both a staunch anti-Semite as well as a convinced Nazi to explicate the Shoah is a dilemma that apparently leaves Di Cesare untroubled. Here, instead of the "oblivion of Being" (*Seinsvergessenheit*), we are witness to the "oblivion" of reason and common sense.

Complementing Di Cesare's exculpatory labors is Friedrich-Wilhelm von Herrmann's recently published essay, "The Role of Martin Heidegger's *Notebooks* within the Context of His Oeuvre."[76] Von Herrmann, who was Heidegger's last "assistant" as well as the official guardian of the *Nachlass*, has done the Heidegger industry a great service by identifying and enumerating the passages in the *Black Notebooks* in which Heidegger excoriates "world Jewry." (Of course, this exercise overlooks the ideological valences of a discursive frame such as Heidegger's that might qualify as anti-Semitic, even in cases where Jews are not mentioned by name.) Since von Herrmann is unable to find more than twelve or thirteen such instances, he concludes that, when all is said and done, there is really nothing to worry about. Consequently, those who are employed in the business of Heidegger veneration can safely return to their calling.

However, as von Herrmann himself seems to recognize, though few in number, many of the passages in question are quite bloodthirsty and egregious. Hence, supplemental damage control is required. Von Herrmann, having meticulously examined the "twelve or thirteen" passages at issue, arrives again at the Panglossian verdict that there is no real cause for concern or alarm, since the passages in question are entirely *devoid of philosophical significance*—this despite the fact that, as many commentators have pointed out, Heidegger's hypertrophic indictments of "world Jewry" go to the very heart of his critique of Western modernity qua *Machenschaft*.[77]

To cinch his case, von Hermann invokes the name of an obscure Hungarian philosopher who, in a private conversation, has seen fit to vouchsafe von Herrmann's conclusions.

Di Cesare's and von Herrmann's misconstruals of the historical and political valences of Heidegger's thought are worth pondering insofar as they are representative of a more general interpretive orientation, widespread among Heidegger's advocates, that remains resolutely textual and ahistorical. However, if one seeks to understand those aspects of Heidegger's philosophy that are avowedly *weltanschauulich* (ideological) in nature, in keeping with the philosopher's own stress on the historicity of thought (*Denken*), one must examine the ways that his conceptual framework intersects with complementary discourses of his time. As I have sought to show, *Being and Time* is suffused with elements of the "conservative revolutionary" mentality, which had become a type of lingua franca among extreme right circles during the 1920s,[78] Hence, the semantic register of so many of the "Existentials" or "formal indications" contained in Heidegger's 1927 masterpiece—terms such as *Entschlossenheit, Eigentlichkeit, Vorlaufen-zum-Tode, Generation, Gemeinschaft,* as well as the critique of "transcendental subjectivity" in general—cannot be understood when isolated from these kindred lexical idioms, with which, as we are now keenly aware from letters, testimonials, and other supporting documents, Heidegger was intimately familiar.

As has recently come to light, during the early 1930s, Heidegger was an avid reader of the notorious far right publication, *Die Tat*, edited by the radical conservative publicist Hans Zehrer.[79] Zehrer's review, whose circulation skyrocketed to 30,000 during the early 1930s, gave voice to a fascist-authoritarian worldview that was in many ways akin to Hitler's. However, Zehrer's standpoint was more elitist and less populist than that of the NSDAP. Zehrer was also archly critical of the National Socialists for participating, albeit in bad faith, in the corrupt rituals of bourgeois parliamentarism.

It also turns out that, during the mid-1930s, Heidegger enthusiastically assimilated the lessons of the Italian fascist Julius Evola's influential work, *Revolta contra il mondo moderno* (*Revolt Against the Modern World*), whose arguments he utilized to reinforce and amplify his (one-dimensional) critique of modernity qua *Machenschaft*: the instrumental fabrication of Being in its totality, the wholesale reduction of entities to the status of "standing reserve" (*Gestell*).

What is additionally troubling about Heidegger's veneration of Evola's doctrines and views is that, following the war, Evola's "spiritual fascism" (in contrast with the "materialism" of the bourgeois-democratic worldview) became the cornerstone for the hate-filled discourse European New Right (*Nouvelle Droite*).[80] On these grounds, it behooves those who seek to uncritically adopt the standpoint of Heideggerian *Zivilisationskritik* for the ends of left-wing cultural criticism—a practice that is extremely widespread in the contemporary academy—to seriously rethink their orientation and commitment.

Since the *Black Notebooks'* publication two years ago, Heidegger's defenders have used the strategy of blaming the messenger with increasing frequency. They claim that the reception of the *Black Notebooks* in the international public sphere has been predominantly malicious, ill-tempered, and hostile; and that, as a result of this prejudicial interpretive frame, the criticisms of Heidegger's work that have emerged are neither worth considering nor taking seriously. Thus instead of seeking to critically reevaluate Heidegger's thought in light of the *Black Notebooks'* publication, Heidegger's defenders rest content with a meretricious effort at damage control.

One of the most disturbing aspects of these apologetics is that they ape the discourse of "Holocaust inversion," whereby the roles of victims and executioners are reversed. Thus Heidegger, insofar as he has purportedly been subjected to a wide array of unjust and calumnious denunciations, is turned into the victim. Meanwhile, the plight of the actual victims—those who suffered directly at the hands of the regime that Heidegger vigorously supported as an activist, a party member, and a titled official (Rektor-Führer of Freiburg University)—is trivialized or suppressed. Thereby, the imaginary anti-Heideggerian zealots— "imaginary," insofar as they almost always remain unnamed—who have subjected the Master to this battery of unfair indictments and insinuations become the new perpetrators. According to this new revisionist template, it is Heidegger's critics who have blood on their hands. As one Heidegger devotée has alleged (without providing any supporting references), "Even when [the *Black*

Notebooks] were still in page proofs, the verdict of some leading experts was clear: . . . anyone who afterward still was preoccupied with Heidegger's work was ipso facto excommunicated from the intellectual community if not from the human race."[81]

According to this new paradigm of exculpation, it is these nameless and unidentified Heidegger critics who have become the new censors—in essence, the new Nazis, insofar as their nefarious aim is to "purge" Heidegger's thought from the canon of acceptable discourse. Or, to echo the analogous complaint of Jeff Malpas, the coeditor of *Reading Heidegger's "Black Notebooks 1931–1941"*: "[the *Black Notebooks*] have been taken by many to . . . establish once and for all the unacceptability of Heidegger's work within the canon of respectable thinking."[82] In this case, too, although we are told that "many" persons have advanced such irresponsible claims and accusations, no corroborative evidence or documentation has been provided.

Of course, efforts to vindicate Heidegger vis-à-vis the wrath of his more intemperate critics should not be rejected a priori. What will ultimately determine the viability of such allegations of mistreatment and persecution is whether they can be empirically and discursively substantiated. What is remarkable is that none of these insinuations of unfair treatment is buttressed by documentation: there is nary a footnote to support them, not a single reference or citation to substantiate them.

One is, therefore, led to conclude that these charges are entirely spurious. For the most part, they are fabrications that have been expressly contrived in order to portray Heidegger—and by association, the philosophy he represents—in a more sympathetic light: that is, as an innocent victim of nameless, ill-willed tormentors.

A related consequence of the Heidegger-as-victim strategy is that the philosopher's champions and defenders have felt justified avoiding the effort to confront the depth of Heidegger's Nazism. Instead, when the topic inevitably arises, it is immediately buried, parried, or deliberately masked in a shroud of interpretive haze.

One might concede that Heidegger's thought has been maligned or treated unfairly in specific instances, but it is entirely different to contend that there is a systematic anti-Heidegger crusade afoot, and that efforts to unmask and discredit this fictitious campaign should become one of the primary foci of contemporary

Heidegger scholarship. The numerous enthusiastic conferences, hagiographic monographs, and supportive anthologies devoted to Heidegger's philosophy belie the claim that his work has been the targeted for suppression or intellectual quarantine.

In this respect, it would be ill-advised to overlook the fact that it was Heidegger himself who, both in his capacity as Rektor-Führer of Freiburg University and in his philosophical writings, made the odious declarations and pronouncements for which he is now being held accountable. It was Heidegger himself who repeatedly insisted that his support for National Socialism was grounded in the innermost precepts and claims of his philosophy. Why not let Heidegger take the witness stand on his own behalf?

> From a "metaphysical" perspective [i.e., from the standpoint of the history of Being], during the years 1930–34 I understood National Socialism in terms of the possibility of a transition to "another Beginning." . . . However, I mistook and undervalued this "movement's" genuine power and inner necessity. . . . [Thus] as a result of newly gained insight with respect to my earlier disappointment concerning National Socialism's essence and essential historical power, there derives the imperative to endorse it—*and to do so on philosophical grounds.* To say that is also to say immediately that this "movement" remains independent of any given contemporary configuration and from any duration of the forms that are visible just now.[83]

In Heidegger's view, the "essence" of National Socialism—its "inner truth and greatness"—far transcends whatever contingent, empirical failings the "movement" might display at this or that particular historical moment. Thus to contend that Heidegger permanently distanced himself from National Socialism after the failure of his rectorship in 1934 is disingenuous: a deliberate falsification of the historical record.[84]

Another commonplace strategy of exoneration that has consistently surfaced in recent Heidegger literature revolves around the effort to relativize the philosopher's anti-Semitic views by recontextualizing them. For example, Jeff Malpas points out that, circa World War II, the anti-Semitic standpoint that Heidegger embraced in the *Black Notebooks* and comparable texts were widely shared. Apparently, since anti-Semitism was widespread at the time, Heidegger's only sin was to have cast his lot in with the *sensus communis*.[85] (By this insinuation, does Malpas mean to suggest that, since anti-Semitic perspectives were widespread, it is very likely that they indeed contained a kernel of truth?) Since Malpas is a philosopher, he must realize that his duty is not to relativize extant prejudices and past injustices, but instead, à la Socrates, to assist his readers in discerning the truth.

Later on, Malpas reproaches Heidegger's (once again, unnamed) critics for their inattention to the interpretive subtleties of "hermeneutics"—a textual approach that, we are told, is serendipitously associated with Heidegger's name. Here, the implication seems to be that the best remedy for any shortcomings or failings in Heidegger's oeuvre is to read more Heidegger.

Finally, in seeking to exonerate Heidegger, Malpas erroneously asserts that the philosopher's anti-Semitism was of the innocuous, nonlethal "cultural" variety: "Heidegger's anti-Semitism, however crude it may appear . . . seems fundamentally to have been based in a form of *cultural anti-Semitism* of a sort that was widespread in Germany and Europe before the Second World War."[86]

That a reputable scholar could hazard such a manifestly insupportable claim following the publication of the *Black Notebooks* is astonishing. As other researchers have shown, the anti-Semitic invective one finds in the *Black Notebooks* and other Heidegger texts of this period was of a piece with the "annihilationist anti-Semitism" that undergirded the National Socialist *Endlösung*.[87] Already in his 1934 seminar on "The Essence of Truth," Heidegger openly called for the "total annihilation" (*völlige Vernichtung*) of the domestic enemy—that is, the Jews. There is no circumventing the fact that, for a member in good standing of Hitler's NSDAP to publicly accuse an entire people or *Volk* of "planetary criminality"—the idiom that Heidegger employed to indict "world Jewry" in his 1938 lecture course, *Die Geschichte des Seyns*—is tantamount to a "warrant for genocide."[88]

Moreover, as we have seen, during the 1930s and 1940s Heidegger's abiding fear was not that National Socialism would succumb to extremes, but that it was insufficiently radical. Thus as the Wehrmacht opened a second front against Russia in 1941, Heidegger callously observes that, "Extermination ensures us against the prospect of defeat" (*Das Vernichten sichert gegen den*

Andrang aller Bedingungen des Niedergangs).[89] And in the *Black Notebooks (Überlegungen II-VI)*, he stresses the paramountcy of "breeding [*Züchtung*] higher and the highest modalities of thought"—a task that, in Heidegger's view, is more important "than the mere communication of knowledge [*Kenntnismitteilung*]."[90] All of which drives one to conclude that the main objective of the "hermeneutical" approach vaunted by the editors of *Reading Heidegger's "Black Notebooks 1931–1941"* is to sow doubt where none exists and to obfuscate the substantive questions at stake concerning Heidegger's deep-seated and enduring National Socialist allegiances by focusing on irrelevant semantic ambiguities as opposed to the disconcerting particulars of Heidegger's case.

Lastly, if it is true, as so many of the contributors to *Reading Heidegger's "Black Notebooks 1931–1941"* contend, that Heidegger "[broke] with National Socialism" in 1934, why is it that he continued to pay his NSDAP dues until the very end, 1945? Moreover, how can one explain the fact that, although Heidegger's Nazi sympathies had purportedly diminished, his anti-Semitism "spiked" during the late 1930s and early 1940s? And how might one account for the fact that, in 1953, Heidegger vaunted the "inner truth and greatness of [National Socialism]"? Finally, what about the multiple passages in *Überlegungen XII-XV* (*Gesamtausgabe* 96) where one finds Heidegger cheering the Wehrmacht and the *Einsatzgruppen* on to the *Endsieg* or "final victory," despite the atrocities that were being perpetrated in the East? Brusquely put: this is not how someone who has distanced himself from the worldview of National Socialism acts and thinks.

Malpas goes on to suggest that, were Heidegger found to be a committed Nazi, this is a merely "biographical" fact that is "not relevant to his philosophy."[91] However, as a Heidegger scholar, he must be aware that on numerous occasions the Master claimed that the "existential" basis of his philosophy was his own "facticity": the *Jemeinigkeit* or particularity of his own *Existenz*. On these grounds, the relationship between these two dimensions of Heidegger's persona—life and thought—would seem integral rather than fortuitous. In essence, Heidegger scholar Karsten Harries settled this question several decades ago, observing appositely that "authenticity, as Heidegger understands it, rules out a separation of the political stance of the author and his philosophy."[92]

In conclusion, when such weighty questions of historical and moral responsibility are at issue—questions bearing on Heidegger's relationship to Nazism and the Holocaust, as opposed to some long forgotten instance of petty larceny—the interpretive stakes are enhanced. It behooves scholars to respond with an integrity and seriousness of purpose that transcends the consolations and rationalizations of conventional academic corporatism.

Notes

1. Richard Wolin, ed., *The Heidegger Controversy: A Critical Reader* (Cambridge, Mass.: MIT Press, 1991); Karl Löwith, *Martin Heidegger and European Nihilism*, ed. Richard Wolin, trans. Gary Steiner (New York: Columbia University Press, 1995); Richard Wolin, *Heidegger's Children: Hannah Arendt, Karl Löwith, Hans Jonas, and Herbert Marcuse* (Princeton: Princeton University Press, 2001); and Herbert Marcuse, *Heideggerian Marxism* (Lincoln: University of Nebraska Press, 2005).

For the French edition of *The Politics of Being*, see *La Politique de l'être: la pensée politique de Martin Heidegger*, trans. C. Goulard (Paris: Éditions Kimé, 1991); German: *Seinspolitik: das politische Denken Martin Heideggers*, trans. Rainer Forst (Vienna: Passagen Verlag, 1992); Portugese: *Politica do Ser: Pensamento Politico de Martin Heidegger* (Lisbon: Instituto Piaget, 1996); Japanese: *The Politics of Being: The Political Thought of Martin Heidegger* (Tokyo: Iwanami Shoten, 1999); Chinese: *The Politics of Being: The Political Thought of Martin Heidegger*, trans. Zhou Xian (Jianshu: Jianshu Education Publishing, 2000).

2. As an author, one of the most gratifying aspects of the reception of *The Politics of Being* was its resolutely international tenor. For a representative sample of the most substantive critical discussions and reviews, see Mitchell Aboulafia, review of Richard Wolin, *The Politics of Being*, *International Studies in Philosophy* 25, no. 3 (1993): 153–154; T. H. Adamowski, "Self-Appointed Legislators to Mankind: Intellectuals and Tyranny," *University of Toronto Quarterly* 72, no. 2 (Spring 2003): 585–614; Alan Apperley, review of Richard Wolin, *The Politics of Being*, *Australian Journal of Politics and History* 39, no. 1 (April 1993): 139; Josef Chytry, "The Timeliness of Martin Heidegger's National Socialism," *New German Critique*, no. 58 (Winter 1993): 86–96; Pascal David, review of Richard Wolin, *The Politics of Being*, *Les Études philosophiques*, no. 4 (October-December 1995): 569–570; Frank Field, review of Richard Wolin, *The Politics of Being*, *German History* 10, no. 1 (January 1992): 120–121; Bärbel Frischmann, review of Richard Wolin, *The Politics of Being*, *Deutsche Zeitschrift für Philosophie* 40, no. 12 (December 1992): 1476–1478; Karsten Harries, review of Richard Wolin, *The Politics of Being*, *Philosophy and Literature* 15, no. 2 (October 1991): 357–359; David Ingram, "Wolin on Heidegger and 'The Politics of Being,'" *Praxis International* 12, no. 2 (July 1992): 215–228; Michel Kail, *Temps Modernes* 47, no. 543 (October 1991): 149–164; Michel Kail, "Review of Richard Wolin, *La politique de l'être, la pensée politique de Martin Heidegger*," *L'Homme et la société* 107, no. 1 (1993): 199–200; David Michael Levin, "Review of Richard Wolin, *The Politics of Being* and *The Heidegger Controversy: A Critical Reader*," *Political Theory* 21, no. 2 (May 1993): 325–331; Michael Löwy, review of Richard Wolin, *The Politics of Being*, *La Quinzaine littéraire*, no. 594 (February 1992): 20; Michael Löwy, *Thesis Eleven*, no. 36 (August 1993): 182–185; Horst Mewes, review of Richard Wolin, *The Politics of Being*, *American Political Science Review* 86, no. 2 (June 1992): 519–520; Ernst Nolte, review of Richard Wolin, *The Politics of Being*, *Historische Zeitschrift* 258, no. 1 (February 1994): 123–124; Paul Thomas, review of Richard Wolin, *The Politics of Being*, *Theory and Society* 21, no. 2 (April 1992): 298–304; Klemens von Klemperer, review of Richard Wolin, *The Politics of Being*, *American Historical Review* 97, no. 2 (April 1992): 517–518; Sonya Sikka, "The Philosophical Bases of Heidegger's Politics: A Response to Wolin," *Journal of the British Society for Phenomenology* 25, no. 3 (October 1994): 241–262; Brian Singer, "The 'Heidegger Affair': Philosophy, Politics, and the 'Political,'" *Theory and Society* 22, no. 4 (August 1993): 539–568; Mark Warren, review of Richard Wolin, *The Politics of Being*, *The Journal of Politics* 54, no. 2 (May 1992): 626–629; Sabine Wilke, review of Richard Wolin, *The Politics of Being*, *German Studies Review* 15, no. 2 (May 1992): 414–415; and Michael Zimmerman, review of Richard Wolin, *The Politics of Being*, *Dissent* 38, no. 3 (Summer 1991): 438–442.

3. See Thomas A. Kohut, *A German Generation: An Experiential History of the Twentieth Century* (New Haven: Yale University Press, 2011). See also my review of Kohut's study, "A Century in Retrospect," in the *Wall Street Journal*, February 27, 2012.

4. For the relevant background, see the important work by Gerd Faulenbach, *Ideologie des deutschen Weges* (Munich: C. H. Beck, 1980).

5. Martin Heidegger, *Überlegungen II–VI (Schwarze Hefte, 1931–1938), Gesamtausgabe* 94 (Frankfurt: Klostermann, 2014), 523.

6. Heidegger, *Being and Time*, trans. J. Macquarrie and E. Robinson (New York: Harper Row, 1962).

7. For a pioneering argument to this effect, see Jürgen Habermas, "Work and Weltanschauung: The Heidegger Controversy from a German Perspective," in *The New Conservatism: Cultural Criticism and Historians' Debate*, ed. and trans. Shierry Weber Nicholsen (Cambridge, Mass.: MIT Press, 1989), 43–72.

8. See, for example, Theodore Kisiel, "Heidegger's *Gesamtausgabe*: An International Scandal of Scholarship," *Philosophy Today* 39, no. 1 (1995): 3–15. See also Rainer Marten, "Grabhalter mit letzter Treuebereitschaft," *Die Zeit*, 18 March 2015: "Seit Jahren nehmen die Herausgeber Martin Heideggers Werk in Beschlag. Das ist ein Skandal, der endlich ein Ende haben muss." See also Lorenz Jäger, "Allesamt Spielarten der Seinsvergessenheit," *Frankfurter Allgemeine Zeitung*, March 3, 2015.

9. See Sidonie Kellerer, "Rewording the Past: The Postwar Publication of a 1938 Lecture by Martin Heidegger," *Modern Intellectual History* 11, no. 3 (2014): 575–602.

10. See Julia Ireland, "Naming 'Physis' and the 'Inner Truth of National Socialism': A New Archival Discovery," *Research in Phenomenology* 44 (2014): 315–346. Such instances of reworking and retouching occurred with greater frequency in the case of Heidegger's lecture courses than with his treatises and other published texts. In part, this is consistent with Heidegger's own understanding of the relationship that his various approaches to philosophical writing had with one another. He viewed the lecture courses as exoteric versions or propaedeutics to his more demanding essays and treatises.

11. See Adam Soboczynski, "Was heisst 'N. Soz.'?" *Die Zeit*, March 26, 2015.

12. Cited in Peter Trawny, *Heidegger und die jüdische Weltverschwörung* (Frankfurt: Klostermann Verlag, 2014), 51.

13. See Ireland, "Naming 'Physis' and the 'Inner Truth of National Socialism,'" 315–346.

14. Heidegger, *Überlegungen II–VI (Schwarze Hefte, 1931–1938), Gesamtausgabe* 94 (Frankfurt: Klostermann, 2014); Heidegger, *Überlegungen VII–XI (Schwarze Hefte, 1938–1939), Gesamtausgabe* 95 (Frankfurt: Klostermann, 2014); Heidegger, *Überlegungen XII–XV (Schwarze Hefte, 1939–1941), Gesamtausgabe* 96 (Frankfurt: Klostermann, 2014); Heidegger, *Anmerkungen I–V (Schwarze Hefte, 1942–94), Gesamtausgabe* 97 (Frankfurt: Klostermann Verlag, 2015).

For more information, see my article, "Heidegger's *Black Notebooks*: National Socialism, World Jewry and the History of Being," *Jewish Review of Books* (June 2014): 40–45. See also my other contributions to the growing international debate: "Heideggers Schwarze Hefte: Nationalsozialismus, Weltjudentum, und Seinsgeschichte," *Vierteljahrshefte für Zeitgeschichte* 63, no. 3 (2015): 370–410; "Addio Heidegger," *Corriere della Sera*, April 17, 2015; "Heidegger's Philosophy of Violence," *Chronicle Review*, March 3, 2015; "La Corercia filosofica del Nazismo di Heidegger," *MicroMega*, March 2015; "Heidegger: l'olocaust come autoannientamento di ebreico," *MicroMega*, February 2015; "Heidegger hielt Endlösung für notwendig," *Hohe Luft: philosophische Zeitschrift*, March 2015; "Heidegger: L'Antisemitisme en toutes lettres," *Books*, October 2014; "Un Heidegger sans Autocensure," *Critique* 811 (2015): 39–58.

15. Heidegger, *Being and Time*, 436; Heidegger, *Sein und Zeit* (Tübingen, Germany: Max Niemeyer, 1979), 384–85: "In der Miteinandersein als ein zusammenvorkommen mehrerer Subjekte begriffen werden kann. In der Mitteilung und im Kampf wird die Macht des Geschickes erst frei. Das schicksalhafte Geschick des Daseins in und mit seiner 'Generation' macht das volle, eigentliche Geschehen des Daseins aus." For an illuminating study of paragraph 74 and its sources during the Weimar era, see the important book by Johannes Fritsche, *Historical Destiny and National Socialism in Heidegger's* Being and Time (Los Angeles: University of California, 1999).

16. See Hugo Ott, *Martin Heidegger: Unterwegs zu seiner Biographie* (Frankfurt: Campus Verlag, 1988), 104, 151. See also Thomas Sheehan, "Everyone Has to Tell the Truth: Heidegger and the Jews," *Continuum* 1 (1) (1990): 30-44.

17. Karl Löwith, "The Political Implications of Heidegger's Existentialism," *The Heidegger Controversy: A Critical Reader*, 103–104.

18. Heidegger, *Zur Bestimmung der Philosophie, Gesamtausgabe* 56/57 (Frankfurt: Klostermann Verlag, 1999), 109. Emphasis added.

19. Ibid., 91.

20. Oswald Spengler, *The Decline of the West, Volume II: Perspectives of World History*, trans. C. Atkinson (New York: Alfred Knopf, 1932), 144. Heidegger grapples with Spengler's legacy on and off during his lecture courses during the 1920s—a fact that is unsurprising given his unconcealed scorn of professional philosophy and Spengler's towering influence. *Decline of the West* was one of the best-selling German nonfiction books during the 1920s; confronting Spengler's claims about Western decline became a rite of passage for the German *Bildungsbürgertum*.

21. Gertrud Heidegger, ed.,*"Mein liebes Seelchen!" Briefe Martin Heideggers an seine Frau Elfride, 1915–1970* (Munich: Deutsche-Verlagsanstalt, 2005), 51.

22. See Kurt Sontheimer, *Antidemokratisches Denken in der Weimarer Republik: die politischen Ideen der deutschen Nation* (Munich: Nymphenburger Verlaganstalt, 1962).

23. See Faulenbach, *Die Ideologie des deutschen Weges*, 6–13. As Faulenbach observes: "With the founding of the Second Empire in 1871, among the *Bildungsbürgertum* (educated middle-classes), but also—and not least of all—among conservative German historians, it became de rigueur to reread German history as a process culminating in the glorious victory over the French at Sedan (1870) and subsequent unification. Thereafter, the Wilhelmine era was defined by a markedly ideological image of Reich or Empire. In light of the many tensions and divisions that were operative in a newly unified Germany (confessional, linguistic, and political), the new monarchical system was promoted as a specifically *German* form of political rule that was distinctly superior to less effective (and tendentially disunified and chaotic) Western parliamentary models. Soon, these perceptions were elevated to the status of unchallengeable political dogma. Correspondingly, German thinkers celebrated the specific characteristics of German spiritual life and German culture—German idealism, German romanticism, historicism, and so forth—as a characteristically *German* form of cultural-political achievement. Thereafter, as the First World War erupted—a conflict, one should recall, that was also fought under the banner of a *Kulturkrieg* or 'Culture War'—the unique, salvific mission of of *Germanentum* (Germanness) congealed into an *idée fixe*. In sum, among historians, philosophers, and theologians such views hardened into what may be denominated *the German ideology*" (7).

24. Heidegger, *Überlegungen II–VI*, 22.

25. Heidegger, *Being and Truth*, trans. G. Fried (Bloomington: Indiana University Press, 2010), 9; translation slightly altered.

26. See Heidegger, *Introduction to Metaphysics*, trans. Ralph Manheim (New Haven: Yale University Press, 1999), 199.

27. Heidegger, *Sein und Wahrheit, Gesamtausgabe* 36/37 (Frankfurt: Klostermann, 2001), 12, 89.

28. Heidegger, *Heraklit, Gesamtausgabe* 55 (Frankfurt: Klostermann Verlag, 1994), 123. Emphasis added.

29. Heidegger, *Überlegungen XII–XV*, 146; Heidegger, *Nietzsche*, vol. IV: *Nihilism*, trans. F. Capuzzi (New York: Harper Row, 1982), 144–45.

30. Hegel, *Phenomenology of Spirit*, trans. A. V. Miller (New York: Oxford University Press, 1977), 110-111.

31. See the classic study by Ernst Tugendhat, *Self-Consciousness and Self-Determination*, trans. Paul Stern (Cambridge, Mass.: MIT Press, 1989). Georg Wilhelm Friedrich Hegel, *Phenomenology of Spirit*, trans. A. V. Miller (New York: Oxford University Press, 1977).

32. Heidegger, *Überlegungen XII–XV*, 96, 82.

33. See Heidegger, *Der Begriff der Zeit, Gesamtausgabe* 64 (Frankfurt: Vittorio Klostermann, 2004).

34. Heidegger, *Reden und andere Zeugnisse eines Lebensweges (Gesamtausgabe* 16) (Frankfurt: Klostermann Verlag, 2000), 53.

35. Heidegger, "Vom Wesen der Wahrheit," in *Sein und Wahrheit, Gesamtausgabe* 36/37, ed. Hartmut Tietjen (Frankfurt: Klostermann Verlag, 2001), 83–264.

36. This is the title of Wilhelm Marr's anti-Semitic diatribe of 1879, in which the term "anti-Semitism" was coined. Also typical in this respect is the sociologist Werner Sombart's influential treatise on *The Jews and Modern Capitalism* (Glencoe, Ill.: Free Press, 1951). Max Weber's monograph, *The Protestant Ethic and the Spirit of Capitalism*, trans. Talcott Parsons (New York: Charles Scribner, 1930), represents an important rejoinder to Sombart's standpoint.

37. Heidegger, *Fundamental Concepts of Metaphysics: World, Finitude, Solitude*, trans. W. McNeill and N. Walker (Bloomington: Indiana University Press, 1995), 177.

38. See Heidegger, *Logik als Frage nach dem Wesen der Sprache, Gesamtausgabe* 38 (Frankfurt: Klostermann Verlag, 1998), 81: "Wenn wir die Frage nach dem Wesen der Geschichte aufnehmen, so gibt es den Einwand, dass unsere Behauptung: dass Geschichte das Auzeichnende für den Menschen sei, willkürlich ist. Neger sind doch auch Menschen und haben keine Geschichte. Und es gibt auch eine Geschichte der Tiere, Pflanzen, die Tasusende von Jahren alt ist und wohl alter als all die der Menschen."

39. On this point, see my article, "Heidegger's Philosophy of Violence," *Chronicle Review*, March 3, 2015.

40. Heidegger, *Überlegungen VII–XI*, 97.

41. See note 26.

42. See the definition of redemptive anti-Semitism provided by Saul Friedlander in *Nazi Germany and the Jews: The Years of Persecution, 1933–1939* (New York: HarperCollins, 1997), 2: "Especially with regard to the Jews, Hitler was driven by ideological obsessions that were anything but the calculated devices of the demagogue; that is, he carried a very specific brand of racial anti-Semitism to its most extreme and radical limits. I call that distinctive aspect of his worldview quote 'redemptive anti-Semitism'; it is different, albeit derived, from other strands of anti-Jewish hatred that were more common throughout Christian Europe, and different also from the ordinary brands of German and European racial anti-Semitism. It was this redemptive dimension, the synthesis of a murderous rage and an 'idealistic' goal shared by the Nazi leader and the hard core of the party, that led to Hitler's ultimate session to exterminate the Jews."

43. "Wäre zu fragen, worin die Vorbestimmung der Judenschaft für das planetarische Verbrechtertum begründet wird." Heidegger, *Geschichte des Seyns, Gesamtausgabe* 69 (Frankfurt: Klostermann, 2009), cited in Peter Trawny, *Heidegger und der Mythos der jüdischen Weltbeschwörung* (Frankfurt: Klostermann, 2014), 51.

44. Heidegger, "Overcoming Metaphysics," in *The Heidegger Controversy: A Critical Reader*, 49.

45. For more on this point, see Peter Trawny, *Heidegger und der Mythos einer jüdischen Weltverschwörung*.

46. Karl Jaspers, *Philosophische Autobiographie* (Munich: Piper, 1978), 101.

47. For another important explication of the nature of German "distinctiveness," or the *Sonderweg*, at the time of the Second Empire or Kaiserreich, see Hans-Ulrich Wehler, *The Second Empire: 1871–1918* (New York: Bloomsbury Academic, 1997).

48. Heidegger, *Überlegungen und Winke II–VI (Schwarze Hefte 1931–1938)*, 194.

49. Heidegger, *Sein und Wahrheit*, 90–91. Emphasis added. For a perceptive gloss on this passage and its significance in Heidegger's oeuvre, see Emmanuel Faye, *Heidegger: The Introduction of National Socialism into Philosophy*, trans. D. Smith (New Haven: Yale University Press, 2009), 168.

50. See note 43.

51. W. H. Auden, *Another Time* (New York: Random House, 1940). The second stanza of Auden's poem reads as follows:

> Accurate scholarship can
> Unearth the whole offence
> From Luther until now
> That has driven a culture mad,
> Find what occurred at Linz,
> What huge imago made
> A psychopathic god:
> I and the public know
> What all schoolchildren learn,
> Those to whom evil is done
> *Do evil in return.*

(Linz, of course, is the Austrian town where Hitler grew up.)

52. For the details, see Walter Asmus, *Richard Kroner, 1884–1974: Ein Philosoph und Pädagoge unter dem Schatten Hitlers* (New York: Peter Lang, 1990), 62–93.

53. See Heidegger, *Introduction to Metaphysics*, 68: "*Polemos* and *logos* are the same. . . . The struggle (*Kampf*) meant here is originary struggle. . . . Struggle first projects and devel-

ops the unheard-of, the hitherto un-said and un-thought. This struggle is then sustained by the creators by the poets, thinkers, and statesman. Against the overwhelming sway, they throw the counterweight of their work and capture in this work the world that is thereby opened."

54. Heidegger, *Überlegungen XII–XV*, 218.

55. See Donatella Di Cesare, *Heidegger e gli ebrei* (Torino: Bollati Bolinghieri, 2014). See her contribution to *Reading Heidegger's "Black Notebooks 1931–1941,"* eds. Ingo Farin and Jeff Malpas (Cambridge, Mass.: MIT Press, 2016), 181–194.

56. For more on this episode, see Hugo Ott, *Martin Heidegger: Unterwegs zu seiner Biographie* (Frankfurt: Campus Verlag, 1991).

57. See Vittorio Klostermann, "Allesamtspielarten der Seinsvergessenheit," *Frankfurter Allgemeine Zeitung*, April 4, 2015.

58. "Only on the basis of a clear awareness of [my] earlier disillusionment concerning the essence and historical power of National Socialism does the necessity of its affirmation arise—and, at that, *on philosophical grounds,*" Heidegger proclaimed in 1938. Heidegger, *Überlegungen VII-XI*, 209. Emphasis added.

59. Hannah Arendt, "What is Existential Philosophy?" in *Essays in Understanding, 1930–1954: Formation, Exile, and Totalitarianism* (New York: Harper Row, 1994), 178.

60. See Kant, "Answer to the Question: What is Enlightenment?" in *Kant: Political Writings*, ed. Hans Reiss (New York: Cambridge University Press, 1991), 54. See also Horace, *Satires and Epistles*, ed. John Davie (New York: Oxford University Press, 2011), Book I, Epistle II, 68.

61. On this point, see Charles Taylor, *Sources of the Self* (Cambridge, Mass.: Harvard University Press, 1989).

62. For more on this topic, see Max Horkheimer, "Egoism and Freedom Movements," in *Between Philosophy and Social Science: Selected Early Essays* (Cambridge, Mass.: MIT Press, 1993), 49–110.

63. Theodor Adorno, "Education After Auschwitz," in *Critical Models: Interventions and Catchwords*, trans. H. Pickford (New York: Columbia University Press, 2005), 191.

64. Karl Jaspers, "Letter to the Freiburg University De-Nazification Committee," in *The Heidegger Controversy: A Critical Reader*, 149.

65. See Karl Jaspers, *The Question of German Guilt* (New York: Fordham University Press, 2001). See also Karl Jaspers, *Notizen zu Martin Heidegger*, ed. Hans Saner (Munich: Piper Verlag, 1978).

66. For an overview of the initial debates concerning Heidegger's *Black Notebooks*, see the following articles, most of which have appeared in the feuilleton sections of various European dailies or weeklies: Philip Oeltermann, "Heidegger's Black Notebooks Reveal Anti-Semitism at Core of His Philosophy," *Guardian*, March 12, 2014; Jennifer Schuessler, "Heidegger's Notebooks Renew Focus on Anti-Semitism," *New York Times*, March 30, 2014; Markus Gabriel, "Der Nazi aus dem Hinterhalt," *Die Welt*, March 8, 2014; Francois Rastier, "Il n'y a pas d'Affaire Heidegger," *LeNouvel Observateur*, March 7, 2014; Jürg Altwegg, "Antisemitismus bei Heidegger: Ein Debakel für Frankreichs Philosophie," *Frankfurter Allgemeine Zeitung*, December 12, 2013; Thomas Assheuer, "Das vergiftete Erbe," *Die Zeit*, March 21, 2014; Jürgen Kaube, "Martin Heideggers Schwarze Hefte: Die Endschlacht der planetarischen Verbrecherbanden," *Frankfurter Allgemeine Zeitung*, March 12, 2014; Peter Gordon, "Heidegger in Black," *New York Review of Books*, October 9, 2014; Jürgen Kaube, "Martin Heidegger: Die Allierten—Schlimmer als Hitler?" *Frankfurter Allgemeine Zeitung*, March 3, 2015; Markus Gabriel, "'Wesentliche' Bejahung Nationalsozialismus: Seine 'Schwarzen Hefte' von 1939–1941 Zeigen Martin Heidegger als Antisemiten und Antiwestler," *Die Welt*, April 7, 2014; Thomas Assheuer, "Genie und Niedertracht: Denker der Inhumanität: Eine Tagung in Siegen deutet Martin Heideggers 'Schwarze Hefte,' *Die Zeit*, 29 April 2015; David Krell, "Heidegger's *Black Notebooks*," *Research in Phenomenology* 45, vol. 1 (2015): 125–160.

67. Heidegger, *Überlegungen VII-XI*, 408–09.

68. See the interview with Marion Heinz, "Er verstand sich als Revolutionär," in *Die Zeit*, March 12, 2015, 50.

69. Pierre Bourdieu, "Back to History," in *The Heidegger Controversy*, edited by Richard Wolin (Cambridge, Mass.: MIT Press, 1993), 266.

70. Donatella Di Cesare, "Das Sein und der Jude: Heideggers metaphysischer Antisemitismus," *Heidegger, die Juden—noch einmal*, eds. P. Trawny and A. Mitchell (Frankfurt: Klostermann, 2015), 55–74. See also Di Cesare, *Heidegger e gli ebrei* (Torino: Bollati Boringhieri, 2014). The English version of Di Cesare's essay, "Heidegger's Metaphysical Anti-Semitism," may be found in *Reading Heidegger's Black Notebooks 1931–1941*, eds. Ingo Farin and Jeff

Malpas (Cambridge, Mass.: MIT Press, 2016), 181–194. It would be interesting to know the reasons that the title was changed in the English version (i.e., the elision of "Being and the Jew.")

71. Martin Heidegger, *Nietzsche: Der europäische Nihilismus, Gesamtausgabe 48* (Frankfurt: Klostermann Verlag, 1986), 333; emphasis added.

72. On this point, see Axel Honneth, "An Aversion Against the Universal," *Theory, Culture, and Society* 2 (November 1985): 147–155.

73. Di Cesare, "Das Sein und der Jude," 74.

74. See Karl Jaspers, *The Question of German Guilt*, trans. E. B. Ashton (New York: Capricorn Books, 1961).

75. Jürgen Habermas, "Work and Weltanschauung: the Heidegger Controversy from a German Perspective," in *The New Conservatism: Cultural Criticism and the Historians' Debate*, ed. Shierry Weber Nicholsen (Cambridge, Mass.: MIT Press, 1989), 159, 163. See also Heidegger, "Das Gestell," in *Bremer Vortäge 1949, Gesamtausgabe 79* (Frankfurt: Klostermann Verlag, 1994), 27.

76. See Friedrich-Wilhelm von Herrmann, "The Role of Martin Heidegger's *Notebooks* within the Context of His Oeuvre," in *Reading Heidegger's "Black Notebooks 1931–1941"* (Cambridge, Mass.: MIT Press, 2016), 89–94.

77. See Emmanuel Faye, "Heidegger und das Judentum: Vom Aufruf zur 'völligen Vernichtung' zur Thematisierung der 'Selbstvernichtung,'" *Deutsche Zeitschrift für Philosophie* 63, vol. 5 (2015): 877–899; Sidonie Kellerer, "Kampf der Besinnung," *Deutsche Zeitschrift für Philosophie* 63, vol. 5 (2015): 941–957.

78. This point has been definitively made by Daniel Morat in *Von der Tat zur Gelassenheit: konservatives Denken bei Martin Heidegger, Ernst Jünger, und Friedrich Georg Jünger, 1920–1960* (Hamburg: Wallstein, 2007). I have combed through *Reading Heidegger's "Black Notebooks 1931–1941,"* and nowhere have I found a reference to Morat's standard work on Heidegger's rapport with conservative revolutionary thought.

79. See Marion Heinz, "Die geheimen Briefe," *Hohe Luft* 3, (2015): 82–83. For more on the "Tat Kreis," see Kurt Sontheimer, "Der Tatkreis," *Vierteljahresheft für Zeitgeschichte* 3, vol. 7 (1959): 229–260.

80. See Thomas Vasek, "Ein spirituelles Umsturz-Programm," *Frankfurter Allgemeine Zeitung*, December 30, 2015, 32. See Julius Evola, *Rivolta contro il mondo moderno* (Milan: Hoepli, 1934). Evola's book was translated into German in 1935, and it was this edition that Heidegger read. See also Andrea Mammone, *Transnational Neofascism in France and Italy* (New York: Cambridge University Press, 2015), 239: The National Front in France "owes a debt to the old MSI [Movimento Sociale Italiano—the heir to Mussolini's Partito Nazionale Fascista]. . . . The Italian activists Giorgio Almirante and Julius Evola were a vital force in the European Extremist milieu." Among leaders of the Nouvelle Droite, such as GRECE founder Alain de Benoist, Evola's disparagement of liberal democracy in the name of a "fascismo spirituale" possessed a status akin to holy writ. As Tamir Bar-On has noted in *Where Have All of the Fascists Gone?* (New York: Routledge, 2007), 186–87, Nouvelle Droite intellectuals, "whether they engage in metapolitics, *apoliteia* [one of Evola's pet terms], or eventually turn to the political realm, seek the hasty arrival of anti-egalitarian, and anti-liberal alternatives to the hated materialism and decadence of liberal parliamentarism and global capitalism. . . . All revolutionary and idealist opposition to the existing system is essentially positive because it heralds the end of the old system and arrival of an allegedly splendid age after the ruins."

Heidegger's philosophy has also been a central inspiration for the leading eminence of the Russian New Right, Alexander Dugin. Dugin, who directs the Center for Conservative Research at Moscow State University, is also Russia's leading Heideggerian. Under Vladimir Putin's rule, he has been the leading exponent of the geopolitical doctrine of "Eurasia," based on the concept of "spatial politics" (Raumpolitik) of Karl Haushalter, Carl Schmitt, and Heidegger. Heidegger's *Zivilisationskritik* has also proved serviceable for Dugin's virulent attacks on Western liberalism. During the 1990s, Dugin was quite unabashed about his admiration for Nazi racial politics. However, once these avowals proved to be a source of tension with his New Right brethren in Western Europe, he gradually sought to mask his admiration for the Third Reich. In its stead, Dugin has advocated the idea of *The Fourth Political Theory* (see his book with that title, London: Arktos Media, 2012, with a preface by the French Nouvelle Droite ideologue, Alain Soral): an authoritarian national populist approach to politics meant to succeed the (failed) paradigms of liberalism, communism, and fascism—although, for all practical purposes, the "fourth political theory" differs from fascism in name only.

Dugin is also the author of *Martin Heidegger: The Philosophy of Another Beginning*, trans. Nina Kouprianova (Washington, D.C.: Washington Summit Publishers, 2014). For a discussion of Dugin's standing among other proponents of the Nouvelle Droite, see *Eurasianism and the European Far Right*, ed. Marlene Laruelle (Lantham, Md.: Lexington Books, 2015). For a good overview, see Laruelle, "Dangerous Liaisons: Eurasianism, the European Far Right, and Putin's Russia," 1–31. Laruelle summarizes Dugin's far-right ideological orientation as follows: "[Dugin's] definition of Eurasianism entirely overlaps with the [German] Conservative Revolution *à la Russe*. Yet contrary to the founding fathers of Eurasianism, Dugin borrows from the whole spectrum of far-right doctrine and does not limit himself to Third Way theories. He is directly inspired by so-called Esoteric Nazism and his metaphorical language calls indeed for violence. He borrows also from some of the New Right theories. He offers a complex doctrinal spectrum that is always in intimate dialogue with movements coming from Western Europe" (xi–xii).

81. Fred Dallmayr, "Heidegger's *Notebooks*: A Smoking Gun?" in *Reading Heidegger's "Black Notebooks 1931–1941,"* 23; emphasis added.

82. See Jeff Malpas, "On the Philosophical Reading of Heidegger: Situating the *Black Notebooks*," in *Reading Heidegger's "Black Notebooks 1931–1941,"* 4.

83. Heidegger, *Überlegungen VII–XI, Gesamtausgabe 95*, 408–09. One of the significant aspects of this statement is Heidegger's avowal that his intellectual preoccupation with National Socialism dates from the year 1930—in other words, several years earlier than we had originally been led to believe.

84. Introduction to *Reading Heidegger's Black Notebooks "1931–1941,"* x: "The [Black] Notebooks . . . [demonstrate] Heidegger's increasing estrangement from National Socialism . . . following 1934."

85. Malpas, "On the Philosophical Reading of Heidegger," 6.

86. Ibid., 6; emphasis added.

87. See Thomas Assheuer, "Heideggers *Schwarze Hefte*: das vergiftete Erbe," *Die Zeit*, March 21, 2014. See also Richard Wolin, "Heidegger's *Black Notebooks*: National Socialism, World Jewry, and the History of Being," *Jewish Review of Books*, June 2014.

88. Heidegger, *Sein und Wahrheit, Gesamtausgabe 36/37* (Frankfurt: Klostermann, 2001), 90–91; emphasis added. For a perceptive gloss on this passage and its significance in Heidegger's oeuvre, see Emmanuel Faye, *Heidegger: The Introduction of National Socialism into Philosophy*, trans. D. Smith (New Haven: Yale University Press, 2009), 168. See also Norman Cohn, *Warrant for Genocide: the Myth of the Jewish World Conspiracy and the Protocols of the Elders of Zion* (New York: Harper & Row, 1967).

In "Heidegger's *Black Notebooks* in Their Historical and Political Context," Ingo Farin seeks to downplay the gravity of Heidegger's commitment to National Socialism by claiming that it is unfair to evaluate Nazism's early years through the lens of the Holocaust. However, in many respects this genocidal terminus—whose desirability Hitler never sought to conceal in his speeches nor in *Mein Kampf*, which Heidegger read enthusiastically—was evident from its totalitarian beginnings. The first concentration camps date from March 1933 and the anti-Jewish boycott began in April of the same year. Within the first few months of the Nazi *Machtergreifung*, the German trade unions had been smashed, oppositional political parties banned, and the Enabling Act, allowing Hitler to rule by decree, had been passed. In other words, the groundwork of the Nazi dictatorship was already firmly in place. Given the opportunity to address the nature of the National Socialist *Endlösung* after the war, Heidegger either could not be bothered, or else he pursued the relativizing strategy of dismissing German responsibility by claiming that the Holocaust was just another expression of modern technology (*Technik*).

89. Heidegger, *Nietzsches Metaphysik, Gesamtausgabe 50*, ed. Petra Jaeger (Frankfurt: Klostermann, 1990), 70.

90. Heidegger, *Überlegungen II–VI*, 125.

91. Jeff Malpas, "On the Philosophical Reading of Heidegger," *Reading Heidegger's "Black Notebooks 1931–1941,"* eds. Ingo Farin and Jeff Malpas (Cambridge, Mass.: MIT Press, 2016), 7.

92. Karsten Harries, "Heidegger as a Political Thinker," *Review of Metaphysics* 29, vol. 4 (1976): 642–669.

PREFACE

A colleague of mine who is a specialist in English literature tells the story of his mother's reaction upon being informed that her son's next book would be a study of the use of metaphor in Shakespeare: "That's all the world needs," she interjected without missing a beat, "another book on Shakespeare!" I would be less than honest if I didn't admit to the frequency with which the words of my friend's mother echoed—*mutatis mutandis*—in my own mind while I was engaged in writing the present study of Martin Heidegger's political thought.

Of course, my friend's study of Shakespeare was going to be "different"; and presumably so would my own study of Heidegger. But would the "difference" (in both our cases) truly make a *difference*?

Perhaps the manner in which this study originated (its *Entstehungsgeschichte*, as the Germans might say) would be of some relevance and interest in the context at hand. It was a chance encounter with a French colleague while I was on leave in Paris during the 1986–87 academic year that set my own Heidegger-labors in motion; a meeting that, ironically, might be taken as a confirmation of Heidegger's own category of "thrownness" or "existential contingency." For it was as a result of this accidental meeting that I was told of an August 1986 article in the German news magazine *Der Spiegel* in which the theme of Heidegger's National Socialist allegiances had surfaced once again.

My initial reaction was one of pronounced skepticism: hadn't the same charges—most of them unfounded—after all been repeatedly raised in the past? Like many, I was more or less satisfied by the customary apologiae that had been dispensed by Heidegger and his followers: that Heidegger's "fling" with National Socialism had been episodic and insincere; that he'd taken over as Rector of Freiburg University under the Nazis only with great reluctance and following the repeated urgings of his colleagues; that, moreover, his fundamental intention as Rector had been to *preserve* the university from politicization and external encroachments; and that once these efforts failed, he resigned in vehement protest. Finally, hadn't all prior attempts to raise the issue of Heidegger's Nazism—thinly veiled efforts to discredit a philosophy on the basis of considerations that were clearly "extraneous to thought"—received their consummate refutation through one of Heidegger's own characteristic dicta concerning the controversy: "They can't attack the philosophy, so they attack the philosopher!"

The evidence cited in *Der Spiegel* was primarily culled from a series of provocative archival studies published in out-of-the-way German journals by the Freiburg historian Hugo Ott; and it was largely on the basis of these materials that Victor Farias composed his (rather prosecutorial) work, *Heidegger et le Nazisme*. But the *Spiegel* article made it clear that the evidence recently amassed concerning Heidegger's political allegiances during the early 1930s was of a qualitatively different nature; and that his commitment to the National Socialist cause could no longer be passed off as either "ephemeral" or "insincere." Instead, it had become impossible to deny that there was a more sinister and enduring set of elective affinities at work. And it was at this moment that I recalled a conversation I'd once had with the Frankfurt School sociologist of literature Leo Lowenthal, who recounted that for the Critical Theorists (as well as for many others familiar with Heidegger's philosophy at the time), Heidegger's turn toward National Socialism in the early 1930s came as little surprise. But if this were true, then what might it have been about the philosophy itself that permitted—or at the very least, proved incapable of forestalling—the philosopher's coming to feel so at home in a brown uniform?

And it was precisely this question concerning the intricate and elusive filiations between philosophy and life-conduct that came to determine the thematic point of departure of my own work on Heidegger.

There are literally thousands of studies of the various aspects and phases of Heidegger's philosophy. Many of these—as one might well expect—are extremely erudite and accomplished pieces of work. For the prospective newcomer to the land of Heidegger-scholarship, this presents a somewhat daunting picture.

Yet, on closer inspection, one finds that with a few significant exceptions, the vast majority of the secondary literature on Heidegger is of a peculiarly "exegetical" character: the Master has set forth his wisdom, and it falls due to the disciples to interpret and transmit the truths that have been received. To be sure, with a thinker as demanding and recondite as Heidegger, such labor of conceptual reconstruction and transmission is indispensable. However, an outsider cannot help but be struck by (1) the "self-referentiality" of Heideggerian discourse, and (2) the extent to which the intellectual bases of the Heideggerian enterprise itself remain seemingly immune to challenge or contestation. To those schooled in different intellectual traditions, it seems at times as though a charmed circle has been drawn, which no one dares—upon pain of excommunication—step outside. Of course, the conceptual incommensurabilities between Heideggerian and non-Heideggerian discourse, far from being an "external" matter, speak to the essence of the philosophical considerations at issue: throughout his work, Heidegger sought to explode from within the inherited definitions of philosophical truth; above all, the idea that the vocation of philosophy would be adequately realized through an exclusive emphasis on "correspondence," "judgment," or "propositional adequacy." Instead, in his view, there is a more fundamental or "primordial" substratum of philosophical questioning that remains concealed as a result of our habitual, prejudicial equation of "truth" with "propositional truth." This "substratum" pertains to what Heidegger refers to as the "question of Being": that pristine, quintessentially Greek capacity for wonder or amazement (*Thaumazein*) about what it means "to be" or "to exist" as such; a sensibility that precedes Being's historical desecration and parceling out by philosophical categories, systems, and academic disciplines. And however much one elects to disagree with Heidegger's specific elaboration of this insight throughout the twists and turns of some fifty years of philosophical reflection, it would take a peculiar in-sensitivity to philosophical questioning in general to remain un-moved by the originality, rigor, and profundity with which he sets this enterprise of philosophical interrogation in motion.

It would, at the same time, perhaps be too easy to interpret the aforementioned "conceptual incommensurabilites" between Hei-deggerian and traditional philosophical discourse as symptomatic of an *absolute impermeability* in consequence of which "never the twain shall meet." And despite the fact that Heidegger himself is so convinced of the deficiencies of traditional philosophy that he goes to no small lengths to reinvent both the terms and terminol-ogy of philosophical study, there may exist more points in common between the two than may appear on first view; an impression that is especially confirmed by an examination of his lecture courses from the 1920s and 1930s (a good number of which have only re-cently been published), in which Heidegger's own positions are only set forth following a meticulous reading of and confrontation with "the tradition."

Thus, despite the stunning originality of many of his insights, it is essential to recognize that Heidegger's own claims to philo-sophical greatness are made on the basis of a putative "overcom-ing" (*Überwindung*) of the Western philosophical tradition. And it is precisely at this point that the problems of "discursive incom-mensurability" begin to dissipate; for we see that it is in terms of his life-long debate with this philosophical legacy that Heidegger's own theoretical project is best understood and evaluated. Hence, by scrutinizing this "debate with the tradition," it becomes ap-parent that Heidegger's philosophy itself presents a set of *internal standards* in terms of which an immanent analysis and critique of his work might be grounded. And it may prove the case that it is in those specific dimensions of his philosophy in which he departs most radically from certain aspects of the philosophical tradition—dimensions, moreover, that his disciples have tended to shield from criticism—that Heidegger's philosophical project becomes in truth most vulnerable.

Perhaps, then, one of the most important ways in which the study that follows diverges from many of the extant Heidegger commen-taries is its willingness to contest many of the apparent self-evidences of Heidegger's avowedly daunting categorial edifice; that is, to critically "think through" Heidegger's philosophy in a man-ner that parallels his own rigorous dialogue with so many other key Western thinkers. And while I have tried to limit the focus of my inquiry to the leitmotif of Heidegger's "political thought," it is with the hope that this heretofore somewhat neglected aspect of his philosophical enterprise may in fact yield a kind of privileged insight into the tensions and contradictions of his philosophy as a whole.

In a colorful 1979 review-essay on the theme of "Heidegger and practical philosophy," the philosopher Hans Ebeling urges that, insofar as the central categories of Heidegger's early philosophy such as "freedom" and "death" are, as a result of a "despair over metaphysics . . . solipsistically perverted," such themes in the future be treated like a "Schwarzwald cuckoo-clock": as "ornaments from the philosophical junk-heap, which many like, but which hardly anyone who is serious about punctuality will rely on." And while I am less confident than Ebeling that the "philosophical junk-heap" would be the proper resting place for the Heideggerian categories in question, there is another statement in the same review with which I thoroughly agree: his urgent appeal for a *"philosophical pendant to Pierre Bourdieu's sociological study, L'ontologie politique de Martin Heidegger."*

In fact, were I asked to summarize in a word or two the book I have sought to write, I would reply: "the philosophical complement to the book of Bourdieu." For while Bourdieu's study of Heidegger's "political ontology" convincingly details the intellectual historical basis of the Heideggerian philosophical "habitus," what is missing in his account is a concomitant *immanent philosophical analysis* of the philosopher's political thought as such. And as a result of the failure to incorporate this immanent philosophical dimension, in Bourdieu's work Heidegger's thought threatens to become indistinguishable from that of any one of a number of his German "conservative revolutionary" contemporaries—Ernst Jünger, Carl Schmitt, Moeller van den Bruck, Oswald Spengler, etc. Hence, what is lacking in Bourdieu's otherwise thorough study is the moment of "philosophical specificity," which in so many respects determines the "conditions of possibility" or the "transcendental ground" for Heidegger's empirical political attitudes and convictions.

According to my original plan, this book was intended to be a study of "decisionism" as a figure of twentieth-century ethical and political thought. But I soon came to realize once work on the Heidegger chapter had begun that the themes involved were of sufficient complexity and interest to warrant book-length treatment. However, the conclusion I had reached by no means met with universal approbation. For example, a grant application to a major national funding organization was turned down with the following explanation: "We have a high regard for the applicant's academic achievements and acknowledge the importance of his topic. But Dr. Wolin is not out simply to understand [Heidegger's] theories and to place them in historical context. *He is out to judge them.* He is an *advocate* and a *social theorist.*"*

But on the whole, I was probably more fortunate than most when it came to receiving financial support for my labors. I would thus like to acknowledge the generosity of Allen Matusow, Dean of Humanities, Rice University, and the Andrew W. Mellon Foundation for granting me a semester's leave during the 1986–87 academic year. And I would also like to express my gratitude to the Alexander von Humboldt Foundation of Bonn, West Germany for a year's fellowship during which most of the writing and rewriting of *The Politics of Being* was completed.

I owe a special debt of thanks to Jürgen Habermas, who proved a gracious host during my year as Alexander von Humboldt Fellow in the Department of Philosophy of Goethe University, Frankfurt am Main. I arrived in Frankfurt well aware of Professor Habermas' greatness as a philosopher and intellectual. I left with an awareness of his greatness as a man.

I would also like to express my sincere gratitude to the persons who evaluated and commented on the manuscript at various stages of completion: Professors Karsten Harries, Agnes Heller, Martin Jay, Otto Pöggeler, and Peter Steinberger. I'm convinced that their respective close readings have saved me from a good deal of—if not all—public embarrassment. Thanks is also due my editor at Columbia, Louise Waller, for her efficient and professional handling of all manuscript-related concerns. And to Ulysses Santamaria for his invaluable assistance in helping me keep abreast of the Heidegger debates in France.

Earlier drafts of chapters 1 and 2 appeared in French translation in the October 1987 and January 1989 issues of *Les Temps Modernes* under the titles "Recherches récentes sûr la relation de

---

*Upon reading these words I could not help but recall the plea with which Michel Foucault concludes his introduction to *The Archaeology of Knowledge*: "Do not ask who I am and do not ask me to remain the same: leave it to our bureaucrats and our police to see that our papers are in order. At least spare us their morality when we write."

Martin Heidegger au national socialism" and "La philosophie politique de *Sein und Zeit.*" I am grateful to the editor of *Les Temps
Modernes,* Claude Lanzmann, for permission to reprint as well as
for his generous hospitality during my recent visits to Paris.

This book is dedicated to my wife, Melissa Cox. For it was she
who, time and again, as I tottered at the edge of the proverbial
Heidegger "abyss" (*Ab-grund*), by way of a glance, a smile, or
sometimes a sigh (yes, I think it was very often a sigh) never failed
to remind me of the things that are truly important in life.

THE POLITICS OF BEING

ONE

Heidegger and Politics

> Was it not through a definite orientation of his thought that Heidegger fell—and not merely accidentally—into the proximity of National Socialism, *without ever truly emerging from this proximity?*
>
> Otto Pöggeler, "Afterword to the Second Edition,"
> *Martin Heidegger's Path of Thinking*

In the passionate debate that has raged over the course of the last several years concerning the National Socialist convictions of the German philosopher Martin Heidegger, many facts of great significance have come to light. At the same time, it is to be regretted that amid the din of partisan accusation "for and against," the paramount *theoretical* questions at stake in this controversy have for the most part been shunned.

For example: did Heidegger's partisanship for the National Socialist cause stand in an essential relation to his own "philosophy of existence" as elaborated in *Being and Time* and other writings? If so, what was the nature of this relation? What were the historico-philosophical conclusions that Heidegger would ultimately draw—if any—concerning the failure of his own National Socialist involvement? And, more importantly, what role would these conclusions play in his reevaluation of the fundamental premises of his own philosophical project from 1936 on?

Otto Pöggeler's observation that it was "through a definite orientation of his thought that Heidegger fell—and not merely accidentally—into the proximity of National Socialism," strongly suggests that our initial query concerning the likelihood of an integral relation between Heidegger's philosophy and his political involvement can be answered in the affirmative. But in conclusion, Pöggeler goes on to make a more sweeping, somewhat shocking claim: that Heidegger never truly *emerged* from this "proximity" to National Socialism; that in a crucial respect—which Pöggler leaves tantalizingly undefined in the context at hand—Heidegger's experience with Nazism in the early thirties continued to have a *defining influence on his thought.* Circumstantial support for Pöggeler's assertion would seem to be provided by the fact that in his later writings, Heidegger resolutely abstained from furnishing an explicit renunciation of his earlier National Socialist allegiances.[1]

It would, however, be unjust to attempt to play off the sublimity of the "philosophical stakes" of the Heidegger controversy vis-à-vis the "subaltern" biographical data that have been newly unearthed. In this respect, both despite and because of the fact that neither work possesses philosophical pretensions, the recent books by Victor Farias and Hugo Ott have performed an extremely valuable service: it is primarily in consequence of their tenacious archival probings that a momentous reappraisal of Heidegger's entire philosophical legacy has been set in motion.[2] The most significant change that has been brought about by the publication of their findings is that a number of facts concerning Heidegger's political involvement, which for decades had either been downplayed by the Heideggerian faithful (following the dissembling tactics of the Master himself) or simply denied, have been established irrefutably. In sum, only thanks to the overwhelming mass of evidence compiled simultaneously by Messrs. Farias and Ott has the full extent of Heidegger's commitment to the Nazi cause become a matter of public record.[3]

Indeed, the evidence, as most by now are aware, gives no small cause for alarm. When it came to the *Gleichschaltung* (the Nazi euphemism for the elimination of political opposition) of the modern German university system, which could proudly trace its origins back to the philosophies of Wilhelm von Humboldt and the German idealists, Heidegger, in his capacity as Rector of Freiburg University, proved well nigh *plus royaliste que le roi*—the *"roi"* in this case being Hitler himself. Or as we read in the personal telegram of May 20, 1933 that Heidegger sent to Hitler: "I faithfully request the postponement of the planned meeting of the executive committee of the German University League until a time when the especially necessary *Gleichschaltung* of the leadership of the League is completed."[4] In August of the same year, Heidegger personally assisted in the redrafting of the university charter at the provincial level in accordance with demands of the *Führerprinzip*. In the future, the rector, who had previously been elected by the university senate, would be known as the *Führer* of the university and would be directly appointed by the state minister of culture—thereby ending a long-standing tradition of university self-government at Freiburg. The various deans would likewise be referred to as the *Führer* of their respective disciplines and would be appointed by the new "Rector-*Führer*."

Heidegger would also prove a vigorous agitator on behalf of the policies of the new regime. In one speech in Heidelberg, he declared that the present generation of university professors was unfit; consequently, it was necessary for a new generation to replace them in ten years' time, one that would prove capable of meeting the demands and challenges of the "National Awakening." It was this brand of right-radical posturing that would seal the fate of his fouteen-year friendship with the philosopher Karl Jaspers, who was present in the audience when the speech was given.[5] Or as he would proclaim in another of his addresses, the university should be *"integrated again into the Volksgemeinschaft and joined together with the State."*[6] In early November 1933, he would on three separate occasions make ardent public appeals on behalf of Hitler's (*ex post facto*) plebiscite on Germany's withdrawal from the League of Nations. Nor does his ideological zealotry in these addresses leave much to the imagination of the audience. As he begins one speech: "The National Socialist Revolution is bringing about the total transformation of our German Dasein."[7] A "yes" vote in the referendum signaled for Heidegger a "decision" for "authenticity."

The unfortunate cases of Heidegger's political "denunciations" in his influential capacity as "Rector-*Führer*" have been well documented by Farias and Ott.[8] Nor did Heidegger ever conceal his conviction that, in keeping with the goals of the new Reich, "political" criteria were of foremost importance in making decisions regarding appointments and promotions. As he would remark on one occasion: "With reference to future appointments, first of all the question arises which of the candidates, presupposing his scientific and personal suitability, offers the greatest guarantee for the fulfillment of National Socialist educational goals."[9] Or as Heidegger, with unabashed candor, formulates his "educational philosophy" under the Nazi regime in a December 1933 memo circulated to the university deans: "Since the first days of my acceptance of office, the defining principle and the authentic (if only gradually realizable) goal [of my rectorship] has been *the fundamental transformation of scholarly education on the basis of the forces and demands of the National Socialist State.* . . . The individual by himself counts for nothing. The fate of our Volk in its State counts for everything."[10]

The vexing question of Heidegger's anti-Semitism—once thought to have been settled in the philosopher's favor—has recently resurfaced (a theme, moreover, that is surprisingly absent in Ott's otherwise thorough study). Charges of this nature were first made in Toni Cassirer's 1950 autobiography, *Mein Leben mit Ernst Cassirer*, where she speaks of having heard of Heidegger's "inclination toward anti-Semitism" as early as 1929.[11] In addition, there has been a longstanding rumor that while Rector, Heidegger barred his former teacher, Edmund Husserl, from utilizing the university libraries on the grounds that Husserl was a Jew; charges that have been denied as "calumny" by Heidegger in the 1966 *Spiegel* interview.[12] Heidegger's supporters point out that until 1933, the philosopher had many Jewish students—among them, Hannah Arendt, Hans Jonas, Karl Löwith, and Herbert Marcuse. And in the *Spiegel* interview, Heidegger emphasizes his support for embattled Jewish professors during the early years of the Hitler regime.

But here, too, evidence that has recently come to light weighs heavily against the philosopher's self-exculpatory strivings. We now know that Heidegger's July 1933 intercession on behalf of two dismissed Jewish professors, the classicist Eduard Fraenkel and the chemist Georg von Hevesy (who was awarded the Nobel prize in 1945), had an exclusively pragmatic basis: he was merely concerned that the summary dismissal, on racial grounds, of two internationally renowned scholars might have deleterious consequences for Germany's foreign policy interests. In his letter of July 12, 1933, moreover, Heidegger assured the Ministry of Education of his full support for the National Socialist ordinance barring Jews from civil service professions—the *Säuberung* ("cleansing") actions, as they were known.[13]

Although Heidegger–supporters have always considered Toni Cassirer's remarks regarding Heidegger's anti-Semitism as little more than unsubstantiated conjecture, a significant confirmation of her claims has recently surfaced in the form of a 1929 letter of recommendation composed by Heidegger on behalf of one of his students, Eduard Baumgarten. There, Heidegger attempts to bolster his appeal on Baumgarten's behalf with the following observation: "at stake is nothing less than the urgent awareness that we stand before a choice: once again to provide our *German* spiritual life with genuine, indigenous [*bodenständige*] manpower and educators, or to deliver it over definitively . . . to increasing Judification [*Verjudung*]."[14] When taken together, the testimony of Toni Cassirer and the Baumgarten letter suggest the degree to which Heidegger's political attitudes in the late 1920s were preconditioned by a set of well-defined, traditional cultural prejudices; and in the light of a growing body of corroborating evidence, his embrace of the Nazi cause in 1933 would seem far from adventitious.

Ironically, another well-documented instance of anti-Semitic conduct on Heidegger's part also concerns Baumgarten; though on this occasion, Baumgarten was the victim rather than the beneficiary of Heidegger's prejudicial sentiments. Thus in December 1933, after the two had had an intellectual falling out, Heidegger tried to block Baumgarten's appointment to Göttingen University by writing an unsolicited letter to the head of the National Socialist professors' organization there. Baumgarten should be disqualified for the position, argued Heidegger, insofar as he hailed from a "liberal-democratic" milieu in Heidelberg, had become excessively "Americanized" during a sojourn in the United States, and, lastly, owing to his associations with "the Jew [Eduard] Fraenkel."[15]

More recently, it has come to light that upon his accession to the Rectorship in May 1933, Heidegger immediately severed contact with all his Jewish dissertation students. And thus, according to the philosopher and former Heidegger student Max Müller, "From the moment that Heidegger became Rector, he allowed no Jewish students who had begun their dissertations with him to receive their degree."[16] According to the testimony of another Heidegger student in the early 1930s, Leopoldine Weizmann, he dashed the hopes of one highly touted doctoral candidate with the words, "You understand, Frau Mintz, that because you are a Jew I cannot supervise your promotion."[17]

Despite the well-documented incidents of anti–Semitic conduct on Heidegger's part,[18] it would be precipitate to conclude that "racial thinking" occupied an essential niche in his "world-view"— let alone in his philosophy. Instead, as one commentator has suggested, it is more likely that Heidegger's anti-Semitism was of the

5

"customary, cultural variety."[19] Nevertheless, it would at the same time be misleading to deny that so-called traditional "cultural anti–Semitism" formed the necessary historical precondition for the racial–biological anti–Semitism that had been germinating in German society since the late nineteenth-century; that is, for the virulent strain of anti–Semitism that proved to be the direct precursor of National Socialist racial doctrines.[20] What such flagrant displays of anti–Semitic sentiment suggest for our understanding of Heidegger's political maturation is that his intellectual world-view was much more profoundly conditioned than one might have initially believed by the vehement, latently fascistic "critique of modernity"—of "Western" values, the Enlightenment, "cosmopolitanism," and so forth—that was shared by both the German intellectual mandarinate and the provincial Volk alike.[21] Moreover, it suggests a question that is essential from the standpoint of the inquiry at hand: *viz.*, to what extent might this antimodernist world-view have impinged on the hypothetical purity of Heidegger's philosophical outlook itself (a question we shall pursue at some length in the following chapter)?

In 1945, the de-Nazification commission at Freiburg University would provide a cogent summation of both Heidegger's activities as Rector as well as the motivations underlying his actions. The most damning charges against him were formulated as follows:

> Before the revolutionary upheaval of 1933, the philosopher *Martin Heidegger* lived in a fully unpolitical, spiritual world; however, he maintained friendly relations (also through his sons) with the Youth Movement of that time and with certain literary spokesmen of German youth, such as Ernst Jünger, who proclaimed the end of the bourgeois-capitalist era and the advent of a new German socialism. From the National Socialist Revolution he expected a spiritual renewal of German life on a *völkisch* foundation and, like many German intellectuals, a reconciliation of social antagonisms and a preservation of Western culture in face of the dangers of communism. He did not have a clear understanding regarding the parliamentary political forms that preceded the National Socialist seizure of power [and] believed it was Hitler's historical mission to bring about the spiritual transformation that he [Heidegger] himself envisioned. . . .
>
> By virtue of the fact that he spoke of "labor service" and "military service" as having equal rights with "service in knowledge"

[in his Rectoral Address], he provided Nazi propaganda with the means to exploit his speech for political ends. While he envisioned the spiritual deepening and restructuring of the German university system . . . the Party used the mere fact that a scholar of his stature had joined its ranks and celebrated its victory in public addresses as a highly welcome propaganda tool. He himself had made its task an easy one, insofar as he sought to ensure a reliable following among the academic youth and allowed himself to be carried away to the point of inciting the students against their so-called "reactionary" professors. He hoped thereby to further his own plans for reform and also to gain a conspicuous standing within the Party, which would make it possible for him to maintain his own line, and where possible, to influence the internal development of the Party in a beneficial fashion. Naturally, these hopes were rapidly disappointed; the students were arrogant and insolent, the majority of professors were deeply offended by his often tactless and, in their eyes, impudent decrees, and were quickly driven into the opposition; the Party distanced itself from him the more it gradually recognized the internal opposition of his goals in the sphere of university politics to their own. The fact that he also enthusiastically participated in the transformation of the university constitution in accordance with the new *Führerprinzip*, in the introduction of the external forms of Hitlerism (e.g., the so-called "German greeting" [*Heil Hitler!*]) into academic life, replaced or exposed persons with anti-Nazi sentiments, even directly participated through newspaper appeals in National Socialist election propaganda, would change nothing of this estrangement. . . . In spite of this later estrangement, there can be no doubt that Heidegger, in the fateful year of 1933, consciously placed the great prestige of his scholarly reputation and his characteristic discursive style in the service of the National Socialist Revolution, and thereby made an essential contribution to the legitimation of this revolution in the eyes of educated Germans.[22]

After a lengthy series of hearings, the verdict handed down by the university commission was severe: Heidegger, who had suffered a nervous breakdown requiring hospitalization during the course of the proceedings, was both stripped of his *venia legendi* (i.e., his right to teach at the university level) and denied emeritus status, by virtue of which he would have still been allowed to participate in university activities. In essence, he was summarily banned from university life; although this judgment was rescinded in 1951, when the political climate in Germany had stabilized.

This significant extension of our factual knowledge concerning Heidegger's "case" has raised new questions concerning the integrity of his philosophical *oeuvre*. And it is in this vein that Pöggeler has suggested that only by thoroughly scrutinizing the premises of Heidegger's philosophical outlook might the intellectual basis of his political commitment first become truly intelligible. If, then, the motivation behind Heidegger's political involvement is in fact philosophically grounded, to what extent might this fact impugn his philosophical achievements? To be sure, the attempt to pose such questions has not sat exceedingly well with Heidegger's more intransigent defenders. Their responses have ranged from intemperate denunciations of the bearer of bad tidings—that is, of Farias himself—to the rigid disavowal that under the best of conditions philosophy might play a role in influencing practical conduct.[23] Or else, as on the previous occasions when the question of Heidegger's Nazism has been raised, one of the preferred strategies of denial has been to proclaim the enduring separation between Heidegger the empirical person—who is fallible and finite—and the philosophical *oeuvre* itself—which is a work of "truth," and as such, "eternal."[24] But given the results of the new biographical researches into Heidegger's past—which have established that Heidegger's National Socialist sentiments, far from being an episodic phenomenon in the philosopher's life, continued to haunt his thinking at least until the mid-1940s[25]—it has become increasingly difficult to avoid the conclusion that Heidegger's Nazi experience stood in an "essential" relation to his philosophical project as a whole.[26]

Moreover, as both Nicholas Tertulian and Jürgen Habermas have convincingly shown, beginning with the Rectoral Address of 1933, Heidegger's philosophy itself undergoes a fundamental transformation: it ceases to be a pristine "first philosophy"; it becomes in addition a veritable *Weltanschauung* or "world-view." From this moment hence, it becomes increasingly difficult to plead a case for the putative purity or "philosophical autonomy" of Heidegger's doctrines. Instead, they become fused with ideological and historico-philosophical considerations that will henceforth prove inseparable from the inner logic of the philosophy itself.[27] One need only consult Heidegger's lecture courses from this period (e.g., *An Introduction to Metaphysics* [1935] and *Hölderlin's Hymns "Germanien" and the "Rhine"* [1934–35]) for ample confirmation of this thesis. As Winfried Franzen has suggested, the crucial step in this process of ideological recrystallization may well have been the intensive debate with the generation of conservative revolutionary thinkers—for example, Oswald Spengler, Ludwig Klages, and, most importantly, Ernst Jünger—undertaken by Heidegger in his 1929 lecture course, *The Fundamental Concepts of Metaphysics*.[28]

For the investigation at hand, the axial relation between fundamental ontology and political engagement is of paramount significance. And thus, as Franzen has remarked, "The more it is shown that [Heidegger's] conduct represents a genuine engagement for National Socialism, the more urgent is the question as to whether the specific roots of this engagement are to be sought out in Heidegger's philosophy."[29] These two facets of Heidegger's life—philosophy and politics—may be said to interact as communicating vessels. However, neither aspect of his life's work passes into the other without leaving a remainder. And while each may rightfully be judged in its own terms, it may also be fruitful to view them as dimensions of a philosophical life that mutually inform one another. Thus, neither aspect can be fully comprehended without recourse to the other. The philosophical doctrine must be understood as a conceptual fundament that, in the last analysis, bears responsibility for its political "effects." And while it would be illegitimate to evaluate that doctrine solely in terms of the "effects" to which it gives rise in an "alien" sphere—the realm of practical life—at the same time, the doctrine itself cannot be understood as existing in an ideational vacuum that is wholly impervious to its effects. Thus, its repercussions in the domain of life-praxis cannot help but significantly influence at a later stage Heidegger's self-understanding as a philosopher. Consequently, whereas to invoke such so-called "external factors" or "effects" can hardly be said to deliver a death-blow to the substance of the philosophy, it would hardly be justifiable to exempt them from consideration entirely.

The relation between philosophy and life-conduct is never direct, but always a highly mediated affair. In Heidegger's case, the element of mediation is provided by his "political philosophy"; or, more adequately expressed—since, for reasons that will later become clear, Heidegger never articulated a political philosophy *per se*—by the "political thought" through which Heidegger seeks to philosophically ground his understanding of the world political situation.

That philosophy and political conduct stand in necessary association with one another is by no means a self-evident truth in the annals of cultural history. An apparent refutation of their causal relation that is often cited is the case of the logician Gottlob Frege, who also happened to be a virulent anti-Semite. Certainly, we are instructed, Frege's anti-Semitism in no way redounds to the discredit of his logical theories. Nor can it in the least be claimed, conversely, that those theories contain the seeds of his anti-Semitism. To be sure, we may well hold Frege the historically existent individual in less esteem as a result of our awareness of his prejudicial sentiments. But it stands beyond doubt that in his case philosophy and life-conduct lie at a safe remove from one another.

Why should things be any different in Heidegger's case? Because of the nature of his philosophy itself. One of the essential components of Heidegger's philosophy is the claim that Being and Time stand in necessary relation to one another, that Being itself contains an inalienable temporal dimension. As a "philosophy of existence," this means that the drama of being human—Dasein's "factical" coming to presence—not only occurs in history, *but is itself historical*. "Historicity" is the term Heidegger coins to describe the intrinsically historical character of human Being-in-the-world. But if this is really the case, then it would be senseless to talk about a "philosophy of existence" for which the relation between philosophy and life-praxis would be a matter of indifference; or in which these two terms could be said to stand at an infinite remove from one another—as seemed to be true with respect to Frege. Such a conclusion, moreover, would seem especially apposite in the case of Heidegger's philosophy, in which the overcoming of the traditional philosophical division of labor between "theoretical" and "practical" reason becomes a programmatic theoretical objective. Indeed, Heidegger is constantly telling us that in its circumspect dealings with the world, Dasein is *already philosophical*; and that "thought" itself is *already practical*. In the cases of epistemology, aesthetics, and logic, the consequences of philosophy for practical life-conduct may well be extremely significant;[30] but, more often than not, the specific character of their interrelation is highly mediated and indirect. Conversely, the overcoming of the traditional diremption between theory and practice sought by *Existenzphilos-*

ophie suggests the likelihood of a more intimate and integral relation between these two spheres.

Heidegger's own metatheoretical observations on the relation between philosophy and political life are diffuse and variegated; but for all that, they are far from unrigorous, let alone "nonphilosophical." *Being and Time,* for example, can hardly be said to contain an independent political theory. However, it does in no small measure harbor a *philosophy of practical life* that suggests important inferences for the organization of political existence— an inchoate and implicit philosophy of political conduct as it were. On the one hand, it would be extremely unjust to attempt to read Heidegger's political engagement of the mid-1930s back into this apparently apolitical treatise of 1927. This caveat should be respected, among other reasons, insofar as Heidegger's own philosophical self-understanding undergoes a series of important transformations during these years. On the other hand, according to all available evidence, Heidegger himself viewed his political endeavors of the mid-1930s as being *of a piece with his philosophy.* That is, he was firmly convinced that his theory of fundamental ontology, as elaborated in *Being and Time* and subsequent works, itself provided the philosophical mandate or grounding in terms of which his political engagement could be justified. The locus classicus in support of this claim is Heidegger's 1933 Rectoral Address, "The Self-Affirmation of the German University." Here, Heidegger expresses with breathtaking clarity what philosophy may expect from the National Revolution—and, conversely, what the National Revolution may expect from philosophy. In a similar vein, he would confirm in a conversation with Karl Löwith in 1936 that "his partisanship for National Socialism lay in the essence of his philosophy."[31]

Thus, while it would be unjust to reduce the "theory of practical life" contained in *Being and Time* to the specific historical realization Heidegger accorded it circa 1933, it is nevertheless fully legitimate to inquire to what extent the philosophical bases of that theory may have facilitated (or restrained) Heidegger's partisanship for the Third Reich. That is, it is certainly valid to reconstruct the inner logic whereby Heidegger's early philosophy of existence provided the conceptual impetus for his turn to National Socialism. This labor of theoretical reconstruction, moreover, may well provide us with valuable insight concerning the internal weaknesses and deficiencies of his early philosophy as a whole.

For Heidegger, the fact that Being comes to presence over the course of time means that Being *has a history*. The theory of *Seinsgeschichte* or "the history of Being" consequently will come to play a seminal role in the course of Heidegger's philosophical development in the 1930s. The more Heidegger comes explicitly to rely on this notion of an autonomous and self-generating "history of Being"—a concept that remained merely implicit in his great work of 1927—the more the theory of practical life elaborated in *Being and Time* falls into partial eclipse. For in keeping with the "Turn" in Heidegger's philosophical development, "destiny" becomes less a product of the resolute decisions—or *Entschlossenheit*—of authentic Dasein and increasingly the result of a mysterious "fate" that has been decreed by Being itself; in Heideggerian parlance, a *Seinsgeschick*.

But if Being can be said to have a "history," might it not also have a "politics"? That is, might there not exist a *Seinspolitik* or a *politics of Being*? Or, to pose the same question in slightly different terms: might there not be determinate forms of political life that would be especially conducive to Being's historical "coming to presence"? We know that the central lamentation of Heidegger's philosophy was directed against the phenomenon of *Seinsvergessenheit*—the forgetting of Being. If the process of *Seinsvergessenheit*, as it comes to pass in the course of the history of Being, is an eminently historical, this-worldly phenomenon, then one might also inquire: what is the role to be played by *politics* in the historico-metaphysical process whereby the "forgetting of Being" is overcome? Can politics with any plausibility be said to function as a "midwife" in the process whereby the truth of Being is historically recovered? The same question can of course be rephrased in the negative with reference to those political structures that prove singularly *unreceptive*—if not actually antagonistic—to the reemergence of Being. And thus, one might further inquire as to the specific contours and shape of the political philosophy that would be appropriate to the project of ontological reclamation envisioned by Heidegger. Though Heidegger has not provided us with a full-fledged political theory, his doctrine of the history of Being certainly contains portentous rudiments of such a theory.

One claim can be made with a fair amount of certainty concerning Heidegger's philosophically grounded conviction that a resurgence of *German* Dasein alone could save the West from a fate of eternal nihilistic decline (a belief he adheres to in his writings as late as 1943): in 1945, it foundered cataclysmically. The historical consequences of Heidegger's theory of the singularity of "western-Germanic historical Dasein"[32] proved disastrous for the world, for Germany, as well as for Heidegger personally. A reevaluation of fundamental philosophical premises thus seemed to be mandated by these events. However, the immediate effect that the world catastrophe seemed to have on his philosophy was a *retreat from the categories of practical philosophy in toto*—for the latter seemed irrevocably contaminated by the events of the recent historical past. Yet, it behooves us to inquire: was it *practical philosophy per se*—associated for Heidegger with the quasi-Nietzschean category of "the will to will"—that was responsible for this world disaster of unprecedented proportions? Or was it not a historically specific *perversion* of the categories of practical philosophy—by that very National Socialist regime whose praises Heidegger had once publicly sung—that must be faulted if true insight into the real causes of the catastrophe is to be gained? Moreover, isn't Heidegger's total *abandonment* of the categories of practical reason in his later philosophy—a stance that is perhaps best epitomized by his infamous proclamation in the 1966 *Spiegel* interview that, "Only a god can save us"—in truth merely a prescription for surrender and resignation: the sad profession of impotence on the part of a once-great thinker?

Out of concern that the later Heidegger has ill-advisedly jettisoned all prospects of political philosophical reflection, the philosopher Leo Strauss has warned that there is "no room for political philosophy in Heidegger's work"; this may be due, Strauss continues, to the fact that "the room in question is occupied by gods or the gods."[33] Thus, in the work of the later Heidegger, *Seinsverlassenheit*—abandonment by Being—simultaneously signifies *Gottesverlassenheit*—abandonment by the gods. His "thought" (*Denken*) occupies the space that has been vacated by a type of *double forsakenness* that has become the distinguishing feature of the modern age: an age that is irredeemably suspended in the no man's land between "the no-longer of the gods that have fled and the not-yet of the god to come."[34] And thus, as Heidegger himself remarks, "The only possibility available to us is that by thinking and poetizing we prepare a readiness for the appearance of a god, or for the absence of a god in [our] decline, insofar as in view of the absent god we are in a state of decline."[35] In this respect, Strauss's observation concerning the conspicuous absence of po-

13

litical philosophical reflection in the later Heidegger seems eminently justified. For the position or space traditionally reserved for political thought gives way in his later work to ruminations concerning our condition of irredeemable secular impotence brought about by the absence of "god" or "the gods"; it gives way to fanciful speculation concerning the "four-fold" (*das Geviert*) of gods and mortals, heaven and earth. And thus, given the cosmologically inspired diagnosis of the human condition proffered by Heidegger, it would be senseless—in truth, an act of unbridled intellectual *hubris*—to engage in systematic reflection on the subject of what would constitute "the best polity" in the sphere of human affairs. Our *Gottesverlassenheit* or "abandonment by the gods" has gone too far for it to be amenable to resolution by the autonomous powers of human thought or will. Hence, "only a god can save us."

At the same time, Heidegger's philosophically conditioned antipathy to the concerns of political theory is a relatively late development: it characterizes his philosophy only after the German *Zusammenbruch* or collapse of 1945, as the *Kehre* or "Turn" in his thinking becomes radicalized. However, earlier (and this is true above all of his "middle phase," from 1933 to 1936) his treatises and lectures contain copious instances of a *"seinsgeschichtlich"* (literally: as viewed from the standpoint of the history of Being) or historico-metaphysically grounded understanding of political reality; an approach to the understanding of political life we have christened *Seinspolitik* or the *"politics of Being."*

One might, however, claim that Heideggerian *Seinspolitik* recaptures the dimension of political philosophical reflection at the expense of its substance. The chief aim of the Heideggerian polis is to make the world safe for the flourishing of Being—not human action. It is our contention that the interests of the former and the latter not only fail to coincide, but in fact prove inimical to one another. In his political thought, Heidegger willfully sacrifices the plurality and difference of human practical life on the altar of an atavistic Eleatic totem—the totem of "Being." And thus, the requisites of human action as an autonomous sphere of life prove unable to come into their own in face of the all-consuming nature of the ontological search. With Heidegger, the tasks of fundamental ontology and those of political philosophy proper are confused; with the result that, in the end, the concerns of political theory are mechanically subordinated to those of the *Seinsfrage* (the "question of Being") itself. The precarious potentials of political life are thereby left to wither under the shadow of this holy ontological quest. In face of the *Seinsfrage* and its incontrovertible metaphysical "primordiality," all other spheres of merely human endeavor cannot help but appear as epiphenomenal and subaltern.

The focal point of the present study is the political philosophy implicit in Martin Heidegger's thought, not his philosophy *per se*. To be sure, a consideration of this specific aspect of his thinking is inseparable from and contingent upon an understanding of his philosophical project as a whole. However, it should be emphasized that the findings of such a partial or "regional" study may only prove transferable to the quintessence of the philosophy itself in a highly qualified and tentative fashion. To conclude from its results that, because Heidegger's *political thought* is critically flawed, the same judgment would hold true for his philosophy as a whole, would be premature.

Nevertheless, as we have sought to show, Heidegger's political thought is in no way isolable and separate from his systematic reflections on human existence, fundamental ontology, the history of Being, etc. Rather, his political judgments and opinions follow from his philosophy with a cogency that is both undeniable and potent. Perhaps, therefore, the interpretive strategy we have elected to follow in addressing Heidegger's formidable philosophical *oeuvre*— which, as a result of its limited focus on the realm of political theory, might be described as pursuing the line of least resistance—may serve to sensitize a critically minded public to some of the more general intellectual failings of the philosopher and his work.

The question of "Heidegger and Politics" has been, and will likely continue to be, one of the most enigmatic themes in the intellectual history of the twentieth century. It is the saga—or tragedy— of a devil's bargain struck between the century's greatest philosopher (at least in the continental tradition) and the most barbarous political regime the world has known. To comprehend the nature of Heidegger's political wager thus requires a tolerance for paradoxes and contradictions. Perhaps the greatest of these may be formulated as follows: how was it possible that the self-proclaimed heir of the Western intellectual tradition could deliberately place his philosophical talents at the disposal of a tyrannical power that represented that tradition's absolute negation?

T W O

Being and Time as Political Philosophy

Now, from personal experience I can tell you that neither in his lectures, nor in his seminars, nor personally, was there ever any hint of [Heidegger's] sympathies for Nazism. . . . So his openly declared Nazism came as a complete surprise to us. From that point on, of course, we asked ourselves the question: did we overlook indications and anticipations in *Being and Time* and the related writings? And we made one interesting observation, *ex-post* (I want to stress that, *ex-post*, it is easy to make this observation). If you look at his view of human existence, of Being-in-the-world, you will find a highly repressive, highly oppressive interpretation. I have just today gone again through the table of contents of *Being and Time* and had a look at the main categories in which he sees the essential characteristics of existence or Dasein. I can just read them to you and you will see what I mean: "Idle talk, curiosity, ambiguity, falling and Being-thrown, concern, Being-toward-death, anxiety, dread, boredom," and so on. Now this gives a picture which plays well on the fears and frustrations of men and women in a repressive society—a joyless existence: overshadowed by death and anxiety; human material for the authoritarian personality.

Herbert Marcuse, "Heidegger's Politics: An Interview"

Between Philosophy and World-View

With his 1927 work, *Being and Time,* Heidegger burst forth on the German philosophical scene with unprecedented vigor and acclaim. Had he never written another book, this pathbreaking study would have assured his position in the history of philosophy—the later doubts of the philosopher himself concerning the philosophical adequacy of this early standpoint notwithstanding. For one can say of *Being and Time* something that one can say of very few works in the Western philosophical tradition: it develops a theoretical framework that fundamentally revolutionizes our understanding of traditional philosophical problems and subject matter. In its wake, the self-evidences of some 2500 years of prior philosophical inquiry seem profoundly shaken—to the point where it could be said that to practice philosophy henceforth in willful disregard of Heidegger's radical challenge to the Western metaphysical legacy would be to risk practicing philosophy "naively."

For all that, *Being and Time* is hardly a study that emerges *ex nihilo* or without important precursors. The very different, yet complementary, critiques of "metaphysical objectivism" proffered by two nineteenth-century thinkers, Kierkegaard and Nietzsche, stand as crucial harbingers of Heidegger's own philosophical program.[1] And Husserl's phenomenological method—its attempt to cut through the network of unwarranted presuppositional assumptions afflicting traditional science in order to yield a nonprejudicial, pristine intuition of "things themselves"—likewise represents an essential *sine qua non* of Heidegger's theoretical approach.

Yet, however dependent he may have been on these previous conceptual breakthroughs, there can be little doubt that Heidegger's recasting of the parameters and language of traditional metaphysical inquiry represents a feat of breathtaking philosophical originality. Two insights—whose ambiguous interrelationship has been a constant source of controversy among Heidegger interpreters—variously elaborated throughout the course of Heidegger's prolonged and demanding 1927 treatise, stand out above all. First, the claim that traditional philosophy, as a result of its inordinate preoccupation with the nature of "entities" or "beings," has perennially bypassed the more fundamental or "primordial" question concerning *the nature of Being in general*. One might refer to this as the "ontological" dimension of Heidegger's work. Second, the contention that the "being" that offers privileged access to the realm of ontological inquiry—human being, which Heidegger dubs "Dasein"—is neither *res cogitans*, nor a "transcendental ego," nor an "intentional consciousness," but, first and foremost, an *embodied* subjectivity: a *Being-in-the-world* that is subject to a prescientific forestructure of practical and social relations. One might refer to this as the "existential" dimension of Heidegger's inquiry. Perhaps even more than the ontological side—the re-thematization of Being—it is this dimension that has had enormous repercussions for the self-understanding of modern philosophy. For Heidegger's "existential" account of the various foundational "world-relations" in which the "there-being" of Dasein is primordially embedded—for example, "understanding," "care," "Being-with," and "everydayness"—throws into serious doubt the standard claims to primacy on the part of theoretical-scientific consciousness—the consciousness that has been so dominant heretofore in our modern Western culture. To uphold Heidegger's existential recasting of human Being-in-the world is to suggest that our prior, predominantly Cartesian self-understanding as *theoretical beings* (as "thinking substance") is in fact something derivative and secondary. Conversely, our status as *self-interpreting beings* would no longer be relegated to the subaltern sphere of unrigorous, nonscientific musings, but would be accorded a new and essential "primordiality"— to use the Heideggerian expression.

Undoubtedly, the most enduring achievement of Heidegger's influential 1927 study is what might be referred to as the "hermeneutical imperative": the claim that Dasein "is ontically distinguished by the fact that, in its very Being, that Being is an issue for it";[2] that human Being-in-the-world is fundamentally characterized by self-interpretation or *understanding (Verstehen)*. And thus, the methodological starting point by which Heidegger allows his inquiry to be guided is the conviction that, in the words of Hans-Georg Gadamer, "*Understanding is the original character of the Being of human life itself.*" This argument constitutes Heidegger's basic appeal for the "universality"—or "primordiality"—of the hermeneutical standpoint. According to Gadamer:

> Heidegger's temporal analytics of human existence (Dasein) has, I think, shown convincingly that understanding is not just one of the various possible behaviors of the subject, but *the mode of Being of Dasein itself*. This is the sense in which the term "hermeneutics" has been used. . . . Not caprice, or even an elaboration of a single aspect, but the nature of the thing itself makes the movement of understanding comprehensive and universal.[3]

In his development of the hermeneutical position, Heidegger certainly had important precursors: above all, Dilthey's deployment of the concept of "life" as the universal basis for historical understanding.[4] However, it would be difficult to overemphasize the originality and rigor with which Heidegger's philosophical elaboration of this idea proceeds. And from our present historical vantage point, it is not difficult to appreciate the enormous intellectual impact this notion has had in the fields of philosophy, sociology, and literary criticism. The so-called "interpretive turn" in the human sciences would be virtually inconceivable apart from Heidegger's emphatic rehabilitation of this concept.[5]

At the same time, it is likely that certain immanent difficulties of presentation have forestalled a more unreservedly positive reception of the idea-complex embodied in *Being and Time*. We have already referred to the potential confusion of levels of philosophical analysis that afflicts the relation between the "ontological" and "existential" dimensions of the work. But in addition, one finds there a studied disregard of traditional modes of philosophical argumentation and discourse, which is a product of Heidegger's own self-understanding as an intellectual iconoclast and breaker of traditions; a self-understanding, moreover, that is responsible for the characteristic amalgamation of blindness and insight that one finds so often in Heidegger's work. It is in this vein that the philosopher Ernst Tugendhat has remarked that the philosophical discourse of *Being and Time* proceeds in a *"non-argumentative and evocative fashion"*; and thus, instead of trying to make his positions plausible through the customary techniques of philosophical argumentation and analysis, Heidegger seeks to convince his readership primarily by recourse to various rhetorical strategies, as well as the employment of neologisms whose conceptual self-evidence is merely assumed. As Tugendhat explains:

> Heidegger's need to disengage himself from the tradition was so strong here [in *Being and Time*] that instead of casting these familiar phenomena [categories pertaining to volition and activity—R. W.] in a new light, he chose to elucidate the subject matter by means of a series of terms that were idiosyncratically adopted and insufficiently explained. This procedure of explication through the sheer accumulation [*Anhäufung*] of words is frequent in *Being and Time*, and it is connected to what I have called the *evocative method*.[6]

A similar point has been raised by Theodor Adorno in his polemical work, *The Jargon of Authenticity*. In Adorno's view, the discourse of Heideggerian *Existenzphilosophie* "sees to it that what it wants is on the whole felt and accepted through its mere delivery, without regard to the content of the words used." Thus, insofar as "the words of the jargon sound as if they said something higher than what they mean . . . whoever is versed in the jargon does not have to say what he thinks, does not even have to think it properly."[7]

In a perceptive commentary on the latent political content of Heideggerian fundamental ontology, Alfons Söllner has reached an analogous conclusion. At issue is a philosophical approach "whose evocative linguistic magic leads to a mimesis of fate rather than to an analysis of concrete social causes of the feeling of crisis." It is at this point, according to Söllner, that "the paradoxical relation between intrinsic [i.e., philosophical] analysis and political meaning becomes comprehensible." For the "mimesis of fate" promoted by Heidegger's imperious and presumptive use of philosophical terminology reveals the latently authoritarian tendencies of his thought in general. Or, as Söllner concludes, "the authoritarian sense or non-sense of Heideggerian philosophy lies in its jargon and its linguistic gestures."[8]

And thus, the "difficulties of presentation" alluded to above, which pertain to both the conflation of levels of discourse (existential and ontological) as well as to what Tugendhat has dubbed Heidegger's "evocative method," are far from irrelevant for an understanding of the political philosophical significance of Heidegger's 1927 work. Even more pertinent to such concerns, however, is the presence of an extraphilosophical, ideological-cultural dimension that plays a critical role in the realization of the conceptual plan of *Being and Time*. For although it has become a fairly standard practice today (especially among Anglo-american circles) to view Heidegger's study primarily as a treatise in continental philosophy (albeit, a fairly radical one), only closer attention to the sociohistorical context in which it was composed will provide the key to its implicit political philosophical makeup. The extent to which Heidegger may have consciously or unconsciously incorporated such putatively "ideological elements" into the philosophical framework of *Being and Time* is contestable; their overall presence, however, is not. Here, I am referring to various components of the so-called *conservative revolutionary world-view* that became so influential among the German mandarin intelligentsia in the middle to late 1920s; a world-view that, in many crucial respects, laid the intellectual foundations for Hitler's rise to power. For a full understanding of the overall cultural significance of *Being and Time*, an appreciation of the work's so-called "ideological" dimension will prove essential. For were this dimension to be omitted from the picture, Heidegger's "existential decision" for National Socialism in 1933 would be explicable solely as a leap of faith; a commitment possessing only the most adventitious and ephemeral connection with his philosophical standpoint of the late 1920s.

Indeed, a good many of the philosopher's champions have pursued precisely this argumentative tack in Heidegger's defense—or, to be more precise, in defense of his philosophy. But just as we spoke earlier about a confusion of ontological and existential levels in his work, one could similarly identify an interlacing of its *philosophical and ideological components*. And while these two aspects of the work are certainly analytically separable, in its factical or actual articulation, they prove *inextricably interwoven*. As we shall attempt to show, the content and structure of the "existential analytic"—the presentation of the constituent features of Dasein's Being-in-the-world—would be unthinkable without both moments, ideological as well as philosophical.

What one might refer to as the "world-view" (*weltanschaulich*) character of Heidegger's 1927 work has been perhaps best captured by the philosopher Winfried Franzen:

> Heidegger's *Being and Time* was written at a time when the first of the great world catastrophes had, more than ever before, shaken confidence in the [Western-scientific] heritage that began with the Greeks. Heidegger's critique of traditional ontology is only comprehensible against the background of an era that had absolutized the 'science' in the sense of the exact, individual sciences, that had made technology into an uncontrollable Moloch, and that had devalued man into a mere functionary of the civilization-process. . . . When viewed in this way, fundamental ontology is in fact a theory and critique of the present age.

However, as Franzen goes on to observe, "It is both of these in a highly problematical way."[9]

We know that during the years 1933–1934, Heidegger went to great lengths to justify his partisanship for National Socialism in categories explicitly culled from the theoretical framework of *Being and Time*; categories such as "decision," "resolve," "fate," "authenticity," and so forth. Indeed, the most cursory glance at his political speeches and writings from this period readily confirms this impression.[10] And thus, the posing of a quasi-Kantian question would seem to be in order. Given the fact that Heidegger himself sought to ground and justify his participation in the National Socialist movement on the basis of his early philosophy of existence, *how was this possible*? Could it be that in a qualified sense, the existential framework of *Being and Time* may have provided a type of "transcendental grounding" for Heidegger's political conduct in the 1930s? If our preliminary reflections concerning the essential interrelatedness of the philosophical and ideological components of *Being and Time* are valid, this would suggest the necessity of submitting the work to a "double reading." One would have to understand it not only as a work of "first philosophy," but also *as a work of its time*. This would require special attentiveness to those aspects of its thematic structure that have internalized constitutive moments of the conservative revolutionary critique of modernity. The result would ideally broaden, rather than narrow, the horizon of our previous understanding of *Being and Time*. It would be read not merely as a philosophical treatise, but—perhaps for the first time—with an eye to its general cultural significance. For the self-conscious radicalism of Heidegger's philosophical project—its indictment of 2500 previous years of Western philosophy, which has been tainted by a deficient understanding of Being—is incomprehensible apart from the deflation of European cultural confidence following World War I.

And thus, as Gadamer has remarked, *Being and Time* "effectively communicated to a wide public something of the new spirit that had engulfed philosophy as a result of the convulsions of World War I."[11] This event more than any other seemed like a Nietzschean prophecy come to pass: *viz.*, the confirmation of his thesis concerning the disqualification of all inherited Western values and the final triumph of nihilism. *Being and Time* is a study in "fundamental ontology," "hermeneutical phenomenology," *Existenzphilosophie*, etc., but it is also emphatically something else: an attempt, based on a re-posing of the "question of Being," to suggest a path of deliverance from the contemporary cultural crisis—the "decline of the West."

"A dominant race can grow up only out of terrible and violent beginnings," observes Nietzsche. *"Where are the barbarians of the twentieth century?"* he goes on to declaim in an oft-cited remark.[12] That is: where are the "modern pagans" who are no longer beholden to the decaying cultural paradigms of bourgeois Europe, and who are thus capable of giving birth to a new set of heroic, life-affirming, *antinihilistic values*? Could it be that Heidegger poses precisely this Nietzschean question in the late 1920s, as the exacerbated chaos of the Weimar years reached its zenith? And could it be that in the National Socialists and their charismatic *Führer*, he believes he has found an answer to the *fin-de-siècle* rhetorical conundrum posed by Nietzsche?

The "Historicity" of *Being and Time*

By emphasizing the historical situatedness of Heidegger's 1927 study, we have implicitly raised the question of the *historicity* of his philosophy itself. Historicity, of course, is one of the central categories of *Being and Time*, a constitutive variant of the theory of "temporality" that figures so prominently in Heidegger's work. In the idiom of Heidegger's 1927 study, historicity signifies the fundamentally historical character of all human Being-in-the-world and life-forms; a nineteenth-century claim to which Heidegger adds an important "existential" twist: not only does Being-in-the-world exist *in* history, but human existence is itself *historical*. That is, "historicity" is not merely a quality of Being-in-the-world that reveals itself *ex post* to the detached and objective observer (this is the fallacy of the way in which the concepts of "life" and *Erlebnis* function in Dilthey's work). Rather it characterizes the facticity of human Dasein itself, which takes the form of an active mediation of a given past in light of a self-chosen, future-oriented potentiality-for-Being (*Seinskönnen*).

It is the category of historicity that ironically provides the basis for an immanent critique of Heidegger's own early philosophical achievements. And thus, the question of historicity, which Heidegger poses in an ontological vein, must be posed with regard to the intellectual historical status of *Being and Time* itself. Yet, to raise the question of the historical determination of Heidegger's philosophical project may pose an immanent threat to its conceptual integrity. For how can a philosophy that understands itself as "fundamental ontology"— as a delineation of the timeless and essential structures that define our Being-in-the world—and hence, which stakes claims to eternal validity, itself be a product of "vulgar" historical circumstances?[13] Certainly, were the historically contingent character of the argument of *Being and Time* demonstrated convincingly, its "ontological" pretensions would be significantly deflated. Yet, as we have already suggested, perhaps in order to be appreciated fully as a philosophical treatise, *Being and Time* must simultaneously be understood as a *historical document*—as a product of determinate historical conditions and of a specific intellectual historical lineage.

One of the keys to understanding the historical determinacy of Heidegger's early work is the entrenched antimodernism of the German mandarin intelligentsia. The practical manifestations of this attitude ranged from a die-hard apoliticism—which sought refuge from the turmoil of contemporary historical reality in the realm of traditional Germanic cultural ideals—to a jingoistic affirmation of German militarism. However, the ease with which the antimodernist apoliticism of the cultural elite could, under adverse historical conditions, pass over into a virulent German nationalism was illustrated time and again in the case of World War I—Thomas Mann's *Confessions of an Unpolitical Man* being perhaps the classical example. The historian Wolfgang Abendroth has described the essential traits of this so-called apoliticism in the following terms: "To be 'unpolitical' meant to uncritically acclaim the power of the dominant classes in Germany and the power of the German Reich against other states; to [sanction] the use of force against the democratic powers of the lower classes as well as against other states; thus [it meant] not only the acceptance of existing power relations, but also the acceptance of the expansionist political designs of the holders of power."[14]

Heidegger's career may be treated as a paragon of the cultural dynamic described by Abendroth. The smug apoliticism of the Weimar years gives way to a period of radical engagement on behalf of the National Socialist cause in 1933. His eventual disillusionment with Nazism is then followed by a return to an apparently unshakable apoliticism in the postwar years. But this later "apoliticism" is preserved in name only, insofar as Heidegger retains to the end—for example, in his frequent lamentations concerning the universal fate of *Seinsvergessenheit* that characterizes the modern age—the basic categories of the antimodernist critique of posttraditional societies.

One of the distinguishing features of the antimodernist attitude of the German mandarin intelligentsia is the contrast between *Kultur* and *Zivilisation*, where the former term connotes the sublimity of spiritual cultivation and the latter signifies the superficial materialism of the decadent capitalist West.[15] The antithesis was originally used by the German middle classes in the eighteenth century in polemical opposition to the frivolity of courtly life: the aristocrats behaved with propriety and hence, were externally "civilized"; but they knew no profound inner cultivation, and were thus "uncultured." Yet, with the Napoleonic conquest, *Zivilisation* became permanently associated in the German mind with France and the merely outward trappings of social refinement; whereas *Kultur* signified the profound spiritual superiority of German *Innerlichkeit* or inwardness.[16] However, with Germany's feverish rush toward industrialization toward the end of the nineteenth century, the privileged social position of the intellectual elite was increasingly threatened by an upstart bourgeois class, whose wealth quickly translated into enhanced political power and social prestige. It was at precisely this juncture that the *Kultur/Zivilisation* dichotomy assumed a more virulent, neonationalist significance, and thus *Zivilisation* was equated with the crass, materialistic outlook of the capitalist West *tout court.*

But what is of especial importance about the uncompromising anti-Westernism of the mandarin intelligentsia—and here, Heidegger is merely a typical case in point—is that the rejection of capitalism as an economic ethos rapidly translated into a dismissal of Western political values *simpliciter:* liberalism, individualism, and democracy were all dismissed as alien to the German spirit; they were essentially regarded as *undeutsch.* And thus, for example, in the 1936 *Beiträge zur Philosophie,* Heidegger remarks that the world-view of liberalism is "tyrannical insofar as it requires that everybody be left to his own opinion." It promotes an "arbitrariness" that is only "the slavery of 'contingency' [*die Sklaverei des 'Zufälligen'* "].[17] Enlightenment rationalism—associated with a superficial mental disposition that was at best conducive to utilitarian economic calculus—similarly fell victim to this dichotomous manner of perceiving the world. An antidemocratic predisposition was already firmly implanted in German soil as a result of Germany's status as a *verspätete Nation,* its belated arrival at nationhood: Germany never had its bourgeois revolution, its nineteenth-century status as a constitutional state had been imposed from above, and a latently feudal, authoritarian social structure—the traditional Prussian *Obrigkeitsstaat*—remained very much intact throughout the Wilhelmine era.[18] The *Kultur/Zivilisation* opposition thus served in many ways to codify a set of traditional, diffusely held, pan-Germanic cultural and political attitudes.

That the German idealist tradition was given a decisively nationalistic twist by the academic intelligentsia in the years prior to World War I may well have sealed the fate of the nation concerning the prospect of democratic alternatives. In the eyes of Fritz Stern:

This *Kulturreligion* embraced nationalism as well, for it insisted on the identity of German idealism and German nationalism. The essence of the German nation was expressed in its spirit, revealed by its artists and thinkers, and at times still reflected in the life of the simple unspoiled folk. In imperial Germany, this type of cultural nationalism grew, until it found

25

expression in the First World War, when German intellectuals insisted they were culturally independent of the West and that the German empire as then constituted fully embodied the supreme cultural values of the German people.

As Stern goes on to remark, these attitudes constitute "the main link between all that is venerable and great in the German past and National Socialism."[19]

As the onset of World War I neared, the apolitical cultural elitism of the German intelligentsia increasingly gave way to an attitude of jingoistic fervor. One of the most important factors in the politicization of the German academic community along reactionary lines stemmed from the increasing threat to its position of social privilege posed by both the parvenu bourgeoisie as well as the politically organized working classes. When these domestic sociological factors are coupled with the traditional geopolitical hostilities vis-à-vis France and England—not to mention the specter of a Bolshevik threat from the East following 1917—one gains an image of a nationalistically inclined intelligentsia seemingly besieged from all quarters.

The academic mandarins were driven to two conclusions as a result of this state of affairs, both of which boded extremely ill for Germany's political future. The first conclusion was that *culture and democracy are antitheses*, since the former concept is necessarily elitist, while the latter promotes a leveling of values that is conducive to vulgarity. The second conclusion followed from a reactive and militant assertion of German cultural superiority, in response to the perceived political and intellectual threat posed by the Western powers. It held that German *cultural* greatness mandated an enhanced *political* role for Germany on the international scene; and thus, that German expansionist ambitions could be justified in cultural terms.[20] Here, too, an observation by Stern is apposite:

> To many Germans, with their honest confusion of culture and religion, a superior culture was as much a legitimate reason for ruling others as the Christian missionary impulse had once been. Goethe, after all, was almost as good as God—just as pushpin had always been inferior to poetry. The German intelligentsia came to believe that the moral justification of expansion was a guarantee of political success as well, and thus revealed anew the dangers of the unpolitical mind.[21]

It is impossible to understand the decisive historico-philosophical impulses behind Heidegger's 1927 work, the profound impact it had on an entire generation of German intellectuals, as well as the specific political choices made by Heidegger in the early 1930s, apart from the peculiar sociocultural problematic of German mandarin antimodernism just described. This was a generation for which Ferdinand Tönnies' celebrated distinction between *Gemeinschaft* and *Gesellschaft* loomed large, where *Gemeinschaft* stood for social relations that were direct, organic, and natural, and *Gesellschaft* represented an organization of life that was impersonal, routinized, and mechanistic. In the years that followed the appearance of Tönnies work (1887), the aforementioned dichotomy between *Kultur* and *Zivilisation* was read into this sociological antithesis, resulting in the apocalyptical vision of a prosaic and disenchanted modern world, insensitive to considerations of national or cultural greatness—in brief, the iron cage of mechanized petrifaction so movingly described by Max Weber in the concluding paragraphs of *The Protestant Ethic and the Spirit of Capitalism*. Repelled by the vast social changes wrought by modernity and modernization, a generation of "German academics reacted to the dislocation with such desperate intensity that the specter of a 'soulless' modern age came to haunt everything they said or wrote, no matter what the subject. By the early 1920s, they were deeply convinced that they were living through a profound crisis, a 'crisis of culture,' of 'learning,' of 'values,' or of the 'spirit.' "[22]

It would be difficult to overestimate the importance of the "crisis mentality" that gripped the German intelligentsia in the years immediately following World War I.[23] So thoroughgoing seemed the bankruptcy of all inherited belief-structures that only a transformation of values that was radical and total seemed worth entertaining. With a bourgeois world that was irredeemably corrupt and "fallen," no compromise could be made. By the same token, the preoccupation with radicalism in both politics and philosophy meant that authentic republican sentiment was in exceedingly short supply during the crucible years of Weimar democracy—limited for the most part to the so-called *Vernunftrepublikaner*, republicans of the intellect rather than of passionate conviction.[24] As one critic has remarked, "With reference to the 'target-date' of 1933, it was only a short step from the ideology of the German professors to that of the fascists, and many were so enthusiastic that they made a quick leap into a brown uniform."[25]

Already as a young theology student, Heidegger's own radical antimodernism seems fully articulated. In one of his first published writings, a review of F. W. Foerster's *Autorität und Freiheit*, he remarks: "And the church, if it wants to remain true to the treasure of its eternal truth, will rightly counteract *the destructive influences of modernism*, which is unaware of this sharpest of oppositions in which its modern conceptions of life stand in relation to the established wisdom of the Christian tradition."[26]

Following his final rupture with the church in the late 1910s, the idea of a total break with the past becomes a prominent theme in Heidegger's philosophy over the course of the next decade. Thus, in a letter of 1923, he speaks emphatically of the need for "radical dismantling" and of finding the "one thing that is necessary" through "destruction."[27] Like many of his generation, he was dismayed by the patent unresponsiveness of the "school-philosophy" of the prewar years, neo-Kantianism, when it came to addressing the ultimate problems of human existence; above all, since the answers provided to such questions in the prewar period seemed manifestly irrelevant and valueless in face of the changed realities of the postwar situation. Or as Gadamer has freely acknowledged with regard to the reception of *Being and Time*: "the radicalism of Heidegger's inquiry produced in the German universities an intoxicating effect that left all moderation behind."[28]

Of course, the quasi-apocalyptic, antimodernist sentiment of the German intellectual elite had both its "left" and "right" variants.[29] Those theorists with whom Heidegger's critique of modernity bore the greatest affinities were the oxymoronic "conservative revolutionaries:" Oswald Spengler, Moeller van den Bruck, Carl Schmitt, and—most importantly—Ernst Jünger; so-called because, unlike the traditional German conservatives, they maintained no illusions about the preferability of traditional, organic, precapitalist forms of life.[30] Instead, they based their hopes for a revitalized German Reich on the proto-fascistic vision of a militant, expansionist, authoritarian state. The spiritual godfather of this generation of right-wing radicals was Friedrich Nietzsche—albeit, on the basis of a rather tendentious transmission of his doctrines. The conservative revolutionaries were thoroughgoing believers in the (Nietzschean) rites of "active nihilism": bourgeois values of commerce, materialism, security, constitutionalism, intellectualism, and toleration, which were already on the decline, needed to be given a final push. Only then could a new series of *heroic* values emerge, based on the pseudo-Nietzschean concepts of will, power, struggle, and destiny. Already in Nietzsche, we find the judgment that, "Life is a consequence of war, society itself a means to war." For Spengler, similarly, "war is the primary politics of everything that lives." With Jünger, "War is an intoxication beyond all intoxication, an unleashing that breaks all bonds. It is a frenzy without cautions and limits, comparable only to the forces of nature." And for Schmitt, "War, the readiness for death of fighting men, the physical annihilation of other men who stand on the side of the enemy, all that has no normative, only an *existential meaning*."[31] When Heidegger, while praising the virtues of "military service" in his 1933 Rectoral Address, opines that "all powers of the heart and all capacities of the body must be deployed *through* struggle [*Kampf*], intensified *in* struggle [*Kampf*], and preserved *as* struggle [*Kampf*]," he inserts himself without reserve in this bellicose intellectual lineage.[32]

In his study of Heidegger's "political ontology," Pierre Bourdieu suggests that the affinities between Heidegger and the conservative revolutionaries were predominantly "ethicopolitical" in nature:

> The assertions of academics like Werner Sombart or Edgar Salin, Carl Schmitt or Othmar Spann, or of essayists like Moeller van den Bruck or Oswald Spengler, Ernst Jünger or Ernst Niekisch, and innumerable other variants of the conservative or "conservative revolutionary" ideology that the German professors produced daily in their courses, public lectures, and essays . . . represent an approximation . . . of [Heidegger's] own ethicopolitical disposition.[33]

The "ethicopolitical" axis described by Bourdieu proves crucial insofar as Heidegger, along with many of the thinkers and polemicists named by Bourdieu, embraced a quasi-Nietzschean approach to ethics, a valorization of "radical will" or heroic self-assertion commonly known as "decisionism." Thus, for example, in a November 1933 political address, Heidegger, basing himself on one of the central concepts of *Being and Time*—the category of "resolve" or "decisiveness"—will characterize the plebiscite called by Hitler on Germany's withdrawal from the League of Nations as *"the highest free decision [Entscheidung]* of all: whether it—the entire Volk—wants its own existence *[Dasein]* or *not*." And he goes on to add that, "What is unique about this election is the simple

29

greatness of the decision that is to be executed."[34] Turning to Jünger's 1934 essay collection, *Blätter und Steine*, we find the observation that, "To the extent that the race degenerates, *action takes on the character of decision.*"[35] For Carl Schmitt, the importance of a decision is that it abrogates conditions of "legitimacy" or "political normalcy"—that is, "rule of law"—and thereby establishes the preconditions for political dictatorship. Thus, in *Political Theology* (1922) he praises the counterrevolutionary philosophers of state—de Maistre, Bonald, and Donoso Cortés—for "emphasizing the moment of decision to such an extent that the notion of legitimacy . . . was finally dissolved." The result is a politics grounded in "a pure decision": "not based on reason and discussion and not justifying itself," but valid alone in terms of "*an absolute decision created out of nothingness.*" Or as Schmitt concludes, "this decisionism is essentially *dictatorship*, not legitimacy."[36]

But just as striking as the aforementioned "ethicopolitical" bonds linking Heidegger and the conservative revolutionaries is what one might describe as a shared disposition, mood, or *aesthetic sensibility*; a general fascination with "limit-situations" (*Grenzsituationen*) and extremes; an interest in transposing the fundamental experiences of aesthetic modernity—shock, disruption, experiential immediacy; an infatuation with the sinister and forbidden, with the "flowers of evil"[37]—to the plane of everyday life, thereby injecting an element of enthusiasm and vitality in what had otherwise become a rigid and lifeless mechanism. And thus, the aesthetic influences of the artistic avant-garde—Baudelaire, futurism, expressionism—on conservative revolutionary *Kulturkritik* proved far-reaching.[38] The "war experience" of 1914–18, graphically celebrated in the writings of Jünger such as *In the Storm of Steel* (1920) and *Struggle as Inner Experience* (1922), added a crucial dimension of apocalyptical urgency to their entire manner of thinking and writing.[39]

Yet, it was, once again, the writings of Nietzsche that in many ways proved the determinative influence on the intellectual sensibility of the conservative revolutionaries. For it was Nietzsche who had first transformed the "aesthetic" problematic just described into an "existential" matter of the highest order, thereby laying the foundations for a highly influential "aesthetics of existence." By effacing the distinction between appearance and reality, illusion and truth, art and life, and declaring that *appearance alone* or *"Schein" was all there was*, he proclaimed the obsolescence of traditional normative paradigms and justified the practice of *evaluating life itself in aesthetic terms*. Thus, his celebration, in the notes and drafts that comprise *The Will to Power*, of "the world as a work of art that gives birth to itself." "We possess art," observes Nietzsche, "lest we *perish of truth.*"[40]

In his comprehensive study of the conservative revolutionary sensibility—felicitously titled *The Aesthetics of Horror*—Karl Heinz Bohrer has superbly demonstrated the affinities between Nietzsche and his conservative revolutionary heirs:

> The aesthetic justification of existence that is established in *The Birth of Tragedy* is the *a priori* principle which, on the basis of the proclamation of the death of God as the "greatest modern event," laid the foundations for the advent of modern nihilism. The fantasy of catastrophe projects an apocalyptically structured temporal semantics "of impending rupture, destruction, decline, ruin [*Abbruch, Zerstörung, Untergang, Umsturz*]. . . ." Nietzsche's aggressive and eccentric self-interpretation in *Ecce Homo* as someone whose name will be associated with a "decision that was conjured up *against* everything that up until then has been believed," who is "not a man," but "dynamite," who wants to see his four "Untimely Meditations" viewed as "four assassination attempts," forces itself directly into the anarchistic-individualistic disposition of Jünger's early style.[41]

According to Bohrer, the shock-laden structure of temporal experience found in Nietzsche's aesthetics, the emphasis on the disruption of temporal continuity that may be identified as "suddenness" or "abruptness" (*Plötzlichkeit*), is "renewed in the 1920s through the works of Max Scheler, Carl Schmitt, and Martin Heidegger."[42] In Heidegger's case, support for this thesis is provided by an examination of the strictures of "existential temporality." Thus, for example, whereas the "They" (*das Man*) experiences time helplessly ("un-ecstatically") as a serial succession of empty "nows," authentic Dasein is elevated above this routinized temporal stasis in the "moment of vision" (*das Augenblick*)—a concept that seems to approximate very closely the Nietzschean "temporal semiotics" of radical discontinuity and rupture described by Bohrer. The "moment of vision" is a type of secular epiphany that both explodes and transcends the "fallen" character of routinized, inauthentic temporality, which Heidegger refers to as "world time" or "public time." Just as in the political philosophy of Carl Schmitt,

31

the "exception" plays a role analogous to that of the "miracle" in theology,[43] in existential ontology, the "moment of vision" introduces a "state of exception" into the benumbing familiarity of bourgeois "everydayness." And by disrupting the hegemonic hold of inauthentic temporality, it provides Dasein in its "situation" with a point of orientation for the realization of an authentic potentiality-for-Being.[44]

Nominally, *Being and Time* subordinates the existential analysis of Dasein or Being-in-the-world to the ontological question concerning the meaning of Being. Thus, the analysis of Dasein—that being for which its own Being is constantly at issue—is, strictly speaking, merely a necessary propaedeutic to the primary, ontological question under investigation. However, there can be no doubt that it is the existential dimension that occupies pride of place in the inquiry and that galvanized the interest of the first generation of readers. Yet, this "existential" point of departure can be fully understood only in terms of the generational crisis already discussed—in relation to which *Existenzphilosophie* presented itself as a radical response.

A philosophy of existence such as Heidegger's presupposes that all traditional contents and truths have lost their substance; and thus all that remains is *naked facticity*, that is, the sheer fact of existence. Thus, unlike traditional hermeneutics, which believes that the past contains a store of semantic potentials that are inherently worthy of redemption, *Existenzphilosophie* in its Heideggerian variant tends to be inherently destructive of tradition.[45] In medieval philosophy all created being is separated into existence and essence, and God alone exists perfectly or essentially. Heidegger's secular ontology does away with the perfection of the creator. All that remains is existence as such, "factical Dasein," awash in temporal flux. As Heidegger remarks in a letter of 1921: "I work from my 'I am' and my spiritual, generally factical origin. Existence rages with such facticity."[46]

According to the philosopher Karl Löwith, the total devaluation of traditional meanings and inherited beliefs that is presupposed by the existential approach has a direct bearing on Heidegger's future political orientation. For one need only jettison the quasi-solipsistic, individualist basis for decision that one finds in *Being and Time*—which is always contingent on the parochialism of my "ownmost potentiality-for-Being"—and replace it with a "collectivist" orientation in which the "national community" or *Volks-*

gemeinschaft provides the basis for decision, and one arrives without difficulty at the political course chosen by Heidegger in 1933. As Löwith observes:

> Whoever . . . reflects on Heidegger's later partisanship for Hitler, will find in this first formulation of the idea of historical "existence" the constituents of his political decision of several years hence. One need only abandon the still quasi-religious isolation and apply [the concept of] authentic "existence"—always particular to each individual—and the "duty" which follows from it to "specifically German existence" and its historical destiny in order thereby to introduce into the general course of German existence the energetic, but empty movement of existential categories ("to decide for oneself," "to take stock of oneself in face of nothingness," "wanting one's ownmost destiny," and "to take responsibility for oneself") and to proceed from there to "destruction" now on the terrain of politics.[47]

Moreover, as we shall attempt to show, the move from an "individual" to a "collective" standpoint is expressly prefigured in the argument of *Being and Time* itself; specifically, in the discussions of "destiny," "repetition," and "choosing one's hero" as they figure in Heidegger's elaboration of the category of "historicity."

Although an understanding of Heidegger's political thought should in no way be reduced to the concrete political choices made by the philosopher in the 1930s, neither is it entirely separable therefrom. And while the strategy of his apologists has been to dissociate the philosophy from the empirical person, thereby suggesting that Heidegger's Nazism was an unessential aberration in the hope of exempting the philosophy from political taint, this strategy will not wash for several reasons.

To begin with, Heidegger's philosophy itself would seem to rule out the artificial, traditional philosophical separation between thought and action. In truth, much of *Being and Time* is concerned with overcoming the conventional philosophical division between theoretical and practical reason; a fact that is evident above all in the "pragmatic" point of departure of the analytic of Dasein: "Being-in-the-world" rather than the Cartesian "thinking substance."

More importantly, though, what is perhaps the central category of Heidegger's existential ontology—the category of "authenticity"—automatically precludes such a facile separation between philosophical outlook and concrete life-choices. As a work of fundamental ontology, *Being and Time* aims at delineating the essential, existential determinants of human Being-in-the-world. Heidegger refers to these structures (e.g., "care," "fallenness," "thrownness," "Being-toward-death") as *Existenzialien*. The category of authenticity demands that the *ontological* structures of *Being and Time* receive practical or *ontic* fulfillment; that is, the realization of these categorial determinations in actual, concrete life contexts is essential to the coherence of the Heideggerian project. This conclusion follows of necessity from the nature of the category of authenticity itself: it would be nonsensical to speak of an "authentic Dasein" that was unrealized, existing in a state of mere potentiality. Authenticity requires that ontic or practical choices and involvements—concrete decisions, engagements, and political commitments—become an essential feature of an authentic existence. Their correlation with the *Existenzialien* of *Being and Time* is in no way accidental, but follows directly from the "resolve" (*Entschlossenheit*) of authentic Dasein. Ontic (existentiell) decisions, therefore, prove an indispensable moment of existential analysis, insofar as they reflect the authenticity/inauthenticity of the individual in question.[48]

At several points in his narrative, Heidegger is emphatic about the necessary correlation between these two planes of argumentation, "existential" (ontological) and "existentiell" (ontic). For example, as he remarks in the course of his initial characterization of the concept of authenticity: "What we are seeking is an authentic potentiality-for-Being of Dasein, which will be attested in its *existentiell* possibility"—thereby suggesting the paramount importance of bridging the gap from an ontological to an ontic standpoint.[49] Just as for Aristotle, the virtuous individual must be so not merely "potentially" but in the domain of life-praxis itself,[50] for Heidegger, though authenticity originates as a category of fundamental ontology, the imperatives of existential inquiry propel it inherently beyond the sphere of pure theory: it demands to be actualized in concrete situations and real-life decisions.

The conclusion to be drawn from what we might define as the "existentiell imperative" of *Being and Time*—from the fact that its ontological categories necessitate ontic realization—is of great moment for an understanding of Heidegger's own political experiences. It suggests the possibility that Heidegger intended his political involvements of the 1930s as *the existentiell consummation of the categorial framework of his 1927 book*; more specifically, that the philosopher viewed his entry into the Nazi Party as a concrete, historical manifestation of authentic, resolute existence. This conclusion, already suggested in the remarks by Karl Löwith cited above, is forcefully borne out by Heidegger's numerous political writings and speeches, in which he has gone to no small lengths to articulate his support for National Socialism in categories explicitly gleaned from the existential analytic of his 1927 work. This having been said, however, the question of the specific, constituent aspects of Heidegger's philosophy that may have predisposed him toward a "National Revolutionary" course in the early 1930s requires a good deal of further specification.

Authenticity and Decision

The gateway to Heideggerianism as a political philosophy is the category of "resolve" or "decisiveness" *(Entschlossenheit)*. The "resolve" that characterizes authentic Dasein is intended as a polemical counterconcept to the irresolution of inauthentic existence, which Heidegger refers to as the "They" *(das Man)*. The bar to authenticity immediately confronting Dasein is that its "natural"— one might almost say "instinctual"—manner of existing is that of the "They-self." The resolve toward authentic existence can only be attained by way of surmounting the inertia of the They. In a passage describing the passing of Dasein from an inauthentic to an authentic mode of existing, Heidegger phrases the problem thusly: "For the most part *I myself* am not the 'who' of Dasein; the They-self is its 'who.' Authentic Being-one's-Self takes the definite form of an existentiell modification of the 'They.' "[51]

Since authentically resolute Dasein can only be understood in polemical contrast with the deficiencies of the They-self, we must begin with a preliminary characterization of the latter. The fundamental trait of the They is the attempt to escape from its "Self" and the responsibilities attendant to being a "Self" through a vast array of ruses and rationalizations that for Heidegger define "everydayness." This is merely another way of saying (as a familiar refrain from *Being and Time* reminds us) that "primarily and for the most part" *(zunächst und zumeist)* Dasein exists in a deficient or inauthentic state; a state Heidegger also describes as "falling."

A somewhat fuller treatment of the They-self must wait until our discussion of what may be referred to as the "social ontology" of *Being and Time*. What is important in the context at hand—for the sake of the contrast with authentic Dasein—is that the Being of the They busies itself with various tasks of self-oblivion in order to obliterate from consciousness the most fundamentally disturbing aspects of Being-in-the-world: for example, the ineradicable *Angst* that seizes Dasein when it realizes the sheer contingency of human existence, that is, that its particular existence is *groundless*, devoid of metaphysical guarantees or consolation.[52] Heidegger describes the various mechanisms of self-forgetting as "averageness," "leveling down," "publicness," "being-distant," and "accommodation." In the end, one is left with a "dictatorship of the They," in which "one's own Dasein [is dissolved] into the kind of Being of the 'others,' " where "every other is like the next."[53] "In these modes one's way of Being is that of inauthenticity and failure to stand by one's Self."[54]

Heidegger's highly critical portrayal of the predominantly inauthentic modes in which human Being-with-others comes to presence immediately raises questions about the relationship in which this analysis might stand vis-à-vis the conservative revolutionary critique of modern political life. For in its more extreme formulations concerning "publicness," "leveling," etc., the argument of the existential analytic tends toward a total repudiation of the public world and its projects. The "fallen" nature of those life-forms that characterize "publicness"—our Being-with or *Mitsein*—seems permanent and irreparable. And in this respect, Heidegger's analysis appears to dovetail fully with the antidemocratic abhorrence of "publicity" (*Öffentlichkeit*—a term that itself becomes a type of deprecatory shorthand for the totality of modern political forms) that proved such a common theme in the discourse of the conservative revolutionaries.

Thus, the initial problem Dasein must confront in making the transition from an inauthentic to an authentic existence is a surmounting of the They and its various techniques of self-deception. Heidegger formulates the problem as follows:

> The They has always kept Dasein from taking hold of [its] possibilities of Being. The They even hides the manner in which it has tacitly relieved Dasein of the burden of explicitly *choosing* these possibilities. It remains indefinite as to who has 'really' done the choosing. So Dasein makes no choices, gets carried along

by the nobody, and thus ensnares itself in inauthenticity. This process can be reversed only if Dasein specifically brings itself back to itself from its lostness in the 'They'. . . . When Dasein thus brings itself back from the 'They,' the They-self is modified *in an existentiell manner* so that it becomes *authentic* Being-one's-Self. This must be accomplished by *making up for not choosing*. But 'making up' for not choosing signifies *choosing to make this choice*—deciding for a potentiality-for-Being and making this decision from one's own choice.[55]

With this "choice" of an authentic Self, we are on the threshold of Heideggerianism as a *decisionism*.[56]

To identify Heideggerianism as a decisionism would seem, *prima facie*, inadvisable. For Heidegger's followers have generally esteemed his philosophy as a renunciation of precisely that notion of self-affirming subjectivity that has dominated Western philosophy since the time of Descartes. The glorification of the faculty of will, the celebration of the powers of human volition implicit in the very concept of decisionism, would seem directly to contravene the inherited understanding of the antisubjectivist thrust of Heidegger's doctrines.

The contradiction just raised, far from being chimerical, pertains to the essence of the philosophy of *Being and Time*. For the relationship of the early Heidegger to the legacy of philosophical subjectivism is itself aporetic. He is, on the one hand, repulsed by its *"reductio ad hominem"* tendencies, which serve only to exacerbate the obfuscation of Being perpetrated by previous metaphysics. On the other hand, he finds it impossible as a philosopher of *existence* (a description certainly unsuited to the later Heidegger, where the question of "Being" occupies pride of place, and allusions to "Dasein" become only a distant, unsentimental memory) to do without the semblance of subjectivity—as is clear from his frequent employment of terms such as "Selfhood," "ego" (*das ich*), and "mineness" throughout the existential analytic. For otherwise the longing for philosophical concreteness inherited from earlier variants of *Lebensphilosophie* (e.g., Bergson, Nietzsche, Dilthey) would remain unrealized. And thus, the logic of *Being and Time* oscillates indecisively pro and contra the heritage of philosophical subjectivism. Perhaps it is Heidegger himself who has best formulated the stakes of the philosophical dispute at issue when he observes that, "if Selfhood belongs among the essential traits of Dasein—whose 'essence,' however, lies in *existence*—then ego and Selfhood must be construed *in an existential sense.*"[57]

As a category of modern political and ethical theory, decisionism is of fairly recent vintage. Although its first employment derives from a 1928 work on the concept of "dictatorship" by the German political philosopher and jurist Carl Schmitt (it is now known that in August 1933, Heidegger wrote to Schmitt trying to solicit his participation in the "National Awakening"),[58] one might legitimately trace the intellectual pedigree of the concept back to Hobbes' claim in *Leviathan* that, "*Autoritas, non veritas facit legem*"—authority, not truth, is the basis for legitimacy. But it was in Schmitt's political and legal writings of the 1920s that the concepts of "decision" and "decisionism" received their fullest elaboration. In opposition to the "legal positivism" or "normativism" of jurists such as Hans Kelsen, Schmitt claimed that because a legal system fails to provide an all-encompassing, closed system of juridical norms, in the last instance, one must rely on a "decision" on the part of those in authority to bridge the gap between the law and the specificity of the concrete case. When transferred to the domain of political theory, the authoritarian implications of the doctrine are clear: a decision *ex nihilo* on the part of the sovereign authority constitutes the ultimate basis of right. Or as Schmitt expresses this thought with clarity and directness in his 1922 work, *Political Theology*, "Sovereign is he who decides on the state of exception."[59]

In his essay on "Philosophy as Rigorous Science and Political Philosophy," Leo Strauss indicates that historically, existentialism and decisionism have existed in a symbiotic relation. This fact may in a large measure be attributed to the radical historicism that traditionally undergirds existentialism. Or as Strauss observes, "Existentialism appears in a great variety of guises but one will not be far wide of the mark if one defines it . . . as the view according to which all principles of understanding and of action are *historical*, i.e. have no other ground than *groundless human decision*."[60] With these remarks, Strauss identifies a crucial intellectual historical dynamic. For once the essential arbitrariness and contingency of human belief-structures has been demonstrated—once traditional moral claims have been dissolved amid the eternal flux of historical emergence and passing away—"values" themselves become an arbitrary posit, and the only power that is capable of establishing them proves to be a *sovereign act of human will*.

Strauss's remarks suggest that existentialism promotes a radical devaluation of traditional values and life-forms—a tendency that comes through forcefully, for example, in the critical verdict Heidegger reaches concerning "everydayness." This rejection of tradition helps account for the radical isolation experienced by Dasein: the abyss of "nothingness" or existential contingency with which it finds itself confronted once it realizes that, like the Nietzschean conception of "truth," all traditional claims to meaning are little more than socially necessary illusion. "Decision" thus provides a quasi-heroic alternative to the abyss of "meaninglessness" that threatens to overwhelm a Dasein permanently awash in radical historical flux. It signifies a voluntaristic transcendence of both "existential contingency" as well as the indecisiveness of the "They." For once the inauthenticity of all traditional social norms has been existentially unmasked, the only remaining basis for moral orientation is a *decision ex nihilo*, a *radical assertion of will*; a will, moreover, that is pure and unconstrained by the impediments of social convention. Schmitt expresses this insight correctly when he observes that, "The decision frees itself from all normative ties and becomes in the true sense *absolute*. . . . [The] *norm is destroyed in the exception.*"[61] Thus, decisionism is a voluntarism whose affinities with the Nietzschean ideal of "the will to power"—itself oriented in no small measure toward a radical devaluation of bourgeois normalcy—are far from coincidental. Or as Nietzsche himself remarks at one point, "*I assess a man by the quantum of power and abundance of his will.*"[62]

With this observation Nietzsche singles out one of the most essential features of decisionism as a philosophy of human conduct: at issue is not the specific material content or direction of the will, but *the sheer quantity of volitional force with which a decision is realized.* Thus, as Schmitt remarks in *Political Theology*, "*making a decision is more important than how a decision is made.*"[63]

It was left to the writings of Carl Schmitt in the 1920s to render the hitherto implicit relation between decisionism and *Existenzphilosophie* explicit and conscious. Like the *Lebensphilosophie* out of which existentialism develops, decisionism emerges as an "antirationalism": or as Schmitt proclaims, the decision on the state of exception "confounds the unity and the order of the rationalist scheme."[64] Decisionism thus represents the prospect of an existential transformation of life in its routinized everydayness, its elevation to a higher plane. The norm must be destroyed insofar as it represents the reign of the merely "conceptual," the "abstract," the "average." Under such conditions, the substance of life itself, its pulsating fluidity, is prevented from coming to the fore. The cardinal virtue of the sovereign decision, therefore, is that it *explodes* the routinization to which life is subjected under the conditions of bourgeois normalcy or Heideggerian "everydayness." Or as Schmitt tells us in a statement that might be taken as a clarion call of vitalism in all its manifestations: "The exception is *more interesting than the rule.* . . . In the exception *the power of real life* breaks through the crust of a mechanism that has become torpid by repetition."[65]

The Call of Conscience

In the thought of Heidegger, it is the category of the "call of conscience" (*Ruf des Gewissens*) that paves the way for authentic decision or *Entschlossenheit*, thereby elevating Dasein above the fallenness of the They. Yet, the discussion of the "call of conscience" is disappointingly vague. When the question is posed as to whence the call emanates, the specific content of the call, or how it might be recognized, we are provided with only the most roundabout and tenuous hints. Indeed, Heidegger seems to treat the nebulousness of the call as a virtue.

In part, this evasiveness is an honest reflection of the requirements of existential analysis, which should in principle bear no responsibility for supplying "existentiell" particulars. For were specific "ontic" directives provided, the whole question of the "decision" at issue—the *Wozu* of resolve—would become superfluous. In a very real sense, it is not up to fundamental ontology to make our choices for us. It is "we" who must *decide*, in accordance with what Heidegger is fond of calling our "ownmost potentiality-for-Being." Nevertheless, these caveats should by no means exonerate existential analysis from the charge of vacuity or insufficient concreteness.

In one of his more revealing and explicit discussions of the call, Heidegger specifies its content as follows: "Conscience summons Dasein's Self from lostness in the 'They.' The Self to which the appeal is made remains *indefinite* and *empty* in its what." And further: "The call dispenses with any kind of utterance. It does not put itself into words at all; yet it remains nothing less than *obscure* and *indefinite*."⁶⁶ What emerges clearly in this account of the call is a deliberate, "wordless" ambiguity concerning the direction and constitution of the Self that has been "summoned" as well as that entity responsible for the summoning. It is this very indefiniteness, moreover, that is itself repeatedly praised. Yet, according to the strictures of Heidegger's own categorial scheme, "ambiguity" signifies a *lack of decisiveness or resolve*. For "ambiguity" is one of the distinguishing features of *inauthentic* Dasein. In introducing the call, Heidegger is at pains to emphasize the fact that it must show itself "unambiguously." Nevertheless, his initial depiction of this category would seem to fall short of his own desideratum. One cannot help but react with dismay to the discovery that the very "ambiguity" that plagued inauthentic Dasein can be found at the heart of authenticity itself.

And thus, the "whence" of the call remains both indeterminate and unforeseeable. It descends upon Dasein from on high, as it were, taking the latter by surprise. As Heidegger explains, "If the caller is asked about its name, status, origin, or repute, it not only refuses to answer, but does not even leave the slightest possibility of one's making it into something with which one can be familiar when one's understanding of Dasein has a 'worldly' orientation." He continues: "Indeed, the call is precisely something which *we ourselves* have neither planned nor prepared for nor voluntarily performed. . . . 'It' calls, against our expectations and even against our will. . . . The call comes *from* me yet *from beyond me and over me*."⁶⁷

The call (*der Ruf*) thus appears as something other-worldly and mystical—comparable only to a religious epiphany. The (highly secularized) Lutheran overtones of the concept are pronounced: it is markedly reminiscent of Luther's concept of "calling" (*Beruf*). Those who are "called" have the superioristic glow of the Calvinist elect. Despite an ever-present possibility of relapse—for as phenomenal beings, we are never wholly free of the temptation of "falling" that characterizes the They-self—they have become "authentic."

Heidegger thus goes to no small lengths to emphasize the obscurity of the call, its unintelligibility from the standpoint of a "this-worldly," human understanding, its status as something "transcendent" vis-à-vis normal capacities. In effect, the call assumes the form of a heteronomous force, impenetrable to the faculties of human reason and will. Indeed, Heidegger does not shrink at one crucial point from characterizing it as *"an alien power by which Dasein is dominated."*[68] His abandonment of modern philosophical doctrines (in this case, the Kantian category of human autonomy) reaches so far that he runs the risk—even more apparent in the later writings—of endorsing a type of secularized mysticism as the avowed goal of philosophical inquiry.

The expressly "noncommunicative" nature of the call of conscience further attests to its esoteric allure. According to Heidegger, the call "dispenses with any kind of utterance." Disregarding the constraints of formal logic, Heidegger states that, *"Conscience discourses solely and constantly in the mode of keeping silent."*[69] Thus, another Heideggerian first: "silence" as a "mode of discourse." Heidegger, moreover, sets great store by the fact that the call cannot be rendered intelligible in ordinary linguistic terms: one of its more seductive features is the *incommunicability of its contents,* that is, the fact that it transcends the powers of human ratiocination in their normal, mortal employment. As Heidegger affirms: "That which calls the call simply *holds itself aloof from any way of becoming known.* . . . To let itself be drawn into getting considered and talked about goes against its kind of Being."[70]

The "wordlessness" of the call, its pronounced aversion to discursive communication, presages one of the essential characteristics of authentic Dasein in general: its *Verschwiegenheit* or "reticence," a taciturn aloofness in face of the prosaicism and frivolity of everyday human affairs.

When viewed according to the strictures of analytical reason, the structure of Heidegger's argument—for example, his attempt to classify "silence" as a mode of "discourse"—may seem gratuitous and unwarranted. However, in fairness to Heidegger, whose integrity as a thinker is certainly above suspicion, there are compelling intratextual reasons, related to the structure and goals of the existential analytic, that explain why he characterizes the call in such a manifestly obscurantist manner.

His main reason for refusing to characterize the call in direct and unambiguous terms is his fear of associating it with the degraded Dasein of the They—an association that would merely precipitate a relapse into inauthenticity. So much depends on the call that, at all costs—even that of excessive abstraction—it must not be confused with the platitudinous nostrums of the They-self. As the hallowed portal of authentic Dasein, the call must first and foremost steer clear of assimilation to something "present-at-hand" (*vorhanden*): the Being of inertia, the inertia of Being, with which the They-self so often shows affinity. The hallmark of the They-self is its concerted efforts to escape from the demands of authentic temporality; for example, by refusing to face up to the prospect of its death and the demands of authentic futurity in general. For this reason, Heidegger strives concertedly to avoid falsely hypostatizing the call in terms of a specific and familiar "caller"—e.g., the "voice of God." Identifications of this nature would only signify a relapse into "ontotheology"; it would provide another escape-mechanism for Dasein in its attempts to avoid the implications of "choosing to be a Self."

Yet, as compelling as the aforementioned reasons may be, we— the critical inheritors of Heidegger's philosophical legacy—certainly need not feel bound to accept his conclusions as articles of faith. For the extremely abstract nature of the call, its wholesale lack of determinate content, raises grave doubts about its serviceability as a viable philosophical concept. Its status as an oblique, other-worldly emanation, its inscrutability to the faculty of human reason in its normal employment, cannot help but suggest that Heideggerianism, at a pivotal juncture, wittingly lapses into a type of secularized mystical fatalism. One can accept, in accordance with the strictures of existential analysis, his unwillingness to provide a concrete set of *ontic* directives for the category. That would be a task for the individual "Selves" in question, whose act of "decision" fundamental ontology must not usurp. However, this qualification should in no way immunize Heidegger from having to provide a rudimentary set of *existential* directives, in lieu of which the call cannot help but seem spectral and vacuous. For without some minimal measure of criterial determinacy, we are provided with no basis for distinguishing an *authentic* "call of conscience" from an *inauthentic* one. The problem of a lack of material criteria, moreover, is one that will haunt Heidegger's decisionism in all its aspects.

The peculiar aversion of the call to discursive articulation thus seems to indicate little more than a willful obscurantism on Heidegger's part. That Heidegger seeks to make a virtue out of the call's incommunicability, that he goes out of his way to laud its "conspicuous indefiniteness,"[71] suggests a deliberate infatuation with the forces of unreason. Whereas the ethos of modernity makes a virtue out of insights that can be linguistically redeemed, and thereby subjected to the approval of the *sensus communis*, Heidegger disappoints us by dogmatically regressing behind the terms of this program.[72] In fundamental ontology, the idea of the *sensus communis* is flatly degraded to the "publicness" of the "They"—in Heideggerian parlance, a term of derision from which no conceivable good can emerge. In his thought, the metaphor of the "light of reason" has no place.[73] We are once more provided with evidence for Tugendhat's claim concerning the predominantly "nonargumentative and evocative" character of Heideggerian discourse.

Moreover, the debasement of spoken discourse and communication in the discussion of the call seems to contradict the earlier, positive emphasis on "discourse" (*Rede*) in Division I. There, "discourse" and "language" are treated as inherently essential phenomena: as indispensable, positive constituents of our Being-in-the-world with others, as one of the fundamental "Existentials" of human Dasein. "As an existential state of Dasein's disclosedness," remarks Heidegger, "discourse is constitutive of Dasein's existence. . . . Discoursing or talking is the 'meaningful' articulation of the intelligibility of Being-in-the-world, to which Being-with belongs; it maintains itself, in a definite way, in all concernful Being-with-one-another."[74] Were it not for "discourse," the ontological project of *Being and Time* would collapse, and not merely in the trivial sense that the book itself could never be written. Rather, the revelation of Being in its unconcealedness could never occur, would fall short of articulation. The "disclosive" capacities of human linguistic expression are a *sine qua non* for this task. Without spoken discourse there would be no "un-covering" (*Ent-decken*) of Being-in-the-world.

Moreover, spoken discourse is an indispensable precondition for all human sociation. It is an obligatory prerequisite for all "Being-with" (*Mitsein*) to such an extent that the very concept of "Being-with-others" becomes unintelligible without it. For in that case our existence would possess the mute indeterminacy of subhuman life.

How, then, is one to explain the devaluation of spoken discourse or language in the case of authentic Dasein, in light of its favorable consideration earlier in the text as a constitutive mode of our "Being-with-others"?

What has transpired is that the fundamental *Existenzialien* that ground our everyday Being-in-the-world—"language" and "communication" included—*have been so thoroughly appropriated by the*

They that the entire realm of human "Being-with-others"—the entire life-world of human intersubjective affairs—must be *consigned a priori to the subaltern sphere of inauthenticity*. The realm of human linguistic expression has been so completely monopolized and distorted by the They that the only recourse left for authentic Dasein is a smug posture of silent superiority—Heideggerian "reticence." As Heidegger explains: "The call discourses in the uncanny mode of *keeping silent*. And it does this only because, in calling the one to whom the appeal is made, it does not call him into the public idle talk [*Gerede*] of the 'They,' but *calls* him *back* from this *into the reticence of his existent* potentiality-for-Being."[75]

And thus, the social world as conceived by Heidegger appears to be radically dichotomous. On the one hand, there is "everydayness," which seems irredeemably characterized by inauthentic modes of Dasein—"publicness," "idle talk," "ambiguity," and so on. An unbridgeable gulf, however, appears to separate this sphere from the realm of authenticity, which, as we have seen, shuns "publicness" altogether, to the point where "reticence" is preferred to speaking a language that has been defiled by vulgar Theyselves. In effect, authentic Dasein subsists in a sphere above and apart from the social world: so degraded is the latter by the *Existenzialien* of inauthenticity. Unlike an Hegelian phenomenology of spirit, the existential phenomenology of *Being and Time* is devoid of a *Bildungsprozess* whereby the They in its fallen state could elevate itself to the sublimity of authentic existence. As a fundamental *ontology*, Heideggerianism eternalizes the dichotomous character of human social life; the latter becomes an unalterable *condition humaine*, impervious to the transformative capacities of human reason and will. Such conclusions follow logically once intersubjectivity (*Miteinandersein*) and language are *a priori* relegated to the nefarious sphere of "everydayness."

At the same time, under the cover of an objective and neutral depiction of Dasein in its unchangeable, basic structures, there lurk in truth sizable value-judgments concerning the nature of human sociability, the prospect of forming meaningful human collectivities, and the likelihood of genuine human self-determination. There can be little denying that the evaluation of these prospects provided by Heidegger is an especially resigned and joyless one—as the opening citation by Marcuse suggests.[76] A cynical consciousness might well dismiss the aforementioned categories as liberal shibboleths. Yet, a political doctrine that blithely dispenses

45

with such values translates into a potentially ruinous defeatism of reason.

In point of fact, the purportedly "timeless" categories of fundamental ontology seem to be based upon a prejudicial, antihumanist philosophical anthropology, whose political implications are distinctly unsavory. The *a priori* division between authentic and inauthentic spheres essentially condemns the inhabitants of the latter realm to a life of perdition; Heidegger is quite explicit on this score, insofar as their lot is generally described by variants of the German *fallen*. On the basis of this division, the vast majority of men and women are deemed incapable of meaningful self-determination.

The political philosophical implications of this theory are as unequivocal as they are distasteful to a democratic sensibility. On the basis of the philosophical anthropology outlined by Heidegger, the modern conception of popular sovereignty becomes a sheer *non sequitur*: for those who dwell in the public sphere of everydayness are viewed as essentially incapable of self-rule. Instead, the only viable political philosophy that follows from this standpoint would be brazenly elitist: since the majority of citizens remain incapable of leading meaningful lives when left to their own devices, their only hope for "redemption" lies in the imposition of a "higher spiritual mission" from above. Indeed, this was the explicit political conclusion drawn by Heidegger in 1933. In this way, Heidegger's political thought moves precariously in the direction of the *"Führerprinzip"* or "leadership principle." In essence, he reiterates, in keeping with a characteristic antimodern bias, a strategem drawn from Platonic political philosophy: since the majority of men and women are incapable of ruling themselves insofar as they are driven by the base part of their souls to seek after inferior satisfactions and amusements, we in effect do them a service by ruling them from above.[77] To date, however, there has never been a satisfactory answer to the question Marx poses concerning such theories of educational dictatorship: "Who shall educate the educators?"[78]

A Self-Canceling Social Ontology; The Aporias of "Decisiveness"

As manifestations of authenticity, the call and resolve are responses to the fundamental "lack" or the "nullity" that pervades the Being of Dasein. According to Heidegger, the "nothingness of the world," the terrifying nullity that lies at the heart of Dasein's existence, reflects our "Being-guilty." The concept of "Being-guilty" (*Schuldigsein*) speaks to the fact that our existence is never something that is wholly self-willed, that our responsibility for our own fate always in part escapes our control. As such, Being-guilty addresses the problem of the *irreducible contingency* of all human Being-in-the-world.

"Being-guilty" thus stands in an essential relation to the category of "thrownness" (*Geworfenheit*). As Heidegger explains, "As being, Dasein is something that has been thrown; it has been brought into its 'there,' but not of its own accord."[79] The concept of "thrownness" bespeaks both the sheer arbitrariness of our lot in life and also the ultimate *groundlessness* of human existence—in the German sense of "*Grund*," being without reason or foundation. Heidegger gives an account of thrownness in the following passage: "Every Dasein always exists factically. It is not a free-floating self-projection; its character is determined by thrownness as a fact of the entity which it is; and, as so determined, it has in each case already been delivered over to existence and it constantly remains so. . . . As something thrown, Dasein has been thrown *into existence*. It exists as an entity that has to be as it is and as it can be."[80] Rather than being a free-floating Self, the existence of each Dasein is determined in advance by a set of inescapable, "factical" preconditions (e.g., geographical and historical, familial and class, looks, intelligence, etc.) that go far toward influencing its future course in life.

For Heidegger the "groundlessness" of our thrownness, the basis of our "Being-guilty," possesses a two-fold significance. On the one hand, it is the source of a pervasive existential disquiet or "estrangement" (*Unheimlichkeit*), insofar as it produces an awareness that our Being-in-the-world is devoid of foundational, metaphysical guarantees. With this thought Heidegger seeks to convey the essentially *terrifying contingency* of all human existence, the "Angst" we feel not over this or that particular aspect of human life but about *existence in general*. Yet, it is precisely this lack of an *a priori*, metaphysical determination of our Being-in-the-world that is simultaneously the source of our *freedom*: our capacity to choose or will our own potentiality-for-Being. In this respect Heidegger endows "existential Angst" with a paramount positive function. For it is this all-enveloping Angst that first leads us to call into question the inauthentic nature of our run-of-the-mill, existentiell, worldly commitments. Existential estrangement alone causes us to step back from our normal immersion in the routine of worldly affairs and to view these with mistrust. It thereby represents the precondition for our receptiveness to the call and the prospects for authenticity contained therein.

As such, a willingness to directly confront the phenomenon of Being-guilty becomes a crucial indication of authentic Dasein; just as, conversely, the attempt to conceal this inescapable dimension of existential contingency becomes one of the hallmarks of the They. The They finds the prospect of having to own up to its own nullity unbearable. It attempts to flee the horror of this realization by seeking refuge in a series of benumbing, prosaic, worldly involvements: in general "busy-ness" (*Betrieb*) and in the modern fascination with novelty (*das Neue*). It engages in a discourse of concealment—"idle talk"—to ensure that all such disquieting insights remain suppressed. It seeks to reinterpret "Being-guilty" as something devoid of existential gravity and import, that is, as essentially something "existentiell"—as something thing-like and present-at-hand.[81]

Thus, on the one hand, the guilt of thrownness accounts for the fact that Dasein "constantly lags behind its own possibilities." It signifies that Dasein can never achieve perfect self-mastery. It means "*never* to have power over one's ownmost Being from the ground up." On the other hand, the "nullity" that results from our Being-guilty has a uniquely positive significance for authentic Dasein, insofar as this ineliminable measure of existential contingency grounds Dasein's possibilities for freedom: "The nullity we have in mind belongs to Dasein's Being-free for its existentiell possibilities," observes Heidegger.[82] For were the "ground" of Dasein, instead of being "null," accorded a positive determination, Dasein's freedom (which should never be confused with arbitrariness; its ability to choose possibilities freely is itself conditioned by the vagaries of thrownness, as well as the "situation" of each particular Dasein) would prove dependent on a prior, superordinate set of categorial precepts. For existentialism, therefore, the category of freedom is preserved as a result of the proviso that *existence* is ontologically prior to *essence*: that is, as a result of the fact that the facticity of our Being-in-the-world is more "primordial" than the subsequent categorial determinations through which we are defined.

At the same time, however, the discussion of Being-guilty reconfirms the fact that the sphere of existentiell reality remains the province of the They. As Heidegger explains: "The common sense of the They knows only the satisfying of manipulable rules and public norms and the failure to satisfy them. It reckons up infractions of them and tries to balance them off. It has slunk away from its ownmost Being-guilty so as to talk more loudly about making 'mistakes.' But in the appeal, the They-self gets called to the ownmost Being-guilty of the Self."[83]

The realm of everyday "rules" and "public norms" is that of the "common sense" of the They. Its control of everydayness is so thoroughgoing, however, that authentic Dasein, it would seem, is left with *nary an existentiell leg to stand on*. In fact, so suspect is Dasein's entanglement in worldly events that the call is "more authentic, the more *non-relationally* Dasein hears and understands *its* own Being-appealed-to, and the less the meaning of the call gets perverted by what 'one' says or what is fitting and accepted"[84]—that is, the more thoroughly removed Dasein remains from "worldliness" in general.

We have already remarked that Heidegger places great store in the "existential" dimension of his work: *Being and Time* is intended to be more than a lifeless theoretical treatise; it is a document meant to have great historico-philosophical relevance. And thus as we have already seen, in his discussion of the category of authenticity, Heidegger emphasizes that the latter concept demands an *existentiell* transformation of life conduct and not just a change in one's habits of thought.

And yet, Heidegger's characterization of everydayness is so disproportionately negative that we are seemingly left with no immanent prospects for realizing our authentic natures in the domain of ontic life as such. For on the basis of his phenomenological descriptions, it would seem that the ontic sphere in general—"worldliness" in its entirety—has been "colonized" by the They. Here, we see that Heidegger's pessimistic philosophical anthropology and his "joyless" social ontology ultimately join forces. The result is a *radical devaluation of the life-world*, that delicate substratum of everyday human sociation which existential phenomenology claims to redeem. At this point, one might raise against Heidegger's social ontology the same charge he levels against Husserl's theory of the pure, transcendental ego: *it suffers from an impoverishment of world-relations*—a fact clearly evinced in Heidegger's self-defeating celebration of the "non-relational" character of authentic Dasein cited above. For how can the authenticity of a Dasein that is essentially "non-relational" ever attain realization in the sphere of ontic life?

The problems of Heidegger's attempt to delineate a viable social ontology were already fully apparent, however, in his deprecatory treatment of the problem of human intersubjectivity or "Being-with-others." For inasmuch as the salient characteristic of inauthentic Dasein is a studied neglect of its *"mineness" (Jemeinigkeit)* and, correspondingly, a voluntary self-surrender vis-à-vis the way in which the nameless "others" think, speak, and act—a self-surrender vis-à-vis the "dictatorship of the They"—the category of Being-with-others seems relegated *a priori* to the sphere of inauthentic dealings. In his study *The Other*, Michael Theunissen confirms this fact when he observes: "With respect to what concerns the inauthentic Self: there can be no doubt that as a 'self,' *it is preoccupied with the Other*. . . .Dasein-with is encountered methodologically *only on the way to the They*." And thus, as Theunissen concludes, "fallenness in the 'world' is itself nothing other than *being fascinated by the Others*."[85]

The more closely one examines the role played by "Being-with-others" in Heidegger's existential ontology, the more unequivocally it appears as a *deficient* mode of Selfhood or Being-a-Self. Heidegger himself is fairly explicit on this point: " 'Fallenness' into the 'world' means an absorption in Being-with-others, inasmuch as the latter is guided by idle talk, curiosity, and ambiguity"—in sum, the various modes of *inauthenticity*.[86] Thus, in the remarks just cited, Heidegger falls into the trap of conflating both "fallenness into the world" and "Being-with-others" with *inauthenticity as such*; a series of false equivalences that ultimately results in *a self-canceling social ontology*, insofar as "world-relations" in general—Being-with-others included—are narrowly identified with the inauthentic modalities of the "They" and "everydayness."[87]

To return momentarily to the call of conscience: perhaps it will provide no special cause for astonishment, then, when we realize that, in the last analysis, the call comes across as an empty, tautological assertion. Or as Heidegger remarks, "The call says *nothing* which might be talked about, gives no information about events. . . . When the call gives us a potentiality-for-Being to understand, it does not give us one that is ideal and universal; it discloses it as that which has been individualized and belongs to that particular Dasein."[88] With this philosophical gesture, Heidegger explicitly renounces the prospect of establishing a set of general criteria that might help us distinguish the true nature of the call. Instead, we learn only that it is something wholly particularized and singular, tailored to each individual Dasein. Yet, for want of a more detailed characterization, in its present articulation the call remains entirely arbitrary and discrete. We are left merely with the tautological assurance that it will manifest itself in a way appropriate to each specific Dasein. But in point of fact, the debilitating lack of material determinacy to this category threatens to turn it into an uncognizable will-o'-the-wisp.

In the end, one cannot help but speculate: is the vacuousness of the call, its disturbing lack of material specificity, in some way a direct consequence of Heidegger's own thoroughgoing denigration of "worldliness" and "everydayness"? That is, has Heidegger's disparagement of everydayness gone so far that he has rendered the ontic sphere in its entirety unserviceable for the existentiell possibilities of authenticity itself?

The category of "resolve" or "decisiveness" is defined by its capacity to heed the call. In approaching "resolve," it is important to keep in mind that we are dealing with a concept that is at least as important ontologically as it is ethically: *Ent-schlossenheit* ("unclosedness") literally signifies Dasein's "openness for Being." Of equal etymological significance, therefore, are its affinities with the category of *Erschlossenheit* or "disclosedness," the process through which the Being of beings stands revealed. Or as Heidegger reminds us, "Resolve is a distinctive mode of Dasein's disclosedness."[89] Hence, only by way of the "openness for Being" characteristic of resolute Dasein does the Being of beings get disclosed.

Heidegger's most important description of resolve is provided in the following passage:

> Resolve, by its ontological essence, is always the resolve of some factical Dasein at a particular time. The essence of Dasein as an entity is its existence. Resolve only exists as a decision [*Entschluss*] which understandingly projects itself. But on what basis does Dasein decide in resolve? On what basis does it make its decision? *Only the resolve [Entschlossenheit] itself can give the answer. . . . The resolve is precisely the disclosive projection and determination of what is currently factically possible.* To resolve, the *indefiniteness* characteristic of every potentiality-for-Being into

which Dasein has been factically thrown, is something that necessarily *belongs. Only in a decision is resolve sure of itself.* The
existential indefiniteness of resolve never makes itself definite except in a decision.[90]

The problems presented by the category of resolve are for the
most part familiar by virtue of our prior analysis of the call. For
the description of resolve is analogously tautological. When the
question is posed as to the "basis" for Dasein's resolve—when the
crucial question of criterial determinacy is raised—we are once
more left in the lurch: all we are told is that, *"Only the resolve itself
can give the answer. . . . Only in a decision is resolve sure of itself."*
The indeterminacy that characterized the call is also lauded in the
case of resolve: "indefiniteness," we are informed, is one of its essential features. Heidegger intends for the category of resolve to
provide the definitive response to the perennial dilatoriness and
"ambiguity" of the They, which is deemed constitutionally "irresolute": "irresoluteness merely expresses that phenomenon which
we have interpreted as a Being-delivered-over to the way in which
things have been prevalently interpreted by the They. Dasein as a
They-self, gets 'lived' by the common sense ambiguity of that publicness in which nobody decides but which has always made up
its mind. Resolve signifies letting oneself be summoned out of one's
lostness in the They."[91] However, the sheer dearth of material determinacy to this category makes it, in the last analysis, seemingly
no less "ambiguous" and "irresolute" than the They.

Our analysis of the call and resolve, of the problem of criterionlessness that plagues them both, suggests some preliminary
conclusions concerning the concept of decisionism in general. For
what might be described as the *normative impoverishment* of the
Heideggerian category of "resolve" or "decisiveness" goes far toward explaining the failings of decisionism in all its forms. For
when it is devoid of any and every normative orientation, "decision" can only be *blind* and *uninformed*—ultimately, it becomes a
leap into the void. Without any *material criteria* for decision, it becomes impossible to distinguish an *authentic* from an *inauthentic*
decision, *responsible* from *irresponsible* action—let alone on what
grounds an individual would even prefer one course of action to
another. Indeed, at times, Heidegger seems to openly glorify the
irrationalist bases of decision; for example, when he observes:

"Every decision bases itself on something not mastered, something concealed, confusing; else it would never be a decision."[92]

Both resolve and the call are putatively bound to the "factical particularity" of a specific Dasein and its "situation." But as a result, decision takes on an entirely arbitrary character; it becomes something particularistic and discrete, unamenable to evaluation according to more general, publicly accessible standards. Insofar as traditional moral imperatives have been rejected either as the prerogative of the They or as instances of an outmoded "value-philosophy," the ontological primacy of "decision" seeks to promote a "teleological suspension of the ethical." Like the Nietzschean *Übermensch*, resolute Dasein is beyond good and evil and must thus establish its own law.

"Destiny" or the Incorporation of Dasein within a Historical Community

According to the formidable Heidegger interpretation set forth by Reiner Schürmann, the antinormativism of fundamental ontology is in truth an antifoundationalism: it represents a thoroughgoing assault against philosophical "essentialism," i.e., against all metaphysical doctrines in which fixed, eternally valid meanings are proclaimed. In Schürmann's view, Heidegger understands Being as something inherently "polyvalent" which must be thought of as an "ever-new event." Heidegger's significance as an ethical thinker thus lies in the fact that he devalues the "teleological model of action." This means that action (and by implication, politics) can have no final goal or purpose: the Heideggerian *Holzwege* are "paths that lead nowhere." The central notion of Heideggerianism as a political philosophy would thus be *anarchy*. Here, the etymological basis of the word—an-archē, without first principle—assumes decisive significance. As a theory of anarchy, Heideggerian politics "withdraw legitimating ground from all central authority." The preconditions of human freedom would be established by this new emancipation from all "static ideals." In a more positive vein, anarchic politics implies that "power has no intrinsic purpose, that playfully reaching ever new social constellations is an end in itself; that its essence is boundless interplay without a direction imposed by central authority."[93]

However, there is a respected tradition in the history of political thought—beginning with Plato's criticism of democracy in the *Republic* and including modern critics of the vacuity of bourgeois, "negative freedom"—which has taken serious issue with the idea of equating "freedom" with "anarchy." In the eyes of these critics, the conception of freedom as the "right to do whatever one will" is tantamount to licentiousness. Thus, we could attribute unrestricted freedom of movement—or, following Schürmann, a life that is led at a safe remove from the strictures of "central authority"—to certain *nonhuman natures*, yet, in an important sense, we would be rather unlikely to categorize their actions as "free." And similarly, we would be more likely to consider "unfree" someone whose life, insofar as it was predominantly governed by "impulse" or "desire," seemed characterized by a nonteleological randomness, and thus devoid of a fundamental coherence or *raison d'être*.[94] It would thus seem that for the concept of freedom to be *meaningful*, it must have a determinate *content*. It presupposes a quasi-coherent set of—self-chosen—principles, values, and norms. Indeed, the very idea of a social order devoid of underlying principles or normative foundations, predicated on "boundless interplay without direction," would be sociologically incoherent. It would be a social order based on "anomie."

These objections notwithstanding, were Heideggerianism as a political philosophy correctly characterized as an "anarchism" in Schürmann's sense, there would be seemingly few meaningful links between the political implications of his thinking and National Socialist doctrines. Instead, his embrace of the regime would be a fortuitous excrescence, untraceable to any of the fundamental impulses of his thought.[95]

Moreover, the preceding analysis of the decisionistic elements of *Being and Time* suggests a certain plausibility for the "anarchist" reading proposed by Schürmann. For our discussion of "resolve" emphasized the antinormative, hence "an-archic" thrust of that category. As a voluntarism, decisionism implies that radical manifestations of will alone should be esteemed, without regard to the content or direction of the will. The will becomes essentially *unprincipled*. Were one therefore to interpret "anarchism" primarily in its etymological sense of "being without first principles," then the Heideggerian concept of resolve would seem to bear distinct affinities with it.

The "anarchist" reading of resolve is apparently supported by two other points. First, by the radically "non-relational" character of resolute Dasein, which is deemed more authentic the more dissociated it remains vis-à-vis the "existentials" of everydayness—the They and its various inauthentic modalities. In this sense, resolute Dasein displays certain "an-archist" trappings in its staunch refusal to go along with the prevailing existentiell *règles de jeu*. Second, Heidegger's repeated emphasis on the "Self" and on the "potentiality-for-Being-a-Self" would seem to confound attempts at an "organicist" or "*völkisch*" reading of his early work and push in the direction of "anarchic freedom" as hypothesized by Schürmann. And thus, by virtue of its radically voluntaristic connotations, resolve would seem to suggest affinities with the Nietzschean ethos of "heroic individualism."[96] In sum, if in *Being and Time* Heidegger propounded "the quasi-religious decision of private, self-individuated existence as finite autonomy" (as Jürgen Habermas has argued in an early essay),[97] then there would apparently be a considerable *break* between the political thought of his 1927 work and his National Socialist convictions of six years hence. Or, at the very least, one would have to fall back on Löwith's claim that the glorification of *individual* will in *Being and Time* was given a "collectivist" rereading with the onset of the Nazi period.

However, a more attentive reading of *Being and Time* will show that Heidegger consciously seeks to avoid an exclusively voluntarist interpretation of categories such as "resolve," "potentiality-for-Being-a-Self," and so forth; and that the antisubjectivist impulses of fundamental ontology remain strong enough to forestall a "radical individualist" or "anarchist" reading of the notion of "Selfhood" as it appears in Heidegger's early work.

In the discussion of resolve itself, for example, Heidegger is at pains to ensure that the category of "Selfhood" is not interpreted in line with the Cartesian tradition of "self-positing subjectivity." As he remarks in one key passage: "Resolve, as *authentic Being-one's-Self*, does not detach Dasein from its world, nor does it isolate it such that it becomes a free-floating 'ego'. . . . Resolve brings the Self right into its current concernful Being-along-side what is ready-to-hand and pushes it into solicitous Being-with-others. . . . Even 'decisions' remain dependent on the They and its world."[98]

Here, Heidegger seeks to relativize considerably the "non-relatedness" of authentic Dasein vis-à-vis the sphere of Being-with-others. To be sure, whether his attempts at relativization are entirely successful is another question. For the tendency to equate "Being-with" and "everydayness" that we remarked on earlier would seem to jeopardize the prospects of recapturing a dimension of authentic *Mitsein*. Nevertheless, Heidegger's insistence on this possibility would seem to raise some legitimate doubts about the tenability of an "anarchist" or "radical individualist" interpretation of *Being and Time*.

And thus, even though, as we have seen, authentic Dasein must provisionally attempt to distance itself from the multifarious *inauthentic* modes of Being-with-others, it is doubtful whether it can extricate itself entirely from its innate character as a *social being*. For its nature as a "being" whose Being is "with-others" is its inalienable birthright. Moreover, as the preceding citation attempts to suggest, *decisiveness itself first makes possible authentic Being-with-others*—even if the particulars of Heidegger's existential analysis make the existentiell likelihood of authentic Being-with seem truly remote.

Hence, the rudiments of a "collectivist" interpretation of the social ontology of *Being and Time* are to a certain extent confirmed by the category of resolve. However, as we have already noted, the political implications of this social ontology are anything but benign given the unabashedly elitist motifs that inform the existential analytic. The *de facto* separation of human natures into authentic and inauthentic is radically undemocratic. The political philosophy that corresponds to this ontological dualism suggests that human beings are divided by nature into leaders and followers. Indeed, this authoritarian conviction was a longstanding precept of the German mandarin intelligentsia and was well reflected in the traditional class divisions of German (especially Prussian) social structure. By celebrating this division between human types and their capacities, Heidegger in effect merely codified in ontological form a time-honored commonplace of German authoritarian political thought. And in this respect, as a work of German interwar *Kulturkritik*, the conservative revolutionary implications of *Being and Time* are telling. When Heidegger summarizes his discussion of *Entschlossenheit* by observing that, "When Dasein is resolute, it can become the conscience of others," it requires no special talent for political forecasting to divine the philosopher's future party loyalties.[99]

The category of *Mitsein* or Being-with thus represents an important corrective to a "radical individualist" interpretation of the early Heidegger. It denotes, as it were, an irrevocable "organicist" fundament to the social ontology of *Being and Time*. It suggests that an understanding of Dasein as an "existential totality" must precede the attempt to analyze the latter in its component parts.

But there is an additional categorial presence in *Being and Time* that equally suggests the untenability of a purely voluntarist reading: the category of *destiny* (*das Geschick*). In fact, in the estimation of Karsten Harries, "*Heidegger's understanding of destiny rules out all attempts to draw anarchistic consequences from Being and Time.*" Or as Harries explains, "Once we recognize that authenticity demands the subordination of the individual to a common destiny, it becomes impossible to see the *Rektoratsrede* as diametrically opposed to *Being and Time.*"[100] The category of "destiny" provides a material point of orientation that serves to intensify the inchoate, existential bond of Dasein in its everyday Being-with-others. In essence, it gives existential meaning and direction to the otherwise lax Being-with of Dasein in its everydayness. And ultimately, as Harries suggests, it is the quasi-collectivist implications of the concept of "being in thrall to a common destiny" that pave the way for Heidegger's later belief that National Socialism represents an appropriate ontic vehicle for the "Existentials" set forth in his 1927 work.

We have previously identified the paucity of material content as a major problem for the category of resolve, and thus, by implication, for the structure of authenticity in its entirety. Inquiries concerning the direction or *Wozu* of resolve met with the tautological response that only resolve itself, as discrete and particular, could provide an answer. The discussion of "authentic temporality," in which the concept of "destiny" figures so prominently, is specifically intended to solve the problem of the self-referentiality of resolve in its preliminary version. In effect, the indeterminacy of resolve is answered by the demand that the individual *subordinate him or herself to a common destiny*. But as we shall soon see, this solution, too, is apocryphal. For the same conceptual aporias that first emerged with the call of conscience and resolve merely repeat themselves on a higher level.

In order to understand the role of "destiny" as an authentic manifestation of Dasein's historicity, some preliminary observations concerning the category of "temporality" (*Zeitlichkeit*) are in order. As a primordial characteristic of Dasein's Being-in-the-world, temporality exists in both authentic and inauthentic modes. If the Being of Dasein is fundamentally characterized by "care," insofar as Dasein is distinguished from all other entities in the world (the "present-at-hand" and the "ready-to-hand") by the fact that "in its very Being, that Being is at issue for it,"[101] it is the *temporal* orientation of Dasein that largely determines whether its care, or existential self-relatedness, will assume an authentic or inauthentic guise.

Here, we shall draw on examples of the relationship between temporality and authenticity taken from Heidegger's own account. One of the basic modalities of authentic Dasein is "anticipation-toward-death" (*Vorlaufen-zum-Tode*). It is this anticipation alone that first confronts Dasein with its own "nullity," its own "Being-guilty," with the radical contingency of is own Being-in-the-world. The contingency of Dasein's thrownness is expressed not only by Dasein's "finitude"—by the fact that it is "mortal"—but also by the indeterminacy of death itself: it is an event that can be *anticipated* but never *foreseen*. As an existential stimulus to authenticity, death serves to radically *individualize* Dasein: Dasein knows that finitude is something it must confront alone, insofar as each death represents the singular, individualized fate of this particular Dasein. Hence, viewed from the standpoint of authentic temporality, "anticipation-toward-death" is a spur toward realizing my ownmost potentiality-for-Being-a-Self. The existential Angst produced by the recognition of our Being-toward-death ensures that neither "life" nor Selfhood will be taken for granted. It is a realization that lends a special intensity and urgency to all our ontic commitments. Henceforth, life is *lived resolutely* or *decisively*.

Heidegger emphasizes that both Dasein's authentic potentiality-for-Being-a-Self as well as authentic resolve are grounded in the phenomenon of temporality. As he avers: "Only insofar as Dasein has the definite character of temporality is the authentic potentiality-for-being-a-whole of anticipatory resolve, as we have described it, made possible for Dasein itself. *Temporality reveals itself as the authentic meaning of care.*"[102]

The basis for this contention can be readily demonstrated via an examination of the category of "anticipation-toward-death." By resolutely anticipating the eventuality of death, Dasein "temporalizes" its existence in an authentic manner. It therefore shows itself to be "*futurally*" directed; and as Heidegger comments at one point, "*The primary meaning of existentiality is in the future.*"[103] Conversely, the temporality of the They is distinguished by the fact that it seeks to *escape* the existential Angst of Being-toward-death, thereby essentially *closing off the future*. Instead, it dwells lifelessly or "un-ecstatically" in the present, irresolutely busying itself with various worldly distractions and factical involvements, covering up its own finitude and drowning out the voice of the call in the bustle of public affairs. However, it is precisely such "un-ecstatic" immersion in the "present" that characterizes the Being of *non-human entities*, that is, the ready-to-hand (equipment) and the present-at-hand (things). Therefore, the Being of inauthentic Dasein, in its renunciation of authentic temporality and futural anticipation, comes to resemble the inert Being of the present-at-hand. It succumbs to the static allure of a timeless, undynamic present and gradually sinks into lifelessness.

The difference between an authentic and inauthentic understanding of Being-toward-death is thus grounded in the phenomenon of temporality. Authentic temporality is *ec-static*: it projects Dasein toward the future, where its ownmost possibilities for Being-a-Self lie in store. Inauthentic temporality is merely *static*: its gaze remains irremediably mesmerized by the present, and thus the realm of possibility becomes for it a dead letter. For Heidegger, *"The primary phenomenon of primordial and authentic temporality is the future."* It is the future that makes possible "the resolute existentiell understanding of nullity"—of thrownness, Being-guilty, and ultimately, Being-toward-death.[104] Conversely, the incapacity for futural projection, which Heidegger defines as a "making-present," constitutes "the *primary* basis for *falling* into the ready-to-hand and present-at-hand with which we concern ourselves."[105]

But it would be misleading to claim that authentic temporality exists solely as futural and in neglect of the past. In truth, Dasein's authentic projection toward the future can be based only on a prior understanding of the past, which itself grounds the possibilities awaiting it in the future. Heidegger expresses this insight as follows: "As authentically futural, Dasein is authentically as 'having-been' [*gewesen*]. Anticipation as one's uttermost and ownmost possibility is coming back understandingly to one's ownmost 'been.' "[106] It is the fundamental significance of the past in the determination of Dasein's self-projection toward the future (after all, Dasein's "factical" character or thrownness lies in its "having been") that accounts for the importance of "destiny" as a category of authentic temporality.

Up until now we have been dealing with radically individualized Daseins. For as we have seen, the redeeming grace of authenticity can only be attained once the totality of everyday assumptions and commitments has been "bracketed." In this respect, Heidegger's problematization of everydayness in its entirety is reminiscent of the epochē performed by Husserl vis-à-vis the "natural attitude" of the impure, "empirical ego." Until the Angst that grips Dasein no longer stems from this or that particular worldly involvement, *but from the entirety of ontic commitments in general*, its attachments to the "world" will remain decisive, and it will not as yet have been sufficiently individualized.

The radical individuation of authentic Dasein is modified and its particular fate is fused with that of a superordinate, collective destiny with the introduction of the category of "historicity" (*Geschichtlichkeit*). Historicity is a mode of *authentic, past-directed temporalization*: Dasein situates itself in relation to a meaningful historical continuum, and this act endows its projection toward the future with content and direction. The categories of "historicity" and "destiny" thus offer a way of surmounting the empty self-referentiality of authenticity in its earlier guises, as well as a concrete solution to the contentless voluntarism that plagued the decisionism of resolve.

Historicity helps answer the question concerning the "who" of Dasein—it is as an "historical" being that its Selfhood is essentially constituted. It also addresses the phenomenon of the "connectedness of life," or the maintenance of a coherent identity over the course of time. Historicity thus provides a response to the problem of material impoverishment that plagued resolve from the outset: it offers, in principle, a concrete basis in terms of which resolve might decide to act. For it is via the transmission of a "heritage" (*Erbe*) alone that decisiveness is provided with a *concrete, factical* basis: "The resolve in which Dasein comes back to itself, discloses current factical possibilities of authentic existing, and discloses them *in terms of a heritage* which that resolve, as thrown, *takes over.* In one's coming back resolutely to one's thrownness, there is a hidden handing down to oneself of the possibilities that have come down to one, but not necessarily *as* thus having come down."[107]

Heidegger then restates this problematic in light of the radically individuating influence exerted by Being-toward-death:

> If everything good is a heritage, and the character of goodness lies in making authentic existence possible, then the handing down

of a heritage constitutes itself in resolve. The more authentically Dasein decides . . . the more unequivocally does it choose and find the possibility of its existence, and the less it does so by accident. Only by the anticipation of death is every accidental and provisional possibility driven out. Only Being-free *for* death gives Dasein its goal outright and pushes existence into its finitude. Once one has grasped the finitude of one's existence, it snatches one back from the endless multiplicity of possibilities which offer themselves as the closest to one—those of comfortableness, shrinking, and taking things lightly—and brings Dasein into the simplicity of its *fate [Schicksal]*. This is how we designate Dasein's primordial historicizing, which lies in authentic resolve and in which Dasein *hands* itself *down* to itself, free for death, in a possibility which it has inherited and yet has chosen.[108]

The historicity of Dasein, prompted by the "anticipation of death" and grounded in categories such as "heritage" and "fate," both frees Dasein for authentic self-individuation and forms the basis for an authentic Being-with-others. For the "connectedness of life" that is actualized in historicity is both synchronic as well as diachronic: "destinies" are connected both *across* time and *within* time (i.e., within the historical present). Authentic Selfhood is thus only fully actualized *within a historically given "collectivity."* The demands of Being-with prohibit resolute Dasein from subsisting in a state of hermetic isolation, however "authentic." There is a greater call that summons it, thus integrating Dasein within a larger historical destiny. Thus, as Heidegger observes in a crucial passage: "If fateful Dasein, as Being-in-the-world, exists essentially in Being-with-others, its historicizing is a co-historicizing and is determinative for it as *destiny*. This is how we designate *the historicizing of a community, a Volk*."[109]

As an individuated Self, Dasein possesses a "fate." Yet, as such, it remains unfulfilled and incomplete. Its true realization of Selfhood will only emerge when its particularity as an individual Dasein is surmounted and the heartland of authentic Being-with-others has been attained. With this move, its individual fate is inserted within a *collective historical destiny* and the existential nature of Dasein has been correspondingly "enriched." As Heidegger explains: "Resolve implies handing oneself down by anticipation to the 'there' of the moment of vision; and this handing down we call fate. This is also the ground for destiny, by which we understand Dasein's *historicizing in Being-with-others*."[110]

Our discussion of resolve brought to the fore a number of distinctly voluntaristic aspects of Heidegger's existential ontology. The analysis of the prominent role played by the categories of "destiny" and "fate" in the discussion of historicity suggests, however, that *Being and Time* simultaneously contains certain *fatalistic tendencies*. This realization may in truth not be as contradictory as it might appear on first view. For in many theories of history, voluntarism and fatalism often go hand in hand. Thus, once the concrete interrelation between historical "agents" and historical "structure" is bypassed, one is left with two autarkic constructs that function relatively independent of one another: "will" and "fate."[111] The Marxist tradition is quite familiar with this antinomy—one need only compare the determinism of Engels with the voluntarism of Lenin on the question of historical change. Similarly, National Socialist ideology emphasized—at times in the same breath—both the importance of German historical "destiny" as well as the unshakable character of the "will" of the German Volk.[112]

It is important to acknowledge that for Heidegger, "fate" is by no means intended as an arbitrary and nameless series of events that "befall" an individual in an external and unpredictable manner. Instead, fate possesses a distinctly *ennobling* character for him or her it envelops; it bestows a type of *dignified coherence* upon the life of authentic Dasein. Without the unifying power of fate, Dasein's existence would be threatened with unrelenting *contingency*—precisely the "fate" of irresolute Dasein. Here, again, we see the forces of "will" and "destiny" intermingle: in order to deserve one's "fate" (as is the case with resolute Dasein), there is a crucial element of conscious "recognition"; and thus, if it would be incorrect to say that we "choose" our fate, nevertheless, we must somehow intentionally take cognizance of its nature in order to merge with it and thus reap the ultimate benefit of its influences. In Heideggerian parlance, individuals have "fates," collectivities have "destinies." Thus, "Our fates have already been guided in advance, in our Being with one another in the same world and in our resolve for definite possibilities. . . . Dasein's fateful destiny *in and with its generation* goes to make up the full authentic historicizing of Dasein."[113]

The opposition between voluntarism and fatalism in *Being and*

Time is never reconciled. Heidegger tries to have it both ways and fails: "destiny" is meant to provide the existentiell basis for the empty self-referentiality of authentic decision, thereby furnishing a measure of content for an otherwise ungrounded, free-floating will. However, the "fatalistic" implications of this category subsequently undermine the autonomy of authentic resolve, an autonomy that was so painstakingly wrested (via the Angst of Being-toward-death) from the inauthentic *Existenzialien* of everydayness. Since this manner of reconciling the opposition is unpalatable, Heidegger at times lurches to the opposite extreme, suggesting that destiny itself can be "chosen" or "willed." But with this move, we have essentially relapsed into the same decisionistic arbitrariness that the concept of destiny was intended to counteract in the first place.

Heidegger grounds the concept of destiny in the category of "repetition": "The resolve which comes back to itself and hands itself down, becomes the *repetition* of a possibility of existence that has come down to us. *Repeating is handing down explicitly*—going back to the possibility of existence that has been-there."[114] Yet, to "repeat" does not mean to reproduce verbatim. Rather it implies an interest in reactivating an inherited historical possibility in the context of the present. The "decision" to repeat occurs in *das Augenblick*, the "moment of vision." Its function is to ensure that the act of repetition is meaningful—that is, "authentic"—that it proceeds in a fashion that has immediate bearing in terms of both Dasein's present "situation" and future possibilities.

To repeat an authentic possibility derived from the past means that "Dasein may *choose its hero*," says Heidegger.[115] The notion of "repetition" is of Kierkegaardian provenance. For the Danish philosopher it implied the idea of living each moment of life to the fullest, so that the prospect of its infinite repetition would be bearable. The "hero-worship" proposed by Heidegger—the search for an archetypal exemplar of human greatness—is suggestive of Nietzsche's *Übermensch*. Both the *Übermensch* and Heidegger's authentic Dasein manifest their "superior natures" by their scorn of moral convention. The *hero* (along with the "bohème," to whom neither Nietzsche nor Heidegger accords much interest) is the quintessential *antibourgeois*. Whereas for the bourgeois, life is a matter of calculation, utility, and narrow self-interest, for the hero, glorious acts of self-affirmation count alone, and utilitarian concerns are beneath contempt.[116]

But the question remains: on what basis is the hero to be chosen? How is one to recognize an *authentic* hero from an icon with feet of clay? Unless some criteria of selection are provided, we run the risk once more of relapsing into the vertiginous arbitrariness of pure decisionism. The only answer Heidegger provides to this question is characteristically unsatisfying. When we inquire as to the *basis* on which authentic repetition is to proceed and in terms of which true heroes might be distinguished from charlatans (how well such criteria might have served Heidegger himself in 1933), we are told that repetition itself is "grounded existentially in anticipatory resolve."[117] Thus, resolve is grounded in repetition (e.g., the choice of a proper hero), and repetition itself is grounded in resolve. Once again, circular reasoning replaces cogent insight and sheer assertion substitutes for compelling argumentation.

Earlier, we described the category of resolve or decisiveness as the "gateway" to Heideggerianism as a political philosophy, insofar as it represents the ontological ground of all authentic ontic commitment. Or, to express the same thought in slightly different fashion, no form of worldly engagement can be authentic that is not *resolute* or *decisive*. With the category of "destiny," the framework of resolve shifts from an individual to a collectivist standpoint; and with this shift the consequences for political life that were already implicit in the earlier discussions of Being-with and authenticity come unmistakably to the fore. We have characterized the political implications of resolve as "aporetic," and it is now time to detail more precisely what this in fact means.

The aporetic character of Heideggerian decisionism may be summarized as follows. On the one hand, there is the problem of its egregious lack of content, which not only presents major conceptual difficulties (e.g., how one determines an authentic from an inauthentic decision), but also crippling problems of a practical nature as well. Here, there is no small irony in the fact that decisionism, which masquerades as voluntaristic bravado incarnate, betrays, *nolens volens*, an extremely servile or obsequious dimension as well. Its servility lies in the fact that, insofar as it is devoid of *intrinsic* orientational precepts, it must survive parasitically by feeding off whatever choices happen to be served up by the contemporary historical hour. Thus, because its own store of material conviction is in such short supply, decisionism must grasp indiscriminately at whatever opportunities for self-realization are provided by the given historical moment. Not only is decisionism thoroughly "unprincipled"; it is also on this account *nakedly opportunistic.* And all voluntaristic bluster about "will," "choice," etc., notwithstanding, opportunism in the end reveals itself often enough as a base and simple conformism. Thus, because it lacks any and every *inherent* basis for choice, decisionism is forced to grasp at random existing opportunities for self-actualization. And as we saw earlier, an authentic resolve that shunned self-actualization would be a contradiction in terms. As innately destitute of inner substance, resolve has no choice but to conform to whatever options are historically available.

The consequences of this decisionistic "ethical vacuum," coupled with the prejudicial nature of Heidegger's conservative revolutionary degradation of the modern life-world, suggests an undeniable theoretical cogency behind Heidegger's ignominious life-choice of 1933. In its rejection of "moral convention"—which *qua* convention, proves inimical to acts of heroic bravado—decisionism shows itself to be distinctly nihilistic vis-à-vis the totality of inherited ethical paradigms.[118] For this reason, the implicit political theory of *Being and Time*—and in this respect, it proves a classical instance of the German conservative-authoritarian mentality of the period—remains devoid of fundamental "liberal convictions" that might have served as an ethicopolitical bulwark against the enticement of fascism. Freed of such bourgeois qualms, the National Socialist movement presented itself as a plausible material "filling" for the empty vessel of authentic decision and its categorical demand for existentiell-historical content. The summons toward an "authentic historical destiny" enunciated in *Being and Time* was thus provided with an ominously appropriate response by Germany's National Revolution. The latter, in effect, was viewed by Heidegger as the ontic fulfillment of the categorical demands of "historicity": it was Heidegger's own choice of a "hero," a "destiny," and a "community."

The aporetic nature of Heideggerian decisionism is thus indicated by its "negative" and "positive" dispositions. Both determined, in a complementary manner, Heidegger's partisanship for the National Socialist cause. For this was a partisanship that was carefully grounded in premeditated philosophical conviction. The "negative" side lies, as we have just seen, in a nihilistic historical opportunism that promotes unprincipled conformity with whatever choices are presented under given historical conditions. It is this side as well that mandates the *a priori* rejection of "bourgeois" political forms—liberalism, constitutionalism, parliamentarianism, etc.—and predisposes Heidegger toward a choice of "extreme" solutions: since bourgeois life-forms—represented by the *Existenzialien* of "everydayness"—are discounted in advance as degraded and profane, only *radical* alternatives to this thoroughly prosaic order of life will suffice.

The "positive" dimension may be discerned in the elitist aspects of the category of authenticity. The repudiation of a routinized modernity, implicit in the search for authenticity (and a judgment that would spur Heidegger's subsequent indictment of "technology"), leads Heidegger to search for "charismatic" alternatives: authentic Dasein alone, as a type of existential "elect," can endow a thoroughly rationalized and disenchanted cosmos with renewed greatness. If authentic Dasein is to lead, inauthentic Dasein must follow. The category of "destiny," as we have seen, suggests an irreducible "collectivist" dimension to this project. Since *structure* is a bourgeois phenomenon inimical to the vitality of *life*, the realization of authenticity on a collective scale will have to assume the character of a "movement" as opposed to traditional institutional form.

Heidegger's involvement with National Socialism—which was of the order of deep-seated, existential commitment—was far from being an adventitious, merely biographical episode. Instead, it was *rooted in the innermost tendencies of his thought*. This claim in no way entails the assumption that Nazism is somehow a necessary and inevitable outgrowth of the philosophy of *Being and Time*. It does suggest, however, that the politics of the Nazi movement emphatically satisfied the desiderata of authentic historical commitment adumbrated in that work.[119]

THREE

"To Lead the Leader": Philosophy in the Service of National Socialism

> We know that Martin Heidegger, with his keen sense of responsibility, in his concern for the fate and future of the German Volk, in his heart stands in the middle of our glorious movement; we also know that he never tried to hide his German sentiments and that for years he supported to the utmost the party of Adolf Hitler in its difficult struggle for Being and power; that he was always ready to sacrifice for Germany what is most precious, and that a National Socialist will always be able to count on his support.
>
> *Der Alemann*
> (the National Socialist daily for the province of Baden),
> May 3, 1933, commenting on Heidegger's entry
> two days earlier into the Nazi Party.

Essential Affliction and the Impoverishment of Bourgeois Normalcy

For a philosophy of existence whose central concept is that of authenticity, and for which the supersession of an academic philosophy divorced from life becomes a *point d'honneur*, a translation of the categorial framework into the terms of concrete life itself becomes an *existential imperative*.[1] Only via such a process of categorial transposition—from the plane of ontological analysis to the domain of life-praxis itself—can the true *existential ramifications* of the philosophical doctrine first become manifest.

In fact, insofar as the conception of fundamental ontology elaborated in *Being and Time* aims at rendering the traditional dichotomy between "philosophy" and "life" obsolete, it is misleading to refer to it as a "philosophical doctrine" in the customary sense. Traditional philosophy prides itself on its *abstraction* from the domain of life-praxis, for only on the basis of such abstraction (from Platonic ideas, to Cartesian radical doubt, to the Husserlian epoché) can its claims to scientific rigor be maintained. The *existentialia* of everyday life become synonymous with an impure sphere of contingency that must be transcended if philosophical science is to make good its claims. For Heidegger, on the contrary, the existential basis of human Dasein is *already philosophical*: by vir-

67

tue of our status of Being-in-the-world, we cannot help but raise ontological questions concerning the meaning of Being. Dasein is thus a "metaphysical being" *par excellence*. Or, as Heidegger himself phrases it: "Metaphysics belongs to the 'nature of man.' . . . Metaphysics is the fundamental event [*Grundgeschehen*] of Dasein."[2]

According to Heidegger, in the history of metaphysics, the raising of such questions has continually been shunted along false paths; a fact repeatedly registered in his claim that, hitherto, philosophers have inquired into the meaning of *beings*, but not that of *Being* itself. This situation is further proof of Heidegger's contention that a "scientific attitude" is in fact derivative and subaltern vis-à-vis the more "primordial" character of existential analysis. The latter is thus the essential "ground" on the basis of which scientific claims may be posited to begin with. In opposition to the ontological claims of a philosophy of existence, the scientific attitude is thus capable of producing only "second order" truths.

In principle, the purely formal "existentials" of *Being and Time* do not necessarily predetermine the direction of their material realization in the domain of practical life. They are, formally considered, open to a plurality of interpretations and an infinite number of factical, "ontic translations."

In point of fact, however, the aforementioned "existentials" might not be as intrinsically pure, as authentically formal, as the project of fundamental ontology itself would lead us to believe. It is Heidegger himself who, in *Being and Time*, on more than one occasion suggests that there is "a definite ontical way of taking authentic existence, a *factical ideal* of Dasein, underlying our ontological Interpretation of Dasein's existence"; and he goes on to refer to this "Fact" as a "*positive necessity* in view of the objects we have taken as the theme of our investigation."[3] Does Heidegger thus imply that, in a manner consistent with his own conception of historicity, the categorial framework of *Being and Time* must itself be interpreted *historically*? That is, that the existential analytic, rather than being purely formal, is itself saturated with historical determinacy? And if this is in fact the case, how is Heidegger's claim concerning the "factical ideal of Dasein" that underlies the existential analysis of *Being and Time* to be interpreted concretely? Could it be that it is the conservative revolutionary world-view of the

Weimar years that largely accounts for the material historical determinacy of Heidegger's 1927 work? We know that, following the publication of *Being and Time*, Heidegger himself came to adopt a specific "factical-historical ideal" of authentic Dasein, an ideal that was integrally tied to the German "National Awakening" during these years. Is it possible that, by carefully tracing the development of this new turn toward a political conception of authentic Dasein, we would succeed in gaining a more concrete idea of the factical, existential ideal presupposed all along by the Heideggerian concepts of authenticity, everydayness, "choosing one's hero," and so forth?

It is known that in the year 1929 Heidegger underwent a deep personal crisis. The crisis was in part provoked by self-doubts concerning the adequacy of the standpoint represented by *Being and Time*, whose third division, "Time and Being" ("The Explication of Time as the Transcendental Horizon of the Question of Being")—which was to have answered the question concerning the "meaning of Being" with which the book began—remained unwritten. The analytic of Dasein, which occupies pride of place in the inquiry, was in truth intended as a type of propadeutic on the basis of which the question of Being itself could be properly posed. But Heidegger increasingly came to have second thoughts about the methodological cogency of the existential point of departure. Above all, he feared the conceptual framework of *Being and Time* had been vitiated by an overreliance on the very metaphysical standpoint he had been seeking to transcend. The conception of truth he sought to advance in *Being and Time* was that of the pre-Socratic *alētheia*: truth as an uncovering or unveiling of the phenomena themselves. In this way he had attempted to counteract the predominant Western philosophical conception of truth as "propositional adequacy," whereby truth is associated with the idea of making "correct statements." In Heidegger's view, traditional Western conceptions of truth had been overly anthropocentric. Or as he would observe in a critical vein in his important essay on "Plato's Doctrine of Truth" (1931–32): "as the correctness of 'looking' truth becomes *the label of the human attitude towards beings*";[4] an attitude that ends up stifling the phenomenal capacity of beings to show themselves in their uncoveredness.

It is precisely in this sense that the fundamental ontology of *Being and Time* was deemed by Heidegger to be overly metaphysical: the entire analytic of Dasein remained excessively beholden to "the human attitude toward beings," and thus insufficiently attentive to the phenomenological capacity of beings *to show themselves.* By means of fundamental ontology Heidegger had sought, in a transcendental spirit, to demonstrate that the "conditions for the possibility of Dasein" represented the "conditions for the possibility of Being" in general. In this way, the existential aspect of the inquiry attained primacy over the ontological aspect. There can be no clearer formulation of this credo than the observation that: " *'There is' truth only insofar as Dasein is and so long as Dasein is.* Entities are uncovered only *when* Dasein *is;* and only as long as Dasein is are they disclosed."[5] However, Heidegger would conclude that in his attempt to ground the question of the meaning of Being existentially, the break with metaphysical anthropocentrism had not been stringent enough; and thus that the standpoint of *Being and Time*—the attempt to re-pose the question of Being on the basis of a philosophy of existence—needed to be rethought. Or as Pöggeler has remarked: "Heidegger failed in his attempt to bring the metaphysical theory of Being back to its ground by means of a fundamental ontology."[6]

On first glance, it may seem peculiar that a work that was apparently the object of such meticulous preparation and forethought could have, in the eyes of its author, foundered with respect to such an essential point: *viz.,* the *Seinsfrage* itself, the nominal *raison d'être* and goal of Heidegger's philosophical program. But a more careful look at Heidegger's intentions in *Being and Time* reveals a fundamental methodological ambiguity; an ambiguity that is reflected in the philosopher's own apparent indecision concerning the relationship between the two dimensions of the inquiry, existential analysis, on the one hand, and metaphysical truth-seeking, on the other.

But there is also another way of understanding this problem. Perhaps these two essential components of fundamental ontology—a philosophy of existence and a quest for the "meaning of Being"—were at cross-purposes from the outset. Perhaps, in truth, Heidegger actually had two very different projects in mind: he sought both to deliver a powerful historical indictment of the "present age" and its various inauthentic modes of embodiment, as well as to raise the metaphysical question concerning the truth of Being with unprecedented radicality. The problem was that these two desiderata proved essentially incompatible, even mutually contradictory. One was eminently historical, "factical," and temporally oriented; the other was ahistorical and metaphysical, a type of renewed *prima philosophia*. It is likely that, in the end, Heidegger felt stymied precisely because of the irreconcilability of these two aspects of the project of fundamental ontology. *Being and Time* represented nothing less than an attempt to square the (hermeneutic) circle: to reinvent the terms of philosophical ontology (Heidegger's "neoscholasticism") on the basis of a historically informed analysis of human finitude. But the purportedly ontological analysis of finitude was itself saturated with elements from the immediate historical present. In the end, *Being and Time* proved to be both a study in fundamental ontology as well as an exercise in radical *Kulturkritik*. And in its global critique of the deficiencies of modernity, it was a far from atypical product of the postwar German spirit. Herein lay much of the reason for the tremendous resonance the book found among German intellectuals in the late twenties and early thirties.

Heidegger's personal/metaphysical crisis of 1929 coincided with a world-crisis: the stock market crash of the same year and the depression that followed in its wake. As the recent testimony of Otto Pöggeler indicates, this was a turn of events that would have far-reaching implications for the future development of his thought.[7] The immediate consequence of this portentous interweaving of personal and historical destinies was an intensive preoccupation on Heidegger's part with the critique of modernity that was first adumbrated in *Being and Time*. What was largely implicit in the latter work now became fully explicit. From this point hence, Heidegger's reflections on the meaning of Being were intimately wedded to pressing historical questions concerning the destiny of the West and the crisis of European Dasein.[8] He regarded Germany's historical role as a "nation in the middle" as crucial if a solution to the crisis was to be found. The framework of *Being and Time* was in no way renounced, but modified—above all, in three crucial essays written between 1929 and 1932, which registered the shift of emphasis from a "philosophy of existence" to the "history of Being": "What is Metaphysics," "The Essence of Truth," and "Plato's Doctrine of Truth." His self-criticism of the overly subjectivist presentation of Dasein in *Being and Time* gained an expressly political content: circa 1932,[9] the ahistorical, individualistic conception of Dasein elaborated in the latter work was given a collectivist twist: the existential "carrier" of the categories of authenticity, historicity, and destiny became the German Volk in its concrete, factical-historical situation.

In the years following the publication of *Being and Time* Heidegger was preoccupied with the philosophical implications of the current historical crisis. During this period, he was involved in an intensive study of the leading conservative revolutionary thinkers—Spengler, Jünger, and Klages. According to Pöggeler, Heidegger's early Freiburg lectures already abounded with references to Spengler's *Decline of the West*.[10]

It was at this point in time that Heidegger's own concern with the historico-philosophical implications of the crisis of European humanity became a veritable obsession. Could the standpoint of fundamental ontology identify objective possibilities for superseding the crisis? To what extent could the *Kulturkritik* inspired by *Lebensphilosophie*, which had become common currency among German intellectuals during the interwar period, itself contribute to an understanding of the crisis? And if not, what were the specific shortcomings of this position that accounted for its failure to address these questions in their metaphysical "primordiality"?

Heidegger's lecture series in the Winter semester of 1929–30— *The Fundamental Concepts of Metaphysics*—sought to raise these questions in their full radicality. Here, he debates the critique of modernity propounded by *Lebensphilosophie*, whose point of departure is the contrast between "spirit" and "intellect," on the one hand, and "soul" and "life," on the other. The foremost representatives of this standpoint according to Heidegger are Spengler, Klages, Scheler, and Leopold Ziegler. Their philosophies lament the fact that in modern life, the former set of terms have been victorious at the expense of the latter, resulting in the triumph of a *Kulturfeindlich* (hostile-to-culture), soulless and mechanized *Zivilisation*.

Although Heidegger certainly sympathizes with the concerns of these authors, he finds their manner of posing the question lacking in depth and insufficiently radical. Their questioning does not begin from the "question of Being," but instead, from that of "beings"—*viz.*, individual "values." Their standpoint is that of "value-philosophy," in which the categories of "soul" and "life" are abstractly counterposed to those of "spirit" and "intellect." By presenting the contemporary historical crisis as one of conflicting "world-views" or "values," their efforts merely become another symptom of the crisis: they promote the superficial conviction that the crisis could be surmounted merely by an adoption of new belief-systems; whereas in Heidegger's view, what is at issue is the question of a more far-reaching and "fateful" (*schicksalhaft*) transformation of life. Much more profound, according to Heidegger, is Nietzsche's insight into the nature of the contemporary historical crisis; especially his discussion of the Greek opposition between the Apollinian and Dionysian attitudes toward life. In comparison to this Nietzschean distinction, the vitalist opposition between "intellect" and "life" proves derivative and sterile.[11]

As Winfried Franzen has shown, Heidegger's lectures of 1929–30 represent a crucial interim stage between the quasi-formal analysis of *Being and Time* and the explicitly political formulations advanced in the 1933 *Rektoratsrede. It is at this point that the existential analysis of Being and Time crystallizes into a determinate world-view.* The merely suggestive talk of authentic existence in the 1927 work here receives substantive material elaboration. The "factical ideal of Dasein" that Heidegger tantalizingly alludes to in *Being and Time* as the work's underlying basis is now for the first time concretely specified. Perhaps it is far from coincidental that it was also in these years that the Nazis emerged from their status as troublesome outsiders to become a legitimate mass party.[12]

Heidegger's most revealing observations occur in section 38 of the aforementioned lecture course, where he discusses "the essential affliction [*Not*] of the whole" and "the absence of essential distress in our contemporary Dasein." It was as though the mood of existential trauma provoked by World War I had undergone a Hegelian transformation from quantity to quality: "Everywhere," laments Heidegger, "there are disturbances, crises, catastrophes, afflictions: the social poverty of today, the political confusion, the impotence of science, the insubstantiality of art, the baselessness [*Bodenlosigkeit*] of philosophy, the powerlessness of religion." But the real problem is that whereas all these *individual* manifestations of crisis are recognized, the remedies proposed to counteract them remain of a piece with the afflictions themselves. The various attempts to "organize" against specific, phenomenal manifestations of "affliction" allow the real underlying nature of *affliction in general* to pass unheeded: "These nervous defensive-measures against the afflictions *prevent one from noticing precisely the affliction of the whole.*"[13]

"Distress" is indeed to be found everywhere; but what is lacking is an awareness of the "essential distress of Dasein," which alone, according to Heidegger, would allow for the emergence of a "community" as a "radical unity of an essential way of acting."[14] "*Mystery* is lacking in our Dasein," observes Heidegger, "and thus the horror which every mystery carries within itself and which gives Dasein its greatness is absent."[15] All the organizing and busy-ness of today's programs and parties serve only to *conceal* the distress—just as in *Being and Time*, the aimless bustle of everdayness serves only to cover-up the essential nature of existential Angst. The result of this concealment is a "generally satisfied contentment with safety and security [*Gefahrlosigkeit*]"—an absence of risk-taking and daring. And thus, "we believe it is no longer necessary in the fundament of our being *to be strong*."[16] "We concern ourselves only with acquired talents and skills," laments Heidegger; "however, force and power [*Kraft und Macht*] can never be replaced by the accumulation of competences."

In his critique of the ineffectiveness of "parties" and "programs," in his appeals to the need for "strength," "force," and "power," in his lamentations concerning the absence of "essential distress" and "extreme demands," Heidegger's impassioned contempt for the life-situation of the Weimar Republic coincides virtually point for point with the conservative revolutionary rejection of bourgeois normalcy. In his criticisms, Heidegger has essentially brought the categorial framework of *Being and Time*—above all, the central opposition between authenticity and inauthenticity—to bear on the "everydayness" of Weimar and found it to be grievously wanting. Weimar normalcy is in truth a state of generalized "affliction." Because it knows no greatness, takes no real risks, shuns "decision," it represents in Heidegger's eyes a state of *inauthenticity incarnate*. On this point, he and the conservative revolutionary thinkers are in complete accord. When the philosopher singles out for special praise the following passage from Nietzsche: "the heroism of the Greek consisted in his struggle with Asiaticism: beauty was not given to him as a gift, nor logic, nor the naturalness of custom—it is *conquered, willed and struggled for* [*eröbert, gewollt, und erkämpft*]—it is his *victory*"—[17] he puts himself in dangerous proximity to a chauvinistic tradition of neonationalist cultural criticism that would flow seamlessly into the National Socialist abolition of bourgeois normalcy.

As Franzen observes, there is little doubt that a vitalist preference for danger, risk, and excess, coupled with a pronounced distaste for conditions of bourgeois "everydayness," may be counted as among the "most important ingredients of the mentality of National Socialism."[18] Nor would it take Heidegger himself long to draw the logical political conclusions from this program of cultural critique.

From "Active Nihilism" to "Total Mobilization"

In a 1936 conversation with Heidegger outside of Rome, Karl Löwith expressed his disagreement with recent reports alleging that there was no intrinsic connection between Heidegger's philosophy and his political option for National Socialism. Instead, Löwith suggested that his former mentor's "partisanship for National Socialism lay in the essence of his philosophy." Heidegger agreed with Löwith "without reservation, and added that his concept of 'historicity' was the basis of his political 'engagement.'"[19]

Löwith's description of his "last meeting with Heidegger" is fascinating not only for the crucial information it supplies toward a proper understanding of the philosopher's political biography. It also contains a striking confirmation by Heidegger himself that his political convictions evolved directly from his philosophy; and that, moreover, it is the concept of "historicity," as elaborated in *Being and Time*, that specifically accounts for his "engagement" on behalf of the National Socialist cause. While Heidegger's claim is far from unambiguous, there is one interpretation that seems to recommend itself above all others.

In *Being and Time*, the category of historicity points to the need for Dasein to immerse itself in a pregiven historical continuum— a "destiny"—while simultaneously engaging in a constructive reappropriation of that historical tradition and its contents. Historicity implies (as we have argued in chapter 2) that the life of an autonomous-individual Dasein will fall short of existential fulfillment—will fall short of *authenticity*—if it persists in a condition of empty self-referentiality, that state of unconnected selfhood that is first suggested by the "call of conscience." In Hegelian terms, this state would be reminiscent of the dialectic of "Self-certainty," the Fichtean *ich gleiche ich*, that begins the discussion of "Self-Consciousness" in *The Phenomenology of Spirit*. Authentic Dasein must "choose itself." But this very decision regarding the "choice of self" must gain a measure of determinate content if it is to avoid lapsing into a potentially debilitating existential narcissism. One of the "answers" Heidegger posits to this dilemma is the category of historicity: only by way of inserting itself within a specific historical continuum can Dasein both avoid the risks of self-referential abstraction and provide its resolve with a concrete, material basis for its orientation toward the world.

It is in this sense that Heidegger's suggestive remark to Löwith concerning the relationship of the category of historicity to his political engagement in the 1930s must be understood. Heidegger's political decision for National Socialism signified an existentiell actualization of the categorial framework of *Being and Time*. Above all, it represented the philosopher's way of providing the concept of authenticity with a measure of material historical determinacy. Thus, it was on the basis of his category of historicity that Heidegger inserted himself seamlessly within the fate of the German Volk. In this sense, the apparently individualistic framework of *Being and Time* is by no means at odds with Heidegger's political stance of the early 1930s. For the category of historicity itself suggests the ultimate need for the individual to actively subordinate him or herself to a supraindividual historical destiny.

In evaluating the relationship between Heidegger's philosophy and his political engagement, we are once again presented with a tantalizing contradiction. On the one hand, the existential analytic of *Being and Time* is sufficiently formal and abstract to allow for a plurality of existentiell readings and translations: on the basis of the existential framework established by Heidegger, as grounded in categories such as the call, authenticity, and resolve, one could virtually imagine the philosopher opting for a *Bolshevist* instead of a *Nationalist* revolutionary course.[20] The critique of bourgeois normalcy is so thoroughgoing that only a political attitude of *radical historical transgression* will satisfy its demands. Correspondingly, the sole political course that seemed to be *a priori* ruled out by this approach was one of accommodation with the liberal democratic status quo—which knew only the reign of a prosaic and unheroic everydayness. On the other hand: if it is true, as we have suggested, that one finds in the early Heidegger—and in the categorial framework of *Being and Time* itself—numerous components of the conservative revolutionary world-view, then the "formalism" of *Being and Time* may in fact be less considerable than is generally assumed. And thus, Heidegger's political engagement would have been in point of fact decisively conditioned by the ideological implications of his own theoretical standpoint.

As we have indicated, Heidegger's interest in the conservative revolutionary position was heightened by the world economic crisis of 1929. Thereafter, the political stability of Weimar became increasingly tenuous, and in the eyes of many, the prospect of authoritarian rule came to be viewed as a political alternative that was both credible and desirable. But it was above all Heidegger's decisive encounter with the work of Ernst Jünger in the early 1930s that facilitated the crystallization of a political world-view that had up until this point only been loosely articulated. According to Pöggeler, Heidegger indicated on several occasions that from this point on, he understood the political implications of the current historical situation on the basis of Jünger's work.[21] One such occasion was the essay, "The Rectorate, 1933–34: Facts and Thoughts," (written in 1945 in the course of a denazification hearing at Freiburg University), where Heidegger sets forth the following reflections concerning the importance of Jünger's theories:

> The way I already viewed the historical situation at that time [i.e., in the early 1930s] may be indicated with a reference. In 1930, Ernst Jünger's essay on "Total Mobilization" appeared; in this essay the fundamental outlines of his 1932 book *The Worker* are articulated. In a small group, I discussed these writings at this time, along with my assistant [Werner] Brock, and attempted to show how in them an essential comprehension of Nietzsche's metaphysics is expressed, insofar as the history and the contemporary situation of the West is seen and foreseen in the horizon of this metaphysics. On the basis of these writings, and even more essentially on the basis of their foundations, we reflected on what was to come, i.e., we sought thereby to confront the latter in discussions. Many other persons also read these writings at that time; however, they were laid aside along with a number of other interesting texts and not comprehended in their true importance.[22]

What is most revealing in Heidegger's account is the avowal that the significance of Jünger's writings lay in their comprehension of the imperatives of the current historical situation—the destiny of the West—on the basis of an understanding of Nietzsche's metaphysics.

We know that in the late thirties, Heidegger would deliver a highly critical verdict concerning the value of "Nietzsche's metaphysics." Correspondingly, his estimation of the worth of Jünger's historical prognoses would also undergo substantial revision at this time (1939–40), when he would once again organize a private seminar around *Der Arbeiter*. But during the period Heidegger describes in the remarks just cited, his attitude toward both Nietzsche and Jünger was unreservedly enthusiastic. As Pöggeler points out, "Nietzsche became decisive for Heidegger. . . . in the years immediately following the appearance of *Being and Time*."[23] More to the point, he viewed the diagnosis of modernity that appeared in the work of these two "essential thinkers" as authoritative prophecies concerning the destiny and future of Western civilization. Moreover, it was on the basis of the doctrine of "heroic nihilism" propounded by both men as a solution to the "crisis of the West" that Heidegger found the intellectual justification for his own engagement in the National Socialist cause.

Nietzsche's "diagnosis of the modern age" is of course present throughout all phases of his *oeuvre*. But the most powerful discussion of this theme in his work—and the one that clearly had the greatest impact on Heidegger—was the section of *The Will to Power* entitled "European Nihilism." The resounding indictment of all inherited Western values—philosophical, religious, aesthetic, and political—proclaimed by Nietzsche in these passages is one that Heidegger—as well as the entire generation of German conservative revolutionary thinkers—will share. And to this generation of German right-wing radicals, the multifarious "afflictions" of Western modernity seemed to be disproportionately concentrated in the everyday reality of the fledgling Weimar Republic.

But the truly provocative aspect of Nietzsche's analysis of modern "nihilism" was to be found in the conceptual opposition he established between "passive" and "active" nihilism. Passive nihilism characterizes the attitude of all those who cling futilely to the traditional Western values that are already in an advanced state of decomposition. The adherents of these values are "mediocrities" fated to perish along with the belief-system of Western humanism in general. Active nihilism, on the other hand, represents the insight of superior character types who realize that "if something is falling, one should give it a shove." This attitude suggests that the process of value-decomposition should not be bemoaned, but welcomed, in anticipation of the new opportunities for historical greatness that would reappear once the decrepit, traditional institutions and values have decayed to a point where they have lost all credibility. The values of a postnihilistic age can be deduced *ex negativo* from those of the dissolute historical present: daring instead of humility, cruelty instead of mercy, rule of the strong rather than the democracy of the weak, the triumph of instinct and sensuality over the timorous rationalism of the modern age. When Nietzsche praises a *"voluntary* desire to contemplate all sorts of distress and transgressions," as well as the need "to give men back the courage to their natural drives," when he claims that "there is nothing in life that has value except the degree of power," his concerns and terminology are one with those expressed by Heidegger in *Die Grundbegriffe der Metaphysik* and many subsequent texts.[24]

Circa 1929, Heidegger made a conscious, existential "decision" for Nietzsche.[25] Nietzsche's prophetic utterance concerning the "death of God," which Heidegger alludes to in the 1933 Rectoral Address, meant that all values that had heretofore given life meaning had become groundless and without substance. Or as he would remark in a gloss on Nietzsche's dictum: "It means: the supersensible world, especially the world of the Christian God, has lost its power of influence in history."[26] For Heidegger, following Nietzsche, the imminent "transvaluation of all values" heralded the possibility that Germany, too, stood before a far-reaching, existential transformation *("unser eigenstes Dasein selbst vor einer grossen Wandlung steht").*[27]

But it was the work of Jünger that would have a more direct and immediate impact on the formation of Heidegger's political world-view. Whereas Nietzsche was able to articulate the nature of the "crisis of nihilism" in general historico-metaphysical terms, it was Jünger who, proceeding from this Nietzschean standpoint, unflinchingly drew the specific sociopolitical conclusions that were at once consequent, bold, prophetic—and potentially terrifying.

"Total Mobilization" is an exercise in "active nihilism."[28] It is a quasi-Nietzschean attempt to embrace the "fatalities" of the modern world, which are defined by Jünger in terms of a tendency toward total organization in an age of world war. For decades, German romantic anticapitalist thinkers on both the right and left sides of the political spectrum had been bemoaning the triumph of the ultrarationalized, mechanistic and soulless world of bureaucratic capitalism. But their lamentations proved little more than clamorous exercises in futility: the desired alternative—a return to a mythologized state of *Gemeinschaft*—was, for reasons that hardly need to be specified, historically unattainable. Toward the end of the 1920s, a growing number of German neonationalist in-

tellectuals—above all, those stemming from the younger generation that had become obsessed by the defeat in the Great War—
began to reevaluate the time-worn *Gemeinschaft/Gesellschaft*
dichotomy. With their outlook sobered by the German defeat, they
came to the conclusion that what Germany needed was a *modern
community*, one whose identity and structure would be forged
through the utilization of the most advanced technological means
in all spheres of life.[29] Ernst Jünger, along with Spengler, was perhaps the most influential among this group of thinkers.

In both "Die totale Mobilmachung" and *Der Arbeiter*, Jünger
conceives of the essence of modern society in terms of a militarization of all aspects of life. What is unique about the modern age
is that the difference between "war" and "peace" has been effaced;
now, "peace" means intensive preparation for the next war. In this
way, Jünger stands Clausewitz on his head: politics in the modern
world becomes the continuation of war by other means. The new
realities of struggle dictate that society in its entirety be fashioned
after a military model. Or as Jünger observes: "In addition to the
armies who encounter one another on the battle-fields originate
the modern armies of commerce, of food-production, of the ar-
maments industry—the army of labor [*Arbeit*] in general." Already
during the concluding phases of World War I, there was hardly an
aspect of social life—down to the housewife with her sewing-ma-
chine—that remained untouched by the drive toward total war.
Jünger continues:

> In this total incorporation of potential energies, which trans-
> forms the warring industrial states into volcanic forges, the be-
> ginning of the "age of work" [*Arbeitszeitalter*] is perhaps most
> strikingly apparent—it turns the World War into a historical
> phenomenon that is superior to the French Revolution in signif-
> icance. In order to unfold energies of such magnitude, it no longer
> suffices to mobilize heavy industry; preparations for war are re-
> quired in the very marrow, in the innermost cell of life. To bring
> about such preparation is the task of total mobilization: an act
> through which the highly differentiated and complex power sup-
> ply of modern life is, by way of a one-time adjustment of the
> control panel, transmitted to the great current of warlike [*krie-
> gerischen*] energies.[30]

The "worker" is the new social type corresponding to an age of
"total mobilization." He is the self-sacrificing cog that makes the

machinery of total mobilization turn. Just as the logic of militarization is extended to the whole of society, so, conversely, is the regimentation of the workplace extended to all spheres of life: in essence, society itself becomes a giant factory whose only "product" is war. The total state of the modern age has succeeded in effacing the distinctions between war and peace, soldier and civilian; and thus in the modern state, the tasks of industrial work dovetail fully with the requirements of modern warfare. The worker is in truth a "worker-soldier," while the soldier is similarly a "soldier-worker." The demands of an era of total war decree that all aspects of social life must be planned—and in this context, it is far from accidental that Jünger lavishes praise on the Soviet "five-year plan."[31] In Jünger's scheme, the worker is the new hero of modern life. His discussion revolves around the concept of the "Form of the Worker" [*Gestalt der Arbeiter*]. With this idea, Jünger disingenuously attempts to ascribe a higher, Platonic reality to that class of persons who in his future society are to be little more than drones. After all, as Jünger himself readily admits, it is ultimately "the state"—or the authoritarian ruler who stands at its summit—that functions as the "supreme architect" of the whole.[32]

Although Jünger's prose-style in *Der Arbeiter* is, as ever, intoxicating—a more accomplished aesthetician of carnage there never was[33]—there is no way of softening the harsh political message the work seeks to convey: martial imperatives dictate that *a totalitarian state alone is the appropriate political form for an age of total war*.[34] This was a message that, in philosophically transmogrified form, would leave an indelible and decisive impression on Heidegger's political self-understanding.

But of equal importance from our perspective is Jünger's attempt in *Der Arbeiter* to extend the Nietzschean/conservative revolutionary critique of modernity in terms appropriate to the contemporary German political context. This is achieved via the basic opposition in the book between two antithetical historical "types": the worker and the bourgeois. Like his image of the worker, Jünger's characterization of the bourgeois is highly artificial and meant primarily to serve ideological ends: the bourgeois becomes the embodiment of all that is prosaic, cowardly, and complacent in modern life; he is a symbol for the liberal-democratic, individualistic, and rational value-paradigms—the triumph of "intellect" over "life"—that the German conservative intelligentsia had railed against since the latter decades of the nineteenth century. He becomes the caricatural scapegoat for all values that, in Jünger's estimation, present an obstacle to Germany's becoming a paramilitary "fortress state." His description of the "bourgeois" is thus of a piece with the conservative revolutionary assault against modernity. The bourgeois is by nature timorous, daring and risk-taking are to him matters of inconsequence, his entire life is spent in pursuit of security, comfort, and material well-being.[35] He is the living embodiment of those decaying values of "passive nihilism" that Nietzsche lambasts in *The Will to Power*. It is on the basis of the same program of conservative revolutionary *Kulturkritik* that Heidegger finds the modern age and its inauthentic character types so profoundly wanting.

It is quite possible that the entire architectonic of Jünger's worker-soldier state was of Nietzschean inspiration. For in *The Will to Power*, we encounter the following lines, which were undoubtedly well known by Jünger: "Concerning the future of the worker: *workers should learn to feel like soldiers.* An honorarium, an income, but no wages. . . . The workers must learn to live as the middle class does now—but on a higher plane, that is, as the superior caste whose needs, however, are few. Hence they will be poor and live more simply. *Power* will be their sole possession."[36]

The generation of conservative revolutionary thinkers posed a fundamentally Nietzschean question: how can the nihilistic conditions of a bourgeois social order be essentially—i.e., radically—overcome? In his works of the early 1930s, Jünger provided one of the most provocative and consistent responses to this question, one that would become an object of fascination for an entire generation of right-wing intellectuals. He argued that a totalitarian *Arbeitergesellschaft* alone would be capable of surmounting the incapacitating fragmentations and divisions of a liberal political system; that only when it is united with singleness of purpose can a state attain the resolve and power that are required in the contemporary historical world. For Jünger, such political eventualities did not hinge on matters of choice or subjective preference. Rather, modern nation-states found themselves in a quasi-Darwinian situation that had been decreed by fate. Only those nations that swiftly adapted to the unyielding imperatives of this new historical mandate would be capable of survival. This fatalism, at the same time, added an ennobling urgency to his prognoses. Through a macabre twist, the total rationalization of social life now seemed to herald the triumph of a "new organicism"—a "modern community." The bourgeois virtues of intellectualism, circumspection, and equity would now be supplanted by the heroic values of struggle, risk, and hierarchy. The Nietzschean opposition between "passive" and "active" nihilism was to be overcome via the "will to power" of a bellicose, totalitarian state.

In point of fact, Nietzsche would likely have viewed this recasting of his critique of modernity with extreme suspicion. His writings are filled with sarcastic jibes directed at the shallowness of German nationalism. His own defense of the warrior-ethos valorized a heroic individualism whose greatness lay precisely in its superiority vis-à-vis the group or herd mentality. To be sure, the Nietzschean distinction between the "superman" and the "herd" cannot help but seem in retrospect an ominous anticipation of the Nazi *Führerprinzip*. Yet, one of the defining traits of the Nietzschean superman was a seeming disinclination to partake in collectivist undertakings.[37] Nor was Heidegger's own appropriation of Jünger's doctrines a straightforward affair. Instead, he sought, in a highly idiosyncratic manner, to integrate the latter's apocalyptical historical prophecies with his own philosophical conception of the history of Being.

But there also exists a significant intraphilosophical basis for Heidegger's turn toward a conservative revolutionary solution to the ills of modernity circa 1930; a fact evident above all in the radicalization of his interpretation of the history of metaphysics. In *Being and Time*, Heidegger is especially critical of the degradation metaphysics has suffered at the hands of modern, Cartesian-scientific approaches. But there is little suggestion that the enterprise of metaphysics itself is irredeemably flawed. In fact, *Being and Time* may be plausibly read as a fusion of the two great legacies of the philosophical tradition, the ancient and modern. In this view, fundamental ontology represents a reconciliation of the approaches of Aristotle and Kant to yield a type of "transcendental ontology." That is, the Kantian "conditions of the possibility of experience" no longer correspond to a set of disembodied mental categories, but are now grounded existentially.

But a qualitatively different attitude toward the legacy of metaphysics is revealed, for example, in his 1931–32 essay on "Plato's Doctrine of Truth." Heidegger, operating now much more directly under Nietzsche's influence, comes to view the entirety of metaphysics as "a history of error." Moreover, following Nietzsche, he locates the "fall of philosophy" no longer with the objectivating attitude of Descartes, but at the very dawn of the metaphysical enterprise itself: with Plato's act of shifting the truth-content of metaphysics to an other-worldly, supersensible sphere. Whereas the original Greek conception of *a-lētheia*—truth as "unhiddenness"— "refers persistently to what is always openly present in the region in which man abides," Plato's cave allegory tells a story that locates truth in another "abode"—the world of *ideas*.[38] The Platonic theory of truth is thus a tale according to which, *"alētheia* comes under the yoke of the idea," with the result that the entire relationship of philosophy to the pre-Platonic conception of "truth as unhiddenness" has been lost: "When Plato says that the idea is the master permitting unhiddenness, he banishes to something left unsaid the fact that henceforth the essence of truth does not unfold out of its own essential fullness as the essence of unhiddenness, but shifts its abode to the essence of the idea. The essence of truth relinquishes the basic feature of unhiddenness." And by virtue of this new equation of knowledge with the "idea," "Truth becomes *orthotos*, correctness of the ability to perceive and to declare something"[39]—that is, truth becomes propositional truth. Truth is no longer a property of beings themselves—of their capacity to hide and show themselves—but rather is made contingent on the capacity of the human "subject" to produce "judgments" about them. Or as Heidegger explains, "From now on the mold of the essence of truth becomes, as the correctness of representing through an assertion, the standard for all of Western thinking."[40]

Heidegger's renunciation of "propositional truth" in preference for the idea of truth as "unhiddenness" has been the target of a number of cogent criticisms whose content will concern us at a later point.[41] What is important in the context at hand, however, is that the radicalization undergone by his critique of metaphysics leads to a corresponding heightening of his perceptions concerning the gravity of the contemporary sociocultural crisis. From this point on, he will understand the origins of the crisis as pertaining not only to specific failings of the modern world; instead, their roots will be traced back to the first stirrings of Western philosophy itself. The crisis of metaphysics, as it is reflected in the collapse of traditional Western values, assumes in Heidegger's eyes a *world-historical* or *epochal* nature. The historical reversal this situation requires must itself be correspondingly global and radical. The political solution—if one is to be found—must itself be of an *eminently metaphysical character*: it must establish *an entirely new re-*

lationship between man and Being. Hence, it must be *non-Platonic*; it must base itself on an entirely different conception of truth from the one that has dominated the West for 2500 years. An authentic politics of Dasein must therefore aim at a restoration of the pre-Platonic Greek polis in modern attire. For under such conditions alone has the notion of "truth as *alētheia*" been able to thrive.

The *Rektoratsrede* or "The Glory and Greatness of the National Awakening"

The consummate fusion of the conservative revolutionary and metaphysical dimensions of Heidegger's thought may be found in the 1933 Rectoral Address, "The Self-Affirmation of the German University"; a work, according to Löwith, whose interweaving of Nazi rhetoric with the language of classical philosophy was so extreme that at the end "the listener was in doubt as to whether he should start reading the pre-Socratics or enlist in the SA."[42]

From a contemporary political standpoint, Heidegger's acceptance of the rectorship in May 1933 was a far from innocent affair. It provided a tacit semblance of cultural respectability for the fledgling Nazi dictatorship: Heidegger, its most prestigious convert to date from the world of letters, was then at the very crest of his renown.[43] Despite his own repeated claims that he took on the position only in order to *prevent* the politicization of university life (a fact that can now be easily refuted on the basis of the evidence compiled by Farias and Ott), his appointment was widely perceived as an instance of political *Gleichschaltung*.[44]

It is with the 1933 Rectoral Address that Heidegger, in his public utterances, passes over from the language of conservative revolutionary cultural criticism to the *Sturm und Kampf* vocabulary of National Socialism proper.[45] From a purely rhetorical standpoint, the evidence is telling enough. Though direct appeals to the theme of "race" are absent from the speech, there is hardly an additional Nazi shibboleth that Heidegger fails to invoke. The content of the address revolves around categories such as *Volk, deutsches Volk, Volksgemeinschaft, volklich,* "the forces of earth and blood" (*erd- und bluthäftigen Kräfte*), followers and leaders, "fate," "mission," "affliction," and "hardness." There are detailed discussions of "will," the "essential will," "decisiveness," and "power." Some of these terms, were they to appear in a different historical and cultural context, would present no great cause for alarm. However, in 1933 Germany—with the nation swarming with Brown Shirts, the Reichstag in ruins, parliament suspended, the trade-unions broken, and the first Jewish boycotts of the previous month fresh in memory—the stakes were of an entirely different order.

On the one hand, it is precisely the innovative mixture of existential categories and Nazi oratory that prevents the address from degenerating into one of the standard professions of faith—so fashionable at the time—in the virtues of the National Revolution. On the other hand, it is the same seamless interlacing of philosophical and political motifs that creates the impression that the categorial framework of *Being and Time* had found its consummate historical embodiment in the total state of Adolf Hitler.

Löwith describes the Rectoral Address as a "minor stylistic masterpiece."[46] It is indeed a marvel of radical concision, a type of politico-philosophical manifesto that concentrates the philosopher's most pressing historico-philosophical concerns in an explosive, ten-page document. The familiar lamentations of the existentialist/vitalist critique of modernity—the sterility of traditional academic knowledge and of a "culture" separated from "life"; the "abandonment" of contemporary man by God—are prominently displayed in the address. The situation in Heidegger's view is wellnigh apocalyptical: "The spiritual power of the West breaks down and [the West] cracks apart at the seams. . . . the decrepit sham-culture [*Scheinkultur*] collapses into itself, drags all powers into the confusion, and causes them to be suffocated in madness."[47] At the same time, there exists the prospect of an imminent, positive, historical resolution: *viz.*, "the will of the German Volk [to fulfill] its historical-spiritual mission." "We want our Volk to fulfill its historical mission. *We want ourselves*,"[48] declaims Heidegger near the end of his speech—in a phrase that Dolf Sternberger has described as an unconscionable avowal of collective narcissism.[49] Heidegger's claim merely echoes an analogous proclamation by Spengler some twenty years earlier: "We don't want principles any more, we want ourselves."[50]

Wherein in fact does that "historical mission" (*geschichtlicher Auftrag*) lie? "In the power of the *beginning* of our spiritual-historical Dasein. . . . This beginning is the awakening [*Aufbruch*] of Greek philosophy."[51] Or as Heidegger explains further: "The beginning still *is*. It does not lie *behind us*, as the distant past, rather it stands *before* us. . . . The beginning has broken in upon our future, it stands there as the decree from afar that we recapture its greatness."[52]

The meaning of Heidegger's (*prima facie* surprising) claim is less obscure when viewed against the background of the categorial scheme of *Being and Time*. The reenactment of the Greek beginning is to be a type of *authentic repetition*. The historicity of German destiny is to express itself as a recreation of the glory of the Greek polis. This justifies Heidegger's observation that "the beginning . . . stands before us." For historicity means precisely this: the repetition of an "essential historical moment" that serves to inform and guide the "futurity" of a given historical collectivity. There is nothing fortuitous or merely subjective about this contemporary historical mission. Rather, it corresponds to the "destiny of the German Volk."[53]

In retrospect, of course, one cannot help but be shocked by Heidegger's historical myopia. How could he have so egregiously misjudged the nature of the contemporary historical situation? Could his blindness be attributable to the megalomania of his own personal political ambitions? According to Jaspers, Heidegger viewed National Socialism as standing in an essential relation to Being. And thus, he believed it should be his responsibility to "lead the leader"—*den Führer führen*—in the manner of a contemporary philosopher-king.[54] Or does this lapse in judgment instead have deeper, philosophical roots? Was the level of abstraction of the conceptual framework of fundamental ontology so extreme as to invite delusive interpretations when applied to the realm of historical facticity itself? For example, might the lack of determinacy of his category of historicity—e.g., the lack of cogent evaluative foundations in light of which we are to "choose our hero"—disqualify it as a legitimate basis for making decisions in the sphere of concrete historical life? Might a similar judgment also prove cogent with respect to Heidegger's conception of the history of metaphysics as a *Verfallsgeschichte* (a "history of decline")—a philosophical night in which all cats are gray, that is, in which all historical epochs are considered to be victimized in equal measure by *Seinsverlassenheit* ("abandonment by Being")?[55]

Heidegger's admiration for Greek traditions is commendable. At the same time, this admiration may have been woefully selective. According to H. W. Petzet, Heidegger shared the historian Jacob Burckhardt's view that democracy was the cause of the downfall of the ancient polis. The conclusion he drew from this fact was that in the modern world, too, the status of the authoritative few was jeopardized by democracy from below;[56] a judgment, of course, that is perfectly consonant with the critique of "das Man" and "everydayness" in *Being and Time*. And it is precisely in this vein that in *What is Called Thinking*, he will cite with approval Nietzsche's characterization of "modern democracy" as a *"degenerate form of the state"* (*Verfallsform des Staats*).[57] It was above all pre-Socratic philosophy that Heidegger deemed of value in the Greek tradition. Even the institution of the polis, which Heidegger often singled out for praise, was not admired for its intrinsic political character, that is, the democratic conduct of political life.[58] It was merely the historical locus where the "thinking of Being" began. A less parochial view of the Greek heritage—not only an appreciation of democracy, but a greater respect for another Greek "first," the "rational concept"—might have mitigated his proneness to irrational political judgments.

In the second half of the Rectoral Address, Heidegger provides an idealized account of the "Great Awakening" that has seized German Dasein. Here, the critique of degenerating bourgeois lifeforms leads directly to an appeal for a new set of heroic values. Foremost among these are a set of existentially redeeming "extreme situations"—Heidegger's own version of "active nihilism." Thus, if the nonessential character of traditional academic knowledge is to be surmounted, university instructors must advance to *"the most extreme posts of danger* amid the constant uncertainty of the world."[59] Similarly, the "essential will" (*Wesenswille*) to knowledge requires that the Volk be subjected to "the greatest inner and outer danger" in order to enjoy the benefits of "its true spiritual world." In contrast with the cultural sphere of the bourgeoisie, the spiritual world of the Volk is no idle "superstructure"; instead, it resides in the *"forces of soil and blood as the power of the inmost agitation and greatest shattering [Erschütterung] of its Dasein."*[60]

"German students are on the march," announces Heidegger; and he leaves no doubt about the fact that, in the future, they will be marching to a military beat. "The much ballyhooed 'academic freedom' " (which for Heidegger is only "negative," and therefore "inauthentic") will be replaced in the future by a new series of "obligations" and "services": "labor service," "military service," and (lastly) "service in knowledge." The inordinate emphasis in the speech on the virtues of labor and military service betrays the pronounced influence of Jünger's doctrines. And thus, taking his cue from *Der Arbeiter*, Heidegger decides that if the society of the future will be composed of worker-soldiers and soldier-workers, then the universities, too, must do their part by producing *student-worker-soldiers*. Consequently, via labor service, the students' obligation to the *Volksgemeinschaft* is made binding and thus "rooted in student-Dasein."[61] Military service cultivates the virtue of "readiness for engagement until the end" (*Bereitschaft zum Einsatz bis ins Letzte*). But the many sacrifices will in the end all be worthwhile insofar as they derive from no other source than the *Seinsfrage* itself: "The questioning of Being in general wrings from the Volk *labor and struggle*, and forces it into its State, to which the vocations belong."[62]

The political object of Heidegger's speech is clear. The shallowness of bourgeois life—evident, for example, in the fact that knowledge is shorn of essential ties to the *Volksgemeinschaft*—can only be radically overcome via the *wholesale integration of life* in a society of *total mobilization*. The multiple fragmentations and divisions of bourgeois society—those of political parties, classes, academic disciplines, and competing value-claims—can be resolved only by recourse to a *total state*. Since Heidegger fully shares the conservative revolutionary critique of liberal democracy, not only does he have no reservations concerning a totalitarian alternative; he in fact perceives the latter as a form of political deliverance. The various *Bindungen* he emphasizes in the address—labor service, military service, and service in knowledge—aim at the creation of an all-encompassing, total state in which the (modern) specialization of competences is abolished and all pursuits are integrated by a common goal: the realization of the historical-spiritual destiny of the German Volk. The three "obligations" (which Heidegger insists are *equiprimordial*; none—not even "service in knowledge," in which the question of Being is presumably addressed—is superior to another), however, are not ends in themselves; rather, they are dependent on the state for authentic leadership, integration, and direction. Or as Heidegger expresses it, they obtain their true meaning, "*through* the Volk *in relation to* the State *in* [its] spiritual mission."[63]

Heidegger ends his speech with a series of encomiums to the virtues of *Kampf* or struggle. He would later attempt to defuse the significance of this word choice by claiming that he had meant it in the sense of the Greek *polemos*, that is, as "strife" or "conflict"—

in the sense of Heraclitus's well known dictum in Fragment 53 that "Polemos is the father of all things."[64] Given his earlier insistence on the need to recapture the "Greek philosophical beginning," Heidegger may well have had such a definition partially in mind (though Heraclitus is nowhere mentioned in the text itself).[65] But both the context and content of Heidegger's formulations tend to belie such transparent, *post festum* apologetics.

In truth, these multiple concluding allusions to the glories of *Kampf* contain little intrinsic philosophical merit. Instead, they serve to depict the bellicose readiness of the *Volksgemeinschaft* as newly forged by the three "obligations." Here, the allusions to *Kampf* unambiguously refer to the virtues of "military service" for the everyday life of a university corps that forms an integral part of a Volk in search of its historical destiny. Thus, Heidegger announces that the "essential wills" of both teachers and students "must mutually ready themselves for battle [*Kampf*]."[66] He speaks of the students and teachers together as forming a *Kampfgemeinschaft*—a "fighting community"—in service to "the Volk in its State." And thus: "all faculties of will and thought, all powers of the heart and capacities of the body must be unfolded *through* struggle, intensified *in* struggle, and preserved *as* struggle."[67] In this way, the opening paean to the sublimity of the Greek beginning has metamorphosed into an fawning apologia for the *Kampf* and *Sturm* mentality of the reigning powers. The concluding sentence, in which Heidegger celebrates "the glory and greatness of this awakening [*Aufbruch*]," certainly leaves little to the imagination of the listener or reader.

Finally, in the motto with which he concludes the address, Heidegger—the philhellene for whom etymology is *everything*—commits the ultimate sacrilege: philological apostasy. He deliberately falsifies a translation from Plato's *Republic* to preserve the illusion of ideological homology between Greek philosophy and Nazi thuggery. Plato's remark (*Republic*, 497d) reads "*ta . . . megala panta episphalā*"; for which the standard English translations are "everything great is at risk" (Grube) or "everything great is precarious" (Shorey). But Heidegger has rendered it in German as "*Alles Grosse steht im Sturm*," thus willfully misreading the Greek *episphalā* in conformity with the *Sturm* and *Kampf* metaphors he has been promoting throughout the address. When one recalls that the initials "SA"—used to refer to Hitler's "Storm Troopers"—actually stand for *Sturm*abteilung (according to eyewitness accounts, moreover, we know that the SA was well represented at Heidegger's speech), and that one of the most virulently anti-Semitic Nazi publications at the time was called *Der Stürmer*, Heidegger's manifestly tendentious gesture loses all its innocence.[68]

Heidegger would later defend the content of the Rectoral Address by referring to its title—"The Self-Affirmation of the German University"—as an illustration of his true intentions as rector. He had accepted the rectorship, he claimed, in order to *defend* the university against the National Socialist idea of "politicized science," adding, "No other rectoral discourse of the time bore a title as audacious as this."[69] However, as our analysis suggests, the title of the address is a grotesque misnomer. It was precisely the long-standing autonomy of the university ("so-called academic freedom") that came in for numerous direct attacks in the course of Heidegger's speech. His critique of the inherited view of knowledge as belonging to a "cultural superstructure" (that of a "sham-culture," moreover) fed directly into his plea for a reintegration of knowledge within the life of the Volk. The key to the entire program was the appeal to the three "equiprimordial obligations," labor service, military service, and service in knowledge. For only once the "world of the intellect" (*die geistige Welt*) would draw its strength once more from the "forces of soil and blood" residing in the German Volk could it attain renewed greatness. It is at this point that the puzzling parallels Heidegger seeks to draw with "the Greek beginning" become clear. For one of the aspects of classical Greece that Heidegger admired most was the fact that its cultural greatness was rooted in the concrete life of the polis.

In truth, the purported theme of the lecture, "the self-affirmation of the German university," was a cover for a political program demanding that the university restructure its goals so as to coincide with those of the National Revolution. Heidegger leaves no doubt about this conclusion in a June 30, 1933 article entitled "The University in the New Reich." After praising the fact that, by virtue of the newly created labor camps, the university "has been relieved of educational tasks to which it has till now believed it had an exclusive right," he goes on to reiterate the main argument of the Rectoral Address, *viz.*, that *"the university . . . must be integrated again into the Volksgemeinschaft* and *be joined together with the State."*[70]

Heidegger's commitment to the National Socialist program of

radical social reform as articulated in the Rectoral Address can be seen in both his future conduct as Rector as well as in the numerous political articles and speeches he composed during his year in office. In this respect, there can little doubt concerning the sincerity of his support for the policies of the new regime. As he says at one point, "The National Socialist Revolution brings the total transformation of our German Dasein. . . . Let not propositions and 'ideas' be the rules of your Being. The *Führer* alone is the present and future German reality and its law."[71] As his former student, Herbert Marcuse, would later comment about these lines: such a claim is "actually the betrayal of philosophy as such and of everything it stands for."[72] What Marcuse found incomprehensible about this and similar claims was how this matchless interpreter of the Western philosophical tradition could come to view the National Socialist movement as the positive culmination of this intellectual heritage.

In his many speeches on behalf of the new regime—a stylistic analysis would show to what extent these addresses represent a striking fusion of Heidegger's own existential categories with the National Socialist jargon that was current at the time—one thing that stands out is a repeated emphasis, following the precedent set by the Rectoral Address, on the virtues of "labor service." Two entire speeches are devoted to this theme, and several others allude to it as well. One would be justified in concluding that here, too, the influence of Jünger is in evidence, *viz.*, his theory of the state of the future as an *Arbeiterstaat*; and that this is a reality that Heidegger seeks to promote in his capacity as spokesman for the new society.

For example, in his speech, "The Call to Labor Service," Heidegger praises the "experience of hardness [and] closeness to soil" that results from labor as an activity. Foremost among his concerns is the surmounting of the one-sidedness of so-called "intellectual work" [*geistige Arbeit*] which, he claims, will "completely disappear" in the sense of a separate stratum of "intellectual producers." He continues:

> So-called "intellectual work" is not spiritual because it relates to "higher spiritual things." It is spiritual because, *as work*, it reaches back more deeply into the afflictions [*Not*] that are part of a people's historical Dasein and because it is more di-

rectly—because more knowingly—beset by the hardness and danger of human Dasein.

> There is only *one single* German "life-estate" [*Lebensstand*]. That is the *estate of labor* [*Arbeitstand*] which is rooted in and borne by the Volk and which has freely submitted to the historical will of the State. The character of this estate is being preformed in the National Socialist *Workers Party* Movement.[73]

Or as he will remark in a later speech, "For us, 'work' is the title of every well-ordered action that is borne by the responsibility of the individual, the group, and the State and which is thus of service to the Volk. . . . The work of a field-worker [*Erdarbeiter*] is basically no less spiritual than the activity of a scholar."[74] And in "Labor Service and the University," the point is driven home with unambiguous clarity:

> A new institution for the direct realization of the *Volksgemeinschaft* is being realized in the work camp. In the future, young Germans will be governed by the knowledge of *labor*, in which the Volk concentrates its strength in order to experience the hardness of its existence, to preserve the momentum of its will, and to learn anew the value of its manifold abilities. . . . [Work] camp and school are resolved to bring together, in reciprocal give and take, the educational forces of our Volk into that new rooted unity from which the Volk in its State will commit itself to act in accordance with its destiny.[75]

The discussions of labor service that dominate Heidegger's public statements in the years 1933–1934 represent far more than a series of political obéisances made in order to appease the ideological watchdogs of new regime. Instead, he had his own immanent *philosophical reasons*—an "intellectually grounded anti-intellectualism," as it were— for wanting to make labor service a compulsory part of the both the university curriculum and German life in general.

Heidegger's reconceptualization in the early 1930s of the history of metaphysics as a "history of decline" led to the conviction that science itself (*Wissenschaft*) was implicated in a 2500-year fate of *Seinsvergessenheit*. The academic division of labor that dominated university studies was only the contemporary, epiphenomenal manifestation of this dilemma of longstanding. Science could analyze and reconstruct to its heart's content; it would, however, never attain to an understanding of *essence*, that is, an appreciation of the primordial thought of "truth as *alētheia*" as it emerged with the pre-Socratics. "Affliction" was everywhere apparent; yet, all contemporary programs for reform that took their bearings from the situation of modern life were merely part of the problem.

In Jünger's vision of a dynamic modern state to be based on a new social type, the "worker," Heidegger thought he saw the radical alternative that was needed to overcome the manifold, hated divisions of bourgeois society: the division between the state and civil society, between worker and employer, and finally, between intellectual and manual labor. Herein lies the basis for Heidegger's "anti-intellectualism"; his desire, through the institutionalization of "labor service," to reintegrate "science" with the tasks of the worker and his world. Only a "total state," organized as a *Volksgemeinschaft*, could resolve these antagonisms—and wasn't this precisely the solution that National Socialism was offering? From the Nazi camp there echoed a critique of precisely those facets of modern life that Heidegger himself found irredeemably bankrupt—not least of all, an indictment of a "sterile" cultural and intellectual life that had lost its ties to the forces of blood and soil. There was a revival of secular mythology—a pseudo-Nietzschean, heroic, pan-German paganism—that must have struck Heidegger as a promising alternative to a moribund Christian culture. And though Heidegger may not have shared the Nazi emphasis on race, he, too, was convinced that Germany and the Germans occupied a special niche in world-history—they had a "destiny" to fulfill. Thus, only German *Kultur*, as opposed to the *Zivilisation* of the Western nations, offered the prospect of a true revival of the "Greek beginning." His belief in a special affinity between German language and culture and that of the ancient Greeks was one shared by many of his countrymen since the end of the eighteenth century. When viewed from this perspective, there was unquestionably an inner conceptual logic behind his "enlistment" for the National Socialist cause in the 1930s.

Heidegger's preoccupation with the virtues of labor service, moreover, coincided with a crucial aspect of the Nazi program of social reform: above all, with its plans for the *Gleichschaltung* of German society. The most threatening source of social antagonism that needed to be defused if a totally integrated society was to be realized was that between labor and the privileged classes. And although the Nazis claimed to be the National Socialist German *Workers* Party, they of course ran into frequent resistance from the left-wing parties in their attempts to secure the allegiance of the working class. Thus, the idea of "labor service" was instituted in the early phases of the regime as a vehicle of mass socialization, primarily for the young and the unemployed. The paramilitary "labor camps" of which Heidegger speaks (and which he on occasion helped organize)[76] were to serve not only as a combination vocational training/public works program. They were an important means of "reeducating" members of society in accordance with the political precepts of National Socialism. Moreover, one of their essential functions was to bring about the leveling of differences between Germans of various social groups and classes, thereby ensuring that the Nazi need for a homogeneous, integral Volk would not falter on the issue of social differentiation.[77]

Similarly, Heidegger's forceful appeals for an end to the antagonism between "intellectual" and "manual" labor (ironically, of course, a central component of the Marxian program for social change as well) are fully comprehensible only in light of the National Socialist program of a totally integrated society. They betray, moreover, a sinister convergence with the verdict against intellectuals as *volksfremd* expressed on numerous occasions by Hitler himself in *Mein Kampf* and elsewhere.[78]

Heidegger's involvement with National Socialism has often been described as a misunderstanding or an error that had little to do with his basic philosophical orientation. But as Franzen observes:

> Such a misunderstanding and error were only possible because of those "consonances," hidden and manifest, between National Socialist ideology and Heidegger's philosophy. . . . Only because so many "depth-dimensions" in Heidegger's thought— in *Being and Time* and then in his investigation of the "history of Being"—were related to those of the National Socialist world-view could Heidegger fall victim to the illusion that National Socialism was something greater and larger than it was in fact.[79]

FOUR

"The Inner Truth and Greatness of National Socialism"

[O]ne would do well to read nothing of Heidegger's anymore without raising political questions. . . . [O]ne must re-read his works—particularly but not exclusively from 1933 on—with strict attention to the political movement with which Heidegger himself chose to link his ideas. To do less than that is, I believe, finally not to understand him at all.

Thomas Sheehan, "Heidegger and the Nazis"

A Politics of Authenticity

Heidegger's tenure as rector lasted only a year. He would later strive to present his resignation as a heroic act of defiance.[1] However, it seems that, in truth, it had finally dawned on Heidegger that his grandiose ambitions as "philosopher laureate" of the new Reich were condemned to failure. He thus seized on an administrative dispute as a pretext to slip quietly from the political stage in April 1934.[2] Apparently, his prestige in the academic world was of use to the Nazis for a brief period of time. But as Heidegger himself soon realized, the regime had little interest in becoming philosophically enlightened concerning the destiny of Being. Hannah Arendt provides an appropriate epitaph for the saga of Heidegger's delusions of political grandeur when she observes:

> The consistent persecution of every higher form of intellectual activity by the new mass leaders springs from more than their natural resentment against everything they cannot understand. Total domination does not allow for free initiative in any field of life, for any activity that is not entirely predictable. Totalitarianism in power invariably replaces all first-rate talents, re-

gardless of their sympathies, with those crackpots and fools whose lack of intelligence and creativity is still the best guarantee of their loyalty.[3]

But Heidegger's enthusiasm for the National Socialist revolution persisted for quite some time. In a 1936 conversation with Karl Löwith, he reaffirmed his conviction that "National Socialism was the proper course for Germany; one only had to 'hold-out' long enough."[4] Moreover, his published lectures of this period are replete with positive allusions to the historical course pursued by contemporary Germany. To be sure, the unreserved enthusiasm for the "National Awakening" that suffused the 1933 Rectoral Address as well as his political speeches of the same year was mitigated in his subsequent political pronouncements. But even when he attempts to distance himself from the pedestrian and vulgar currents of National Socialism which had assumed responsibility for providing the movement with "philosophical direction" (e.g., the Rosenberg-Krieck faction, which on occasion took to attacking Heidegger's own philosophy), the break Heidegger makes never goes far enough.

Thus, for example, when in the 1936 *Beiträge zur Philosophie* Heidegger proffers an incisive polemic against the perils of "Weltanschauung-thinking" and "nihilism,"[5] he makes it immediately clear that the *true* carriers of nihilism in the contemporary world are "Christianity" and "Bolshevism"—which are, moreover, only *apparently* opposed to one another—*not the National Socialists*.[6] And despite his legitimate criticisms of the "world-view philosophers"—National Socialism's "false friends"—in his own historico-philosophical speculations during the 1930s and 1940s, Heidegger himself would never abandon the concepts and rudiments of *völkisch* thought. Instead, in his estimation, what is necessary is that such concepts be tied to a more primordial and essential dimension of reflection. Thus, for Heidegger, "Reflection on the Volk [*das Volkhafte*] is an essential passage. . . . [An] uppermost rung of Being will be attained if a '*völkisch* principle,' as something determinative, is mastered and brought into play for historical Da-sein."[7] What is of paramount importance—and herein lies his main critique of "really existing" National Socialism—is that the relation between the "Volk" and "philosophy" be properly established. That is, the Volk itself must be led by a higher, ontological self-understanding—by a *seinsgeschichtlichen Auftrag*—which Heidegger identifies as "the guardianship of the truth of Being."[8]

The key to comprehending Heidegger's political judgments in his postrectorship phase is a distinction he makes toward the conclusion of *An Introduction to Metaphysics* (1935) between "the inner truth and greatness of National Socialism" as opposed to the "works that are being peddled about nowadays as the philosophy of National Socialism."[9] That is, Heidegger comes to view the movement in terms of a dialectic of "appearance" and "essence," whose true nature the philosopher himself is best able to discern. *Potentially*, the movement contains the prospect of the "radical overcoming of Western nihilism" that had been prophesied by Nietzsche. In *actuality*, its ultimate philosophical "truth and greatness" has been perverted by epigones and pretenders—by Heidegger's philosophical opponents (E. Krieck, A. Bäumler, and A. Rosenberg), who threaten to banish this potential for greatness back to the nether world of everydayness.

The same differentiation between the appearance and essence of the movement is implicit in his 1936 claim that "These two men, Hitler and Mussolini, who have, each in essentially different ways, introduced a countermovement to nihilism, have both learned from Nietzsche. The authentic metaphysical realm of Nietzsche has not yet, however, been realized."[10] The statement itself is a reaffirmation of Heidegger's conviction that the fascist movements of the 1920s and early 1930s represent the only real historical alternatives ("countermovements") to the darkness of European nihilism so presciently diagnosed by Nietzsche. However, whether they have learned *enough* from Nietzsche is by no means clear, since the "authentic metaphysical realm" that would embody the true epochal overcoming of nihilism has yet to be realized.

That Heidegger continued to adhere even after the war (and very likely, until the end of his life) to the distinction between the original historical potential of National Socialism as a "countermovement" to nihilism and its subsequent factual degradation is evidenced by the following unguarded admission in "The Rectorate 1933–34": "I saw in the movement that had come to power the possibility of an inner gathering and renewal of the Volk and a way for it to find its western-historical [*geschichtlich-abendländischen*] destiny."[11] Similarly, when questioned as late as 1966 in the *Spiegel* interview about the paean to the "greatness and glory of the

[National] Awakening" with which the Rectoral Address concludes, Heidegger simply confesses, "Yes, I was convinced of that."[12]

These considerations suggest that the philosophical course pursued by Heidegger in the mid-thirties is only fully comprehensible in light of the political concerns that preoccupied him since his accession to the rectorship in the spring of 1933. Thus, as Pöggeler has remarked, "Whoever does not want merely to judge Heidegger, but also to appropriate initiatives and to learn from him, must realize that in the thirties, *Heidegger himself placed the decision about the truth of Being as he sought it in a political context.*"[13] That Heidegger came to view the *Seinsfrage* in the mid-1930s as essentially related to a series of epochal political questions and exigencies suggests the legitimacy of inquiring into the "politics of Being."

As we suggested in the preceding chapter, Heidegger's understanding of the meaning of politics possesses an inalienable "epochal" dimension: it is inseparable from his understanding of history as essentially *Seinsgeschichte*, "the history of Being." From this vantage point, the ultimate matter of consequence in politics is whether the *Seinsvergessenheit* that pervades contemporary European Dasein can be surmounted. In comparison to this theme, all other political questions shrink to matters of indifference: they represent political perspectives that are essentially "regional" and hence *inauthentic*. However, the attempt to understand contemporary historical events from the ethereal standpoint of *Seinsgeschichte* will have an extremely deleterious effect upon Heidegger's capacity for political judgment. It is this standpoint that not only induces him to mistake the political character of National Socialism for a potential embodiment of that "saving power" of which Hölderlin speaks, but also to persist in the conviction—until quite late in life—that the "inner truth and greatness of National Socialism" lay in its status as a "countermovement" to nihilism.

But just as Heidegger's philosophy in the postrectorship years can be understood only in light of his political concerns, so his political ideas cannot be understood apart from his philosophy. The philosophical "Turn" of 1929–32 is accentuated during these years. Increasingly, it is no longer "human being" or Dasein that serves as the prime mover with respect to the paramount "encounter" between "Being" and "beings" (*das Ereignis*). Instead, with increasing autonomy, *Being itself* establishes the conditions for the destining of beings—Dasein among them. Or as Heidegger warns already in "On the Essence of Truth" (1930), "man . . . is all the more mistaken the more exclusively he takes himself, as subject, to be the standard of all beings."[14]

However, the most important categorial innovation to appear in Heidegger's thought during the mid-1930s—and a concept that is indispensable for understanding his political thought during these years—is that of the "work." It is the "work" that provides the locus, that facilitates the "clearing" (*Lichtung*), for the all-important encounter between beings and Being, between what is finite and the truth. The original question in *Being and Time* concerning the "meaning of Being," which still seemed tied to the interpretive capacities of human subjectivity, recedes in favor of that of the "truth of Being." And it is the "work"—rather than Dasein itself—that now stands out as the privileged agent of mediation for this epochal reckoning between beings and the truth.

During this period, Heidegger refers above all to three types of "works" that possess privileged status with regard to the encounter between Being and beings: the work of art (*Kunst–werk*), the work of thought (*Denk–werk*), and, lastly—what is of foremost importance for the purposes of our inquiry—the state-work (*Staats–werk*).

The concept of the work is predicated on what one might refer to as Heidegger's "cosmology": the agonistic relationship between "world" and "earth" that establishes the boundaries of the phenomenological field within which the encounter between Being and beings transpires. In general (Heidegger's descriptions of the meaning of these terms tend to vary), the earth signifies a concealing, but also a "sheltering" element: "world" must carve out a space against the all-enveloping background of the "earth" in order for unconcealment to take place. The earth is inexhaustible, vast, and unindividuated; and although Heidegger himself never expresses this thought explicitly, it often seems that he employs it as a synonym for Being itself. Such an interpretation is suggested by the fact that he associates "earth" with the Greek *physis*, the conceptual basis for the pre-Socratic reflection on the nature of Being:

> Tree and grass, eagle and bull, snake and cricket first enter into their distinctive shapes and thus come to appear as what they are. The Greeks early called this emerging and rising in itself and in all things *physis*. It clears and illuminates, also, that on which and in which man bases his dwelling. We call this ground

the *earth*. What this word says is not to be associated with the idea of a mass of matter deposited somewhere, or with the merely astronomical idea of a planet. Earth is that whence the arising brings back and shelters everything that arises without violation. In the things that arise, earth is present as the sheltering agent.[15]

The counter-concept to earth is that of world. Unlike earth, world already figured prominently in the Dasein-analysis of *Being and Time*, where it determined the environmental coordinates for Dasein's "totality of involvements" (*Bewandtnisganzheit*), for example, its practical dealings with the ready-to-hand.[16] Thus in *Being and Time*, world established the navigational parameters for a type of Dasein-based "existential geography." However, Heidegger strives to ensure that in its post-*Kehre* incarnation, the concept of world is divested of all possible anthropological residues. It is no longer Dasein that "possesses" a world; instead, a world is erected—anonymously—via the unconcealment activity of the work.

The relationship between world and earth is one of inherent conflict or strife according to Heidegger. Thus, "The work-being of the work consists in the fighting of the battle between world and earth."[17] The openness of the world established by the work seems always under threat of slipping back into the unnameable, concealing embrace of the earth. However, this manner of describing the *polemos* between world and earth is not intended to prejudice either term. For the ontological struggle between these two forces, in Heidegger's view, unquestionably issues forth in a fruitful tension. In truth, it is *the most fruitful tension*. For it is by virtue of this conflict alone—as mediated by the disclosive capacities of the work itself—that the epochal encounter between Being and beings occurs. "To be a work means to set up a world," remarks Heidegger. "World is never an object that stands before us and can be seen. World is the ever-nonobjective to which we are subject as long as the paths of birth and death, blessing and curse, keep us transported into Being."[18] The world provides a type of ever-shifting, nonfinite ontological frame of reference on the basis of which our experience of Being is grounded.

It may seem as though our excursus on "Heideggerian cosmology"—the interrelationship between earth, world, and work—has placed us at a considerable remove from the theme of Heidegger as a political thinker. In truth, however, it has delivered us to the very threshold of this theme: *viz.*, Heidegger's reformulation, circa 1935, of the relationship between political life, the destiny of Being, and the "historical fate of a Volk." For when Heidegger speaks of "works," he is referring neither to art for art's sake nor to academic philosophy. Rather, the ultimate purpose of the work—be it in the case of the work of art, the work of thought, or the state-work—is to define *the historical destiny of a nation*. And in this sense, it may be said that all works possess an intrinsically political function. As Heidegger comments with reference to Hölderlin: *"Poetry is the foundation which supports history*, and therefore it is not a mere appearance of culture, and absolutely not the mere 'expression' of a 'culture-soul.' "* Instead, poetry is the *"voice of the Volk."*[19] The *works* of a nation establish its *historicity*; and it is this historicity that ultimately determines whether or not a Volk stands in an *authentic or an inauthentic relation to Being*. In Heidegger's view, the work sets up a world; and the world established by the work becomes "the self-disclosing openness . . . of the simple and essential decisions in the destiny of a historical people." And thus, it is by virtue of the expanse or openness created by the work that "a Volk first returns to itself for the fulfillment of its destiny."[20]

With the incorporation of the category of "the destiny of a historical Volk" into the very heart of his theory of the history of Being, Heidegger undertakes a final retreat from the quasi-solipsistic, Kierkegaardian theory of subjectivity advanced in *Being and Time*. Not only is the question of Being thoroughly historicized; but now the very posing of the question has become inseparable from the capacity of a *collective megasubject*—a historically situated Volk— to heed Being's call. Given the influence of the conservative revolutionary critique of modernity on Heidegger, as well as his own longstanding conviction concerning the innate superiority of Germany as a nation of "poets and thinkers,"[21] it is clear that his theoretical justification of the "inner truth and greatness of National Socialism"—far from being a random biographical error—was rooted in the essence of his thought.

The numerous historico-philosophical observations contained in *An Introduction to Metaphysics* provide ample confirmation of the sinister political conclusions to which this Volk-oriented understanding of the history of Being would lead. For Heidegger, to reflect on the "forgetting of Being" means to inquire into the universal affliction of the contemporary historical world as well as to identify those forces specifically responsible for its loss of essence, its essential "abandonment." The question of Being, therefore, must be taken out of a scholastic setting and viewed historically if it is to be properly posed. As he observes, "We maintain that this preliminary question [concerning the truth of Being] and with it the fundamental question of metaphysics *are historical questions through and through.* . . . Philosophy is historical only insofar as it—like every work of the spirit—realizes itself in time."[22] For when properly understood, this question, far from being a theoretically idle postulate, speaks to "the spiritual destiny of the Western world."[23]

However, by all accounts, the contemporary historical lie of this "spiritual destiny" could hardly be more grim. Heidegger describes it as follows: "The spiritual decline of the earth is so far advanced that the nations are in danger of losing the last bit of spiritual energy that makes it possible to see the decline. . . ." When viewed from the standpoint of the history of Being, our fate has become so dire—"the darkening of the world, the flight of the gods, the destruction of the earth, the transformation of men into a mass, the hatred and suspicion of everything free and creative"—that the traditional categories of "optimism" and "pessimism" have been outstripped.[24] Heidegger then sets forth his own geopolitical description of the contemporary dilemma facing Europe, an imaginative combination of metaphysics and traditional German *real*political thinking:

> This Europe, in its ruinous blindness forever on the point of cutting its own throat, lies today in a great pincers, squeezed between Russia on one side and America on the other. From a metaphysical point of view, Russia and America are the same; the same dreary technological frenzy, the same unrestricted organization of the average man. . . . [And thus] the farthermost corner of the globe has been conquered by technology and opened to economic exploitation.[25]

But Heidegger is also a believer in Hölderlin's maxim: "where danger grows, so grows the saving power."[26] Thus, all is not lost as long as Germany—which is both "the nation in the middle" and "the most metaphysical of nations"—can reestablish its authentic, epochal-historical relation to the primordial powers of Being:

> We are caught in a pincers. Situated in the middle, our Volk incurs the severest pressure. It is the Volk with the most neighbors and hence *the most endangered*. With all this, it is *the most*

metaphysical of peoples. We are certain of this mission, but our Volk will only be able to wrest a destiny from it if *within itself* it creates a resonance, a possibility of resonance for this mission, and takes a creative view of its tradition. All this implies that this Volk, as a historical Volk, must move itself and thereby the history of the West beyond the center of their future "happening" and *into the primordial realm of the powers of Being.* If the great decision [*Entscheidung*] regarding Europe is not to bring annihilation, that decision must be made in terms of new spiritual energies unfolding historically from out of the middle.[27]

There is nothing especially subtle—or metaphysical—about Heidegger's depiction of Germany as a nation "in the middle." It is an allusion to a standard component of German neo-nationalist political thought that gained currency circa World War I. At that time it received its most consequential formulation in Friedrich Naumann's influential work, *Mitteleuropa,* a justification of Austro-Hungarian/German geopolitical aspirations written in 1915. (It may be of more than passing interest to point out that in the *Spiegel* interview, Heidegger refers to the "national" and "social" attitudes of Naumann as an important basis for his own understanding of German politics in the early 1930s).[28] The notion *Mitteleuropa* itself, however, harks back to the controversy during the Bismarck era over a German *Sonderweg*: a special course of German state-formation that is neither Western (in the sense of England and France) nor Eastern (in the sense of Russia). In certain respects, then, the concept implied a specifically political extrapolation of the *Kultur/Zivilisation* dichotomy. It was, in the main, a conservative idea that had its "expansive, indeed imperialist, aspects, inasmuch as it served as a justification for a renewed German *Drang nach Osten* [drive toward the East]."[29] But it also had a more perverse, proto-fascistic side: for example, as a legitimation of German claims to European hegemony in the work of Paul de Lagarde, the virulent German nationalist and anti-Semite who was one of the most important and direct precursors of National Socialist ideology.[30] The concept subsequently underwent a radical, conservative revolutionary refashioning in the post–World War I era, becoming a catchword for Germany's expansionist territorial designs.

What is especially fascinating about Heidegger's allusion to this term is his attempt to unite the conservative revolutionary ideal of *Mitteleuropa*—which, by this time, had been thoroughly incorporated within the standard, bellicose refrains of National Socialist ideology as a justification of the German need for *Lebensraum*—with his own metaphysical idea of the history of Being—resulting in an, as it were, bastardized conception of *Seinspolitik*—the "politics of Being."

Heidegger could readily justify the belief that the politics of *Seinsgeschichte* led of necessity in a *National Revolutionary direction* (the foreign policy of the Nazis, after all, was predicated on the idea of Germany as being an "endangered nation in the middle") on the basis of the aforementioned distinction between the "inner truth and greatness of National Socialism" and its flawed, present actuality. He would make what he meant by this *prima facie* cryptic allusion unequivocally clear in the parenthetic explanation he appended to the 1953 edition of the lecture (which, ironically, in no way redounds to Heidegger's credit): *viz.*, that National Socialism's "inner truth and greatness" refers to "the encounter between planetary technology and modern man." By this claim Heidegger meant that the "inner (i.e., philosophical) truth" of National Socialism, when viewed from the standpoint of the history of Being, lay in its potential as a vehicle of the metaphysical-historical transcendence of the dilemmas of "planetary technology"; above all, as such prospects of "transcendence" had been portrayed in the prophetic work of Ernst Jünger. Whereas from a *metaphysical* standpoint, Russia and America are the same—they exhibit "the same dreary technological frenzy, the same unrestricted organization of the average man"—Germany alone, because of a more primordial relation to the thought of Being—a spiritual superiority that was for Heidegger evinced in the incomparable greatness of its poets, its thinkers, in the very structure of its language—possessed the capacity to deliver European destiny from the specter of perpetual spiritual decline. Thus, according to one commentator, Heidegger believed that "Philosophy is for Hitler, because Hitler stands on the side of Being."[31]

What was it specifically that attracted Heidegger as a philosopher of Being to the National Socialist cause? Wherein lay the "philosophical promise" of National Socialism as an empirical, historical movement? In other words, what were the qualities of the movement as a "lived phenomenon" that convinced Heidegger that it was endowed with such tremendous metaphysical potential as a countermovement to the dilemmas of European nihilism?

In part, many of the virtues of National Socialism were deduced by Heidegger *ex negativo*: they pertained more to what National Socialism was against than what it advocated in a positive sense. Among these components must be numbered its disdain for democratic institutions, political parties (it always strove to present itself as a "movement" rather than as a political party in the traditional sense), "intellectualism," bourgeois egalitarianism, aesthetic modernism, and "cosmopolitanism." In sum, the movement seemed in many ways to be the legitimate political heir to the conservative revolutionary critique of Western modernity with which Heidegger identified in so many crucial respects.

However, another undeniable factor in Heidegger's enthusiasm for the movement was his personal attraction to Hitler as an archetypal embodiment of charismatic leadership. In this connection, the following exchange between Heidegger and Karl Jaspers in June 1933 may be of more than merely anecdotal import. To the latter's query, "How could you think that a man as uncultivated as Hitler can govern Germany?" Heidegger responds: "It's not a question of culture. Take a look at his wonderful hands!"[32] When understood within the framework of *Seinspolitik*, the meaning of this claim is clear: *existential* qualifications are more important than *intellectual* ones. It would be unfair to overburden with theoretical significance an offhand conversational remark made by Heidegger. But in a far from trivial sense, Heidegger's response is superbly illustrative concerning the pitfalls involved in employing "irrationalist," existential criteria in the formulation of political judgments.

Heidegger will express a similar thought five months later, this time in a public context, when, in view of the upcoming plebiscite called by Hitler (*ex post facto*) on Germany's withdrawal from the League of Nations, he implores his student audience: "Let not doctrines and 'ideas' be the rules of your Being. The *Führer* alone is the present and future German reality and its law."[33] According to Heidegger's logic, the greatness of the National Socialist movement is ultimately irreducible to a given set of intellectual precepts or "ideas." It is not so much "ideological," but *existential, rooted in the authenticity of the Führer as an individual, historically existent Dasein.* In this sense, Heidegger would have undoubtedly seconded Carl Schmitt's proclamation that "On this day [January 30, 1933] one can say that 'Hegel died' "—*viz.*, the idea of the German *Rechtsstaat* as an entity based on universal principles and norms.[34] Heidegger's claim on Hitler's behalf, far from representing merely an ad hoc political opinion, is thus philosophically over-determined by the imperatives of *Seinspolitik*. The disparaging allusion to "doctrines and ideas" (*Lehrsätze und Ideen*) expresses a veiled critique of the traditional philosophical theories—from Plato to neo-Kantianism—which Heidegger believes must be eradicated if the glorious promise of Germany's "new beginning" is to succeed. He appeals to Hitler's person, therefore, because he embodies the "new man" who is free of the dead-weight of outmoded convictions, a social type that must flourish if the German Revolution is to be successful. Hitler stands not for antiquated dogmas and ideas, but for a new *politics of authenticity*.[35] A fact that is confirmed by Max Müller, who observes: "[Heidegger] placed [his hopes] not on the Party, but on a person and on a [political] direction, on the 'Movement.' "[36] Heidegger's portrayal of the Hitler regime as an embodiment of "authenticity," moreover, betrays a profound, philosophically grounded affinity with the political self-understanding of the regime itself. As J. P. Stern reminds us: "[Hitler's] originality consists in a deliberate reversal of the functions normally attributed to personal-existential values on the one hand and social-political values on the other. Hitler's discovery . . . is astonishingly simple: it is to introduce a conception of *personal authenticity* into the public sphere and proclaim it as *the chief value and sanction of politics*."[37]

A "politics of authenticity"—although Heidegger never uses this expression *per se*, it accurately captures the *metaphysical transfiguration of politics* he anticipated from the Third Reich. In terms of the categories of *Being and Time*, he viewed the turn toward National Socialism as nothing less than an "authentic decision" based on Germany's *ownmost potentiality-for-Being a nation or Volk*. Because it was an "existential decision" ("from now on, every single thing demands decision," he would go on to observe in the address cited above), Germany was *choosing itself*—affirming its own existential basis and future, opting for an authentic mode of historicity. Just as in *Being and Time*, Heidegger sought to justify the inherent particularity of each individual Dasein, now it is the existential particularity of Germany's Dasein as a Volk that he seeks to underwrite. Only in view of this existential orientation—only in light of a "politics of authenticity"—can one make sense of Heidegger's repeated utterances (e.g., in the Rectoral Address) that engagement on behalf of National Socialism is a question of *"wanting ourselves."*[38] In the same way, in his pre-plebiscite address of November 10, 1933, he will explain that the *Führer*, by summoning the people to vote, accords it "the possibility of making, directly, the highest free decision of all: whether it—the entire Volk—*wants its own Dasein or whether it does not want it.*"[39] In his partisanship for National Socialism, Heidegger has in effect transposed an entire series of categories from Division II of *Being and Time*—resolve, potentiality-for-Being, historicity, and, above all, authenticity—to the contemporary historical situation.

It would of course be ill-advised to exaggerate the intellectual responsibility of existentialist thought for the ideology of Hitler's Reich; and there were certainly aspects of that ideology (most notably, "racial thinking") that would seem *prima facie* opposed to existentialist doctrines. At the same time, there exists a considerable dispute in the literature on National Socialism over the general role played by ideology within the Third Reich, as well as whether or not one can in fact identify a coherent body of political dogma that would in fact fit the label "Nazi ideology."[40]

Franz Neumann, for example, has argued in *Behemoth* that National Socialist ideology was largely incoherent and opportunistic, and that whatever role ideology may have played in the early stages of the regime declined markedly in significance as time wore on. At the same time, Neumann suggests that in the absence of cohesive ideological vision, it was often specific "existentialist premises"—such as those we have just been discussing—that provided a self-justification for the aims and practices of the totalitarian state. And in this connection, he cites Heidegger's thought as prototypical. Toward the end of a long discussion of the intellectual origins of Nazi imperialist geopolitical doctrines, Neumann offers the following observations:

> What is left as justification for the [*Grossdeutsche*] Reich? Not racism, not the idea of the Holy Roman Empire, and certainly not some democratic nonsense like popular sovereignty or self-determination. Only the Reich itself remains. It is its own justification. The philosophical roots of the argument are to be found in the existential philosophy of Heidegger. Transferred to the realm of politics, existentialism argues that power and might are true: power is a sufficient theoretical base for more power. Germany lies in the center, it is well on its way toward becoming the mightiest state. Therefore, it is justified in building the new order. An acute critic has remarked about [Christoph] Steding [au-

thor of the 1938 work, *The Reich and the Sickness of European Culture*]: "From the remains of what, with Heidegger, was still an effective transcendental solipsism, his pupil constructs a national solipsism."[41]

The Ontological Vocation of Art

Heidegger's attempt to interpret the political stakes of the contemporary world from the rarefied philosophical perspective of the "history of Being" results in repeated distortions and misjudgments in other respects as well: for example, with reference to his views concerning art and culture. For art to be authentic, it must participate in the encounter between Being and beings: "The work opens up in its own way the Being of beings," remarks Heidegger. "Art is truth setting itself to work."[42] But since the main function of both art and philosophy, qua authentic "works," is to facilitate the onto-ontological encounter that Heidegger calls the *Ereignis*, the difference between these two forms of cultural expression threatens to sink into oblivion. In the last analysis, the independent claims of the aesthetic sphere are sacrificed as a result of the primacy of ontological considerations, that is, for the sake of the unveiling of truth. The integrity of artistic endeavor is, moreover, further relativized by virtue of its "founding function" in relation to the historical life of a Volk. Or, as Heidegger expresses this thought in the course of his 1934–35 Hölderlin lectures, "The essential disposition [*Grundstimmung*], that is, the truth of the Dasein of a Volk, is originally founded by the poet."[43]

And thus, modern art as a whole is dismissed by Heidegger as "destructive": it lacks both a relation to Being as well as to the historical life of a people.[44] In the end, of course, these two dimensions are integrally related to one another. The modern concept of "culture"—as we have already seen—becomes simply a term of derision: it is an idle "superstructure" lacking in existential-historical rootedness. As Heidegger phrases it: "The attitude of the littérateur and esthete is merely a late consequence and variation of the spirit falsified into intelligence."[45] Or as he will inquire on another occasion, in a thinly disguised attack against the spirit of "cosmopolitanism": "does not the flourishing of any genuine work depend upon its roots in a native soil?"[46] His critique of aesthetic modernism coincides in its essentials with Nietzsche's critique of art for art's sake: it is decadent and nihilistic, a postromantic manifestation of spiritual decline. Or as Nietzsche himself expresses it with inimitable candor: *"L'art pour l'art*: the virtuoso croaking of shivering frogs, despairing in their swamp."[47]

According to Weber's classical description of aesthetic modernity, modern Western culture produces an art that is privatized and self-enclosed. Thus, "the ultimate and most sublime values have retreated from public life." "It is not accidental," Weber continues, "that our greatest art is intimate and not monumental." Today, it is "only within the smallest and most intimate circles . . . in *pianissimo*, that something is pulsating that corresponds to the prophetic *pneuma*, which in former times swept through the great communities like a firebrand, welding them together."[48] Heidegger will have no part of this enfeebled culture of refined interiority. In this respect—but also politically—his standpoint is that of an *intractable antimodernism*. In his view, poetry must once again become *epic*, it must govern and determine the historicity of a Volk. Thus, Hölderlin is proclaimed to be the poet of "German destiny." He is the "voice of the Volk" in the same way that Homer was the "bard of the Greeks," an "authentic repetition" of the Greek beginning. And in the same spirit of neo-national parochialism, Heidegger will invoke the name of Heraclitus as a symbol of the "primordial power [*Urmacht*] of western-germanic Dasein."[49]

In general then, art, if it is, qua work, to reestablish an essential relationship to Being, must become *monumental*, it must rediscover a relationship to historical greatness. It was, therefore, undoubtedly the neomonumentalist façade of National Socialism that went far toward seducing Heidegger.

Heidegger seeks to illustrate the world-creating, history-founding vocation of art via the example of a Greek temple. It is, to be sure, a highly serviceable example for his purposes, since, among the arts, architecture alone possesses an inherently public character, establishing the spatial coordinates in which all human social interaction occurs. "The temple, in its standing there, first gives to things their look and to men their outlook on themselves," remarks Heidegger. He continues:

> Standing there, the building holds its ground against the storm raging above it and so first makes the storm itself manifest in its violence. The luster and gleam of the stone, though itself apparently glowing only by the grace of the sun, yet first brings to light the light of day, the breadth of sky, the darkness of the night.

The temple's firm towering makes visible the invisible space of air. . . . It is the temple-work that first fits together and gathers around itself the unity of those paths and relations in which birth and death, disaster and blessing, victory and disgrace, endurance and decline acquire the shape of destiny for human being.[50]

To be sure, these lines are among the most lyrical and compelling in Heidegger's voluminous *oeuvre*. His description convincingly portrays the manner in which the architectural ordering of public space forms a type of transcendental precondition for our experience of the world. The temple serves as a type of monumental, man-made prism by means of which the cycles of human life, as well as our contact with the environing natural world, are ordered and experienced. As a "work," it places at a temporary and fragile remove the sheltering and concealing powers of the earth. "The work-being of the work consists in the fighting of the battle of the world and earth," observes Heidegger.[51] The more this architectural space is impoverished, the more impoverished the totality of our world-relations become. Certainly, this is one aspect of Heidegger's critique of modernity that still speaks to us in a meaningful way.[52]

The State as "Work for the Works"

Heidegger never attempted to develop a political philosophy *per se* any more than he sought to articulate an ethics or an aesthetics. In this respect, his prejudices against the traditional academic division of labor extended to the customary divisions of philosophical subject matter as well. In Heidegger's view, the traditional academic ordering of philosophical competences was irredeemably marred by ontotheological assumptions—for example, the modern philosophical distinction between subject and object, which conceived of beings after the model of the "present-to-hand." The very idea that there somehow exists a natural and legitimate distinction between ethics, aesthetics, and epistemology already presupposes that these concerns should be judged as "beings"—hence, as something present-to-hand—rather than, in the first instance, in terms of their relation to Being. For Heidegger, the original sin of all philosophizing is the forgetting of the primordiality of this relation to Being; and the ultimate consequences of such forgetting are nihilistic: "To forget Being and to cultivate only beings—that is nihilism."[53] Hence, his persistent critique of so-called "value-philosophies." The world will not be regenerated by the creation of a new ethics, or a new philosophy of culture, or a new political theory; all of which, when all is said and done, essentially leave everything as it is. Instead, only by reflection on the extreme oblivion into which Being has fallen in contemporary life can these individual spheres of human endeavor regain their true ontological significance.

However, the fact that one fails to find a developed political theory in Heidegger's work does not mean that systematic political philosophical reflection is entirely absent from his thinking. The increasingly important role played by the category of "the historical life of a Volk" in his lectures and essays during the mid-1930s implicitly suggests that the question as to whether or not humanity will enter into closer proximity with Being in the foreseeable future is at least partially tied to the emergence of a new political order. That is, it is to a considerable degree dependent on the creation of a political infrastructure or framework that is conducive to posing the type of philosophical questions Heidegger has in mind. *Politics essentially makes the world safe for the posing of the Seinsfrage.* And in this respect, it seems that one of the results of the personal/intellectual crisis Heidegger underwent in 1929—a personal crisis that happened to coincide with a world economic crisis of historical proportions—was a realization that the question of Being was in truth inextricably intertwined with historical considerations; a fact that also explains his preoccupation with the conservative revolutionary critique of modernity during these years. The omnipresence of the inauthentic structures of everydayness, the understanding of the historical present as an era of universal "affliction" and "distress," seemed effectively to militate against all serious attempts to pose again the question of Being.[54] Such convictions in turn appear to have heightened his belief that a critical historical turning point had been reached. In quasi-apocalyptical, Nietzschean fashion, this turning point seemed to herald either the dawning of a new era or total collapse.

Political philosophical reflection in Heidegger's work primarily takes the form of a justification of the state as a paramount carrier of historical-ontological truth. The state, therefore, plays an indispensable meta-ontological role in the unconcealment of beings. Why "*meta*-ontological"? Because the state as "work" appears as the essential prerequisite, the *sine qua non*, for all subsequent labor of unconcealment. Thus, Heidegger at times speaks as though the Being of the state were more "primordial"—*ursprünglicher*—than that of all other works—the works of poetry, of architecture—even those of philosophy.

It is Heidegger's concept of the "work" that represents the indispensable key for understanding his theory of the ontological role of the state; more specifically, his conception of the work as establishing a "clearing" (*Lichtung*), a type of transcendental-ontological openness, by virtue of which the unconcealment of beings first becomes possible. As an essential presupposition for the unconcealment of beings, the clearing possesses a type of ontological superiority vis-à-vis the world of ontic reality, that is, in relation to the world of beings themselves. And thus in the following passage, Heidegger describes the clearing as a type of metaphysical ground for the encounter between Being and beings: "In the midst of beings as a whole an open place occurs. There is a clearing, a lighting. Thought of in reference to what is, to beings, this clearing *is* in a greater degree than are beings." He continues: "That which is can only be, as a being, if it stands within and stands out within what is lighted in this clearing. Only this clearing grants and guarantees to us humans a passage to those beings that we ourselves are not, and access to the Being that we ourselves are."[55]

The clearing represents for Heidegger a primordial truth, a precondition for the emergence for all particular claims to truth, insofar as unless an open space is first "cleared," nothing can be said about the beings at issue. As long as they remain unilluminated by the clearing, they are essentially inaccessible to us. In this sense, too, propositional truth is derivative of and subaltern to the clearing as an original act of unconcealment. Before propositions can be formulated and states of affairs can be represented, beings must first be "cleared."

"Clearings" are produced by works of art; for example, the environmental openness established by the Greek temple as "work." But they are produced by other types of works as well. As Heidegger observes: "One essential way in which truth establishes itself in the beings it has opened up is truth setting itself to work. Another way in which truth occurs is *the act that founds a political state*."[56] With this claim, we have arrived at the threshold of Heidegger's political philosophy proper: *viz.*, *the role played by the state in the setting to work of truth*. The state—in a way that remains as yet unspecified—participates in the work of unconcealment. It, too, is a type of work, a rescuing of openness from the shadows of concealment, a clearing in which the phenomenal glory of truth first comes to light.

But what does Heidegger mean when he speaks of the state as a "work"? What he intends by the "setting to work of truth in the work" is readily comprehensible with regard to the examples of poetic, architectural, or philosophical works. The implications of his attempt to categorize political life in the same way, however, are far from immediately apparent.

In this connection, it might be of help to recall once again the example of the Greek temple. The world it established was a type of clearing: that is, it erected or set to work a network of spatial relations in which the concealment and unconcealment of beings— gods and mortals, heaven and earth[57]—as such took place. As the ground or ontological precondition of this momentous "event"— the encounter between Being and beings—the temple, as a work of unconcealment, would seem to possess a type of *ontological priority:* the "event" itself could not come into being without the clearing established by the temple. The temple would stand as the primordial *sine qua non* of that encounter.

But this characterization of the temple as a setting for the ontological encounter between Being and beings inexorably leads to the more basic question: what, in turn, serves as the "ontological ground" of the temple itself? Is there an entity (a "being") that is in fact prior to the temple and on the basis of which its unconcealment activity is predicated? A being that, in terms of Heidegger's analysis of the "clearing" discussed above, would apparently possess a *higher ontological value* than the temple itself? This entity, should it be found or itself "unconcealed," would thus constitute a type of "clearing for the clearing."

The being we are in search of is of course *the state*; or, in terms of the categories of the "Greek beginning" that Heidegger seeks to mobilize in a contemporary historical context, *the polis*. The state is the historical presupposition for *all* works that come into Being, *all* unconcealment, *all* human world-relations. It is the *indispensable presupposition for all setting truth to work*, the primordial ground and *sine qua non* for all possible ontic-ontological encounters. The state is the foundational ontological-historical framework in terms of which the human experience of Being and beings comes to pass. As Aristotle knew well, the polis, though it might have been a later development in the temporal sense, is always *logically prior* to its individual citizens, their social institutions (religion, art, commerce, etc.), and municipalities.[58] The state is therefore the *work for the works*. It is that act of "setting truth to work" which, in and of itself, makes all other individual works of truth possible. It is the transcendental-existential framework in which all truth-relations occur.[59]

This is precisely the relationship between unconcealment, works, and politics that Heidegger seeks to articulate in the mid-1930s: "Unconcealment occurs only when it is achieved by work: the work of the word in poetry, the work of stone in temple and statue, the work of the word in thought,the work of the polis as the historical place in which all this is grounded and preserved."[60] That the polis represents the historical site in which all other works are "grounded and preserved" seems to confirm its claims to ontological primacy.[61] It is the primordial work that provides the clearing within which all other works—poetic, artistic, and philosophical—occur.[62]

A more detailed explanation of this conception of the polis/state as a historical basis or ground within which all other social and cultural activities may be found in the following passage:

> The foundation and the scene of man's being-there, the point at which all these paths meet [is] the polis. Polis is usually translated as city or city-state. This does not capture the full meaning. Polis means, rather, *the place, the there, wherein and as which historical being-there is*. The polis is the historical place, the there *in* which, *out of* which and for which history happens. To this place and scene of history belong the gods, the temples, the priests, the festivals, the games, the poets, the thinkers, the ruler, the council of elders, the assembly of people, the army and the fleet. All this does not first belong to the polis, does not become political by entering into a relation with a statesman and a general and the business of the state. No, it is political, i.e., at the site of history, provided there be (for example) poets *alone*, but then really poets, priests *alone*, but then really priests, rulers *alone*, but then really rulers.[63]

There are many dangers lurking in the statist conception of politics advanced by Heidegger in the preceding citation. The specifically *political* danger of this theory of the polis/state is that it is latently totalitarian: when the state—and the "destiny of a historical Volk" that is its *raison d'être*—are accorded unchallenged ontological primacy as "the work for the works," the autonomy and integrity of the other spheres of life (social, cultural, religious) disappears: they are *gleichgeschaltet* or immediately subsumed within the political sphere. The Greeks could solve this potential danger via the institution of direct democracy: by virtue of this medium, political space was opened up to its maximum extent. But in Heidegger's contemporary pan-Germanic "repetition" of the ancient polis, the opposite is true: since his twentieth century polis/ state is integrally tied to the *Führerprinzip*, it becomes a *Führerstaat*, a new form of political tyranny, in which political space shrivels up into the person of the *Führer* and his sycophantic entourage.[64] As the remarks just cited suggest, for Heidegger, the concept of a *Führerstaat* is unproblematical provided there be "rulers *alone, but then really rulers.*" That is, the rulers must be "authentic" and not imposters. And as we will soon see, Heidegger develops a theory of world-historical "leader-creators" in order to ground his partisanship for the *Führerprinzip* philosophically.

Many similar objections to Heidegger's political philosophy have been raised by Karsten Harries in his essay on "Heidegger as a Political Thinker":

> Unfortunately this project [i.e., the extension of Heidegger's analysis of the work of art to the state] became intertwined with a rejection of the modern conception of the state, with its separation of the ethical and the political, of the private and the public, separations which are difficult to reconcile with the kind of unity and self-integration demanded by Heidegger's conception of authenticity. Recalling Nietzsche's hope for a creative resurrection of Greek tragedy, Heidegger calls for a state which would be a "repetition"—in his sense of the word—of the Greek *polis*, a state which would assign man his *ethos*, his place as member of a genuine community. It is this romantic conception of the state with its fusion or confusion of the political and the social which we must question. The attempt to restructure the modern state in the image of the *polis* will tend towards totalitarianism.[65]

Another major dilemma for Heidegger's theory of politics is the way in which the activities of the state are rigidly subordinated to the realization of philosophical ends. In Heidegger's schema, political life is in essence stripped of all intrinsic content: such content fades into insignificance in face of the more exalted *philo-*

sophical mission with which the state is entrusted, that is, the role
it is to play in the encounter between Being and beings, in the
setting to work of truth. Absent from this theory is any reference
to the various activities of politics that account for its specifically
political nature: voting, speeches, popular assemblies, public debate. All such considerations shrink to matters of supreme indifference given Heidegger's distaste for democracy in general, and
modern democracy in particular.

Moreover, as Harries indicates, Heidegger's theory of the state
as a "work" is modeled upon his theory of the work of art. Thus,
as we have seen, in Heidegger's view, both works of art and the
state are examples of the "setting-to-work of truth." In essence, the
state becomes a *giant work of art*: like the work of art, it participates in the revelation of truth, yet on a much more grandiose and
fundamental scale, since it is the *Gesamtkunstwerk* within which
all the other sub-works enact their preassigned roles. However, the
idea of basing political judgments on analogy with aesthetic judgments is an extremely tenuous proposition. Though we may readily
accept and even welcome Heidegger's claim that works of art reveal the truth or essence of beings ("The work [of art] . . . is not
the reproduction of some particular entity that happens to be present at any given time," observes Heidegger; "it is, on the contrary,
the reproduction of the thing's *general essence*"),[66] we must question the attempt to transpose aesthetico-metaphysical criteria to
the realm of political life proper. Is it in point of fact meaningful
to speak of the "unveiling of truth" as the *raison d'être* of politics
in the same way one can say this of a work of art or a philosophical
work? Is not politics rather a nonmetaphysical sphere of human
interaction, in which the content of collective human projects, institutions, and laws is articulated, discussed, and agreed upon? Is
it not, moreover, in some sense *dangerous* to expect "metaphysical
results" from politics? For is not politics instead a sphere of human plurality, difference, and multiplicity; hence, a realm in which
the more exacting criteria of philosophical truth must play a subordinate role? And thus, would it not in fact be to place a type of
totalitarian constraint on politics to expect it to deliver over truth
in such pristine and unambiguous fashion? And even if Heidegger's
own conception of truth (which we shall turn to shortly) is sufficiently tolerant and pluralistic to allay such fears, shouldn't the
main category of political life be *justice* instead of *truth*? Undoubtedly, Heidegger's long-standing prejudices against "value-philos-

ophy" prevented him from seriously entertaining this proposition; and thus, as a category of political judgment, justice would not stand in sufficiently close proximity to Being. In all of the afore-mentioned instances, we see that Heidegger's political philosophy is overburdened with ontological considerations that end up sti-fling the inner logic of politics as an independent sphere of human action.

The Equiprimordiality of Truth and Error

Heidegger's incapacity for political judgment that is the result of his attempt to conceive of the state (the "state-work") on analogy with the truth-grounding function of the work of art has a more fundamental and potentially debilitating origin in the internal dy-namic of his philosophy itself: *viz.*, a deep-seated theoretical in-ability to differentiate between *truth* and *untruth*. That Heidegger consciously and deliberately flaunts the sanctity of this most fun-damental of philosophical distinctions is far from accidental: rather it pertains to the very essence of his critique of the representa-tional function of propositional theories of truth. The notion that truth could be represented by the determinate propositional con-tent of statements—an image of truth that purportedly dates back to the Platonic theory of ideas—becomes for Heidegger a form of *metaphysical sacrilege*, the "Fall" of western philosophy, a sin against the more "original" Greek philosophical ideal of truth as *alētheia*. Consequently, Heidegger seeks to unearth a more "primordial" doctrine of truth: one with greater ontological resonance, in which both the *Seinsfrage* and beings as they truly are, are not immedi-ately covered up by grammatico-syntactical statements contrived by "man," but instead are allowed to shine forth in a more pristine and unspoiled state.

This breakthrough (as we have already indicated) is to be achieved via Heidegger's conception of truth as "unconcealedness." But in the end, one cannot but doubt whether the overall losses are not greater than the partial gains. For the rash dismissal of the idea of propositional truth at the same time entails a wholesale rejec-tion of the truth/untruth dichotomy; the net result being that Hei-degger has rendered himself intellectually (and morally) defense-less against the "absolute historical evil" of the twentieth century: the genocidal imperialism of German National Socialism. Heideg-ger is not merely defenseless in face of this evil, but remains sufficiently deluded to defend its true "inner potential" even at a point where the horrific truth of the movement was unveiled for all to see.

How does this incapacitating confusion—an inability to distinguish truth from untruth—actually work itself out in Heidegger's thought? We have already seen how Heidegger argues for the more "primordial" epistemological rank of the "clearing" vis-à-vis propositional truth: beings must first stand in the open—they must be "unconcealed"—before they can be made into objects of philosophical judgment. However, it is in consequence of this attempt to conceptualize truth primarily as an act of "unconcealment" that the distinction between truth and untruth is blurred to the point of indistinguishability.

"Freedom for what is opened up in an open region lets beings be the beings they are. Freedom now reveals itself *as letting beings be*," observes Heidegger, in an initial formulation of his later philosophical doctrine of *Gelassenheit* or "releasement."[67] This greater philosophical willingness (a type of philosophical *Ent-schlossenheit* or "un-closedness") to "let beings be the beings they are" presumably yields greater fidelity to the "Being of beings" as such. It thus represents a first significant step toward a solution to the *Seins-frage*; whereas in the case of philosophical thought from Plato onward, the Being of beings was essentially covered up or concealed by the distortional influence of various philosophical "first principles": the "idea," the "cogito," "substance," "monad," "the transcendental subject," "spirit," etc. However (and what follows constitutes a crucial admission by Heidegger), insofar as letting beings be always lets beings be in a specific way—that is, because letting be is itself always perspectival or selective—*its very manner of disclosing beings also conceals them*. Thus, *every act of unconcealment is simultaneously an act of concealment*. Or as Heidegger himself expresses this thought: "Precisely because letting be always lets beings be in a particular comportment which relates to them and thus discloses them, *it conceals beings as a whole*."[68] With this claim, Heidegger seems to suggest that there are fundamentally two types of concealing, an essential and an inessential. The latter would pertain to the type of "covering up" that occurs as a result of our employment of faulty philosophical concepts (such as those just enumerated) in our understanding of beings; whereas *essential concealing* would refer to the inevitably partial and incomplete manner in which our phenomenological letting beings be occurs. Hei-

119

degger further ennobles the latter type of concealing by referring to it as the *mystery* (*Geheimnis*) that lies at the heart of Being. Once the "mystery" is forgotten, observes Heidegger, "the world is filled out by proposing and planning," and "Being as a whole is forgotten."[69]

But the truly radical insight that emerges from Heidegger's suggestion that a countervailing process of concealment is at work at the heart of our laborious efforts toward unconcealment is the idea that *untruth*—in the form of concealment—*is inseparable from truth.* Thus, as Heidegger remarks, "untruth [derives] from the essence of truth," that is, untruth conceived of as "errancy" (*Irrnis*). Or as he observes in a similar vein, "errancy and the concealment of what is concealed belong to the primordial essence of truth."[70]

Heidegger would reaffirm with renewed vigor the doctrine of the equiprimordiality of truth and error in "The Origin of the Work of Art," where the same theory is articulated with reference to the relationship between "world" and "earth." The conflict between world and earth, that which brings light and that which shelters, is an eternal, "primal" conflict in which neither party is able to gain the upper hand. Or, as Heidegger himself describes this primordial ontological antagonism: "the clearing is pervaded by a constant concealment in the double form of refusing and dissembling. . . . The nature of truth, that is, of unconcealedness, is dominated throughout by a denial. . . . *This denial, in the form of a double concealment, belongs to the nature of truth as unconcealedness. Truth is in its nature untruth.*"[71]

However promising Heidegger's ontological critique of the traditional philosophical ideal of propositional truth may have been, it ultimately founders in consequence of his inability to distinguish between "truth" and "error." In fact, as a result of the radicalism with which Heidegger seeks, from the standpoint of the history of Being, to re-pose the question of philosophical truth, he comes to perceive the inseparability of truth and error explicitly as a *gain in metaphysical profundity.* In point of fact, however, it is precisely the complacency with which he allows this fundamental intellectual distinction to blur into meaninglessness that accounts for his egregious errors of political judgment. Just as the Nietzschean superman is "beyond" the traditional moral divide between good and evil, so Heidegger's political judgments—by virtue of a claim to greater metaphysical profundity—are able to imperiously disregard all conventional, modern standards of political and intellectual judgment.

Ultimately Heidegger's theory of truth succumbs to the same problem of criterionlessness that was at issue in the decisionistic approach to human action in *Being and Time*. On the one hand, Heidegger seems at first to be claiming that unconcealment is merely an ontological *precondition* of truth—which is, as far as it goes, certainly a plausible and valuable insight. In point of fact, however, the nature of truth is conceptualized in terms of the dialectic of concealment and unconcealment that occurs within the phenomenological horizon that has been opened up by a work, a world, etc. In the end, his thoroughgoing antisubjectivism, which is radicalized in the "Turn," results in a type of ineffectual positivism: objects (beings) are no longer to be "judged" (for this would be to subject them to subjective criteria, or, worse still, to "values"), but "disclosed" or "unveiled." Yet, once the lines between truth and error become blurred, the distinction between *authentic* and *inauthentic unveiling* essentially evaporates: both are victimized by error in an unspecifiable way. Heidegger could conceivably redeem his theory of truth by an attempt, however minimal, to distinguish a true from an untrue act of unconcealment. A true unconcealment would thus unveil a being "essentially" or as it is "in itself." But no such distinction between genuine and non-genuine unveiling is forthcoming in his work. Instead, error (*Irrnis*) is paradoxically deemed a mode of unconcealment that is valid in its own right and thus "equiprimordial" with truth. Or again, Heidegger might have claimed that unconcealment presents a type of privileged or *exemplary* disclosure of beings; and judgments of truth, in turn, could have been predicated on this exemplary mode of disclosure. But no such claim is made. Instead, all we are left with is an unexalted, positivistic affirmation of "givenness," "beings in their immediacy," "disclosure as such."

In this respect, Heidegger's theory of *Seinsgeschichte* regresses behind both the Husserlian and the ancient Greek conceptions of truth. For in both cases, truth resides not in the "givenness" of beings as such, but in a supramundane or *superior* mode of givenness.[72] As a result of his obsession with providing a "topography" of truth—with defining the clearing or openness as a sufficient condition for the appearance of truth as "untruth"—to the wholesale exclusion of all traditional predicative considerations,

Heidegger lays himself open to extreme judgmental incapacities. And it was this *philosophically induced* lack of discernment that would lead to his fatal misapprehension of the intellectual as well as the political essence of National Socialism.

Many of the aforementioned themes concerning Heidegger's portentous misunderstanding of the relationship between politics, truth, and error have been intelligently summarized by the Heidegger-scholar Werner Marx:

> Heidegger conceived the institution of the *polis* in the first [i.e., the Greek] beginning, on the basis of *alētheia*, as an occurrence of truth in which man is violently involved. Likewise, in the "basic event of the realization of the National Socialist state" he saw an "incipient" foundation of a state, a "state-founding act," which he expressly characterized in the essay on the work of art (1935) as one of the ways in which "truth essences" [*die Wahrheit west*]. That the "National Socialist revolution" as the "total transformation of our German Dasein" could take place only violently, and that it was pervaded by evil as well as by error and sham, for Heidegger might thus have simply resulted from an "occurrence of truth." And it might have for him been merely a consequence of the *coordination* of evil and good in the clearing of Being, such that the founders of the state followed the directives of evil without [Heidegger] being able to hold them guilty on the basis of "moral considerations." These references touch on the difficult, disturbing, and painful problem of the relationship of this thinker to National Socialism and the effect of his related speeches, writings, and actions insofar as they cast doubt on the often heard view that he "erred" with regard to the violence and evil of the National Socialist revolution. On the contrary, he must have *a priori* assessed it correctly, since he viewed it as an "occurrence of truth."
>
> These considerations are especially appropriate in bringing to light the extremely perilous character of Heidegger's concept of truth. They forcefully raise the question of whether Heidegger actually viewed the matter correctly when he recognized not only "the mystery" but also error, sham, and evil as equal partners within the occurrence of truth.[73]

Thus, for Marx, the "perilous character" of Heidegger's concept of truth derives from its obstinate insistence on treating "error, sham, and evil" as coexistent moments of truth.[74] The central dilemma of this theory of truth is that it is essentially *non-falsifiable*: since error and truth are for Heidegger equiprimordial aspects of the *Ereignis*, we are given no criteria on the basis of which we might distinguish between them. Only the philosopher himself, who possesses privileged access to the history of Being *qua* "Mystery," is capable of determining authentic from inauthentic manifestations of truth and error. The philosopher thus becomes a "high priest of Being" who no longer need prove his case by reason or force of the better argument. Instead, his status as an "initiate" of the secret rites of Being should suffice to allay all questions and doubts (except in the case of nonbelievers, who are beyond redemption in any event). Since the 1929 conversation with Cassirer in Davos, Heidegger had imperiously dismissed the results of the social and natural sciences, insofar as they can attain only knowledge of beings and never of Being. As such, they have nothing to say to us that is truly meaningful, that addresses the roots of the contemporary crisis. Instead, the variety of knowledge they proffer is inferior, *nihilistic*—a term that, for the later Heidegger, becomes synonymous with all types of thought other than his own—insofar as its results are merely culled from the nether world of "beings." But as Löwith has observed:

> Philosophical reflection on the whole of what exists in nature, which is the world . . . cannot merely "pass science by" without falling into the void. It is easily said, and it would be a relief, if philosophical thought were to dwell beyond what is provable and refutable; if, however, the realm of "essential thinking" were to surpass all proof and refutation, then philosophy would have to do neither with truth nor with probability, but rather with uncontrollable claims and allegations.[75]

Heidegger ceaselessly accuses the history of philosophy, and the present age in particular, of *Seinsvergessenheit*. But one could just as easily turn the tables: his own philosophical *oeuvre* seems at times to come perilously close to a monumental instance of *Logos-Vergessenheit*—the "oblivion of reason."

A Spiritual Aristocracy of Leader-Creators; Violence as an Ontological Imperative

Given his philosophical self-understanding as someone in possession of privileged access to the mysteries of Being, it is far from

123

mere chance that in the mid-1930s, Heidegger attempts to formalize the notion of an elite cadre of poets, thinkers, and statesmen—a cadre of authentic "leader-types"—who stand in a more immediate proximity to Being, and whose historical responsibility it is to lead the unenlightened many into the vicinity of such "nearness" (*Nähe*). The *Führerprinzip*—refunctioned as an existential theory of authentic leadership—thus serves as the essential ground for Heidegger's thinking about the way in which politics, philosophy, and poetic creation should become historically actualized. In vintage Nietzschean fashion, the nihilism of the indigent historical present can only be vanquished via the iconoclastic heroism of a creative elite, referred to by Heidegger as the "great creators" (*die grossen Schaffende*). And in consequence of the *a priori* divide between authentic and inauthentic natures, it is in the hands of this clique of superior human types that the destiny of Being rests.

Nietzsche elaborates his own theory of the "superman" as a counterweight to nihilism in the following passage from *The Will to Power*:

> The need to show that as the consumption of mankind becomes more and more economical and the "machinery" of interests and services is integrated ever more intricately, a countermovement is inevitable. I designate this as the secretion of a luxury surplus of mankind: it aims to bring to light a stronger species, a higher type that arises and preserves itself under different conditions from those of the average man. My concept, my metaphor for this type is, as one knows, the "superman". . . . In opposition to the dwarfing and adaptation of man to a specialized utility, a reverse movement is needed—the production of a synthetic, summarizing, justifying man for whose existence this transformation of mankind into a machine is a precondition, as a base on which he can invent his *higher form of being*.[76]

The Heideggerian version of this doctrine of a new, dominating caste of leader-types is developed in connection with his theory of the "work." In his view, this caste represents an aristocracy of creators. They are the warriors in the "primordial struggle," the struggle for Being:

> It is this conflict that first projects and develops what has hitherto been unheard of, unsaid and unthought. The struggle is

then sustained by the creators, poets, thinkers, statesmen. Against the overwhelming chaos, they set the barrier of their work, and in their work they capture the world thus opened up. It is with their works that the elemental power, the *physis*, first comes to stand. . . . This world-building is history in the authentic sense.[77]

The works established by Heidegger's leader-aristocracy of poets, thinkers, and statesmen have an eminently historical function: they bring the primordial Heraclitean conflict (*polemos*) to a temporary standstill by virtue of the stability of their works, which in turn ground the historical destiny of a nation. The role of the leader-caste is indispensable, for in Heidegger's quasi-Nietzschean epistemology, the mysteries of Being will only deign to reveal themselves to the heroic few: "The true is not for every man but only for the strong."[78] "Nowadays, a little too much fuss is made over the Greek polis," remarks Heidegger; that is, the Greek polis as the historical origin of the democratic idea. Instead, all Heidegger can find to admire about the polis as a political entity is the primacy of "rank and domination," the traces of that same *Führerprinzip* he wishes to see transposed to the modern political context.[79]

But just as the Nietzschean superman is justified in utilizing the average man as a "base on which he can invent a *higher form of being*," so, too, in the case of Heideggerian leader-creators does rank have its privileges. They are "violent men" (*Gewalt-tätige*) who "use power to become pre-eminent in historical Being as creators, as men of action." They are the great misunderstood geniuses of civilization who stand above and outside of the law, which, after all, they have brought into Being to begin with: "Pre-eminent in the historical place, they become at the same time *apolis*, without city and place, lonely, strange, and alien . . . without statute and limit, without structure and order, because they themselves as creators must first create all this."[80] The leader-creators embody a kind of *law-creating violence*: they are a self-justifying elect who ultimately become *laws unto themselves*. Their status as "perpetrators of violence" is by no means a dispensable or nonessential aspect of their Being. According to Heidegger, it is only by virtue of such violent acts that the encrusted powers of convention and everydayness can be broken, that authentically creative natures can truly assert themselves, and that the otherwise concealed, primordial powers of Being can come to the fore: "The violence of poetic speech, of thinking projection, of building configuration, of the action that creates states, is . . . a taming and ordering of powers by virtue of which what is opens up as such as man moves into it."[81]

Thus, in Heidegger's metaphysical schema, violence takes on the character of an *ontological imperative;* it is an essential means possessed by the *Führer*-elite to combat the forces of everydayness and routine, whose predominance prevents the posing of the question of Being. However, what comes through unmistakably in this philosophical glorification of violence are the patent affinities between Heidegger's *Gewalt-tätige*—the "shock-troops of Being," as it were—and the National Socialist rhetoric of *Sturm und Kampf.* Whatever its intrinsic philosophical merit, this theory of a creative elite who are "apolis" and "without statute" cannot help but strike one as a fanciful but crude, *post festum* justification of the Nazi *Führerprinzip* and its train of illegalities. As devoid of any underlying moral or legal restraints, Heidegger's glorified image of a *Führerstaat* zealously underwrites the totalitarian claims of the ruling elite. The elevated metaphysical terms of discussion cannot mask the ease with which his approach lends itself to abuse: despite Heidegger's qualification that "rulers *alone*" must rule, the theory represents *carte blanche* for authoritarian licentiousness. Because the only claim to "right" possessed by the creative elite is their own intrinsic charismatic-existential superiority, because they are self-justifying "laws unto themselves," the basis for their authority is essentially decisionistic. The original ontological separation between leaders and followers is the abyss out of which all other nefarious consequences of the theory subsequently emerge.

That the actions of the leader-creators cannot be judged in normal human terms is emphasized time and again by Heidegger—perhaps most emphatically in his discussion of the creative elite as a group of "demigods," whose exalted mission it is to mediate between the concerns of gods and men. As demigods, the leader-creators occupy a position analogous to the Nietzschean superman: they are, on the one hand, superior to the world of everyday human affairs; on the other hand, they fall short of the divine excellence of the gods themselves. As Heidegger describes them, they qualify as *"supermen"* and *"lesser gods"* (*Übermenschen und Untergötter*): "Demigods—not gods themselves, but beings directed toward the gods, and, to be sure, in a direction that leads beyond human life; *supermen,* who nevertheless remain below the greatness of the gods—*lesser gods.*"[82] And thus, in an allusion to the contemporary German political situation (1934–1935), Heidegger illustrates how his theory of demigods might gain concrete historical application: "The true and only *Führer* points by virtue of his Being toward the realm of the demigods. To be *Führer* [*Führersein*] is a fate and therefore finite Being."[83]

Heidegger's incessant references to this suprahuman avant-garde of demigods and leaders by no means constitute a nonessential deviation from his philosophy proper, but instead serves to delineate the *historical conditions of its realization*. Given the "existential" motivation underlying his entire philosophical project, it was inconceivable that the question of the historical actuality or nonactuality of that project could remain for him a matter of indifference. The question of Being gained its uniqueness precisely from the fact that it could not be "answered"—let alone "posed"—by arm-chair philosophers in a traditional university setting. Instead, its nature was for Heidegger eminently *epochal* and *historical*: its posing depended on the concrete relation of a nation or Volk to the question of its own historicity as well as, ultimately, on the question of whether a new relation to a more primordial understanding of Being could be regained. Because of the *a priori* separation between authentic and inauthentic natures, between leaders and led, that dominated his ontology of the life-world, hope for the historical realization of this philosophical desideratum hinged on the emergence of a violent, creative elite—Heidegger's "great creators"—who, like the biblical prophets of old, would be capable of leading the people along the path of metaphysical salvation. Consequently, for Heidegger, "The authentic idea of the state must necessarily be antiliberal, requiring . . . a new ruling caste which can lay the foundations for the coming of a new kind of man, the superman."[84] Even then, of course, there was the real danger that "the many" would remain immobilized in their inauthentic torpor, failing to recognize the prospects for historical greatness awaiting them. Thus, the *Führerprinzip*, as it manifested itself in Heidegger's own philosophical theory, far from being an expendable, subaltern component, took on the role of a *sine qua non*, the indispensable key to the authentic unfolding of history as the "history of Being." For unless there exist ("real") poets, philosophers, and statesmen to catalyze and celebrate the metaphysical (*seinsgeschichtliche*) mission of a historical Volk, its relation to "essence" threatens to fall into historical eclipse: it invites a fate of *Seinsverlassenheit*, abandonment by the powers of Being. Given the magnitude of the historical struggle, as well as the immensity of the stakes involved, Heidegger felt compelled to emphasize the *violent* nature of the process, going so far as to identify his leadership clique as *"the violent ones"* (*die Gewalt-tätige*). And thus in his reading of Heraclitus' fragment 53, *violence* (along with "struggle," "strife," and "conflict") is interpreted as the midwife of Being: "Violence against the preponderant power of Being *must* shatter against Being, if Being rules in its essence, as *physis*, as emerging power. . . . Therefore the violent one knows no kindness and conciliation. . . . To him disaster is the deepest and broadest affirmation of the overpowering."[85]

But perhaps the clearest account of the role to be played by the vanguard of authentic creators in the overall historical scheme of *Seinspolitik* is provided by Heidegger in the course of his 1934–35 Hölderlin lectures. As he expresses it:

> The historical Dasein of nations—their emergence, flowering, and decline—originates from poetry; out of the latter [originates] authentic knowledge in the sense of philosophy; and from both of these, the realization of a Volk as a Volk through the state—politics. This original, historical age of peoples is therefore the age of poets, thinkers, and state-founders [*Staatsschöpfer*], that is, of those who authentically ground and establish the historical Dasein of a Volk. They are the *authentic creators.* . . . The Being of beings is comprehended and ordered as Being, and thereby first exposed, by the thinker; and Being thus comprehended is placed in the ultimate seriousness of what is—that is, in *determinate* historical truth—so that the Volk is thereby brought to itself qua Volk. This occurs via the creation by the state-founder of the state that is appropriate to its essence.[86]

According to a charitable reading of Heidegger's doctrine of *Seinspolitik*—his theory of the integral interrelationship between creators, the Volk, and the state as viewed from the standpoint of the history of Being—the philosopher is merely advocating a theory of national self-determination to be based on the "higher powers" of poetry, philosophy, and statesmanship; a doctrine that, thus understood, is essentially unobjectionable. In truth, however, the historical and conceptual bases of Heidegger's theory are decidedly more complex. They are inseparable from his acceptance of the (proto-fascistic) conservative revolutionary critique of modernity, including the imperialist vision of Germany as "master of *Mitteleuropa*"; from a systematic devaluation of all conceivable institutional checks vis-à-vis the eventuality of totalitarian state power; and from a glorification of the ideals of authority, hierarchy, and rank that in its essentials is indistinguishable from the Nazi *Führerprinzip* itself. When these systematic aspects of his philosophical theory are in turn viewed against the background of the philosopher's own numerous observations and asides in support of Germany's National Revolutionary course in the 1930s, the portrait of the man and the thinker that emerges is far from innocent. Philosophy and politics are not related in a contingent or nonessential fashion. Instead, as our theoretical reconstruction has attempted to show, they exist as communicating vessels.

And thus there can be little doubt that, in the mind of the philosopher himself, there existed profound affinities between his project for the historical reclamation of Being and German National Socialism—despite Heidegger's own increasing misgivings concerning the determinate empirical form the movement had assumed in actual practice. That his confidence in the ultimate historical mission of Germany as a "nation in the middle" remained unshaken at least through the mid-1940s is illustrated by a number of startling observations from his lecture courses of 1942–43. Though these years signify the historical turning point in the course of World War II, this fact seemed to be of little consequence for Heidegger's own political sensibilities. Instead, as late as the summer of 1942, he astonishingly persists in alluding to the "historical singularity [*geschichtlichen Einzigkeit*] of National Socialism."[87] Similarly, in his Parmenides lectures of the following semester, he observes: "Thus it is important to realize that, when it comes to victory, this historical Volk [*i.e.*, Germany] has already triumphed and is unconquerable [*schon gesiegt hat und unbesiegbar ist*] if it remains the nation of poets and thinkers that it is essentially, as long as it does not fall victim to the dreadful—because always threatening—deviation from, and thus misunderstanding of, its essence."[88] And in his Heraclitus lectures of the same year, Heidegger reaffirms his delusory conviction—against a massive weight of historical evidence to the contrary—that Germany and the Germans represent the only force capable of redeeming the West from a fate of impending catastrophe: "the Germans and they alone can save the West for its history," he declaims. "The planet is in flames. The essence of man is out of joint. Only from the Germans can there come a world-historical reflection—if, that is, they find and preserve 'Germanness' [*das Deutsche*]."[89]

As these lines were composed, the German army stood in ruins before Stalingrad, and there could no longer be any doubt about the gruesome nature of Hitler's *Endlösung* to the "Jewish question": the entire Jewish population of Germany had been forcibly removed, and the reports from the death-camps had already made the rounds among the civil population. That the world conflagration alluded to by Heidegger had been *unleashed by Germany itself*—specifically, by a political movement that Heidegger had once vigorously and wholeheartedly supported—which thus represented the "cause" of the catastrophe rather than its "solution," is a fact that—appallingly—seems beyond the pale of the philosopher's powers of historical comprehension.

As a disillusioned former student would write of his fallen mentor shortly after the Rectoral Address:

> Existentialism collapses in the moment when its political theory is realized. The total-authoritarian state which it yearned for gives the lie to all its truths. Existentialism accompanies its collapse with a self-abasement that is unique in intellectual history; it carries out its own history as a satyr-play to the end. It began philosophically as a great debate with western rationalism and idealism, in order to redeem the historical concretion of individual existence for this intellectual heritage. And it ends philosophically with the radical denial of its own origins; the struggle against reason drives it blindly into the arms of the reigning powers. In their service and protection it betrays that great philosophy which it once celebrated as the pinnacle of western thinking.[90]

FIVE

Technology, Antihumanism, and the Eclipse of Practical Reason

> There is no room for political philosophy in Heidegger's work, and this may well be due to the fact that the room in question is occupied by gods or the gods.
>
> Leo Strauss, "Philosophy as Rigorous Science and Political Philosophy"

> Whoever seeks to replace the question of truth with that of "openness to Being" relinquishes the idea of "critical responsibility" which is presupposed by every rational concept of practice.
>
> Ernst Tugendhat, *Der Begriff der Wahrheit bei Husserl und Heidegger*

> Heidegger doesn't know what freedom is.
>
> Karl Jaspers, *Notizen zu Martin Heidegger*

Rethinking Nietzsche

Heidegger's middle phase—the period lasting roughly from "What is Metaphysics?" (1929) to "The Origin of the Work of Art" (1935–1936)—is characterized by a major shift of emphasis away from a Dasein-centered philosophy of existence and toward an independent theory of the history of Being. Thus, when the term "Dasein" appears, it is frequently hyphenated to read "Da-sein"—Heidegger's way of indicating that the term is best understood as the "there" of "Being," rather than as an autonomously existent entity. The discussion of *physis* in *An Introduction to Metaphysics* is also symptomatic of Heidegger's new approach. As portrayed by the pre-Socratics, *physis* is understood as a self-actualizing phenomenon that anticipates Heidegger's own category of *Sein*. Thus conceived, *physis* possesses a metaphysical primordiality in face of which the petty, "worldly" concerns of Dasein itself seem to fade into insignificance.

This middle phase, however, rather than representing a sudden or total *break* with his early work, is genuinely transitional: elements from both the "later" and "early" periods intermingle in ways that are both fruitful and contradictory. On the one hand, the question of Being is posed in its own right in works such as

"On the Essence of Truth" and *An Introduction to Metaphysics*. On the other hand, Heidegger's political reflections on Germany's privileged role in the history of Being, as well as his theory of an aristocracy of leader-creators, both suggest that Dasein, rather than being a merely passive receptacle of a prior metaphysical "destining," possesses the capacity to actively influence and shape its own "fateful" relation to the powers of Being.

Another crucial categorial innovation in this so-called transitional phase is the concept of the "work," which is the focal point of Alexander Schwan's important study of Heidegger's political thought.[1] In many respects, this concept serves as an emblem of Heidegger's philosophical preoccupations during this period: the "work" acts as an ideal mediating agency between the transcendence of *Sein* and the immanence of Dasein. It becomes the privileged locus of their historical commingling, the ideal site of the "Ereignis," and thus the authentic construct in terms of which the truth of Being is disclosed. However, insofar as Heidegger eschews the notion of "subjective spirit" espoused by German classical philosophy, the work—be it of art, philosophy, or politics—seems less a product of autonomous human fashioning than a result of Dasein's solicitous attunement to the call of Being itself. As a producer of works, Dasein thus serves as a passive "midwife of Being." Or as Heidegger explains, "It is precisely in great art . . . that the artist remains inconsequential as compared with the work, almost like a passageway that destroys itself in the creative process for the work to emerge."[2]

In 1936, however, the transitional "middle phase" discussed at length in chapter 4 comes to an abrupt end: with the onset of Heidegger's intensive Nietzsche studies that date from this year, the *seinsgeschichtliche* Turn first adumbrated in "What is Metaphysics?" is brought to a dramatic completion. So extreme is the philosopher's reconceptualization of the relationship between Being and Dasein that one could plausibly interpret the *Kehre* as a "Reversal" rather than a "Turn" in Heidegger's thinking. In this final phase,[3] many of the ambiguities that characterized the Being/Dasein nexus in the middle period have seemingly disappeared: the capacity of Dasein to influence or alter the history of Being in the slightest respect is all but ruled out. Instead, humanity, it seems, has been unilaterally delivered over to a fate of absolute "meaninglessness" and "abandonment by Being" (*Sinnlosigkeit* and

Seinsverlassenheit), a fate which is deemed *implacable*, insofar as Heidegger characterizes it as a *Seinsgeschick*—the "destiny of Being." In face of this "destiny," the aristocracy of authentic leader-creators, in whom Heidegger had once placed an abundance of trust, proves as powerless as those who are fully at home in the fallen world of everydayness.

However, Heidegger's later metaphysical judgments, far from being philosophically autonomous, have a powerful and immediate historical point of reference: the failure of Germany's National Revolution. The Heideggerian *Kehre* therefore betrays both an intraphilosophical as well as an external, historically conditioned motive. And thus, the Turn must at least in part be understood with reference to Heidegger's attempt to come to terms with his National Socialist past. In the last analysis, however, this attempt proves radically deficient—to a point where one might be justified in interpreting his later doctrine of the history of Being as an involuted philosophical rationalization of his own failed National Socialist involvement. Thus, although Heidegger's later thought and conduct are marked by a conscious abstention from the quandaries of political life—whose complexities the philosopher had so badly misjudged in the early 1930s—the strategy of avoidance he practices is itself highly revelatory—both philosophically as well as biographically.

During the five-year period from 1936–1941 Heidegger was obsessed with the work of Nietzsche. During these years, he offered four lecture courses on various aspects of Nietzsche's philosophy and composed at least six other lectures or essays attempting to situate Nietzsche's work within the context of the history of Being. The two-volume 1961 work in which these materials were assembled runs well over 1100 pages.

Heidegger was convinced that Nietzsche's philosophy alone offered privileged insight into the nature of contemporary historical conditions, which the author of *The Will to Power* had accurately diagnosed as "nihilistic." In his lecture course on "European Nihilism," Heidegger cites approvingly Nietzsche's famous definition of nihilism in the opening pages of the *The Will to Power*: "What does nihilism mean? *That the uppermost values devaluate themselves.* The aim is lacking; the 'why?' receives no answer."[4] And with the analysis that followed, Nietzsche captured with visionary acumen the world-weariness of *fin-de-siècle* Europe.

To be sure, many other contemporary thinkers had contemplated and bemoaned the decline of the "uppermost European values." And in Germany, which had long prided itself as a bulwark of traditionalism and a staunch foe of Western influences, the seemingly inevitable transition from a traditional, religiously oriented world-order to a modern secularized "society" seemed an especial cause for alarm. But Nietzsche's historical diagnosis contained a brilliant and original twist. While other thinkers were claiming that the "cause" of nihilism was to be found in the deterioration of time-honored European precepts concerning reason, faith, morality, etc., Nietzsche took the whole question a step further: it was not the *decline* of those values *per se* that was responsible for the advent of nihilism; instead, *these values themselves were, according to their essence, intrinsically nihilistic*; and thus their current state of decomposition merely reflected their original nature and potential. Nietzsche's own shrewd diagnosis of the fate of European modernity—which is articulated in almost all of his works of the 1880s—has to do above all with his critique of the "life-denying" character of the traditional Platonic-Christian, metaphysical view of the world. According to Nietzsche, its hatred of "life" is expressed by the fact that its most exalted values—the Platonic theory of ideas, the Christian doctrine of salvation, the Kantian notion of the moral subject—are relegated to an otherworldly, supersensible sphere. And thus "worldly" concerns are correspondingly devalued—they are slandered as "impure."

In his lectures of the late 1930s, Heidegger seeks to do Nietzsche one better. Whereas Nietzsche claims that by virtue of his insight into the afflictions of European modernity, he is able to prophesy the "self-overcoming of European nihilism" via his doctrines of the "eternal recurrence," the "superman," and the "will to power," Heidegger stands Nietzsche on his head: Nietzsche takes these ideals to be *postmetaphysical* notions, whereas in reality, Nietzsche is *the last metaphysician*. The truth of Nietzschean philosophy is that it reveals itself to be a species of *inverted Platonism*: whereas the Platonic-Christian tradition posits the supersensuous realm as the fount and ground of all Being, Nietzsche, in his overcoming of this tradition, has merely succeeded in *reversing the metaphysical hierarchy of his philosophical adversaries*. Thus, "sensuousness," "life," and "aesthetic illusion" become the new philosophical *archai*.[5] In the final analysis, however, Nietzsche's "transvaluation of values" remains under the spell of that very Platonism it is seeking to escape; it has merely succeeded in supplanting the realm of super-sensuous, metaphysical truth with a competing realm of sensuous truth that is equally metaphysical. Or as Heidegger argues in "European Nihilism":

> But if the interpretation of beings as a whole cannot issue from a transcendent that is posited 'over' them from the outset, then the new values and their standard of measure can only be drawn from the realm of beings themselves. . . . If the essence of metaphysics consists in grounding the truth of being [*des Seindes*] as a whole, then the transvaluation of all values, as a grounding of the principle for a new valuation, is itself metaphysics. What Nietzsche perceives and posits as the basic character of being as a whole is what he calls the "will to power."[6]

Thus, in Heidegger's view, the stumbling block for Nietzsche is identical to the one that has proved the undoing of all previous metaphysics: the inability to appreciate the onto-ontological difference, the failure to distinguish between Being and beings. However perspicacious his critique of traditional metaphysics may have been, in the last analysis, Nietzsche has merely fallen victim to the same trap as his predecessors: Nietzsche, too, in the end decides to privilege a specific determinate "being" (*Seindes*) and make this entity the foundational or metaphysical point of departure for his understanding of "beings in general."[7] His thought is therefore still fully beholden to metaphysics. For as Heidegger remarks, the distinguishing feature of "metaphysics" is that it "thinks beings as a whole according to their priority over Being."[8] In consequence, the *Seinsfrage* itself is never posed by Nietzsche. Heidegger identifies this Nietzschean "privileged being" as the "will to power," which is itself merely a grandiose inflation of the modern standpoint of self-positing subjectivity. The only difference in Nietzsche's case is that he happens to cull his first principle from the nether sphere of sensuous being rather than the supersensuous plane of noncorporeal reality.

But what is of essential importance about Heidegger's intensive debate with the *Geist* (both "ghost" and "spirit") of Nietzsche in the late 1930s is that as a result of this confrontation, his own theory of the "history of Being" reemerges permanently transformed in a way that will prove determinative for his entire later philosophy.[9] Above all, Heidegger's polemic against the deficiencies of Nietzsche's "metaphysical-anthropological" thinking serves to solidify Heidegger's own emergent conception of Being as that which "essences" (*west*) independently of all human will and endeavor. If in the first half of the 1930s, Heidegger believed, in a genuinely Nietzschean spirit, that the ideal of the "superman" embodied the prospect of an authentic overcoming of nihilism (and this is precisely the sense in which Heidegger's partisanship for the *Führerprinzip* in relation to National Socialism must be understood), his Nietzsche critique in the latter half of the decade led him to a diametrically opposite stance: the deification of the human "will to will" as exemplified by the Nietzschean superman signified not the *overcoming* of European nihilism; instead, it represented nihilism's *consummation*. Thus, whereas heretofore, Heidegger had read Nietzsche in accordance with the latter's own theoretical self-understanding—*viz.*, as the iconoclast and anti-Christ of the European philosophical tradition—henceforth he viewed Nietzsche's doctrines as the inevitable *culmination* of that tradition. More specifically, he regarded the Nietzschean theory of the "will to power" as the apotheosis of the Western "metaphysics of the will."[10] And thus, in Heidegger's eyes, Nietzsche ironically proved to be the *ultimate Cartesian*: his concepts of the "will to power," the "superman," the "blond beast," etc., represent a consummate glorification of the Cartesian *subjectum*, for whom "objects" ("things," "beings") are reduced to the mere "stuff" of subjective domination and control. Or, as Heidegger himself remarks, "Nietzsche's doctrine, which makes everything that is, and as it is, into the 'property and product of man,' merely carries out the final development of Descartes' doctrine, according to which truth is grounded in the self-certainty of the human subject."[11]

It is, moreover, the imperious and grandiose designs of this Cartesian/Nietzschean "will to will"—relentless and implacable—that grounds, according to Heidegger, the "essence" of the modern age—an essence that ultimately proves "nihilistic" insofar as it represents the *ne plus ultra* of *Seinsvergessenheit*. Only once this "essential" dimension is philosophically grasped does the course of modern history become comprehensible. Or as Heidegger remarks in "The Age of the World-Picture" (1938), "Metaphysics grounds an age . . . [and] holds complete dominion over all the phenomena that distinguish the age."[12] Thus, for Heidegger, like Hegel before him, the history of philosophy becomes the philosophy of history.

Only in light of this sustained confrontation with Nietzsche's "metaphysics of the will" in the decade following 1935, therefore, can the "reactive" character of the Heideggerian *Kehre* be fully understood. It consists in the zealous eradication of all remaining subjective-anthropological traces in Heidegger's own thought and a counteremphasis on the quietistic concepts of "releasement," "letting-be," and "openness to the mystery."[13] The philosophical voluntarism implicit in Heidegger's pre-*Kehre* categorial scheme— for example, his discussions of "resolve," "authentic potentiality-for-being," and poets, philosophers, and statesman as "the great creators"—recedes dramatically. His conception of the vocation of man is correspondingly redefined: man is now the "shepherd of Being" (*Hirt des Seins*). Accordingly, it is the virtues of human docility and submissiveness that Heidegger singles out above all for praise. For such comportment proves most propitious in our attempt to remain "attuned" to the "mystery of Being."

If the foregoing reconstruction of Heidegger's Nietzsche critique is accurate, and the philosopher's post-*Kehre* denigration of the possibilities for human action is indeed total, then the question must seriously be posed as to whether any prospects remain in the later Heidegger for salvaging the concept of practical philosophy.

Seinsgeschick as a Strategy of Denial

It is impossible to account for Heidegger's "Nietzsche obsession" in abstraction from the historical context of the late 1930s, or by disregarding Heidegger's own extreme political disillusionment during these years. As a world-renowned philosopher who had concluded his 1933 Rectoral Address with a paean to the "glory and greatness" of the Nazi regime, and who then pledged his organizational and intellectual talents to ensuring the movement's success, Heidegger must have felt acutely betrayed over the historical course taken by the movement. From the standpoint of our interest in the philosopher's political thought, the critical question becomes: in what way would this political disillusionment become a decisive factor in shaping Heidegger's later philosophical project? Were the conclusions he would draw from these political misadventures *philosophically productive*? Or would they lead to a series of biographically overdetermined, theoretical denials which, as it were, only compounded the initial error?

137

Perhaps the work that best documents Heidegger's philosophical response to the mid-century world cataclysm is "Overcoming Metaphysics": a series of Nietzsche-esque jottings set down in thesis-form between 1936 and 1946, and hence contemporaneous with the period of his own intensive preoccupation with Nietzsche.[14] It is far from coincidental that the text selected by Heidegger as the point of departure for his reflections on the contemporary world situation—"the midnight of a world-night"[15]—is once again Ernst Jünger's *Der Arbeiter*, on which Heidegger held a seminar in the winter semester of 1939–40.[16]

In "Overcoming Metaphysics," Heidegger accepts unreservedly Jünger's characterization of modern man as *homo laborans*: a "laboring animal," a fungible cog in a process of "total mobilization" whose domination is omnipresent and inescapable. Indeed, Jünger has faithfully portrayed the way in which modern man, as a "working being," has been "condemned to wander through the desert of the earth's desolation."[17] Not only is Jünger's prophetic work of 1932 *descriptively* accurate; his thesis concerning the "Form" (*Gestalt*) of the worker has captured the degradation of the modern world in its *essential* or *metaphysical* dimensions as well. As Heidegger explains, "For labor (cf. Ernst Jünger, *Der Arbeiter*, 1932) is now reaching the metaphysical rank of the *unconditional objectification of everything present* which is active in the will to will."[18] The category of the "will to will," which occupies pride of place in the Nietzsche lectures, denotes for Heidegger the apotheosis of the Cartesian/Nietzschean "metaphysics of subjectivity" in the modern world. Thus understood, the *Arbeiterwelt* forecast by Jünger—an age of "total reification," as it were[19]—represents the historical fulfillment of a metaphysical world-view originating with Plato and culminating in Nietzsche's concepts of the will to power and the superman; a world-view in which objects or things become "meaningful" only when forced to submit to the will-ful dictates of self-positing subjectivity. It is a world that refuses (to use the language Heidegger first employs in "On the Essence of Truth") *to let beings be*. This world knows no *Gelassenheit*, no "releasement"; it arrogantly spurns the call of Being. As the "unconditional objectification of everything present," the modern world is the result of a logic of subjective self-assertion gone haywire. The total devastation that follows in its wake—"the events of world history in this century" according to Heidegger—are described by the philosopher in the following passages:

The decline of the truth of beings occurs [*ereignet sich*] necessarily, and indeed as the consummation of metaphysics.

The decline [*Untergang*] occurs through the collapse of the world
characterized by metaphysics, and at the same time through the
devastation of the earth stemming from metaphysics.

Collapse and devastation find their adequate occurrence in the
fact that metaphysical man, the *animal rationale*, gets fixed as
the laboring animal.

Before Being can occur in its primal truth, Being as the will
must be broken, the world must be forced to collapse and the
earth must be driven to devastation, and man to mere labor. Only
after this decline does the abrupt dwelling of the Origin take place
for a long span of time. In the decline, everything, that is, beings
in the whole of the truth of metaphysics, approaches its end.

The decline has already taken place. The consequences of this
occurrence are the events of world history in this century. They
are merely the course of what has already ended. Its course is
ordered historico-technologically in the sense of the last stage of
metaphysics. . . . The laboring animal is left to the giddy whirl
of its products so that it may tear itself to pieces and annihilate
itself in empty nothingness.[20]

The essence of the later Heidegger's critique of the modern
Zeitgeist is faithfully represented in the preceding citation. His
standpoint is nothing if not apocalyptical. While the primary "ac-
tor" in the process of universal decline and devastation is apparently "metaphysics" ("the decline occurs as the consummation of
metaphysics"), the other essential components of Heidegger's later
world view—"will," "technology," the *animal rationale qua* laboring animal—are simultaneously present. Also characteristic is the
chiliastic suggestion that a *reversal* of the present state of decline
in favor of a return to "the primal truth of Being" is imminent;
that somehow, "the world must be forced to collapse and the earth
must be driven to desolation" before this primal truth can be re-
captured. However, whether the crisis described by Heidegger is,
as he claims, of *metaphysical provenance*, and more generally,
whether this standard Heideggerian precept—"the consummation
[*Vollendung*] of metaphysics"—is capable of bearing the explanatory force he would like to attribute to it, are two matters that
must be called seriously into question.

In "The Age of the World-Picture" (1938), Heidegger similarly praises Jünger's strategy in "Total Mobilization"—*viz.*, "to set up 'total mobilization' as an absolute once it is recognized as being at hand"—as "an attitude incomparably more essential" than a mere affirmation of technology.[21] But it should be clear from our discussion of "Overcoming Metaphysics" that Heidegger's post-*Kehre* interpretation of Jünger's theories reaches conclusions that are diametrically opposed to the meaning these ideas possessed for him in the early 1930s. At that time, Heidegger was convinced that Jünger's doctrines heralded the birth of a "new age"; that his critique of the nihilism of modern bourgeois life was a genuine continuation of Nietzsche's work; and that, moreover, Jünger's vision of the future as an *Arbeiterwelt* signified a positive alternative to the languid world of bourgeois everydayness, an authentic overcoming of the millennial reign of European nihilism (one need only review Heidegger's many discourses in praise of "Labor Service" to be convinced of this). And it was at least partially on the basis of Jünger's theoretical apotheosis of a heroic new breed of "worker-soldiers" and "soldier-workers" that Heidegger ultimately cast his lot with the National Socialists.

But with the foundering of Germany's National Revolution—which, for Heidegger, meant that ultimately this movement was merely another species of "power politics"; that in its unconcern for the truth of Being, it, too, was essentially "nihilistic"—Heidegger's conception of the *Arbeiterwelt* as portrayed by Jünger underwent a complete transformation. Ironically, he still treated Jünger's 1932 work as an indispensable key for deciphering the contemporary Spenglerian condition of devastation and decline. Its prophetic-descriptive powers remained in his eyes undiminished. Otherwise, it is unlikely that Heidegger would have devoted yet another seminar to it (not to mention his lengthy, 1955 contribution to the Festschrift in honor of Jünger's sixtieth birthday, *The Question of Being*). But what had by now become clear to Heidegger was that the *Arbeiterwelt* described by Jünger portended not the *overcoming* (*Überwindung*) of metaphysics; instead, it represented the *consummation* (*Vollendung*) of metaphysics, an age of total *Seinsverlassenheit*. Thus, it was not the *descriptive* content of Jünger's forecasts that had been misguided, but the *evaluative* significance he accorded them.

However, according to Heidegger's later rereading of Jünger, all was not lost. For as the citations from "Overcoming Metaphysics" indicate, he persisted in the conviction that the *Arbeiterwelt* embraced by Jünger—that "devastation of the earth" resulting from the "unconditional objectification of everything present," which was itself the product of a "metaphysical" understanding of the Being of beings carried to its "completion"—constituted a necessary prerequisite for the return to a more primordial relation to Being. For only once the devastation of the earth by *homo laborans* became *total* would the folly of 2500 years of metaphysical thinking become apparent. Only once the objectification of beings had been "consummated" would that long metaphysical night initiated by Platonism stand a chance of coming to a merciful end; only then might the "forgetting of Being" triggered by metaphysical thinking be replaced by a primordial way of thinking, which Heidegger simply refers to as "thought" (*Denken*). It was as if, according to Heidegger, the total nihilism of technological frenzy objectively engendered its opposite—total salvation.[22] Or, to quote the line from Hölderlin that Heidegger was so fond of citing, "Where the danger is, grows the saving power also."

In our view, it is far from coincidental that in the late 1930s, the Heideggerian *Kehre*, as it were, comes full circle, and at this pivotal moment in his philosophical development, his thought turns anew toward the twin idols of the conservative revolutionary generation, Nietzsche and Jünger. For it was their influence above all that was responsible for convincing him in the early 1930s of the value of Germany's National Revolutionary course. When seen from this perspective, the motivation behind the obsessive concern with Nietzsche in the later years of the decade is unequivocal: in Heidegger's own mind, the Nietzsche-related texts represent *an extensive and impassioned exercise in self-criticism.* They signify the philosopher's own attempt to work through those elements of his thought that led to his "great blunder" (his "*grosse Dummheit,*" as Heidegger himself would later refer to it)[23] of the years 1933–1934. Heidegger himself admits as much in the 1966 *Spiegel* interview, where he explicitly refers to the Nietzsche courses as his "confrontation with National Socialism."[24]

"Nietzsche did me in!" was Heidegger's oft-heard lamentation later in life.[25] In retrospect, we can discern the meaning of this cryptic aside with a fair degree of precision. For it was Heidegger's reading of the National Awakening of 1933 in terms of the Nietzschean doctrines of the "will to power," "self-overcoming," and the "superman" that led to his fervid conviction that National Socialism represented the "saving power" for Western humanity and

Germany, *the authentic countermovement to nihilism* prophesied by Nietzsche's Zarathustra.[26] The preoccupation with Nietzsche (and, to a lesser extent, with Jünger), then, must be viewed as a painstaking labor of self-criticism and self-renewal: it represents Heidegger's attempt to purge his thought of those philosophical influences responsible for his fatal political flirtation of the early 1930s; and the "positive" result was to have been a "purified" reformulation of the question of Being, an approach cleansed of all metaphysical residues. From now on, the thinking of Being would be thought "essentially" for the first time. The "Letter on Humanism" (1946) is perhaps the most representative example of this new "postmetaphysical" approach.

However, in emancipating his later philosophy from all metaphysical vestiges, it is by no means clear that the results Heidegger presents us with are unilaterally constructive. In truth, Heidegger's understanding of the major historical events of our century— and as we have tried to show, these events serve as the crucible in which his later, post-*Kehre* philosophy originates—remains woefully mystified; and this misunderstanding perpetuates itself, as it were, in his later philosophy. But this shortfall in his thinking is not merely a "mistake" or an "error of judgment" on the philosopher's part. It is thoroughly overdetermined. Heidegger believes that by expunging the last traces of a "metaphysics of subjectivity" from his later philosophy, he is combating those influences that were responsible for his lamentable "political error." For in his view, the global conflagration set off by National Socialist militarism was, in the last analysis, of *metaphysical origin*. As the citations from "Overcoming Metaphysics" suggest, the world catastrophe is ultimately explicable as the "consummation of metaphysics." The "essential" responsibility for these events must be borne by the world philosophers—Plato, Descartes, and Nietzsche—who gave birth to the metaphysical paradigm that has held sway over Western humanity for some 2500 years. In the end, the tragic events of the mid-twentieth century are merely an especially severe instance of *Seinsvergessenheit*, the forgetting of Being. It is not real-life men and women who are responsible for the course of history; instead history is a product of *Seins-geschick*, it is "sent" by the powers of Being. And the only one with true insight into the essential course of world events is an unassuming philosopher from the southwestern German province of Baden: "The philosopher knows better; *he* knows the metaphysical status of the National Revolution. . . . he alone can explain what it means in a metaphysico-historical sense to overcome nihilism and set truth to work."[27]

As a direct result of the rarefied, postmetaphysical standpoint from which Heidegger chooses to view the events of world history, his capacity for political judgment is seriously diminished—if not incapacitated. The category of the "destiny of Being" becomes the philosophical catch-phrase by means of which everything is explained, but nothing is understood. The Heideggerian interpretation of history becomes an Hegelian night in which all cats are gray: the specificity of concrete historical events blurs into unintelligibility as a result of the leveling gaze of his ethereal categorial framework. Any attempt to dispute his conclusions runs up against the *a priori* objection that it derives from the nether world of nonessential thinking. And thus, every effort to marshal "empirical" findings that might contradict Heidegger's own standpoint is dismissed with a preemptive sweep of the hand. There is no small measure of irony that such shortcomings must be attributed to a thinker whose claim to philosophical originality in the 1920s was based on an avowed revival of the dimension of existential concreteness that was otherwise so lacking in modern philosophy; a thinker whose great achievement was a purported reincorporation of "history"—via the category of "historicity"—into modern philosophical discourse.

In truth, it is the essential facts of twentieth-century political life that Heidegger, time and again, shows himself incapable of comprehending. Or, as Franzen has remarked, "In Heidegger's late philosophy . . . the avoidance of concrete history is in a certain sense perfected."[28] This dilemma is perhaps nowhere as evident as in his leveling conflation of twentieth-century ideologies: fascism, communism, and democracy all stand under the accursed sign of the "will to will." And thus, on the basis of this assumption concerning the "universal rule" of this "will," Heidegger sets forth the following historical reflections regarding the current historical situation (1945):

> Today everything stands under this reality [i.e., "the universal domination of the will to power"] whether it is called communism or fascism or world democracy.
>
> From the standpoint of the reality of the will to power I saw even then [1939–1940] what *is*. This reality of the will to power

143

can be expressed, with Nietzsche, in the proposition: "God is dead." . . . This means: the supersensible world, more specifically the world of the Christian God, has lost its effective force in history. . . . If that were not the case, would World War I have been possible? Even more: if that were not the case, would World War II have become possible?[29]

It is precisely as a result of such metaphysical pseudoexplanations regarding the course of modern historical life—which is especially significant in the case of a thinker like Heidegger, who stakes so much on the claim of having extirpated all metaphysical residues from his philosophy—that the weaknesses of the Heideggerian standpoint of the history of Being become most transparent. One can only agree with Thomas Sheehan when, with reference to the preceding citation, he observes: "[This] statement has about as much explanatory power, and displays as much historical and political wisdom, as the claim that the world is in the grip of Original Sin. Surely if Adam and Eve had not fallen from grace, neither World War I nor World War II would have happened."[30]

In a similar vein, Heidegger will remark in a 1954 text that the outcome of World War II has "essentially" left the course of the world unchanged. That the victory of the allied powers over the fascist dictatorships of Europe might in fact represent the preservation of that Western cultural legacy with which Heidegger claimed to be so concerned is a thought that manifestly never occurs to him. Indeed, the only specific result of the war that he is willing to contemplate—the fact that the privileged "nation in the middle" has itself been divided in two—is a purely negative one. As he observes:

> What has the Second World War actually decided—not to speak of its terrible consequences for our fatherland, especially the laceration down its middle? This World War has decided nothing, if here we take decision in the strong sense, as it pertains uniquely to the essential destiny of man on this earth. Only the indecisiveness of what remains comes a little more clearly into view.[31]

The later Heidegger's attempt to attribute real explanatory significance to concepts such as the "destiny of Being" and the "will to will," in addition to being a philosophical category mistake, is biographically overdetermined. And while the sincerity of Heidegger's belief in the philosophical cogency of such concepts remains beyond doubt, their important function in Heidegger's own psychological economy must also be addressed. For doesn't this method of philosophical argumentation—explanation through metaphysical abstraction—conveniently serve to deflect personal responsibility from Heidegger the man for all possible errors of political judgment? For if the ultimate ground of the German catastrophe must be sought neither in the actions of the German people, nor in the conduct of Adolf Hitler, much less in the insignificant role of a provincial Freiburg philosopher, but instead, *in the mysterious destining of Seinsgeschichte*—then, with a stroke of the pen, all questions of individual and collective responsibility have been conveniently tabled *ad kalendras Graecas*. There can be no question of "personal" or "national" culpability for Germany's unspeakable crimes against the other European peoples, insofar as larger, impersonal, metaphysical forces are to blame. Heidegger, moreover, has done us the service of identifying these forces for us. In truth, since the other European nations (and along with them, the United States) are equally implicated in the modern rule of metaphysics *qua* "technology," they must bear equal responsibility for the disastrous course of European history in the twentieth century.

In this vein, one must seriously inquire whether Heidegger's own philosophical arrogance did not in fact motivate him to fall back on the specious notion of *Seinsgeschick* as a vehicle of historical explanation.[32] For didn't this theory possess the distinct advantage of absolving both himself and Germany (the privileged "nation in the middle") of all direct historical responsibility for the misdeeds of National Socialism? Is it possible that, in a far from trivial sense, the adoption of this cryptic philosophical standpoint became for Heidegger psychologically necessary as a face-saving device, a type of theoretical subterfuge, as the true historical magnitude of his political blunder gradually became clear to him? For might not this political indiscretion—an error of historical and theoretical judgment of the highest order—threaten permanently to taint his considerable philosophical achievement? Moreover, were Heidegger to have publicly admitted his mistake, his entire self-understanding as a philosopher would have been undermined; that is, his self-image as a thinker whose doctrines possessed unmediated, privileged access to the truth of Being.[33] In this way the theory of the history of Being comes to play an essential role in Heidegger's personal strategy of denial.

Further evidence of this strategy may be found in his arrogant, pseudo-Nietzschean dictum in *Aus der Erfahrung des Denkens* (1954) that, "He who thinks greatly must err greatly";[34] a claim which derives from his theory of "erring" (*Irrnis*) as an essential moment of truth. Yet, by invoking the idea that "error" has a necessary role in the history of Being, one can excuse anything—as well as justify anything. And thus, as Löwith has observed, the theory of error as a necessary feature of the destining of Being enables Heidegger to formulate an *ex post facto* "philosophical grounding and justification" for his "erroneous decision" of 1933:

> Exactly at the moment when it discloses itself in beings, Being withdraws itself, and in this way deceives; yet, for all that, "error" actually belongs to the essence of truth! This is true also and primarily of beings in history. Their "essential sphere" is a realm of error. . . . [Thus] what occurs historically is misinterpreted, not owing to personal errors of judgment for which individuals would be responsible, but "necessarily," according to what has been destined by Being [*zufolge eines Seinsgeschicks*].[35]

In the recent debate spurred by the appearance in France of Victor Farias' book, *Heidegger et le Nazisme*, a number of prominent French intellectuals—Maurice Blanchot, Emmanuel Levinas, Philippe Lacoue-Labarthe—have found the most disturbing aspect of "*l'affaire Heidegger*" to be the philosopher's unpardonable refusal to utter a word of remorse for the victims of the Holocaust.[36] But in light of our reconstruction of Heidegger's post-*Kehre* world view, it becomes clear that this refusal was far from a simple crime of omission; nor as several Heideggerians have claimed—thus perpetuating the duplicity of their mentor—was "silence" Heidegger's way of expressing his solidarity with those who had perished, owing to the "unspeakable" character of the crimes that had been committed. Instead, Heidegger's reticence was fully consistent with his postmetaphysical, philosophical antihumanism. For, according to this view, it was not the conscious acts of men and women that were responsible for the unfolding of historical events, but the "destining of Being." A gesture of penitence or contrition toward the victims of National Socialism would have been wholly superfluous according to the strictures of his theoretical standpoint. Moreover, by means of this conceptual framework, the question of historical "fault" or "blame" could not even be posed. Perhaps nowhere more than in this philosophically engendered reticence vis-à-vis the sins of the German past does "essential thinking" stand convicted of moral bankruptcy: by systematically denying the legitimacy of questions of historical responsibility, it even proves capable of effacing the difference between "victims" and "executioners."[37]

A Philosophy of Heteronomy

As we suggested earlier, the essential thinking of the later Heidegger promotes an "eclipse of practical reason." For his post-*Kehre* reformulation of the relation between Being and Dasein rebels so fervently against the voluntarist dimension of his own earlier thinking that the very concept of "meaningful human action" is seemingly rendered null and void. If the early Heidegger attempted to rally Dasein to "decisiveness" (*Entschlossenheit*), the thought of the later Heidegger appears at times to be a summary justification of human passivity and inaction (*Gelassenheit*)—so prejudicially is the balance between *Sein* and *Mensch* struck in favor of the former term. Thus, in the later Heidegger, the campaign against practical reason develops along a two-fold front: not only is the concept of Being grossly inflated, but the powers of human reason and will are correspondingly devalued. In the later writings, Being assumes the character of an omnipotent primal force, a "first unmoved mover," whose "presencing" proves to be the determinative, ultimate instance for events in the lowly world of human affairs. In its other-worldly supremacy, this force both withdraws from the tribunal of human reason and defies the meager capacities of human description: "A Being that not only surpasses all beings—and thus all men—but which like an unknown God rests and 'essences' in its own truth, in that it is sometimes present and sometimes absent, can never be explained like a being in existence; instead, it can only be 'evoked.' "[38]

According to Karl Jaspers, Heidegger's way of thinking is "essentially unfree, dictatorial, and incapable of communication [*communikationslos*]."[39] Nowhere would this judgment prove more apt than with respect to the articulation of the relationship between Being and human existence in his later philosophy. "But Being—what is Being?" inquires Heidegger in the "Letter on Humanism." "It is It itself," he rejoins in a phrase redolent of the "I am who I am" of the Biblical God. It is as though the tautological definition of the word itself were a self-evident indicator of its philosophical profundity. In *Being and Time*, Heidegger could still claim that, "Only so long as Dasein *is*—that is, the ontic possibility of the understanding of Being—'is there' Being." But if we turn to the afterword to the fourth edition of "What is Metaphysics?" (1943), we run across the claim that, "Being *indeed* essences without beings [*das Seinde*], but beings never are without Being" (Heidegger's italics).[40] Thus, in the later theory of the history of Being, an inverse dependency exists between Being and Dasein. And with this reversal of the existential-hermeneutical point of departure of *Being and Time*, it becomes entirely questionable whether Being—now conceived of in its self-subsistent, self-identical primordiality—is in any meaningful sense in the least dependent on the receptivity of Dasein for its "essencing" and "presencing."

With the deification of Being at the expense of Dasein, Heidegger's later philosophy enters into contradictions that undermine its entire credibility as theoretical project. At certain times, he speaks of *Seinsvergessenheit* as a "fate" that is merely a logical consequence of Dasein's narcissistic obsession with its own "self-assertion" (the "will to will"), as a result of which the question of Being itself never gets posed. In a similar vein, he frequently discusses our abandonment by Being as if it could be directly attributed to a series of category mistakes perpetrated by three "essential" philosophers—Plato, Descartes, and Nietzsche. In both cases, however, there seems to be a direct and consequential relationship between the "conduct" of Dasein and the specific "destiny of Being" that humanity must endure.

Yet, elsewhere, Heidegger discusses the "rule" (*walten*) of Being as if it were a self-positing force that bears absolutely no relation to what is willed or not willed by humankind. Thus, for example, in the Nietzsche lectures, Heidegger affirms that the "essence of nihilism is not at all the affair of man, but *a matter of Being itself*."[41] Nor, apparently, does the "abandonment by Being" stand in any essential relation to human practice. Rather, it is a simple result of the fact that "Being withdraws itself."[42] In truth, "The history of Being is neither the history of man and of humanity, nor the history of the human relation to beings and to Being. *The history of Being is Being itself, and only Being*."[43] Or as Heidegger decrees in a characteristically authoritarian pronouncement from the concluding section of "Overcoming Metaphysics": "No mere action will change the state of the world, because Being as effectiveness and effecting [*Wirksamkeit und Wirken*] closes all beings off in the face of the Event."[44] And returning to the "Letter on Humanism," we find the following illuminating specification of the relationship between "man" and "Being": "Man does not decide whether and how beings appear, whether and how God and the gods or history and nature come forward into the lighting of Being, come to presence and depart. *The advent of beings lies in the destiny of Being.* But for man it is ever a question of finding what is fitting in his essence which corresponds to such destiny. . . . Man is the shepherd of Being."[45]

Instead of drawing the logical consequences from the excessively solipsistic articulation of Dasein in *Being and Time* and attempting constructively to reintegrate the latter in a series of intersubjectively oriented world-relations and goals, Heidegger merely leaps to the philosophically contrary extreme: what was previously *constitutive* of all truth-relatedness and unconcealing—Dasein, as that being for which an understanding of truth is essential for its Being—now becomes that which is wholly *constituted*. The irony here is that in his desperate effort to extirpate the last vestiges of a "philosophy of subjectivity" from his thinking, Heidegger has "succeeded" only by endowing Being with the characteristics of an all-powerful metasubject.[46] Moreover, why Being would have any interest in willing its own "oblivion" (*Vergessenheit*) is merely another unfathomable aspect of the theory of *Seinsgeschichte* as a whole.

For Heidegger, what is of primary importance is that "man is 'the neighbor of Being'—not the neighbor of man."[47] And thus, as Emmanuel Levinas has pointed out, the ethical impoverishment of Heidegger's standpoint derives from the fact that it lacks the all-important counterweight of *the Other*—without which all reflection on the nature of human affairs threatens to succumb to a nihilistic abyss of moral meaningless.[48] By radically privileging "Being," *physis*, and "fate" over the mundane, inner-worldly encounters of sentient human beings—that is, by radically privileging *ontology* over *ethics*—the amoralism to which Heideggerianism succumbs in actual fact seems theoretically foreordained. The tendency to write off the intersubjective character of the human life-world as simply a staging-ground for "inauthenticity" is inherited from *Being and Time*. But this practice is radicalized in Heidegger's post-*Kehre* thought, where all prospects for choosing an authentic potentiality-for-Being are preempted *a priori* by the "world-night" of nihilism and *Seinsverlassenheit*. Similarly, the intersubjective character of language—its role in forging human solidarity and mutual recognition—is a matter of indifference to Heidegger. Instead, language, which he defines as "the house of the truth of Being," is of importance only insofar as it plays a role in the arcane pageant of *Seinsgeschichte*.[49]

Thus, insofar as Heidegger characterizes Being as a self-identical substance whose "coming to presence" occurs in a manner that is independent of human comprehension, the category as a whole threatens to lapse into unintelligibility. If "Being" is the absolute and mysterious *transcendens* that Heidegger makes it out to be, it is not clear how "for us" it can be maintained as a legitimate theoretical concept. Instead, he would do better to heed the practice followed by Kant in the first *Critique* with reference to the "thing-in-itself" and admit that, *qua transcendens*, Being cannot be treated as a meaningful aspect of human experience.

The profound antihumanism of the later Heidegger compels one to inquire in all seriousness whether he has in fact ever surmounted those habits of thought that Jaspers described as "essentially dictatorial and unfree." And thus, as Jaspers observes, "[Heidegger's] manner of speaking and his actions have a certain affinity with National Socialist characteristics; these alone begin to make his 'error' comprehensible."[50] For in the helplessness of Dasein vis-à-vis the mysterious coming to presence of the primordial powers of Being, there survives distinct traces of that masochistic submission of the individual to the collective destiny of the *Volksgemeinschaft* under a totalitarian regime. In the later Heidegger, pride of place is accorded to the idea that only via the total self-prostration of Dasein in face of the superior destining of *Seinsgeschichte* might the truth of Being be preserved. The very capacity of Dasein to receive the truths that the lofty forces of Being on occasion deign to dispense is, moreover, a matter that is ultimately determined by the whims of Being itself. The influence of Dasein on the *danse macabre* of *Seinsgeschick* is negligible to nonexistent. Or as Löwith suggests, since for the later Heidegger, Being is characterized as a self-positing "Being-in-itself," "We are thrown back to the question as to whether or not a thinking and perceiving Dasein is at all essential for [Being] to be 'there' and to be 'cleared.'"[51]

Dasein is no longer responsible for its own fate. Instead, it must assume an attitude of passive obedience vis-à-vis the call of Being, to which it stands in a relation of impotent bondage. Is it not, then, in the conspicuously authoritarian requirement that Dasein abandon itself to the despotic rule of nameless, higher powers, that the spirit of Hitler's *Führerstaat* returns to haunt the work of its former vassal? Is the resolute antihumanism of the coercive doctrine of *Seinsgeschichte* not, at least in part, *politically overdetermined*? Do not the ceaseless polemics against the Enlightenment ideal of autonomous subjectivity represent an unconscious reenactment of Germany's own struggle against Weimar liberalism in the name of a more primal, superordinate destiny? Would it be correct to observe that in a crucial sense, Heidegger's later philosophy has remained "unregenerate"; that, in the last analysis, it has remained a *philosophy of heteronomy*—in a manner strongly suggestive of that politics of "total mobilization" whose rhetoric of *Sturm* and *Kampf* ultimately proved so seductive? This is indeed the uncharitable conclusion reached by Karl-Heinz Haag in *Kritik der neueren Ontologie*. As Haag observes: "The world to which ontology as a system corresponds is the totalitarian world whose social organization it imitates and whose metaphysical hierarchy it glorifies."[52] In a similar spirit, Habermas has depicted the relationship between Being, fate, and authority in the later Heidegger as follows:

> Because Being withdraws itself from the assertive grasp of descriptive statements, because it can only be encircled in indirect discourse and 'rendered silent,' the destinings of Being remain undiscoverable. The propositionally contentless speech about Being has, nevertheless, the illocutionary sense of demanding resignation to fate. Its practical-political side consists in the perlocutionary effect of a diffuse readiness to obey in relation to an auratic but indeterminate authority. The rhetoric of the later Heidegger compensates for the propositional content that the text itself refuses: it attunes and trains its addressees in their dealings with pseudo-sacral powers.[53]

The glorification of authority and submission in the work of the later Heidegger, already remarked upon by Haag and Habermas, has been the target of an equally unsparing critique by the philosopher Hans Blumenberg. Thus, in the context of his prodigious defense of the "legitimacy of the modern age," Blumenberg perceives Heidegger's theory of the history of Being as regressing behind the inherited normative potentials of modernity, which emphasize the spirit of criticism, the capacities of autonomous human insight, and the need for an immanent analysis of the trajectory of worldly events. For Blumenberg, the unchallengeable primacy of Being in Heidegger's later work signifies recourse to an *ersatz* divinity; a divinity, moreover, that assumes vengeful traits in response to the hubristic self-assertion of modern man. The end result is a secularized replay of medieval ontology. In the words of Blumenberg:

> The [modern] age appears as an absolute "fact"—or better: as a "datum"; it stands, sharply circumscribed, outside of any logic, adapted to a state of erring [*Irrnis*]; and in spite of its immanent pathos of domination (or precisely on account of it) finally permits only the one attitude that is the sole option that the "history of Being" leaves open to man: *submission*. The absolutism of "Being" is in truth only *the continuation of the medieval result by other means.*[54]

And thus, if upon turning to the text of a 1953 lecture we find the observation: "Thinking begins only when we have come to know that reason, glorified for centuries, is the most stiff-necked adversary of thought"[55]—we cannot help but conclude that in his later work, Heidegger has only sunk more deeply into the bog of *Logosvergessenheit*. This verdict gives cause for dismay, for it suggests that the philosopher has drawn precisely the *wrong* conclusions from the political events of 1933–1945: instead of participating in the attempt to forge, out of the ravages of postwar Europe, a new conception of reason and truth, Heidegger himself has become an even greater "stiff-necked" advocate of counterenlightenment. His thought seeks refuge in the recrudescence of myth: "openness for the mystery," "the remembrance of Being," and "the mirror-play of the four-fold" (gods and mortals, heaven and earth) becomes the mystified categorial scheme around which his later thinking revolves.[56] The notion that analogous counterenlightenment attitudes and doctrines might have played a key role in the spiritual preparation for the German catastrophe is a thought that has obviously never crossed his mind.[57]

A plausible notion of practical reason presupposes a viable conception of human agency. To this end, we must be able to attribute at least some measure of autonomy to human conduct. Actors must be capable of adjudicating both the ends of their actions as well as the appropriate means to achieve those ends. On the basis of their social traditions and individual life-histories, they must be capable of independently evaluating their own values, motivations, and goals. They must possess the capacity to reflect on their own life-choices, and in this way determine whether or not the latter are appropriate to the conception of the "ideal self" or "the good life" they have fashioned for themselves; a point of orientation which subsequently becomes constitutive for "personal identity." Only on the basis of such distinctions does it make sense to speak of our autonomy as human agents and of our projects as defined by the potential for "free action." A viable conception of practical philosophy thus presupposes an understanding of human beings as "free agents"—as "autonomously acting subjects." For our most basic sense of the prerequisites of meaningful human conduct—of what it means to be a responsible human agent—is necessarily tied to our self-understanding as "self-positing subjects"; as persons who are capable, with at least some regularity, of realizing their projects in the world.[58]

Consequently, the major problem with Heidegger's later philosophy is that the doctrine of Being, in its oppressive omnipotence, causes the conceptual space in which freedom can be meaningfully thought to all but disappear. In light of this fact, Jaspers' verdict concerning Heidegger's inability to grasp the nature of human freedom—"Heidegger doesn't know what freedom is"—becomes readily intelligible. For according to the theory of the "destining of Being," all the worldly events we experience undergo a prior, other-wordly, metaontological determination. Like a *deus absconditus*, Being "essences" or "comes to presence" in ways that are inscrutable to the human understanding. On this point, Heidegger is emphatically clear: "The history of Being"—*and not the decisions of man himself*—"underlies and determines every *situation et condition humaine*."[59] But if this description of the human condition is correct, then human action is essentially *unfree*, and the notion of persons as potentially autonomous actors becomes equally incoherent. For the very possibility of a meaningful correlation between human practice and its desired ends has been disqualified in advance: it is not *we* who are ultimately responsible for the outcome of our actions (for "the advent of beings"); rather, it is the "destiny of Being."

Heidegger's incapacity to comprehend the concept of freedom is merely a logical outgrowth of his post-*Kehre* radical antihumanism.[60] The philosophical economy of *Seinsgeschichte* necessitates that the autonomy of human conduct be negated, for in this way alone can Heidegger reconceptualize Dasein as an abject and pliable conduit for Being's "coming to presence." In order to secure Dasein's compliance with the goals of *Seinsgeschichte*, it must be divested of the capacity for free action. Thus, in his 1936 Schelling lecture, Heidegger essentially proclaims the obsolescence of "freedom" as a viable philosophical category—that is, when understood from the "essential" standpoint of *Seinsgeschichte*: "From the originary perspective of the history of Being, '*freedom*' has forfeited *its role*. For Being [*Seyn*] is more originary than the totality of beings and subjectivity."[61] In the few passages of his philosophical *oeuvre* where the category of freedom does manage tentatively to emerge, its meaning is inverted and thereby despoiled. Consequently, according to Heidegger, freedom is no longer "a property of man"; rather, man is "a possibility of freedom."[62] Freedom is ontologically re-defined as "freedom for what is opened up in an open region"; that is, "Freedom now reveals itself in letting beings be," it is essentially "releasement."[63] However, by redefining freedom neo-ontologically as quiescent compliance with the destining of *Seinsgeschichte*, Heidegger has effectively negated the central category of modern Western political thought.

The project of human freedom, incessantly belittled by "essential thinking," receives its inspiration from the conviction that "it is more honest, courageous, self-clairvoyant, hence *a higher mode of life*, to choose in lucidity than it is *to hide one's choices behind the supposed structure of things*."[64] In this respect, the concept of freedom, as it has been handed down to us on the basis of the Greek ideal of *autonomia* or self-rule, represents an indispensable touch-stone of the Western tradition: it has become a *sine qua non* for the ideal of a meaningful human existence. And thus, in a far from trivial sense, we view a life led under conditions of "unfreedom" as a life deprived of an essential prerequisite for the fulfillment of human potential. It would be a life bereft of those autonomous capacities of decision and choice on the basis of which alone we are able to identify and define our projects as *our projects*. We are of course simultaneously defined by a preexisting network of values, institutions, and belief-systems, which have themselves been shaped and handed-down by the members of a given community or group. Yet, it is our capacity to "choose in lucidity" as to which among these would endow our projects with direction and significance that forms the indispensable basis of a meaningful human life.

Once again following the lead of Jaspers, it would thus seem entirely correct to characterize the philosophy of the later Heidegger as a "philosophy of heteronomy." For its chief concern seems to be that of proving that human existence is a condition of perpetual ontological bondage to the unpredictable destining of the powers of Being. Yet, as a philosophy of heteronomy, the theory of *Seinsgeschick* threatens to turn the notion of "meaningful human action" itself into a *non sequitur*. For if our projects are conditioned *a priori* by the random twists and turns of the "destining of Being," there would no longer be even a minimal causal relation between our intentions and the outcome of our worldly undertakings. As heteronomously "fated," our actions would be bereft of the slightest degree of coherence and intelligibility. It is indeed at this point that Heidegger's antisubjectivism reveals its essentially self-defeating character: for it seems that the philosophical cure (antihumanism, "openness to the mystery," "Gelassenheit") proves worse than the disease ("metaphysical thinking," "the will to will," etc.).

It is precisely in this sense that the philosophy of the later Heidegger runs the risk of lagging behind the inherited ethicopolitical foundations of the Western tradition: in its uncritical celebration of a superordinate, nameless destiny, it strives to circumvent the dilemmas of human fallibility and choice by seeking refuge in the allegedly unalterable "structure of things." Its facile repudiation of the faculty of human will—and of practical reason *simpliciter*—as "metaphysical" finds its logical corollary in a senseless glorification of "fate" that is in point of fact equally metaphysical. Heidegger insists in the *Spiegel* interview that philosophy, as well as human endeavor in general, are powerless when it comes to giving directives for practical life: "philosophy will not be able to effect any immediate change in the current state of the world. This is true not only of philosophy but of all purely human reflection and endeavor. Only a god can save us."[65] But is this proclamation of philosophical impotence not merely a classical instance of "projection": a consequent manifestation of the conceptual impoverishment of Heidegger's own later theoretical standpoint; that is, of his unwillingness to think through the admittedly difficult problem of the role practical philosophy is to play in the modern world?

If, as we have argued, Heidegger's later philosophy actively promotes an "eclipse of practical reason," the attempt to redeem his philosophical legacy on the part of the French Heideggerians must also come to naught. In their efforts to downplay the philosophical underpinnings of Heidegger's Nazism, their gambit has been to "sacrifice" the early Heidegger—the author of *Being and Time*—in order to save the post-*Kehre* Heidegger—the author of the "Letter on Humanism" and "Overcoming Metaphysics." According to this interpretive stratagem (which, it should be pointed out, closely parallels Heidegger's own philosophical self-understanding), Heidegger's political "error" may be explained by the fact that his early work is victimized by a *surfeit of metaphysical thinking*. That is, the philosophical approach of *Being and Time* remains overly indebted to the theoretical paradigm of Western humanism, with its glorification of "man," "subjectivity," "will," and so forth; and it was precisely Heidegger's excessive theoretical dependence on this "essentialist" categorial framework that allowed him to be seduced into believing that the "overcoming of nihilism" could be achieved by an actually existing, collective historical "subject"—National Socialist Germany. Hence, it was an overreliance on "metaphysical subjectivism"—the philosophical paradigm with which Heidegger would break so decisively in his post-*Kehre* phase—that was, in truth, responsible for his partisanship for Nazism. Derrida, for example, finds evidence of such metaphysical-humanist excess in Heidegger's uncritical reliance on the concept of "spirit" during the early 1930s:

> At the moment in which his discourse betrays its most spectacular affinity for Nazism . . . Heidegger returns to the word "spirit" which he had [earlier] intentionally avoided, he does away with the quotation marks in which it had been enclosed. He limits the movement of deconstruction in which he had previously engaged. He engages in a *voluntarist and metaphysical discourse,* which he will subsequently [i.e., in his later antimetaphysical writings—R. W.] view with suspicion. To this extent at least, by celebrating the freedom of spirit, its glorification resembles other European discourses (spiritualist, religious, humanist) that people generally consider opposed to Nazism.[66]

According to Derrida's interpretation, which receives its fullest elaboration in *De l'esprit,* the patent distinction between Nazi and non-Nazi discourse falls by the wayside. It is the eminently humanist concept of "spirit" itself that is at the root of Heidegger's engagement for National Socialism. Thus, Derrida seeks to show that in the conception of German destiny, self-determination, etc., articulated by Heidegger in "The Self-Affirmation of the German University" and elsewhere, the German philosopher merely employs the standard refrains of Western metaphysical thought.[67] For after all, what is "self-affirmation" but the deepest confirmation of the Western, Cartesian-metaphysical longing for self-legislation and autonomy? Consequently, everything Heidegger demands for the German Volk on the basis of the category of "self-affirmation" is perfectly consistent with an Hegelian "metaphysics of spirit"— with that very notion of self-positing *Geist* that informs so much of the Western philosophical tradition. Derrida's conclusion: although many of us are inclined to make a tidy intellectual separation between Nazism and non-Nazism, thus mercifully sparing the legacy of metaphysical humanist thinking from having to own up to its own fundamental deficiencies, this separation cannot at all be maintained. "Nazism" and "non-Nazism" pass over to each other with great frequency and fluidity.

But here one can only react with astonishment at the ease with which Derrida is seduced by the *philosophical veneer* of Heidegger's Rectoral Address—the perfunctory allusions to "spirit," the glory of the "Greek beginning," and so on; as if this veneer itself could explain the philosopher's Nazism better than the rhetorical-ideological core of the speech, which Derrida strangely refuses to analyze. In truth, what is unique about Heidegger's speech (see the discussion in chapter 3 above) is that one finds for the first time in his work the awkward and unabashed attempt to fuse traditional philosophical motifs with the Nazi discourse of *Sturm* and *Kampf.* Heidegger's efforts were unsuccessful, his audience was left dazed and confused (cf. Löwith's remark that students departed the auditorium "wondering whether they should begin reading the pre-Socratics or enlist in the SA"), precisely insofar as these two discourses—one universalistic, the other woefully particularistic; one a discourse of reason, the other a discourse of force—*are intrinsically at odds with one another.* It is in fact much more likely (as Derrida himself virtually admits at one point with reference to Heidegger's implicit critique of Nazi biological theories)[68] that the metaphysical residues of Heidegger's world-view are what in fact *prevented him* from identifying unreservedly with the policies of the Third Reich; and that whatever "spiritual resistance" Heidegger was able to accomplish was due to his *fidelity* to a Western intellectual narrative that began with the Greeks. In attempting to efface prematurely the differences between humanism and antihumanism—and thereby the differences between Nazism and anti-Nazism—Derrida allows himself to be misled too easily by the Nazi

157

"rhetoric of humanism"; that is, by a "pseudohumanism," beneath which a virulent antihumanism—a grotesque *violation* of the belief in the value of men and women as ends in themselves—lies concealed.

A perfect instance of this standard, pseudouniversalist duplicity, which was highly characteristic of National Socialist political rhetoric in the early phases of Hitler's dictatorship, may be discerned in the case of the November 1933 plebiscite on Germany's secession from the League of Nations. The arguments for Germany's withdrawal from the League were theatrically couched in the Wilsonian rhetoric of national self-determination; arguments, moreover, that Heidegger would repeat verbatim in his election-eve appeal of November 11, 1933.[69] But it is not very difficult to discern that the pseudouniversalistic oratory of the regime was largely instrumental in character; and that beneath this rhetorical cover, purposes more sinister and diabolical lay in mind. As Joachim Fest has noted, the plebiscite was "one of [Hitler's] most effective chess moves in the process of consolidating his power within Germany."[70] The insincere appeal to Wilsonian principles tended to reassure Hitler's wavering, middle-of-the-road supporters, and thus brought a crucial semblance of domestic respectability to the regime in its tenuous first year of power. Through recourse to the methods of immanent critique, however, we can certainly distinguish between those who live up to their self-professed ideals and those who merely employ such ideals for self-serving, instrumental gain (the pseudouniversalism of Western imperialism in the second half of the nineteenth century would be another example thereof).

Further, the ideal of self-positing spirit, as elaborated for example by Hegel, is integrally tied to the notion of critical self-reflection; e.g., in the case of the Hegelian "shapes of consciousness" (*Gestalten des Bewusstseins*) whose internal inadequacies are to be measured against the tribunal of Reason. That the claims of self-actualizing spirit admit to evaluation by the criteria of rational self-reflection implies that not *every* claimant to *Geist* can prove worthy of the appellation. Thus, even if National Socialism (or, what is more likely, its philosophically inclined exponents) chose to legitimate itself in terms of the "dialectics of spirit," the "discourse of spirit" itself possesses the conceptual tools by virtue of which it is capable of giving the lie to such assertions; of unmasking this ideology as the regressive phenomenon it is in truth. The tradition of Western rationalism shows its uniqueness precisely by virtue of this capacity for self-criticism.

Derrida goes on to observe that "Nazism would not have been able to develop without the variegated, yet decisive complicity of other European nations, 'democratic' states, religious and academic institutions. Throughout this European network, this hymn to the freedom of spirit—which is at the very least compatible with that of Heidegger, precisely in the Rectoral Address and other analogous texts—is always pompously raised."[71] In such remarks (as well as in his earlier claim concerning the confluence of Nazi and anti-Nazi discourse), Derrida runs the risk of following too closely the mistaken lead of Heidegger's own strategy of denial. For like Heidegger, he too seeks to understand the origins of National Socialism in terms of its status as a *metaphysical occurrence*, that is, primarily in relation to the occidental metanarrative he calls "the hymn to the freedom of spirit." But one of the major problems with this reliance on the "metaphysics of spirit" as an explanatory scheme is that it tends to discount the nature of National Socialism as a *specifically German phenomenon*—as the product of a highly specific set of historical circumstances and conditions (the Versailles treaty, economic collapse, political instability, lack of democratic traditions, authoritarian social structure, etc.). For there are many aspects of the movement—its racial ideology, for example—which are, strictly speaking, incompatible with the other variants of fascism *qua* "normal despotisms," let alone incompatible with those forms of political life we are accustomed to calling democratic. In sum, the explanatory power of this Derridean "hymn to the freedom of spirit" seems much too diffuse to be able to account for the historical success of National Socialism as well as the "decisive complicity of other European nations." Moreover, by focusing so exclusively on this particular metaphysical "hymn," Derrida himself ironically runs the risk of "spiritualizing" the origins and causes of European fascism. Or as Otto Pöggeler warns with regard to recent French attempts to comprehend National Socialism on the basis of the "history of ideas": "That National Socialism was able to come to power and destroy Europe is not comprehensible apart from certain ideological presuppositions or the blindness of people like Heidegger; however, to try to understand politics and history from such [ideological] presuppositions alone is to misuse philosophy."[72]

Like Derrida, for Philippe Lacoue-Labarthe, although Heidegger's political involvement is "absolutely consistent with his thought," in the last analysis, this claim says nothing about the specificity of Heidegger's philosophy *per se*. Rather, his "error" may ultimately be attributed to "metaphysical" habits of thought, which Heidegger shares historically with any number of thinkers. Hence, one would be justified in tracing Heidegger's error back to the misdeeds of the earliest metaphysician, Plato, who was the first to launch the doctrine of "philosopher kings": "The engagement of 1933 derives its legitimacy from the idea of a hegemony of the spiritual and the philosophical over political hegemony itself . . . which goes back at least to the Platonic *basileus*." In this way, Lacoue-Labarthe justifies the "temptation" of explaining Heidegger's "engagement" in terms of *"the pressures of a thought insufficiently disengaged from metaphysics."*[73] Lacoue-Labarthe's logic of argumentation therefore also pushes in the direction of a redemption of the "postmetaphysical" or post-*Kehre* Heidegger.

However, the verdict of both thinkers follows the mystified self-interpretation of Heidegger himself on a crucial point: *viz.*, that "metaphysics" ("spirit," "voluntarism," etc.) is somehow ultimately responsible for the philosopher's foolhardy political engagement. But as we have sought to demonstrate, this method of argumentation in truth "explains away" rather than clarifies. More importantly, however, our conclusions suggest that in consequence of its repudiation of practical philosophy, Heidegger's later thought—which both Lacoue-Labarthe and Derrida celebrate as being free of the metaphysical-humanist residues of *Being and Time*—lacks the necessary conceptual means through which the nightmare of National Socialism (and thus the philosopher's own "error") could be "worked through" in an intellectually fruitful manner. Instead, the theory of *Seinsgeschick* functions as an elaborate mechanism of denial. In their attempt to vindicate the later, nonmetaphysical Heidegger, the French Heideggerians thus play directly into the hands of Heidegger's own apologetic tendencies.

The "Leveling Gaze" of Heidegger's Later Philosophy

Heidegger's critique of technology, the predominant theme in his later work, is of a piece with the critique of modernity originally elaborated in the Nietzsche lectures.[74] There is little doubt that in his treatment of this problem, Heidegger addresses one of the central dilemmas of twentieth-century social life. Here, moreover, his philosophical concerns converge with those of a wide variety of twentieth-century philosophers and cultural critics—ranging from the Frankfurt School and Lewis Mumford to the conservative cultural criticism of Spengler and Arnold Gehlen.[75] And while it would be an act of bad faith to trivialize his contributions toward understanding the theoretical origins and complexities of this problem, one is nevertheless obliged to inquire as to whether the theoretical framework of the history of Being actually enhances our ability to cope with the realities of technology in the modern world, or instead tends to obscure the truly important questions at issue.

For Heidegger, it is essential that technology not be understood as "applied science," that is, as a series of practical capacities and means that would in some way be separable from the perspective of theoretical science *per se*. Rather, the reverse would be true: "modern natural science is grounded in the development of the essence of modern technology."[76] Thus, it is not as though the putative "neutrality" of scientific method has been somehow distorted via improper and thoughtless application. Instead, according to Heidegger, the sham-objectivity of modern natural science must be stripped away. Then alone might we realize that science itself is engaged in a prejudicial mode of "unconcealment" or "presencing," whose results are the pathologies of technological reason to which our century bears manifold and painful witness.

Hence, when viewed "essentially," technology refers to something much more insidious and pervasive than the mere "misapplication" of scientific method: it represents a metaphysical "world-picture" (cf. his 1938 essay, "The Age of the World-Picture") by means of which beings are "unconcealed," but never known in their essence, whose origins may be found in the Cartesian division of the world into *res cogitans* and *res extensa*. In Heidegger's view, this world-picture, whose essence he will characterize as *Gestell* or "enframing," retrospectively defines the totality of modes in which Being has been apprehended since the instauration of modern metaphysics with Descartes. As a process of "enframing," technology signifies a metaphysical standpoint whereby a "subject" counterposes itself to the totality of existing "objects" (*Gegen-stände*) for the purpose of subordinating them to an imperious logic of domination and control. As such, it becomes the signature or defining feature of the modern world in all its aspects. Thus, what "we" call "technology"—including the unprecedented catastrophes (the "devastation of the earth" resulting from the "unconditional objectification of everything present") that have marked the history of this century—is merely the end result of the idea of the "will to will," whose ultimate, metaphysical formulation was provided by Descartes. It is important to keep in mind, however, that this process, which *appears* to be the result of a philosophical false step on the part of Descartes that subsequently becomes determinative for the course of Western modernity as a whole, is in truth a product of the *destining of Being*.

It is precisely in this sense that technology must be understood as the "consummation of metaphysics." For it represents the apocalyptical culmination of over two millennia of *Seinsvergessenheit*; a fate which is itself the result of a metaphysical standpoint in which "beings" are comprehended solely as "Being-for-Other"—for man *qua* "subject" or "master of the earth"—instead of "let be" in the restful simplicity of their Being. Our concepts never reach the essence of beings—their Being—for our metaphysical habits predispose us only to see what we have already put into them: ourselves. As Heidegger explains:

> The basic form of appearance in which the will to will arranges and calculates itself in the unhistorical element of the world of completed metaphysics can be stringently called "technology." This name includes all the areas of beings which equip the whole of beings: objectified nature, the business of culture, manufactured politics, and the gloss of ideals overlying everything. Thus "technology" does not signify here [merely] the separate areas of the production and equipment of machines. . . . [It] is understood here in such an essential way that its meaning coincides with the term "consummated metaphysics."[77]

In Heidegger's estimation, the reign of metaphysics *qua* technology in the modern world is absolute and total. But as we have seen, the universal reduction of all beings to technological enframing finds its "positive" corollary in the fact that the consummation of metaphysics simultaneously represents the precondition for its "overcoming" (*Überwindung*): only the total oblivion of the distinction between Being and beings suggests the prospect that this forgetting will be felt as essential affliction (*Not*).[78] Since enframing becomes the exclusive mode through which beings are uncovered in the modern world, the totality of the real takes on the character of "standing reserve" (*Bestand*): things become entirely devoid of intrinsic meaning and significance; they are not known essentially or in the manner of their "Being." Instead, they become meaningful only as part of the machinery of a gigantic "ordering process" set in motion by the modern economy. Nor is man *qua* "subject" of this process exempted from its all-encompassing logic of domination and control. As Heidegger observes:

> The forester who, in the wood, measures the felled timber and to all appearances walks the same forest path in the same way as did his grandfather is today commanded by profit-making in the lumber industry, whether he knows it or not. He is made subordinate to the orderability of cellulose, which for its part is challenged forth by the need for paper, which is then delivered to newspapers and illustrated magazines. The latter, in their turn, set public opinion to swallowing what is printed, so that a set configuration of opinion becomes available on demand.[79]

In remarks such as these concerning the all-pervasive nature of the forces of "profit-making" and "industry" in the modern world, Heidegger comes close to abandoning his penchant for an abstract-metaphysical analysis of contemporary social conditions in favor of an approach that is both concrete and historical. The passage just cited, for example, contains important rudiments of the Hegelian-Marxist theory of "reification."[80] Were he to expand these insights in conjunction with a sociologically informed "phenomenology of the contemporary life-world," the result might have been an extremely fruitful interweaving of philosophical and sociohistorical motifs. But characteristically, Heidegger prematurely abandons the potential for historical concretion embodied in this theory and immediately relapses into the mystified perspective of neo-ontology.[81]

Thus, for the sake of internal consistency—and in keeping with the antihumanist tenor of the theory of *Seinsgeschichte*—Heidegger must argue against all attempts to understand technology in "anthropological" terms, that is, as a direct result of human action or intention. Hence, the theory of "reification" is disqualified, insofar as the pathologies of technology cannot be explained in terms of the Hegelian, subject-centered paradigm of "alienation" (whereby *Entäusserung* becomes *Entfremdung*). The dilemmas of modern technology have nothing to do with the inability of "humanity" *qua* collective subject to control the technological apparatus. Instead, for Heidegger, as we have already seen, the imperious will to self-assertion that is implicit in the concept of modern subjectivity itself is precisely the problem. Consequently, if the "danger" of technology lies in the "possibility that all revealing will be consumed in ordering and that everything will present itself only in the unconcealedness of standing-reserve," nevertheless, *"Human activity can never directly counter this danger."*[82] Insofar as "modern technology as an ordering revealing is no merely human doing,"[83] its triumph must be mythologically traced back to the "destining of Being" itself: its primordial source is "enframing," rather than, say, a concrete historical social formation—capitalism—that has over the course of time assumed an independent logic. And thus, insofar as the dominion of "enframing" is a "destiny" wholly independent of the powers of human action or will, those powers can play no role in reversing this condition. Thus, *Seinsgeschick is a fate humanity is condemned passively to endure.* Or as Heidegger himself observes, all depends on whether "Being itself reaches its culmination [*ins Letzte geht*] and reverses the oblivion which derives from Being itself."[84]

Heidegger's inability to conceptualize the sociohistorical determinants and character of modern technology raises the oft-discussed question of the "pseudo-concreteness of his philosophy"; that is, its apparent incapacity to fulfill its original phenomenological promise as a philosophy of "existential concretion."[85] The problem was already evident in the tension between the ontological and ontic levels of analysis that dominated the existential analytic of *Being and Time*. For there the sphere of ontic life seemed degraded *a priori* as a result of its monopolization by the "They" and its concomitant inauthentic modalities. As a result, both the desirability and possibility of effecting the transition from the metalevel of ontology to the "factical" realm of ontic concretion seemed problematical from the outset. Nowhere was this problem better illustrated than in the case of the category of historicity. And thus despite Heidegger's real insight into limitations of Dilthey's historicism,[86] the inflexible elevation of ontology above the ontic plane virtually closes off the conceptual space wherein real history might be thought. In truth, it can only appear as an afterthought: as the material demonstration of conclusions already reached by the categories of existential ontology. Consequently, the "ontology of *Being and Time* is still bound to the metaphysics that it rejects. The conventional tension between *existentia* and *essentia* stands behind the difference between everyday (factical) and 'authentic historical existence.' "[87]

The ahistorical "pseudo-concreteness" of the early work reproduces itself in Heidegger's later philosophy, but on an apparently higher plane. And thus, in Heidegger's "metaphysical" (*seinsgeschichtlich*) formulation of the problem of technology, the fundamental deficiencies of his philosophical framework in its entirety come to the fore. For his claim concerning the total domination of technology *qua* enframing, coupled with his wholesale devaluation of the powers of human action, in the end only prove conducive to further resignation and passivity vis-à-vis *Seins-geschick*—the mysterious "fate" that humanity has been "sent."

In this regard, one of the foremost problems of Heidegger's theory of "enframing" is that it results in the *demonization* of technology. And although on several occasions he specifically denies allegations to this effect,[88] the force of his own arguments provides ample testimony to the contrary. Hence, because technology as the "consummation of metaphysics" is primarily conceptualized as an inexorable fate that is "destined" by the history of Being itself, the only alternative we are left with is to submit disconsolately and hope against hope for an eventual shift in the winds of Being. Or as Heidegger remarks in *Gelassenheit*:

> [T]echnological advance will move faster and faster and *can never be stopped*. In all areas of his existence, man will be encircled ever more tightly by the forces of technology. These forces, which everywhere and every minute claim, enchain, and drag along, press and impose upon man under the form of some technical contrivance or other—these forces, since man has not made them, *have moved long since beyond his will and have outgrown his capacity for decision*.[89]

Since the doctrine of the history of Being has already banished all categories of practical reason from its theoretical purview, we are left with two complementary extremes that combine to produce the image of a *totally reified world from which there can be no escape*—for, strictly speaking, there are no "social actors" left to alter its course. On the one hand, there is the implacable advance of technology itself, which "can never be stopped"; on the other hand, there is a wholesale devaluation of the possibilities for human action, which has the performative consequence of encouraging a total submission to fate. In the last analysis, Heidegger's theory ends up reinforcing the logic of technological domination it claims to oppose: technology is ontologized as the modern *con-*

165

dition humaine, and our historical capacities for resisting or re-
shaping this fate are written off *a priori* as merely a further expression of the nefarious and omnipresent "will to will." As Richard
Bernstein has remarked, this standpoint is

> not only totally inadequate, but is itself extremely dangerous—
> dangerous because it seduces us into thinking that all human
> activity (other than the activity of thinking) reduces itself—flat-
> tens out—into *Gestell,* manipulation, control, will to will, ni-
> hilism; dangerous because it virtually closes off the space for at-
> tending to the type of thinking and acting that can foster human
> solidarity and community.[90]

Ironically, for all his criticisms of Nietzsche, Heidegger's own
position remains eminently "Nietzschean" in at least one crucial
respect: he accepts without question the standpoint of "total critique" that Nietzsche himself adopts vis-à-vis the failings of the
modern age. Thus, for both thinkers, the essence of modernity is
faithfully captured by the category of "nihilism": a wholesale dissolution of the structures of value and belief that have traditionally
made life meaningful. The method of "immanent critique" is rejected insofar as there is essentially nothing about modernity as a
social formation that is worth redeeming.

Since according to Heidegger's neo-ontological restatement of
the "decline of the West" (as he remarks at one point, "Nihilism
is the world-historical movement of the peoples of the earth who
have been drawn into the power realm of the modern age"),[91] all
immanent prospects of historical renewal are blocked in advance,
there is only one route remaining by virtue of which the "saving
power" might enter historical life: *viz., transcendence.* Thus, in the
explanatory schema embraced by Heidegger, *praxis* has been disqualified, *technē* has become all-dominant, and consequently
poēsis—in the form of "poetic transcendence"—becomes the only
option available: "The poetical brings the true into the splendor
of what Plato in the *Phaedrus* calls *to ekphanestaton,* that which
shines forth most purely," observes Heidegger.[92] "The only possibility available to us is that by thinking and poetizing we prepare
a readiness for the appearance of a god, or for the absence of a god
in [our] decline, insofar as in view of the absent god we are in a
state of decline."[93] In the end, Heidegger's critique of modernity
ends up by retracing the well-worn path already trod by the German romantics: "poetic transcendence" is abstractly counterposed

to the ills of modern world consumed by the imperatives of technical reason. Thus, "To 'dwell poetically' means: to stand in the presence of the gods and to be involved in the proximity of the essence of things."[94] This is Heidegger's solution to an age of (double) "affliction": an age that is caught between "the no-longer of the gods that have fled and the not-yet of the god to come."[95]

In Heidegger's critique of technology, we see a profound longing to be free of the "rationality imperatives" of the modern world in their entirety. Rather than attempting to isolate the process whereby instrumental reason, as tied to the forces of the modern economy, has been elevated to the status of an end in itself at the expense of its practical corollary, his theoretical orientation seeks instead to promote a *rejection of rationality in toto*. As a result, both practical as well as technical reason are reductively dismissed as merely interchangeable variants of "metaphysical thinking." Heidegger is unwilling (or unable) to contemplate the prospect that it is the historically conditioned *imbalance* between these two rationality types, instrumental and practical, rather than the evils inherent in reason *per se*—which for Heidegger, as we have seen, represents "the most stiff-necked adversary of thought"—that is responsible for modernity's technological excrescences. By opting for "poetic dwelling"[96] as the only valid alternative to *technē* and *praxis*—the latter is erroneously denigrated as a mere variant of the former—his thought proves incapable of reflecting on the nature of this imbalance.

Heidegger's theory of technology ultimately collapses under the weight of its own self-imposed conceptual limitations. And thus, the intrinsic shortcomings of his theoretical framework prevent him from entertaining the prospect that the problem of technological domination owes more to the *dearth* of reason in the modern world rather than an *excess*. For in modern life, the parameters of rationality have been prematurely *restricted*: formal or instrumental reason has attained *de facto* hegemony; practical reason—reflection on *ends*—has been effectively marginalized. Instead of the "overcoming" of reason recommended by Heidegger, what is needed is an *expansion* of reason's boundaries, such that the autonomous logic of instrumental rationality is subordinated to a rational reflection on ends. Similarly, Heidegger's incessant lamentations concerning the "will to will"—the theoretical prism through which he views the modern project of human self-assertion in its entirety—only serve to confuse the problem at issue.[97] That the forces of technology and industry follow an independent logic that remains *divorced* from the tribunal of human reason poses an incomparably greater threat to the quality of life in the modern world than the powers of human will as such, against which Heidegger ceaselessly polemicizes. Thus, it is not human agency *per se* that must be faulted; rather, it is the fact that technical and economic imperatives have been *uncoupled from* the controlling scrutiny of human reason and will, resulting in a seemingly blind and unlimited proliferation of technological development.

The ultimate proof of the bankruptcy of Heidegger's later thought—including the critique of technology that represents an integral moment thereof—may well be contained in a relatively obscure remark from his 1949 lecture series, "Insight into That Which Is." For it is this observation that perhaps best reveals the "leveling" tendencies inherent in his theory of the "destiny of Being," his incapacity for making rational sociohistorical judgments, as well as his insensitivity to the suffering of the victims of Nazism. According to Heidegger:

> Agriculture is today a motorized food industry, in essence the same as the manufacture of corpses in gas chambers and extermination camps, the same as the blockade and starvation of countries, the same as the manufacture of atomic bombs.[98]

That Heidegger can in good conscience equate mechanized agriculture with the genocidal politics of the Nazis is not only a monumental *non sequitur* in historical reasoning; it suggests a fundamental incapacity for both moral and theoretical discernment. It is at this point that his thought fully regresses behind the standards of the healthy human understanding that he treated with unremitting condescension throughout his life.[99] This judgment, far from representing a momentary lapse, is wholly consistent with the "leveling gaze" of the theory of *Seinsgeschick* in general, *viz.*, its endemic propensity for equating incomparables. Ironically, here we see metaphysics at its purest: a theoretically conditioned insensitivity to the concrete specificity of the phenomena of contemporary historical life. Above all, Heidegger's observation proves shocking insofar as it signifies a calculated regression behind the received standards of twentieth-century morality, which have been "indexed" in relation to the unspeakable crimes of the Holocaust. It is as though Heidegger, in a characteristic gesture of philosophical arrogance, has by means of this deliberate provocation intentionally withdrawn from the community of "rational natures"—

and thereby, from the fellowship of other human beings. We have already seen how Heidegger's later philosophy presents us with a series of "false equations" that in turn become the basis for a set of dogmatic historico-philosophical judgments: "philosophy" = "metaphysics" = "the will to will" = "technology" = "nihilism." In the remarks just cited, we are confronted with an analogous series of false parallels that are purportedly illustrative of the un-challenged hegemony of technological domination in modern life. But if these are the practical conclusions toward which Heidegger's philosophy necessarily tends, one cannot help but doubt the underlying cogency of his conceptual framework in its entirety.

If there is some truth to the claim that, "We can, if needs be, distinguish theories according to whether or not they are structurally related to possible emancipation,"[100] then the philosophy of Martin Heidegger must be judged profoundly wanting.

NOTES

1. Heidegger and Politics

1. Pöggeler's "Afterword" appeared only in the 1984 edition of his work, which is widely regarded as the "standard" commentary on Heidegger's philosophical development, and which received the official benediction of Heidegger himself. It would be of interest to trace the trajectory of Pöggeler's own attitudes (he is considered by most to be Germany's leading Heidegger scholar) toward the problem of "Heidegger and Politics" over the course of the last two decades. When his study first appeared in 1963, the theme did not even merit treatment. His 1972 book on the subject, *Philosophie und Politik bei Heidegger*, is disappointingly apologetic. However, in the several essays he has written since the republication of Heidegger's 1933 Rectoral Address in 1983, he has shown himself to be a champion of forthrightness regarding the difficult hermeneutical questions that have recently arisen in connection with Heidegger's politics; questions that will undoubtedly prove central for all future Heidegger interpreters.

2. Victor Farias, *Heidegger et le nazisme*; and Hugo Ott, *Martin Heidegger: Unterwegs zu seiner Biographie*. To their efforts should be added Thomas Sheehan's impressive overview of the controversy in the *New York Review of Books*, "Heidegger and the Nazis."

Unlike Ott, who respects the limitations of strictly biographical research, Farias' study, to its detriment, too often crosses the delicate line between fact-finding and unwarranted philosophical generalization—in effect, "condemnation." I have discussed the relative merits and deficiencies of Farias' account in my essay, "The French Heidegger Debate" (*New German Critique*; Fall 1988). In "Recherches récentes sûr la relation de Martin Heidegger au national so-

171

cialisme," (*Les Temps Modernes*; October 1987), I have attempted to appraise Ott's findings in light of a number of larger questions they suggest concerning Heidegger's overall status as a philosopher.

3. The documentary evidence assembled in Guido Schneeberger's *Nachlese zu Heidegger* (1962) represented an important first step in this process.

4. Cited in Ott, *Martin Heidegger*, p. 187.

5. Reported by Karl Jaspers in his *Philosophische Autobiographie*; an English translation may be found in *The Philosophy of Karl Jaspers*, ed. P. A. Schlipp (La Salle, Ill.: Open Court, 1981), p. 75/8.

6. Heidegger, "The University in the New Reich," in "Political Texts, 1933–1934," p. 100.

7. Heidegger, "German Students," in ibid., p. 101.

8. See Farias, *Heidegger et le nazisme*, pp. 234ff.; Ott, *Martin Heidegger*, pp. 201–213.

9. See Ott, "Martin Heidegger als Rektor der Universität Freiburg i. Br.—Die Zeit des Rektorats von M. Heidegger," p. 108.

10. Cited by Ott in "Martin Heidegger als Rektor der Universität Freiburg i. Br., 1933–1934," p. 356; emphasis added.

11. Toni Cassirer, *Mein Leben mit Ernst Cassirer* (Hildesheim: Gerstenberg, 1981), p. 182.

12. Martin Heidegger, "Only a God Can Save Us," p. 51. Heidegger's denial has been contested by Leopoldine Weizmann, "Heidegger, était-il Nazi?" *Études* 368 (5) (May 1988), p. 638: "Heidegger interdit alors à Husserl l'accès à l'université parce qu'il était juif."

13. See Ott, *Martin Heidegger*, pp. 198ff. ; and Thomas Sheehan, "Heidegger and the Nazis," pp. 40–41.

14. Ulrich Sieg, "Die Verjudung des deutschen Geistes: Ein unbekannter Brief Heideggers," *Die Zeit* 52, December 29, 1989, p. 19.

15. Farias, *Heidegger et le nazisme*, p. 235; see also Thomas Sheehan, "Heidegger and the Nazis," p. 40.

16. See "Ein Gespräch mit Max Müller," p. 23.

17. Leopoldine Weizmann, "Heidegger, était-il Nazi?" p. 638.

18. Additional evidence—such as the claim by Heidegger-intimate Heinrich Petzet that Heidegger felt ill at ease in cities, especially with reference to "the mundane spirit of Jewish circles, which is at home in the metropolitan centers of the West"—has been provided by Sheehan in "Heidegger and the Nazis," p. 41.

19. Jürgen Habermas, "Heidegger: Werk und Weltanschauung," in Victor Farias, *Heidegger und der Nationalsozialismus*, p. 23. An English translation of this essay ("Work and Weltanschauung: The Heidegger Controversy from a German Perspective") has recently appeared in Habermas, *The New Conservatism: Cultural Criticism and the Historians' Debate*, trans. Shierry Weber Nicholsen (Cambridge, Mass. : MIT Press, 1989), pp. 140–172.

20. For more on this theme, see George Mosse, *The Crisis of German Ideology: the Intellectual Origins of the Third Reich*.

21. For an especially vivid example of the extent to which Heidegger personally identified with the *völkisch* mentality of the German provinces, see his essay "Why Do I Stay in the Provinces?" For a more extended discussion of the essential role played by antimodernist attitudes in both Heidegger's politi-

cal thought and his philosophy itself, see the discussion of these themes in chapter 2.

22. Cited by Ott in *Martin Heidegger*, pp. 305–306.

23. Representative of the first tendency is the diatribe by François Fédier, *Heidegger: l'anatomie d'un scandale*; illustrative of the second is Richard Rorty's essay, "Taking Philosophy Seriously," *The New Republic* (April 11, 1988), pp. 31ff.

24. The two previous times the question had been debated extensively in public occurred, significantly, in French journals.

The first exchange occurred in the pages of *Les Temps Modernes* in 1946 and 1947–48. It was provoked by an essay by former Heidegger student and intimate, Karl Löwith, "Les implications politiques de la philosophie de l'existence chez Heidegger." Responses to Löwith's position were composed by Alfons de Waelhens ("La philosophie de Heidegger et le nazisme") and Eric Weil ("Le cas Heidegger"), *Les Temps Modernes* 4 (1947–48); 115—138. Löwith subsequently responded to Waelhens ("Réponse à A. de Waelhens"), who then in the same issue delivered a concluding, "Réponse à cette réponse"; *Les Temps Modernes* 4 (1947–48); 370–377.

The second debate occurred in the mid-1960s in the pages of the review *Critique*. It was set off by François Fédier's 1966 review essay, "Trois attaques contre Heidegger," a critique of three German books on Heidegger (P. Hühnerfeld's *In Sachen Heidegger*, Schneeberger's *Nachlese zu Heidegger*, and Adorno's *Jargon der Eigentlichkeit*). The following year, Robert Minder, Jean Pierre Faye, and Aimé Patri responded to Fédier's position (*Critique* 237 [February 1967]; 672–686). Finally, Fédier delivered a rebuttal to his antagonists in the July 1967 issue of the same journal. A fair summary of the basic positions in this debate has been provided by Beda Alleman, "Martin Heidegger und die Politik," in Otto Pöggeler ed., *Heidegger: Perspektiven zur Deutung seines Werkes*.

25. The most convincing proof of this fact is provided by Nicholas Tertulian, "Quand le discours heideggerien se mue en prise de position politique," as well as the article by Thomas Sheehan cited in note 2.

26. The most concerted efforts to date to reinterpret the foundations of Heidegger's philosophy on the basis of the new awareness concerning the depths of his political engagement may be found in *Heidegger und die praktische Philosophie*, eds. O. Pöggeler and A. Gethmann-Siefert (see especially the essays by, Pöggeler, Franzen, Schwan, and Gethmann). Also worthy of note are three earlier pioneering studies concerning the theme of Heidegger and politics: Alexander Schwan, *Philosophie und Politik bei Heidegger*; Winfried Franzen, *Von der Existenzialontologie zur Seinsgeschichte;* and Karsten Harries, "Heidegger as a Political Thinker."

27. See Tertulian's essay cited in note 25; and Jürgen Habermas, "Heidegger: Werk und Weltanschauung," pp. 11–37.

28. See Franzen, "Die Sehnsucht nach Härte und Schwere," in *Heidegger und die praktische Philosophie*, pp. 78–92.

29. Ibid. , p. 80.

30. This seems to be true in modern life above all in the case of *aesthetics*, which, since the romantic era, under the guise of "aestheticism," has increasingly assumed the character of a full-fledged philosophy of life. It is this conviction that unites various theorists of the aesthetic sphere, from Schiller to

Flaubert to Nietzsche to Oscar Wilde to the Surrealists; who, despite their multiple and sundry divergences, agree on the fact that the aesthetic sphere embodies a source of value and meaning that is superior to "mere life" in its prosaic and routinized everydayness. In this respect, in the modern world aesthetics has become one of the foremost repositories of the *critique of instrumental reason*. Perhaps the philosopher who was most consequent in drawing theoretical conclusions from this state of affairs was Theodor Adorno, who in his *Aesthetic Theory* tries to reestablish the possibility of social theory on an aesthetic foundation.

31. Karl Löwith, *Mein Leben in Deutschland vor und nach 1933*, p. 57.
32. Heidegger, *Hölderlins Hymnen "Germanien" und "Der Rhein,"* p. 134.
33. Leo Strauss, *Studies in Platonic Political Philosophy*, p. 30.
34. Heidegger, *Existence and Being*, p. 289.
35. Heidegger, "Only a God Can Save Us" (the *Spiegel* interview), p. 57.

2. *Being and Time* as Political Philosophy

1. See Hans-Georg Gadamer, *Truth and Method*, p. 228: "The true predecessor of Heidegger in raising the question of Being and thus going contrary to the whole direction of Western metaphysics. . . . [was] Nietzsche."
2. *Being and Time*, p. 32; *Sein und Zeit*, p. 12 (subsequent references to the German original will appear parenthetically).
3. Gadamer, *Truth and Method*, pp. 230, xviii; emphasis added.
4. See Wilhelm Dilthey, *Der Aufbau der geschichtlichen Welt in den Geisteswissenschaften*. On the importance of Heidegger's relation to Dilthey, see Karl Löwith, "Diltheys und Heideggers Stellung zur Metaphysik," in *Heidegger: Denker in dürftiger Zeit*, pp. 258–275; and J. Barash, "Über den geschichtlichen Ort der Wahrheit: Hermeneutische Perspektiven bei Wilhelm Dilthey und Martin Heidegger," in *Martin Heidegger: Innen- und Aussenansichten*, pp. 58–74.
5. For a representative survey of the basic literature concerning the so-called "interpretive turn" in the human sciences, see *Understanding and Social Inquiry*, edited by Fred Dallmayr and Thomas A. McCarthy (Notre Dame: University of Notre Dame Press, 1977).
6. Ernst Tugendhat, *Self-Consciousness and Self-Determination*, pp. 178, 187; emphasis added.
7. Theodor W. Adorno, *The Jargon of Authenticity*, pp. 8–9.
8. Alfons Söllner, "Left Students of the Conservative Revolution: Neumann, Kirchheimer, and Marcuse," *Telos* 61 (1984), p. 59.
9. Winfried Franzen, *Von der Existenzialontologie zur Seinsgeschichte*, p. 10; emphasis added.
10. See Heidegger, "Political Texts, 1933–1934." I discuss these texts in detail in chapters 3 and 4.
11. Gadamer, *Philosophical Hermeneutics*, 214. The radical philosophical iconoclasm of Heidegger's magnum opus of the interwar period has been felicitously portrayed in the following observations by Gadamer: "The contemporary reader of Heidegger's first systematic work was seized by the vehemence of its passionate protest against the secured cultural world of the older generation and the leveling of all individual forms of life by industrial society,

with its ever stronger uniformities and its techniques of communication and public relations that manipulated everything. Heidegger contrasted the concept of the authenticity of Dasein, which is aware of its finitude and resolutely accepts it, with the 'They,' 'idle chatter,' and 'curiosity,' as fallen and inauthentic forms of Dasein. The existential seriousness with which he brought the age-old riddle of death to the center of philosophical concern, and the force with which his challenge to the real 'choice' of existence smashed the illusory world of education and culture, disrupted well-preserved academic tranquility." Ibid., pp. 214–215.

12. Friedrich Nietzsche, *The Will to Power*, no. 868; emphasis added.

13. See Heidegger's own discussion of the "vulgar concept of time" in *Being and Time*, section 81.

14. See the excellent discussion of this theme in Wolfgang Abendroth, "Das Unpolitische als Wesensmerkmal der deutschen Universität," p. 192.

15. For a classical treatment of the genesis of this distinction, see Norbert Elias, *The Civilizing Process*, pp. 3–10.

16. See the discussion in Fritz Ringer, *The Decline of the German Mandarins*, pp. 86–90.

17. Heidegger, *Beiträge zur Philosophie*, p. 38.

18. See the explanations for belated German development in Helmut Plessner, *Die verspätete Nation* and Ralf Dahrendorf, *Society and Democracy in Germany*.

19. Fritz Stern, *The Politics of Cultural Despair*, pp. 18, 15. Concerning the characteristic German equation of capitalism with liberalism, Stern makes the following observation: "They [the conservative revolutionaries] sensed that liberalism was the spiritual and political basis of modernity and they sought to equate liberalism with Manchesterism, with the disregard of man's spiritual aspirations, with the acceptance of economic selfishness and exploitation, with the *embourgeoisement* of life and morals." Ibid., p. 10.

20. In *The Decline of the German Mandarins*, Ringer is careful to point out that a minority of politically moderate mandarins also existed who were more receptive to the demands of the modern world and Western values in general. For this reason he refers to them as the "modernists" or "accommodationists." He numbers among them Friedrich Meinecke, Ernst Troeltsch, Max and Alfred Weber.

21. Stern, *The Failure of Illiberalism*, p. 17. Heidegger would himself attempt to justify the German expansionist idea of *Mitteleuropa* in terms that are remarkably similar to those just discussed by Stern in the mid-1930s. See especially, *An Introduction to Metaphysics*, pp. 47ff., as well as the discussion of these passages in chapter 4.

22. Ringer, *Decline of the German Mandarins*, p. 13. For an excellent discussion of the anticapitalist attitudes of the German intelligentsia, see Michael Löwy, *Georg Lukács: From Romanticism to Bolshevism*, pp. 22–66. See also, *Rédemption et utopie: le judaisme libertaire en Europe centrale*, a more recent book by Löwy on a kindred theme.

23. For an excellent discussion of the way in which this "crisis mentality" plays a crucial role in Heidegger's own intellectual formation, see Allan Megill, *Prophets of Extremity*, pp. 110ff.

24. See the discussion in Peter Gay, *Weimar Culture*, pp. 23ff.

25. Hauke Brunkhorst, *Der Intellektuelle im Lande der Mandarine*, p. 81.

26. *Der Akademiker* (May 1910); cited by Hugo Ott, *Martin Heidegger: Unterwegs zu seiner Biographie*, p. 63; emphasis added.

27. Cited in Karl Löwith, *Mein Leben in Deutschland vor und nach 1933*, p. 28.

28. Gadamer, "The Phenomenological Movement," *Philosophical Hermeneutics*, p. 139.

29. For a discussion of the left-wing version of this mentality, see Georg Lukács' "Preface" to the 1962 edition of *The Theory of the Novel* (Cambridge, Mass.: MIT Press, 1971). Among its exponents, whom he characterizes as possessing a "left ethics and right epistemology," Lukács numbers Ernst Bloch, Walter Benjamin, Theodor Adorno—in addition to himself. For a more detailed treatment of this romantic anticapitalist social type, see Löwy, *From Romanticism to Bolshevism*.

30. First use of the term "conservative revolutionary" is generally attributed to a 1927 speech of Hugo von Hofmannsthal before a student group in Munich. For more on this term, see Jeffrey Herf, *Reactionary Modernism*, pp. 18ff.; George Mosse, *The Crisis of German Ideology*, pp. 280ff.; Klemens von Klemperer, *Germany's New Conservatism*, pp. 153ff.; Kurt Sontheimer, *Antidemokratisches Denken*, pp. 357ff.; and Armin Mohler, *Die konservative Revolution, passim*.

The actual relation of the conservative revolutionaries to National Socialism was complex. Many joined with the National Socialists once it appeared to be the only means available to realize their social and political goals. Two of the movement's main figures, Spengler and Jünger, both refused to join the Nazi Party, largely because they felt its leaders were vulgar and plebeian. Hitler personally tried to recruit Spengler for the movement in 1934, but failed. One of the leading conservative revolutionaries, Edgar Jung, a member of the influential Munich Herrenklub, proudly claimed in a June 1932 essay (*Deutsche Rundschau*, pp. 153ff.) that it was the *conservative revolutionaries*, and not the Nazis, who had created "the spiritual presuppositions for the German Revolution." The Nazis begged to differ, however. On June 30, 1934, the "Night of the Long Knives," Jung, who had served as personal secretary to Franz von Papen during the latter's chancellorship, was murdered along with many others whose political allegiances were suspect.

31. Nietzsche, *The Will to Power*, no. 5; Spengler, *The Decline of the West*, vol. 2, p. 440; Jünger, *Der Kampf als inneres Erlebnis*, p. 57; Schmitt, *Der Begriff des Politischen*, p. 49 (emphasis added).

32. Heidegger, *Die Selbstbehauptung der deutschen Universität*, p. 18. Bourdieu's book represents the most sustained attempt to date to situate Heidegger's philosophy in relation to the German conservative revolutionaries. In his review of Bourdieu (*Philosophische Rundschau* 1–2 [1979]; 143ff.), Hans-Georg Gadamer takes strong exception to the reductionist implications of a sociology of knowledge approach to understanding Heidegger's philosophy, claiming that the philosophical autonomy of Heidegger's thought disappears in the process. For more on the relationship between the conservative revolutionaries and National Socialism, see Kurt Sontheimer, "Anti-democratic Thought in the Weimar Republic," in *The Road to Dictatorship*, Lawrence Wilson ed. (London: Oswald Wolff, 1964), pp. 42ff. As Sontheimer observes, "It is hardly a matter of

conroversy today that certain ideological predispositions in German thought generally, but particularly in the intellectual and political climate of the Weimar Republic, induced a large number of German electors under the Weimar Republic to consider the National Socialist movement as less problematic than it in fact turned out to be." An account of these "ideological predispositions," Sontheimer suggests, will "throw light on the intellectual atmosphere in which, when National Socialism arose, it could seem to be a more or less presentable doctrine." "There is no doubt," he continues, "that, shaped by such authors as Wilhelm Stapel, Oswald Spengler, Arthur Moeller van den Bruck, Ernst and Friedrich Georg Jünger, Ernst Niekisch, August Winnig and many others, the thought of the young right-wing nationalists prepared the intellectual soil for the growth of National Socialism. The Conservative Revolution which they wanted to bring about was exploited by the mass movement of National Socialism. . . . Indeed, some of the conservative revolutionaries became outspoken opponents of the regime and paid for their opposition with death. But though the fact was not admitted, as a political mass movement National Socialism had been able to profit from the hostility to the Republic generated by the anti-democratic intellectuals and derived great strength from it."

33. Pierre Bourdieu, *L'ontologie politique de Martin Heidegger*, p. 24. The title of the book contains a double allusion, which accounts for what is, as it were, Bourdieu's main thesis: that Heidegger's politics are "ontological" and that his ontology is "political."

34. Heidegger, "German Men and Women," in "Political Texts: 1933–1934," p. 103; emphasis added.

35. Cited in Karl Löwith, "Der okkasionelle Dezisionismus von Carl Schmitt," in *Heidegger: Denker in dürftiger Zeit*, p. 32; emphasis added.

36. Carl Schmitt, *Political Theology*, pp. 66–67; emphasis added.

37. Cf. Max Weber, "Science as a Vocation," p. 148: "since Nietzsche, we realize that something can be beautiful, not only in spite of the aspect in which it is not good, but rather in that very aspect. You will find this expressed earlier in the *Fleurs du mal*, as Baudelaire named his volume of poems."

38. These influences are well documented in Karl Heinz Bohrer, *Ästhetik des Schreckens, passim*.

39. For the best discussions of Jünger in English, see Herf, *Reactionary Modernism*, pp. 70ff.; and Gerhard Loose, *Ernst Jünger*.

40. Nietzsche, *The Will to Power*, nos. 796, 822. For a good discussion of aestheticism in Nietzsche's work, see Allan Megill, *Prophets of Extremity*, pp. 29ff.

41. Bohrer, *Ästhetik des Schreckens*, pp. 334–335. As a further illustration of Heidegger's filiations with conservative revolutionary "aesthetics of horror," Bohrer cites Heidegger's brilliant "phenomenology of fear" in Section 30 of *Being and Time* ("Fear as a Mode of State-of-Mind"), which he goes on to compare with analogous discussions of "horror" and "fright" in the work of Jünger: "The constitutive moments of the phenomenon of fear, when viewed as a whole, can vary. Thus in fearing, different possibilities of Being emerge. The degree of proximity in our surroundings of what is threatening [*des Bedröhlichen*] belongs to the encounter-structure of fear. If something threatening breaks in suddenly upon concernful Being-in-the-world (something threatening in its 'not

now, but any moment'), *fear* becomes *alarm* [*Erschrecken*]. Accordingly, in what is threatening we must distinguish between the closest proximity of what is threatening and the way in which this proximity is encountered—its suddenness [*Plötzlichkeit*]. That in the face of which we take fright is to begin with something well known and familiar. But if, on the other hand, that which threatens has the character of something altogether unfamiliar, then fear becomes *dread* [*Grauen*]. And where that which threatens is laden with dread, and is at the same time encountered with the suddenness of the alarming, then fear becomes *terror* [*Entsetzen*]." Similarly, in the *Beiträge zur Philosophie* (p. 46), Heidegger will identify *Erschrecken* ("alarm" or "terror") as the "foundational mood of the new beginning"; i.e., a "mood" that is conducive to overcoming our contemporary *Seinsverlassenheit* or "abandonment by Being." And thus, according to Bohrer, despite their contrasting intellectual vocations (Jünger the "littérateur" as opposed to Heidegger the "fundamental ontologist"), common to the texts of both authors is a "perspective of the *ritual intensification of various modes of 'horror'* [*Schrecken*]" in which "the way that 'terror' becomes manifest is tied to the 'encounter-structure' of 'suddenness' [*Plötzlichkeit*]."

42. Bohrer, *Ästhetik des Schreckens*, p. 332.

43. See Schmitt, *Political Theology*, p. 36.

44. Bohrer, *Ästhetik des Schreckens*, p. 341. In the comparison between Heidegger and Jünger, Bohrer is thinking primarily of Jünger's glorified depictions of the shocks experienced in battle. He mentions both Jünger's graphic accounts of the "rain of shrapnel" as well as his portrayal of the "suddenness" of the soldier's "death-swoon." But he also cautions wisely against extending the parallels between the two men in a way that would efface the important differences between them. In the last analysis, Jünger's celebration of the "war experience" dwells fully in the plane of immediate experience or ontic life; whereas Heidegger's phenomenology of "fear," "terror," etc., is confined to the abstract, metatheoretical plane of existential ontology.

In *The Aesthetic State*, Josef Chytry, in a way that parallels the argument of Bohrer, suggests a more determinate, material relation between the "temporal semiotics" informing the work of Jünger and Heidegger: "Heidegger . . . advanced a breakthrough in ontology that bears remarkable similarities to the Jüngerian intuition of the existential primacy of ecstasis on the horizon of the front as the ritual foundation for the communal bonds of a new heroic order of beings." In this way, Chytry seeks to demonstrate that "Heidegger's ontological discovery of being as timeliness rests on his transformation of an inchoate mass experience of nihilation in the trenches, the 'aesthetics' of mass warfare, into a formal philosophical argument for the primacy of ecstasis as a dwelling in being and proof of man's peculiar vocation of guardianship" (p. 376).

45. A full exposition and justification of this claim will have to wait until our analysis of Heidegger's concept of "resolve" (*Entschlossenheit*) below.

46. Cf. the pertinent reflections of Löwith in "The Political Implications of Heidegger's Existentialism," p. 122.

47. Löwith, *Mein Leben in Deutschland*, p. 30.

48. For an excellent account of the way the category of authenticity in *Being and Time* entails a necessary correlation between the work's ontological and

ontic dimensions, see Karsten Harries, "Heidegger as a Political Thinker."

49. *Being and Time*, p. 312 (267).

50. Cf. Aristotle, *Nichomachean Ethics*, 1099a, where he points out that at the Olympic games medals are not awarded on the basis of which athlete is most beautiful or possesses the best physique, but to the one who performs the best.

51. *Being and Time*, p. 312 (267).

52. For a good discussion of the existential significance of anxiety (*Angst*) and its relation to the nullity or void confronting all human Dasein, see Heidegger, "What is Metaphysics," in *Basic Writings*, pp. 102ff.

53. *Being and Time*, p. 164 (126).

54. Ibid., p. 166 (128).

55. Ibid., p. 313 (268).

56. For the background of this concept see *Historisches Wörterbuch der Philosophie*, vol. 2 (Basel: Schwab, 1971), pp. 477ff.

57. *Being and Time*, p. 365 (317–318); emphasis added.

58. An English translation of Heidegger's letter to Schmitt may be found in *Telos* 72 (1987), p. 132. Schmitt's first use of the term "decisionism" appears in the preface to the 1928 edition of *Die Diktatur*, a work that originally appeared in 1921.

59. Schmitt, *Political Theology*, p. 5.

60. Leo Strauss, *Studies in Platonic Political Philosophy*, p. 30; emphasis added.

61. Schmitt, *Political Theology*, p. 12; emphasis added.

62. Nietzsche, *The Will to Power*, no. 382; emphasis added.

63. Schmitt, *Political Theology*, pp. 55–56; emphasis added. For an excellent discussion of Schmitt's decisionism, see Karl Löwith's essay, "Der okkasionelle Dezisionismus von Carl Schmitt," in *Heidegger: Denker in dürftiger Zeit*, pp. 232ff.

64. Schmitt, *Political Theology*, p. 14.

65. Ibid., p. 15; emphasis added. I have explored the relationship between existentialism and decisionism in Schmitt's work at greater length in my essay, "Carl Schmitt, l'existentialisme politique, et l'état total," *Les Temps Modernes* 523 (1990): 50–88. In *Die Entscheidung* (*The Decision*; p. 76.), Christian von Krockow aptly summarizes those aspects of decisionism held in common by Heidegger, Schmitt, and Jünger in the following terms:

> [Heideggerian] decisiveness is thus separated from every possible content, from every material orientation [*Wozu*]—indeed, this being-separated-from is its goal, its achievement, and the proof of its worth. In this way, we see in Heidegger's case the same process at work as in the articulation of "struggle" [*Kampf*] with Jünger and "decision" with Schmitt. If in Schmitt's case we find that from a normative standpoint, the decision is born out of nothing, Heidegger shows how decisiveness emerges on the basis of "nullity"—i.e., where "norms," which are collectively unmasked as deriving from the fallen world of the "They," can no longer enter into consideration. And just as Schmitt in analyzing the political sphere identifies parliament as a system of avoiding all real decision, Heidegger bears witness to the fact that "They," in the ambiguity of "idle talk," in "publicness"—to which the "reticence" of authentic, resolute Dasein stands opposed—"slinks away from" every decision.

66. *Being and Time*, pp. 319, 318 (274, 273); emphasis added.

67. Ibid., p. 319 (274) and p. 320 (275).

68. Ibid., p. 320 (275); emphasis added.

69. Cf. the argument at p. 316 (271): "Vocal utterance is not essential for discourse, and therefore not for the call either"; emphasis added.

70. Ibid., p. 319 (274–275); emphasis added.

71. Ibid., p. 319 (274).

72. It is of more than passing interest to note that Heidegger's denigration of the idea of the *sensus communis* contrasts sharply with the views of his best known pupil, Hans-Georg Gadamer. See *Truth and Method*, pp. 15ff.

73. Or as Heidegger will lament in a later work: "Philosophy does speak about the light of reason, but does not heed the opening of Being." See "The End of Philosophy and the Task of Thinking," *Basic Writings*, p. 386.

74. *Being and Time*, p. 204 (161).

75. Ibid., p. 322 (277); emphasis added.

76. The "joylessness" of Heidegger's social ontology commented on by Marcuse has been the subject of an especially acerbic critique by Guenther Stern (Anders):

> [Heidegger's] *philosophy is the first and unique sample of the species "philosophy of life hostile to life."* His "Dasein" still suffers from the Christian bad conscience, even from the additional bad conscience of having thrown overboard the Christian concept of sin after all. This doubly evil conscience makes Heidegger's "Dasein" so vile that it begrudges itself all joy. . . . *No man could bestow a worse treatment on his fellow-man than Heidegger's "Dasein" bestows on itself.* Whether the treatment is sadistic or masochistic this question is hard to decide since the social partners are Siamese twins. When "Dasein" sleeps, it wakes itself up, if it wants to read the paper it tears this "tool of mediocrity and average-life" from its own hands. It excludes itself from leisure, friendship, friendliness, in short, from culture. Its *exercitia* fill the twenty-four hours of the day, its drudgery to march toward death lasts the whole life.

Guenther Stern, "The Pseudo-Concreteness of Heidegger's Philosophy," p. 362.

77. Prior to Plato, this argument was used to justify the rule of masters over slaves. With him for the first time it is employed as a justification for rule over one's fellow citizens. The whole theory of the guardian class in the *Republic* is predicated upon it.

78. See Marx, "Theses on Feuerbach," in the *Marx-Engels Reader*, p. 144. Here I have paraphrased Marx (something that is often done in the case of the passage in question). His actual words read: "it is essential to educate the educator himself."

79. *Being and Time*, p. 329 (284).

80. Ibid., p. 321 (276).

81. To illustrate this point, Heidegger gives the example of "wanting to pay back debts"—"*schulden*"—which is also the German word for "guilt," to show how the They turns a fundamental "existential" question into something "vulgar" and "existentiell."

82. Ibid., pp. 330, 331 (284, 285).

83. Ibid., p. 334 (288).

84. Ibid., pp. 325, 326 (280).

85. Michael Theunissen, *The Other: Studies in the Social Ontology of Husserl, Heidegger, Sartre, and Buber*, pp. 175, 184, and 186; emphasis added.

86. Heidegger, *Being and Time*, p. 220 (175).

87. The prospects for authentic Being-with-others in Heidegger's early work has been the subject of some controversy in the secondary literature. My critical account of this aspect of Heidegger's work has been supported by Karl Löwith, in *Das Individuum in der Rolle des Mitmenschen* (1928), as well as by Theunissen in *The Other*. For an excellent summary of the various positions in this debate over the status of Heideggerian *Mitsein*, see Fred Dallmayr, *Twilight of Subjectivity*, pp. 56–71. There, Dallmayr makes a plausible argument for a more positive conception of Being-with in Heidegger's early work; a theme, moreover, to which we shall turn shortly. One must agree that the inchoate rudiments of such a conception can be found in *Being and Time*; however, they are indeed very difficult to reconcile with the extremely harsh verdict Heidegger himself delivers with regard to the categories of worldliness and everydayness. To be sure, the possibility of authentic Being-with is an idea Heidegger never fully relinquishes. However, his general critique of the life-world is so thoroughgoing that one cannot help but wonder how and where such authentic *Mitsein* could in point of fact prosper.

88. Heidegger, *Being and Time*, p. 325 (280).

89. Ibid., p. 343 (297).

90. Ibid., p. 345 (298); emphasis added.

91. Ibid., p. 345 (299).

92. Heidegger, "The Origin of the Work of Art," *Poetry, Language, Thought*, p. 55.

93. The citations are taken from Schürmann, "Political Thinking in Heidegger," pp. 191–221. See also his *Heidegger on Being and Acting: From Principles to Anarchy*. In this work, Schürmann proposes the interpretive strategy of "reading Heidegger backward," i.e., beginning with the later writings and then proceeding to the earlier ones. Of course, this practice suggests a very different series of answers to the question concerning Heidegger and politics than if one reads the works of the Heideggerian corpus in the order in which they were written. In any event, it conveniently bypasses the question of the philosophical basis for Heidegger's "conversion" to National Socialism in 1933: an answer to this question can only be gleaned by scrutinizing the works of this period. Moreover, as many interpreters have suggested, his later disillusionment with National Socialism may very well have precipitated a reexamination of his early philosophy as well as an expunging of precisely those aspects that bore affinities with this political movement.

For another essay emphasizing the political importance of the later writings for Heideggerianism as a philosophy of freedom, see Fred Dallmayr, "Ontology of Freedom: Heidegger and Political Philosophy."

94. Cf. Harry Frankfurt, "Freedom of the Will and the Concept of a Person," *Journal of Philosophy* 67:1 (Jan. 1971): 5–20.

95. For a discussion of the anti-authoritarian implications of Heidegger's later work that is in many points in agreement with Schürmann, see O. Pöggeler, *Philosophie und Politik bei Heidegger*. At the same time, Pöggeler, unlike Schürmann, does not attempt to gloss over the avowedly *völkisch* dimensions of Heidegger's early work.

96. Suffice it to say that the characterization of Heidegger's thought as "anarchist" in the etymological sense of the word has nothing whatsoever to do with historical anarchism. The latter, while virulently antistatist, was far from being "unprincipled." Rather, historical anarchism often emphasized mechanisms of mutual human assistance and cooperation (e.g., Kropotkin's "mutualism") as an alternative mode of social organization intended to supplant traditional vertical and hierarchical models of social power. For a good account, see James A. Joll, *The Anarchists*.

97. Habermas, *Philosophisch-politische Profilen*, pp. 67–75. His remark is taken from a 1953 review of Heidegger's recently published 1935 lecture course, *An Introduction to Metaphysics*.

98. *Being and Time*, pp. 344, 345–346 (298, 299).

99. *Ibid.*, p. 344 (298).

100. Karsten Harries, "Heidegger as a Political Thinker," p. 312; emphasis added.

101. *Being and Time*, p. 32 (12). Or, as Heidegger describes the existential nature of Dasein as care in another passage: "In existing, Dasein understands itself in such a way that this understanding does not merely get something in its grasp, but makes up the existentiell Being of its factical potentiality-for-Being."

102. *Ibid.*, p. 374 (326).

103. *Ibid.*, p. 376 (327).

104. *Ibid.*, pp. 378, 379 (329, 330).

105. *Ibid.*, p. 376 (328). It is of significant interest that Heidegger here identifies the falling of inauthentic temporality into the present-at-hand with a "making-present," since his critique of traditional philosophy focuses upon its status as a "metaphysics of presence," that is, an inquiry in which Being is interpreted as something present-at-hand. See, for example, his important essay "Plato's Doctrine of Truth," pp. 251–270.

106. *Being and Time*, p. 373 (326). At the same time, Heidegger is quick to add that "Only insofar as it is futural can Dasein *be* authentically as having been. The character of 'having-been' arises, in a certain way, from the future." That is, in authentic temporality, the past and the future mutually inform one another. The future can be anticipated only on the basis of Dasein's "having been"; yet the understanding of the past itself is based necessarily on Dasein's self-projection into the future. For it is on the basis of such projection alone that it rescrutinizes its past.

107. *Ibid.*, p. 435 (383). The concluding phrase to this citation is of great interest insofar as it indicates a profound decisionistic residue in the entire discussion of historicity. It implies that the taking up of historically extant possibilities is never something unalterable and merely given, but in the last analysis something codetermined by the autonomous decision of Dasein itself.

108. *Ibid.*, p. 435 (383–384).

109. *Ibid.*, p. 436 (384); emphasis added.

110. *Ibid.*, p. 438 (386); emphasis added.

111. For a recent sociological attempt emphasizing the necessity of conceiving social interaction in terms of the interdependence of "agency" and "structure," see Anthony Giddens, *The Constitution of Society*.

112. In *Hitler: The Führer and the People*, p. 76, J. P. Stern has commented on this aspect of National Socialist ideology as follows:

It is obvious that the more "absolute" the Will becomes, and therefore the further removed from all concrete means, the more ineffectual it will be, and the more its assertion will resemble childish tantrums. . . . [At] the point where the self is so imperiously asserted a curious reversal, from complete subjectivity and arbitrariness to what looks like its opposite is said to take place. In declaring "the Will" absolute, the ideologist makes a show of replacing the subjective self by an objective principle; "the will" is now to be seen as a cosmic "law" *and* as an element of a religious faith.

113. *Being and Time*, p. 436 (384–385); emphasis added.

114. Ibid., p. 437 (385).

115. Ibid.

116. It is of more than passing interest in the present context to note that Werner Sombart contrasts these two types, the "trader" and the "hero," in a militaristic tract written in 1915. Whereas the trader "regards the whole existence of man on earth as a sum of commercial transactions" in which "profit" is always the bottom line, the hero "wants to give things away, wants to spend himself, to make sacrifices—without a return." Of course, here, "hero" and "trader" are meant as code-words for the national characters of the Germans and English, respectively. Cf. Ringer, *Decline of the German Mandarins*, p. 183. Thus, just as the artist was for the early Thomas Mann the quintessential antibourgeois, the *soldier* occupies the same place of honor in the thinking of the conservative revolutionaries (e.g., Jünger).

117. *Being and Time*, p. 437 (385).

118. The correlation between "decisionism" and "nihilism" has been demonstrated by Christian von Krockow in *Die Entscheidung*.

119. The dialectic of "resolve" and "historicity" that led to Heidegger's political decision of 1933 has been astutely characterized in the following remarks by the philosopher and former Heidegger student Hans Jonas:

The criterion of authenticity is decisiveness [*Entschlossenheit*]: one must decide about something for oneself. Decisiveness as such—not that *for which* or *against which* one decides, but *that* one decides—becomes the signature of *authentic* Dasein. The occasions for deciding for oneself, however, are provided by historicity. . . . As the hour of January 1933 struck, history offered the opportunity for decisiveness. . . . It was at this time that the enormous dubiousness of the Heideggerian outlook in its entirety became clear to me. Whereas he accused [German] idealist philosophy of a certain idealism—it claimed to study the forms of thought, the categories, according to which the world is ordered, and thus [did] everything at a certain remove [from the world]—one could accuse him of something much more serious: the absolute formalism of his decisionism, where decision as such becomes the highest virtue.

Cf. Hans Jonas, "Heideggers Entschlossenheit und Entschluss," pp. 226–227.

3. "To Lead the Leader": Philosophy in the Service of National Socialism

1. A crucial way-station in Heidegger's rejection of academic philosophy is his 1929 discussion of the neo-Kantian legacy with Ernst Cassirer in Davos, Switzerland. For Heidegger, neo-Kantianism is to be renounced insofar as it allows only for "scientific knowledge," whereas knowledge of Being remains a matter of indifference to it. The exchange is reprinted in Guido Schneeberger, *Ergänzungen zu einer Heidegger Bibliographie*, pp. 17–27. An English translation of the Heidegger-Cassirer dialogue ("A Discussion Between Ernst Cassirer and Martin Heidegger") may be found in *The Existentialist Tradition*, ed. N. Lagiulli.

2. Heidegger, *Basic Writings*, pp. 111–112. It is important to note that in this essay (Heidegger's Freiburg inaugural lecture held on July 24, 1929), as well as others of the period, Heidegger still utilizes the concept of metaphysics in a positive sense (another good case in point is his 1935 lecture, *An Intro-duction to Metaphysics*; here, too, the concept is employed approvingly). This will cease to be the case circa 1936, *viz.*, with the onset of his Nietzsche critique and a more radical "Turn" (*Kehre*) in his conception of "the history of Being."

3. *Being and Time*, p. 310 (265).

4. Heidegger, "Plato's Doctrine of Truth," p. 265; emphasis added. It should be remarked that the date of composition Heidegger lists for this essay in *Weg-marken* is 1931/32/1940.

5. Heidegger, *Being and Time*, p. 269 (226). And further: "*Because the kind of Being that is essential to truth is of the character of Dasein, all truth is relative to Dasein's Being.*" Ibid., p. 270 (227).

6. Pöggeler, *Martin Heidegger's Path of Thinking*, p. 48. It is important to recognize that despite the misgivings on Heidegger's part concerning funda-mental ontology, he always remained very cautious about suggesting too great a breach between *Being and Time* and his later work, often going out of his way to emphasize the continuities. On this point, see Heidegger's Preface to William J. Richardson, *Heidegger: Through Phenomenology to Thought*, pp. viii–xxiii. See also his account of the *Kehre* in the *Beiträge zur Philosophie*, pp. 84ff. ("Von 'Sein und Zeit' zum 'Ereignis'"). For more on Heidegger's retrospective self-understanding in relation to *Being and Time*, see F. W. von Hermann, *Die Selbst-interpretation Martin Heideggers*, pp. 265ff.

7. See Pöggeler's essay, "Heideggers politisches Selbstverständnis"; above all, the discussion that begins: "the symptoms of the world-economic crisis and its domestic political effects in the winter of 1929–30 coincided with the crisis of Heidegger's own religious and metaphysical convictions"; pp. 22ff.

8. On this dimension of Heidegger's work, see N. Tertulian, "Quand le dis-cours Heideggerien se mue en prise de position politique."

9. As Pöggeler points out, contrary to common belief, Heidegger's decision for Hitler preceded 1933: "Heidegger opted for Hitler before 1933, e.g., in the spring of 1932 on the occasion of the presidential elections." See Pöggeler, "Den Führer führen? Heidegger und kein Ende," p. 62.

10. "In his early Freiburg lectures, Heidegger repeatedly referred to Spen-gler's *The Decline of the West*." On the basis of Heidegger's fascination with Spengler, Pöggeler goes on to inquire: "did he have a political conception al-

ready in *Being and Time* that justified his linking the individual and his fate with the fate of a 'Volk'?" Ibid., p. 26.

11. The discussion of the vitalist critique of modernity, as well as Nietzsche's alternative critique, can be found in *Die Grundbegriffe der Metaphysik*, pp. 103–111.

12. In the Reichstag election of May 1928, the Nazis, with 12 seats, were the smallest party represented. In the elections of September 1929, they captured 107 seats to become the second largest party. See Franzen, "Die Sehnsucht nach Härte und Schwere," p. 91.

13. Heidegger, *Die Grundbegriffe der Metaphysik*, p. 243.

14. Ibid.

15. Ibid., p. 244. It should be remarked that the discussion of "horror" in this context bears affinities with both the function of "Angst" in *Being and Time* as well as a previous description in the same lecture course of the Dionysian attitude in Nietzsche: "Dionysus: sensuousness and cruelty. Transience can be interpreted as enjoyment of creative and destructive power, as constant creation." Ibid., p. 109. For more on Heidegger and the "aesthetics of horror," see Karl Heinz Bohrer, *Die Ästhetik des Schreckens*, pp. 142ff.

16. *Die Grundbegriffe der Metaphysik*, p. 245; emphasis added.

17. Ibid., p. 110; emphasis added (with the exception of the word "*victory*").

18. Franzen, "Die Sehnsucht nach Härte und Schwere," p. 85.

19. Löwith, *Mein Leben in Deutschland vor und nach 1933*, p. 56. An English translation of the Heidegger-Löwith exchange ("My Last Meeting with Heidegger in Rome, 1936") may be found in *New German Critique* 45 (1988); 115ff.

20. In this respect, it would be fascinating to compare the analogous, yet opposite, political paths traversed by Heidegger and Georg Lukács. Lukács was also profoundly influenced by *Lebensphilosophie* in his early years (see above all his 1911 study *Soul and Form*). And in the essay in which he chronicles his moral justification for Bolshevism, "Bolshevism as a Moral Problem," (*Social Research* 44/3 [1977]: 416–24), he describes his engagement for Bolshevik politics as a type of Kierkegaardian "teleological suspension of the ethical," in a way that is suggestive of *Being and Time*'s own critique of ethical normalcy. A philosophical comparison of the two thinkers has been attempted by Lucien Goldmann in *Lukács and Heidegger*.

21. Pöggeler, "Heideggers politisches Selbstverständnis," p. 28.

22. Heidegger, *Die Selbstbehauptung der deutschen Universität*, p. 24

23. Pöggeler, *Martin Heidegger's Path of Thinking*, p. 83.

24. Nietzsche, *The Will to Power*, nos. 119, 124, and 55.

25. Pöggeler, *Philosophie und Politik bei Heidegger*, p. 25.

26. Heidegger, *Die Selbstbehauptung der deutschen Universität*, p. 25.

27. Ibid., p. 13.

28. Indeed, in his contribution to the Festschrift for Jünger's sixtieth birthday, Heidegger would underline the significance of precisely this dimension of Jünger's work. He observes: "Your essay, *The Worker* (1932) has achieved a description of European nihilism in its phase after World War I. It develops out of your treatise *Total Mobilization* (1930). *The Worker belongs in the phase of 'active nihilism'* (Nietzsche). The action of the work consisted . . . in the fact that it makes the 'total work character' of all reality visible from the figure of the worker" (emphasis added). Heidegger, *The Question of Being*, p. 41.

29. This is Jeffrey Herf's thesis in *Reactionary Modernism: Technology, Culture and Politics in Weimar and the Third Reich.*

30. Jünger, "Die totale Mobilmachung," p. 130. In a manner that closely paralleled Jünger's approach, the jurist and political philosopher Carl Schmitt would, in a series of essays in the late twenties and early 1930s, formulate an analogous justification of Germany's turn toward a "total state." See above all, "Das Zeitalter der Neutralisierungen und Entpolitisierungen" (1929), "Wesen und Werden des faschistischen Staates" (1929), "Die Wendung zum totalen Staat" (1931), and "Weiterentwicklung des totalen Staats in Deutschland" (1933). All have been collected in Schmitt, *Positionen und Begriffe: im Kampf mit Weimar-Genf-Versailles, 1923–1939.*

31. Ibid., p. 131: "The Russian 'five-year plan' for the first time presented to the world the attempt to unite the total efforts of a great regime in *one* river bed." In passages such as these, Jünger flirts with the position of the so-called "National Bolshevists" around Ernst Niekisch, who believed that a right-wing version of the Soviet model would be ideal for Germany.

32. Jünger, *Der Arbeiter*, p. 236.

33. On this point see Karl Heinz Bohrer, *Die Ästhetik des Schreckens, passim.*

34. Cf. Gerhard Loose, *Ernst Jünger*, p. 32: "*Der Arbeiter* is a radical, unequivocal statement of militant totalitarianism."

35. Analogous themes are developed in Jünger's 1931 essay, "Über die Gefahr," in *Widerstand* (1931). Technological advances as applied to the infrastructure of everyday life (e.g., means of transportation) would mean the end of bourgeois satiation and complacency, and instead inject a new element of "danger" and excitement into the heart of everyday life itself. Cf. Herf, *Reactionary Modernism*, p. 98: "One no longer needed to go to war to be terrified. Danger was relief, an antipode of security, boredom, and reason."

36. Nietzsche, *The Will to Power*, nos. 763–764; emphasis added.

37. To be sure, the attempt to actualize philosophical ideas in empirical historical contexts is a process that is more often than not fraught with arbitrariness and surprises; and in this regard the annals of historical study are filled with many cruel ironies. It was perhaps the sociologist Max Weber who had the deepest insight into this phenomenon. His concept of "unintended consequences" was coined to account for precisely the divergence between the noblest intentions of men and women and the real historical outcomes of their acts. The young Karl Marx, for example, was an astute and prescient critic of bureaucracy. Yet, his doctrines somehow have been invoked to justify the most sclerotic and encrusted bureaucracies the world has known. And the classical example to be found in Weber's own work is his study of how a religious ethos could turn into the foundation for a thoroughly profane economic system: according to the Protestant leaders, "the care for external goods should only lie on the shoulders of the saint like a light cloak. But fate decreed that the cloak should become an iron cage" (*The Protestant Ethic and the Spirit of Capitalism* [New York: Scribner's, 1958], p. 181). Perhaps it should not really surprise us that the ideas of Nietzsche—who from the beginning had little faith in Hegel's maxim equating world history with justice—as propagated by National Socialism would experience an analogous fate.

38. Heidegger, "Plato's Doctrine of Truth," p. 257.

39. Ibid., p. 265.

40. Ibid., p. 266.

41. Above all, see E. Tugendhat, *Der Wahrheitsbegriff bei Husserl und Heidegger*.

42. Löwith, "The Political Implications of Heidegger's Existentialism," p. 125.

43. Or as the Freiburg University denazification commission charged with evaluating Heidegger's case would conclude some twelve years later: "the mere fact that a scholar of his intellectual caliber had joined the [Nazi] Party and celebrated its victory publicly was used by the Party as a highly welcome tool of propaganda." Cited in Hugo Ott, *Martin Heidegger*, p. 306.

44. Cf. Löwith's commentary on Heidegger's appointment in "The Political Implications of Heidegger's Existentialism": "Heidegger's accession to the rectorship of Freiburg University was an event. It came at a decisive time during the 'German Revolution,' insofar as all the other universities at this critical juncture lacked a leader capable of filling his role—not merely by virtue of his Party membership, but by virtue of his intellectual stature. As a result, his decision took on a more than local significance. It was felt everywhere, for Heidegger was then at the zenith of his fame" (p. 124).

Gleichschaltung (which literally means "synchronization") became the official Nazi word to refer to both the elimination of political opposition as well as the realignment of the entire state and its individual districts under unified National Socialist rule.

45. Pöggeler seeks to account for Heidegger's decision for Hitler in the following way: "The *Führer* appeared to him as the redeemer of a hopeless situation. Not only the shock of the First World War led to this option, but also the way in which Heidegger related science and philosophy as a problem to metaphysics in an undifferentiated way and, as a result of a crisis in his religious beliefs, sought a new myth." Pöggeler thus implies that Heidegger, by indiscriminately subsuming all previous "science" and "philosophy" under the (derogative) rubric "metaphysics," disqualified traditional intellectual paradigms to such an extent that he was really left with only one recourse: a new version of myth. Pöggeler, "Den Führer führen? Heidegger und kein Ende," p. 62.

46. "The Political Implications of Heidegger's Existentialism," p. 124.

47. Heidegger, *Die Selbstbehauptung der deutschen Universität*, p. 19.

48. Ibid., p. 19; emphasis added.

49. Sternberger, "Die grossen Worte des Rektors Heidegger," p. 25.

50. Oswald Spengler, *Preussentum und Sozialismus*, p. 8.

51. Heidegger, *Die Selbstbehauptung der deutschen Universität*, p. 11. It is worth noting that the term *nationaler Aufbruch* was a common expression used by the Nazis and their supporters to refer to the National Socialist revolution itself.

52. Ibid., p. 12.

53. If the outcome of this destiny is "fated" in advance, one might ask why Heidegger's speeches of this period emphasize with such frequency the values of "will," "hardness," and "resolve" (*Entschlossenheit*). The explanation lies in the fact that though "destiny" places great demands on a people, the people itself does not always prove capable of rising to those demands. Hence, only by an extreme display of will and decisiveness can the greatness of those de-

mands be met. On this point, Heidegger's view of fate coincides with that of the Nazis, who also viewed "fate" and "will" as correlatives in numerous speeches and texts of the period.

If one were to pursue the parallels Heidegger is seeking to draw concerning Fifth century Athens and the Germany of his day, Athens would become Berlin, Heraclitus Heidegger himself, and Pericles . . . Hitler!

In point of fact, one of Heidegger's colleagues, the economist Walter Eucken, complained in May 1933 to Heidegger's predecessor as Rector, Joseph Sauer (then pro-rector), that Heidegger saw himself as the greatest philosopher since Heraclitus and that he aspired to become the "spiritual *Führer*" of the new movement. Cf. Hugo Ott, "Martin Heidegger als Rektor der Universität Freiburg i. Br. 1933/34," p. 349.

54. See W. Hochkeppel, "Heidegger, die Nazis und kein Ende," *Die Zeit*, May 6, 1983. See also, Pöggeler, "Den Führer führen? Heidegger und kein Ende," p. 27. A colleague of Heidegger's, encountering the latter immediately after he tendered his resignation from the office of Rector, is reputed to have said, "On your way back from Syracuse, Herr Heidegger?"

55. To be sure, it is the modern era, as dominated by the demons of "technique" and "enframing," that seems to have a negatively "privileged" relationship to *Seinsverlassenheit*.

The possibility that Heidegger's myopic political judgments might be attributable to the leveling gaze to which historical events are subjected when viewed from the standpoint of *Seinsgeschichte* has been raised by Jürgen Habermas in his Introduction to the German edition of Farias' *Heidegger and Nazism* ("Heidegger: Werk und Weltanschauung"). There, Habermas criticizes Heidegger for engaging in a process of "abstraction through essentialization" (*Abstraktion durch Verwesentlichung*), as a result of which historical events of vastly different proportions are deemed equivalents.

56. See Petzet, *Auf einen Stern zugehen*, p. 232. On p. 82, Petzet cites Heidegger's 1974 lament over the "democratized disintegration" (*demokratisierter Verfall*) of contemporary institutions.

57. Heidegger, *Was heisst Denken?* p. 65.

58. For an account of the real functioning of democracy in the Greek polis, see M. I. Finley, *Democracy: Ancient and Modern* (New Brunswick, N.J: Rutgers University Press, 1985).

59. Heidegger, *Die Selbstbehauptung der deutschen Universität*, p. 14; emphasis added. "Die Lehrerschaft der Universität [muss] wirklich vorrücken in den äussersten Posten der Gefahr der ständigen Weltungewissheit." The German original is filled with military metaphors that come through only dimly in English translation.

60. Ibid; emphasis added.

61. *Volksgemeinschaft* was a key propagandistic term that was often featured in Hitler's speeches during the early years of National Socialism. It refers to the Nazi desire to eliminate the appearance of class and status differences in the new Reich, thus paving the way for the realization of a homogeneous national community. To this end, it was common practice for the *Führer* and his propagandists to refer to the citizenry as a whole as "workers" or "soldiers" laboring on behalf of the Volk. As Hitler himself expresses this thought in a 1934 interview: "*Volksgemeinschaft*: this means the community of effective la-

bor, it means the unity of all interests, it means the elimination of private cit-
izenship and a mechanical, union-organized mass" (*Frankfurter Volksblatt*, January 27, 1934.) Of course, the egalitarianism advocated by the term *Volksgemeinschaft* was largely ideological window-dressing that served to mask real
differences in social position that persisted under the Third Reich. Cf. the discussion of *Volksgemeinschaft* in David Schoenbaum, *Hitler's Social Revolution*,
pp. 59ff.

62. Heidegger, *Die Selbstbehauptung der deutschen Universität*, p. 16. Heidegger, who is known for his idiosyncratic German coinages, in this sentence
takes a common German word—*Fragwürdigkeit*, meaning "questionable status"—and gives it an entirely new, yet literal meaning in the context at hand:
Frag-würdigkeit now means "worthy-of-being-questioned."

63. Ibid., p. 16.

64. He claims this in "Das Rektorat: 1933–34," in ibid., pp. 28–29.

65. There is evidence for a Heraclitean reading of *Kampf* in Heidegger's claim
that there must also be "resistance" on the part of the followers against the
leaders, thereby suggesting that some degree of "struggle" between the two
groups is inherently good. He goes on to remark in a similar vein that "struggle
alone holds open the opposition" between students and teachers; *Die Selbstbehauptung der deutschen Universität*, p. 19. But these observations in no way
mitigate the unambiguous political implications of the term in National Socialist Germany, a mere four months after the author of *Mein Kampf* had seized
power.

66. Ibid., p. 18.

67. Ibid.

68. We know that in Heidegger's view, the Nazi Revolution was to recapture the "Greek beginning." But did this also mean that, in light of his translation of "*ta . . . megala panta episphalā*," the Greeks themselves were
proto-National Socialists? (In his lecture courses of the 1940s, Heidegger will
explicitly disassociate himself from such irresponsible speculation).

69. Heidegger, "Only a God Can Save Us," p. 48.

70. Heidegger, "Political Texts, 1933–1934," p. 130. Italics in the original.
Heidegger continues the article with the following observations:

Up to now, *research* and *teaching* have been carried on at the universities
as they were carried on for decades. Teaching was supposed to develop
out of research, and one sought to find a pleasant balance between the
two. It was always only the point of view of the teacher that spoke out
of this notion. No one had concerned himself with the university as a
community. Research *got out of hand* and concealed its uncertainty behind the idea of international scientific and scholarly progress. Teaching
that had become aimless hid behind examination requirements.

A *fierce battle* must be fought against this situation in the National
Socialist spirit, and this spirit cannot be allowed to be suffocated by hu-
manizing, Christian ideas that suppress its unconditionality.

71. Heidegger, "Political Texts: 1933–1934," p. 102.

72. Marcuse, "Heidegger's Politics: an Interview," in *Marcuse: Critical Theory and the Promise of Utopia*, pp. 95–104; see also his letter to Heidegger of
May 13, 1948, reprinted in *Pflasterstrand* 279–280 (January 23–March 5, 1988),
p. 48. For an interesting account of how Marcuse's early philosophy was in-

debted to the thought of Heidegger, see Alfred Schmidt, "Existential Ontology and Historical Materialism in the Work of Herbert Marcuse."

73. Heidegger, "The Call to Labor Service," in "Political Texts: 1933–1934," p. 109 (all italics in the original). In another speech entitled, "National Socialist Education," Heidegger mocks "intellekshuals" [*Geschtudierten*] and stresses the need "to build *a living bridge* between the worker of the 'hand' and the worker of the 'head.'" "Today," he continues, "the will to bridge this gap is no longer a project that is doomed to failure. And why not? Because the whole of our German reality has been changed by the National Socialist State, with the result that our whole past way of understanding and thinking must also become different." Ibid., p. 112.

74. Heidegger, "National Socialist Education," in "Political Texts: 1933–1934," pp. 113–114.

75. Heidegger, "Labor Service and the University," in ibid., p. 98.

76. For a detailed account of Heidegger's enthusiastic participation in such ventures, see Ott, *Martin Heidegger*, pp. 214ff.

77. For more on the Nazi program of labor service, see Martin Broszat, *The Hitler State*, pp. 155, 268. According to Broszat, though it was initially conceived of as a cushion for the unemployed, the *Reichsarbeitsdienst* program, which was made obligatory for young adults as of June 26, 1935, "developed into a new state organization in which National Socialist schooling was closely tied up with the state direction of labor and pre-military training . . . [It] expressed a basic tenet of National Socialist policy: the deliberate ideological, propagandist elevation of manual labor ("work ennobles"), which on the one hand appealed to and stimulated the worker's self-awareness, but chiefly his will to produce and to work, and thus fostered social quietism as well as the mobilization of labor energies."

78. In one speech, "National Socialist Education," Heidegger actually confronts the Marxist image of the worker directly. Its inadequacy lies in the fact that the worker is treated as a "mere object of exploitation." Of course, with the instrumentalization of the working classes under National Socialism (the trade unions were among the first institutions of civil society that Hitler dismantled, a mere three months after seizing power), their exploitation would reach a new extreme.

The standard National Socialist critique of intellectuals was formulated by Hitler in *Mein Kampf* (Munich, 1940), p. 480 : "Our intellectual classes are, especially in Germany, so closed off unto themselves and ossified that they lack a living relation to things below them. This takes its toll in a twofold respect. First, they consequently lack understanding and sensitivity for the teeming masses. They have already been torn away from this context for too long to have the necessary psychological understanding for the Volk. They have become *volksfremd*. Secondly, these higher strata lack the necessary force of will [*Willenskraft*]. For the latter is always weaker in self-encapsulated intellectual circles than in the masses of the Volk."

79. Franzen, *Von der Existenzialontologie zur Seinsgeschichte*, pp. 89–90.

4. "The Inner Truth and Greatness of National Socialism"

1. Heidegger, *Die Selbstbehauptung der deutschen Universität*, pp. 34–38; and Heidegger, "Only a God Can Save Us," p. 52.

2. I have described the events surrounding Heidegger's resignation in "Recherches récentes sûr la relation de Martin Heidegger au National Socialisme," pp.77–78. See also Hugo Ott, *Martin Heidegger*, pp. 224ff.

3. Arendt, *The Origins of Totalitarianism*, pp. 331–332. We still lack a comprehensive account of the way in which Arendt's political philosophy is grounded in Heideggerian categories. For example, the central theme of *The Human Condition*—the "dramaturgical" model of action, whereby revealing oneself in public through speech and deed becomes the highest mode of practical life—remains unintelligible apart from an appreciation of Heidegger's conception of the "clearing" (*Lichtung*) *qua* locus of unconcealment. Thus, for Arendt, the virtues of "publicness" represent the politico-philosophical corollary to the Heideggerian concepts of the "clearing" or "openness of an open region." Or one might further emphasize the derivation of Arendt's conception of "worldliness" from Heidegger's own category of "world" as elaborated in *Being and Time* and "The Origin of the Work of Art."

However, Arendt's appropriation of these Heideggerian concepts often results in a recasting so radical that ultimately their Heideggerian basis appears entirely transformed. Thus, for example, whereas for Heidegger "publicness" is relegated to the sphere of inauthenticity *simpliciter*, for Arendt, publicness, *qua* locus of human "action," becomes the highest form of human activity.

At the same time, it would be a worthwhile task to investigate to what extent the shortcomings of Arendt's political philosophy may be traceable to their Heideggerian origins. Thus, it would be legitimate to inquire whether the dramaturgical model of action advanced by Arendt is itself decisionistic; that is, whether her understanding of the essence of politics in terms of "revealing or showing oneself in public" remains capable of differentiating between legitimate and illegitimate modes of self-unveiling, or on what normative basis such distinctions might proceed.

4. Löwith, *Mein Leben in Deutschland vor und nach 1933*, p. 57.

5. Heidegger, *Beiträge zur Philosophie*, pp. 36ff. See also the related critique in the essay, "The Age of the World-Picture," *The Question Concerning Technology*, pp. 115ff. As Martin Jay has sought to demonstrate in "The Rise of Hermeneutics and the Crisis of Ocularcentrism," Heidegger's critique of visual metaphors in the mid-1930s (e.g., of the concepts of "world-view" and "world-picture" in the works just referred to) is part of a much broader assault against traditional Western theories of representation that is characteristic of the twentieth-century hermeneutic sensibility.

6. See Heidegger, *Beiträge zur Philosophie*, pp. 138ff. For a critical study of National Socialism as essentially nihilistic (written by a former Party member who ultimately broke with Hitler), see Hermann Rauschning, *The Revolution of Nihilism*.

7. Heidegger, *Beiträge zur Philosophie*, pp. 42–43.

8. Cf., ibid., p. 43: "The philosophy of a Volk is that which makes the Volk into the Volk of a philosophy, which establishes the Volk in its Da-sein, and determines it for the guardianship of the truth of Being."

9. Heidegger's remarks read as follows: "The works that are being peddled about nowadays as the philosophy of National Socialism but have nothing whatever to do with the inner truth and greatness of this movement (namely the encounter between global technology and modern man)—have all been written by men fishing in the troubled waters of 'values' and 'totalities.' " *An Introduction to Metaphysics*, p. 199. The phrase in parenthesis has become over the years a matter of considerable controversy; many have alleged (correctly, as it turns out) that this was an addition to the lecture that Heidegger included when it first appeared print in 1953—a fact Heidegger himself always denied. Only recently has one of Heidegger's former assistants, Rainer Marten, confirmed that, indeed, Heidegger, while going over the page-proofs for the lectures in 1953, retouched the passage in question, in addition, changing "National Socialism" to "this movement." Cf. Marten, "Ein rassistisches Konzept von Humanität," *Badische Zeitung*, December 19-20, 1987. See also, Jürgen Habermas, "Heidegger: Werk und Weltanschauung," in Victor Farias, *Heidegger und der Nationalsozialismus*, pp. 30–31.

10. The remark is from Heidegger's Schelling lectures of 1936, cited in Pöggeler, "Den Führer führen? Heidegger und kein Ende," p. 56. See also the letter from Dr. Carl Ulmer in *Der Spiegel*, May 2, 1977, p. 10. That Heidegger left this passage out of the published version of the lectures jibes poorly with his claims that as a matter of principle, he never reedited past lectures for publication.

11. Heidegger, *Die Selbstbehauptung der deutschen Universität*, p. 23.

12. Heidegger, "Only a God can save us," p. 48. In part, one cannot help but admire Heidegger's honesty in these remarks: unlike so many others, he refuses to dissemble the true nature of his convictions during the Hitler years. However, there is a darker side to the coin as well: for nor would Heidegger ever publicly renounce his Nazi involvements during the 1930s.

13. Pöggeler, *Martin Heidegger's Path of Thinking*, p. 278; emphasis added.

14. Heidegger, *Basic Writings*, p. 135.

15. Heidegger, *Poetry, Language, Thought*, p. 42. Cf. also the important discussion of "physis" in *An Introduction to Metaphysics*, pp. 14–15.

16. *Sein und Zeit*, Division I, Part III.

17. Heidegger, *Poetry, Language, Thought*, p. 49.

18. Ibid., p. 44.

19. Heidegger, *Existence and Being*, pp. 283, 287; emphasis added.

20. Ibid., pp. 48 and 42; emphasis added.

21. Cf., Heidegger, *Erläuterungen zu Hölderlins Dichtung*, p. 29, where Heidegger declares that the return home as interpreted by poets is "the future of the historical essence of the Germans. They are the nation [Volk] of poetry *and* thought [*des Dichtens* und *des Denkens*]."

22. Heidegger, *An Introduction to Metaphysics*, p. 43; emphasis added. Heidegger provides another important illustration of his conception of the necessary relationship between metaphysics and history in the following passage: "Our asking of the fundamental question of metaphysics is historical because it opens up the process of human Dasein in its essential relations—i.e. its relations to beings as such and as a whole—opens it up to unasked possibilities, futures, and at the same time binds it back to its past beginning, so sharpening it and giving it weight in its present. In this questioning our Dasein is sum-

moned to its history in the full sense of the word, called to history and to a decision in history"–i.e., a decision about authentic repetition. Ibid., p. 44.

23. Ibid.

24. Ibid., p. 38.

25. Ibid., p. 37.

26. Heidegger cites this remark on numerous occasions. See, for example, his essay "The Turning," in *The Question Concerning Technology and Other Essays*, p. 42. The origin of the citation is Hölderlin's poem "Patmos." See Friedrich Hölderlin, *Poems and Fragments*, trans. M. Hamburger (Ann Arbor: University of Michigan Press), pp. 462–463.

27. Heidegger, *An Introduction to Metaphysics*, p. 38; emphasis added (with the exception of *"within itself"*). Heidegger will return to this theme on a number of occasions in his lecture. For example, p. 42: "That is why we have related the question of Being to the destiny of Europe, where the destiny of the earth is being decided—while our own historic Dasein proves to be the center for Europe itself."

28. Cf. Heidegger, "Only a God Can Save Us," p. 48.

29. K. von Klemperer, *Germany's New Conservatism*, p. 56.

30. See Neumann, *Behemoth*, p. 141: "Lagarde was also the precursor of the Central Europe concept; he saw Germany's future in its expansion into Poland and West Russia and advocated a Middle Europe reaching from the mouth of the Ems to the mouth of the Danube, from Memel to Trieste, from Metz to the River Bug. Even [Alfred] Rosenberg's idea of deporting the Jews to Madagascar derives from Lagarde." Pages 136–147 of Neumann's book contain a good general discussion of the historical origins and subsequent National Socialist adoption of the term. See also Fritz Stern, *The Politics of Cultural Despair*, pp. 25ff.

31. Cf. Paul Hühnerfeld, *In Sachen Heidegger*, p. 98.

32. Cited in *Der Spiegel*, November 23, 1987, p. 212.

33. Heidegger, "German Students!" in "Political Texts: 1933–1934," p. 102.

34. Schmitt, *Staat, Bewegung, Volk*, p. 32. January 30, 1933 is of course the date of Hitler's accession to power. Schmitt views the metaphorical death of Hegel on this date as a phenomenon to be welcomed.

35. The theme of Heidegger's justification of Hitler will be further pursued in the context of our discussion of Heidegger's theory of "great creators" later in the chapter.

36. "Ein Gespräch mit Max Müller," p. 19. And as Müller indicates further, although Heidegger had discerned the false course that National Socialism had assumed as early as 1934, "For a long time he adhered to the belief, as he later admitted, that positive prospects still lay with the so-called 'Führer,' even if his followers remained worthless."

37. J. P. Stern, *Hitler: the Führer and the People*, p. 24; emphasis added.

38. Heidegger, *Die Selbstbehauptung der deutschen Universität*, p. 19.

39. Heidegger, "German Men and Women," in "Political Texts: 1933–1934," p. 103; emphasis added.

40. For a good survey of the basic positions in this dispute, see Herf, *Reactionary Modernism*, p. 238.

41. Neumann, *Behemoth*, pp. 135–136.

42. Heidegger, *Poetry, Language, Thought*, p. 39.

43. Heidegger, *Hölderlins Hymnen "Germanien" und "Der Rhein,"* p. 144.

44. Cf. Heidegger, "Only a God Can Save Us," p. 57: "according to our human experience and history, everything essential and great has arisen only out of the fact that man had a home and was rooted in a tradition. Contemporary literature, for example, is largely destructive." In essence, the remark cited delivers a thinly veiled critique of the "cosmopolitanism" of modern culture; a critique whose unsavory political implications we need not rehearse.

45. Heidegger, *An Introduction to Metaphysics*, p. 47.

46. Heidegger, *Discourse on Thinking*, p. 47.

47. Nietzsche, *The Will to Power*, no. 809. Perhaps it is because of marvelously phrased remarks such as these that, even when Nietzsche's judgments sail woefully wide of the mark, one is nevertheless tempted to agree with him.

48. Weber, "Science as a Vocation," in *From Max Weber*, eds. H. Gerth and C. W. Mills, p. 155.

49. Heidegger, *Hölderlins Hymnen "Germanien" und "Der Rhein,"* p. 134. The citation in full reads: the name of Heraclitus is that of a "primordial power of western-germanic historical Dasein, and indeed in its struggle with the Asiatic."

50. Heidegger, *Poetry, Language, Thought*, p. 42.

51. Ibid., p. 49. Heidegger's conception of the relationship between "world" and "earth" is considerably more complex than we have been able to indicate in the present context. For a more detailed presentation, see F-W von Herrmann, *Heideggers Philosophie der Kunst*. For an excellent discussion of the importance of the "Origin of the Work of Art" essay within the context of Heidegger's later work in general, see Gadamer, "Heidegger's Later Philosophy," *Philosophical Hermeneutics*, pp. 213–228.

52. In this respect, recent efforts have been made to ground a postmodernist critique of modern architecture on the basis of a Heideggerian position. See the essay by Kenneth Frampton in H. Foster, ed. *The Anti-Aesthetic: Essays on Post-Modern Culture* (San Francisco: Bay Press, 1983). A dissenting opinion with respect to such attempts has been registered by Jürgen Habermas in his essay, "Modern and Postmodern Architecture," *The New Conservatism* (Cambridge, Mass.: MIT Press, 1989).

53. Heidegger, *An Introduction to Metaphysics*, p. 203.

54. Thus the position Heidegger takes in this regard circa 1929 represents a significant alteration of his standpoint in *Being and Time*. There, the structures of authenticity and inauthenticity are able to coexist side by side without the latter presenting any ultimate obstacle to the posing of the question of Being. In the years following the composition of *Being and Time*, however, Heidegger seems to be convinced that the afflictions of the modern world result in an environment that is especially unconducive for the posing of metaphysical questions.

55. Heidegger, *Poetry, Language, Thought*, p. 53; emphasis added. There is another important aspect of the clearing—the fact that it serves both to unconceal and to *conceal*—that will concern us in our upcoming discussion of Heidegger's conception of the relationship between "truth" and "untruth."

56. Ibid., pp. 61–62; emphasis added.

57. These are of course the terms which Heidegger will in later works—e.g., "Building, Dwelling, Thinking," *Basic Writings*, p. 328—refer to as "the fourfold" (*das Geviert*).

58. Aristotle, *The Politics*, Book I.

59. See Aristotle, *Nichomachean Ethics*, Book VI. The most comprehensive discussion of the relationship between the categories of "work," "truth," and "politics" in Heidegger is to be found in Alexander Schwan, *Politische Philosophie im Denken Heideggers*. See especially chapters 1 and 5.

60. Heidegger, *An Introduction to Metaphysics*, p. 191; emphasis added.

61. Although it is only fair to note that on other occasions, Heidegger appears to accord "equiprimordial" status to the equally essential "works" of poetry and philosophy.

62. See also the important discussion of the state as a "work of art" in Josef Chytry, *The Aesthetic State*, pp. 371ff. Chytry correctly sees Heidegger's characterization of the polis as a "concrete work of art that draws together all the lesser artworks—thinking, poetry, sculpture, temples"—as a type of neo-ontological (or *seinsgeschichtlich*) counterweight to the baser dimensions of the extant National Socialist state: "This concept, of an ontological site gathering together an explosive concentration of extraordinary human beings that make a clearing for being, Heidegger offers as his 'political' counter to National Socialism. Not the ethnic-*volk*ish Third Reich with its supra-nationalistic chauvinisms, but polis as the ultimate artwork, as aesthetic state, makes up Heideggerian authentic 'politics' " (p. 391).

63. Heidegger, *An Introduction to Metaphysics*, p. 152; first emphasis added.

64. The classic discussion of the way in which tyranny is destructive of public life is Leo Strauss' *On Tyranny* (Ithaca: Cornell University Press, 1968).

65. Harries, "Heidegger as a Political Thinker," p. 327.

66. Heidegger, *Poetry, Language, Thought*, p. 37; emphasis added. Heidegger continues: "The art work opens up in its own way the Being of beings. This opening up, i.e., this deconcealing, i.e., the truth of beings, happens in the work. In the art work, the truth of what is has set itself to work. Art is truth setting itself to work." Ibid., p. 39.

67. Heidegger, *Basic Writings*, p. 127; emphasis added.

68. Ibid., p. 132; emphasis added.

69. Ibid., p. 134.

70. Ibid., pp. 130, 137.

71. Heidegger, "The Origin of the Work of Art," p. 54; emphasis added for the last sentence.

72. See Ernst Tugendhat, "Heideggers Idee von Wahrheit," in Pöggeler ed., *Heidegger: Perspektiven zur Deutung seines Werkes*, p. 293. The article cited is a condensed version of the conclusion to Tugendhat's landmark study, *Der Wahrheitsbegriff bei Husserl und Heidegger*.

73. W. Marx, *Heidegger and the Tradition*, pp. 250–251.

74. Ibid., p. 251.

75. Löwith, "Diltheys und Heideggers Stellung zur Metaphysik," in *Heidegger: Denker in dürftiger Zeit*, pp. 273–274.

76. Nietzsche, *The Will to Power*, no. 866.

77. Heidegger, *An Introduction to Metaphysics*, p. 62.

78. Ibid., p. 133.

79. Ibid. "If Being is to disclose itself," Heidegger continues, "it must itself have and maintain a rank. That is why Heraclitus spoke of the many as dogs and monkeys. . . . What has the higher rank is the stronger."

80. Ibid., p. 153; emphasis added.

81. Ibid., p. 157.
82. Heidegger, *Hölderlins Hymnen "Germanien" und "Der Rhein,"* p. 166.
83. Ibid., p. 210.
84. Chytry, *The Aesthetic State,* p. 393.
85. Heidegger, *An Introduction to Metaphysics,* pp. 162–163.
86. Heidegger, *Hölderlins Hymnen "Germanien" und "Der Rhein,"* pp. 51–52, 144; first emphasis added.
87. Heidegger, *Hölderlins Hymne der "Ister,"* pp. 98 and 106. This remark occurs in the context of a criticism of those vulgar classicists who would like to claim that the Greeks were "already National Socialists." It is significant insofar as it reveals that as late as 1942, Heidegger still adheres to the distinction between "the inner truth and greatness of National Socialism" (which the philosopher alone is able to discern) as opposed to the epigonal, vulgar Nazis who have gained intellectual control over the movement's historical direction. Hence, the claim concerning "the historical singularity of National Socialism" just cited is intended to reinforce precisely this distinction.
88. Heidegger, *Parmenides,* p. 114.
89. Heidegger, *Heraklit,* pp. 108, 123.
90. Marcuse, "Der Kampf gegen Liberalismus im totalitärischen Staat," in *Kultur und Gesellschaft* I, pp. 53–54; *Negations* (Boston: Beacon, 1968), p. 40.

5. Technology, Antihumanism, and the Eclipse of Practical Reason

1. See chapter 4, note 59. The category of the "work" seems to make its first appearance in Heidegger's Rectoral Address, where in the form of *am-Werke-Sein,* he employs it as an equivalent for the Aristotelian concept of *energeia.* Cf. *Die Selbstbehauptung der deutschen Universität,* p. 12.
2. Heidegger, *Poetry, Language, Thought,* p. 40.
3. Strong evidence for dating the "Turn" in Heidegger's thought circa 1930 is provided by the philosopher himself in his 1961 Foreword to the first German publication of his Nietzsche lectures: "Considered as a whole, the publication aims to provide a view of the path of thought I followed from 1930 to the 'Letter on Humanism' (1947). The two small lectures published just prior to the 'Letter,' 'Plato's Doctrine of Truth'(1942) and 'On the Essence of Truth' (1943), originated back in the years 1930–31"; *Nietzsche,* vol. 1, p. xvi. In this way, Heidegger confirms that it makes sense to treat his "path of thought" from 1930 to 1947 as a whole. See also his Preface to William Richardson, *Heidegger: Through Phenomenology to Thought,* pp. xiii–xxiii, for a self-interpretation that tends to emphasize the overall continuity in his philosophical development since *Being and Time.*

That in this 1961 depiction of his "path of thought" Heidegger makes no reference to any of the texts in which his theory of the "work" (not to mention that of the "great creators") is elaborated, might signal an attempt to downplay that phase of his development most replete in political significance.

4. Heidegger, *Nietzsche,* vol. 4, p. 14.
5. See Heidegger, *The End of Philosophy,* p. 92: "The reversal of Platonism, according to which for Nietzsche the sensuous becomes the true world and the suprasensuous becomes the untrue world, is thoroughly caught in metaphysics. This kind of overcoming of metaphysics, which Nietzsche has in mind in the

spirit of nineteenth-century positivism, is only the final entanglement in metaphysics, although in a higher form. It looks as if the 'meta,' the transcendence to the suprasensuous, were replaced by the persistence in the elemental world of sensuousness, whereas actually the oblivion of Being is only completed and the suprasensuous is let loose and furthered by the will to power."

6. Ibid., p. 6.

7. Cf. Pöggeler, *Martin Heidegger's Path of Thinking*, p. 108: "Thus metaphysics seeks that being which in a specific way fulfills the demand for being constantly present. . . . Metaphysics is, therefore, not only ontology, the foundation of beings in Being, but also theology, the foundation of Being in a supreme being. . . . it is onto-theology."

8. Heidegger, *Nietzsche*, vol. 3, p. 7.

9. There are many important aspects of Heidegger's Nietzsche critique that are impossible to pursue in the present context. An excellent overview of what is thematically at stake in the debate is provided by Pöggeler in *Martin Heidegger's Path of Thinking*, pp. 82–106. See also, Karl Löwith, "Heideggers Vorlesungen über Nietzsche," in *Heidegger: Denker in dürftiger Zeit*, pp. 242–247.

10. See Heidegger, *Nietzsche*, vol. 4, p. 147: "*We must grasp Nietzsche's philosophy as the metaphysics of subjectivity.* . . . Nietzsche's metaphysics, and with it the essential ground of 'classical nihilism,' may now be more clearly delineated as a *metaphysics of the absolute subjectivity of will to power.*"

11. Ibid., p. 86.

12. Heidegger, *The Question Concerning Technology*, p. 115.

13. The first and last concepts are developed in *Gelassenheit* (1955), which has been translated into English as *Discourse on Thinking*.

14. Heidegger himself explicitly requested that "Overcoming Metaphysics" be included among a group of three texts culled from the German edition of his Nietzsche lectures. Cf. the editorial remark in *The End of Philosophy*, p. 84.

15. See "Wozu Dichter," *Holzwege*; see also, "Mitternacht einer Weltnacht" (review of A. Schwan, *Politische Philosophie im Denken Heideggers*), *Der Spiegel*, February 7, 1966, pp. 110–112.

16. *Die Selbstbehauptung der deutschen Universität*, p. 24. The seminar would have thus begun only a few weeks following the outbreak of World War II on September 1, 1939.

17. Heidegger, *The End of Philosophy*, p. 85.

18. Ibid; emphasis added.

19. The later Heidegger's description of the world as characterized by "unconditional objectification" (*unbedingte Vergegendständlichung*) prima facie suggests parallels with Lukács' concept of reification (*Verdinglichung*) in *History and Class Consciousness* (Cambridge, Mass.: MIT Press, 1971). A fruitful investigation of the theoretical similarities between these two thinkers—with the category of reification serving as a leitmotif—has been undertaken by Lucien Goldmann in *Lukács and Heidegger*.

At the same time, it would seem important to point out the significant differences between these two great contemporaries as well. Lukács remains indebted to a philosophy of subjectivity deriving from German classical philosophy and Marx. According to this philosophical paradigm, alienation (or reification) results when human beings can no longer recognize themselves in the products of their endeavors, insofar as the form the latter assume is heteronomously determined—the classical example being the fate of the worker under capitalism, who is forced to "alienate" the products of his or her labor to the capitalist. As such, the overcoming of alienation for Lukács would be signified by the retention of control by the workers over the products of their labor, i.e., the socialization of the means of production.

From the standpoint of Heidegger's critique of the modern "metaphysics of subjectivity," on the other hand, the question of *who* is in control of the labor process (and thus the question as to whether labor is "alienated" or not in the Marxian sense) could not be a matter of greater indifference. Because it is the paradigm of self-positing subjectivity *itself* that he attacks, the "socialization of the means of production" would in the end constitute merely a continuation of that paradigm by other means (*viz.*, by "labor" instead of "capital"). In truth, the Lukácsian and Marxist humanist standpoint—the apotheosis of labor—would for Heidegger signify only a further stage in the history of "the will to will." It would be merely the consummation of man's self-understanding as *homo laborans* rather than its abolition.

20. Heidegger, *The End of Philosophy*, pp. 86–87.

21. Heidegger, The *Question Concerning Technology*, p. 137.

22. Compare with the following remark by Adorno: "total socialization objectively hatches its opposite, and there is no telling yet whether it will be a disaster or a liberation." *Negative Dialectics*, p. 346.

23. M. Heidegger, E. Kästner, *Briefwechsel* (Frankfurt: Insel, 1986), p. 10.

24. "Only a God Can Save Us," p. 53.

25. Cited in Pöggeler, "Besinnung oder Ausflucht? Heideggers ursprünglicheres Denken," pp. 240–241.

26. That Heidegger dared to flirt with this Nietzschean perspective of "heroic nihilism" as late as his concluding lecture course on Nietzsche (1940) is illustrated by his observation that:

A new humanity is needed that is thoroughly equal to the fundamental essence of modern technology and its metaphysical truth; that is, which lets itself be totally dominated by the essence of technology, in order to guide and utilize the individual technical procedures and possibilities.

Only the superman is adequate to the unlimited 'machine-economy,' and vice versa: the former is in need of the latter to establish unconditional domination over the earth.

These citations are taken from the *Gesamtausgabe* of Heidegger's work, vol. 48, p. 205, and thus correspond to the original manuscript version of Heidegger's lecture on "European Nihilism" (cf. "Nachwort der Herausgeberin," pp. 337–339). In the 1961 Neske edition of the same lecture course, Heidegger added the words "In the sense of Nietzsche's metaphysics" to the beginning of the last sentence quoted, as a way of distancing himself from the remarks whose content he manifestly endorses in the original version of the lecture. (I am grateful to Nicholas Tertulian for having brought this discrepancy to my attention). The English edition of the Nietzsche lectures, which appeared four years before volume 48 of the *Gesamtausgabe*, follows the Neske version (cf. vol. 4, p. 117).

27. Habermas, "Heidegger: Werk und Weltanschauung," p. 25.

28. Franzen, *Von der Existenzialontologie zur Seinsgeschichte*, p. 130.

29. *Die Selbstbehauptung der deutschen Universität*, p. 25.

30. Thomas Sheehan, "Heidegger and the Nazis," p. 45.

31. Heidegger, *Was heisst Denken*, p. 65.

32. Support for this thesis is provided by Pierre Bourdieu in *"Ich glaube, ich wäre sein bester Verteidiger,"* *Das Argument* 131 (1988): 724: "This absolute thinker, who could think everything better than everyone else, was wholly incapable of thinking himself. To have engaged in self-criticism would have meant that this absolute thinker would have erred absolutely, and that there would have been a connection between his error and the philosophy."

33. See Habermas, "Heidegger: Werk und Weltanschauung," p. 33.

34. See Heidegger, *Poetry, Language, and Thought*, p. 9.

35. Löwith, *Heidegger: Denker in dürftiger Zeit*, p. 171.

36. Their remarks are to be found in "Heidegger et la pensée Nazie," *Le Nouvel Observateur*, January 22-28, 1988: 41ff.

37. A further confirmation of Heidegger's gross insensitivity on the question of the Holocaust is indicated by his January 20, 1948 response to a 1947 letter from Herbert Marcuse complaining of Heidegger's silence about the mass extermination of the Jews by the Nazis: "I can only add that instead of the word 'Jews' [in your letter] there should be the word 'East Germans,' and then exactly the same [terror] holds true of the Allies, with the difference that everything that has happened since 1945 is public knowledge world-wide, whereas the bloody terror of the Nazis was in fact kept a secret from the German people." A French translation of the letters has been published in *Les Temps Modernes* 510 (1989): 1–4. An English translation is forthcoming in *New German Critique*. What is so striking about Heidegger's remarks, in addition to their thoughtlessness (Marcuse, against the advice of fellow German-Jewish émigrés, had continued to send his former mentor care-packages after the war at a time when living conditions in Germany were deplorable), is that they resemble the typical rationalizations contrived by the German population in the postwar years to deal with the question of war-guilt: especially the claims that the German civilian population "knew nothing" about Nazi war crimes and that the Germans should bear no special guilt or responsibility since they had suffered as much as anyone else. For an excellent discussion of the German *"Verdrängung der Vergangenheit"* (repression of the past) in the postwar years, see Theodor Adorno, "What Does Coming to Terms with the Past Mean?" in *Bitburg in Moral and Political Perspective*, ed. G. Hartman (Indianapolis: Indiana University Press, 1986), pp. 114–129.

38. Löwith, *Heidegger: Denker in dürftiger Zeit*, p. 128.

39. Cited in Hugo Ott, *Martin Heidegger*, p. 316.

40. Heidegger, *Wegmarken*, p. 304. This passage has been the object of considerable controversy among Heidegger-scholars, insofar as in the fifth edition of "What is Metaphysics?" (1949), Heidegger then *reverses* the formulation to read: "Being *never* essences without beings, beings are never without Being." Cf., for example, the discussion of this passage in Franzen, *Von der Existenzialontologie zur Seinsgeschichte*, p. 105.

41. Heidegger, *Nietzsche*, vol. 4, p. 221; emphasis added.

42. Ibid., p. 215.

43. Heidegger, *The End of Philosophy*, p. 82; emphasis added.

44. Ibid., p. 110.

45. Heidegger, *Basic Writings*, p. 210; emphasis added.

46. Cf. Franzen, *Von der Existenzialontologie zur Seinsgeschichte*, p. 125: "While

in *Being and Time* there had been in principle no subject of history . . . now [i.e., in Heidegger's later philosophy] Being itself was elevated to the rank of absolute subject of history and man condemned to total subjection to Being and its fateful sendings [*Schickungen*]."

47. Habermas, "Heidegger: Werk und Weltanschauung," p. 29. Habermas goes on to observe that Heidegger's thoroughgoing rejection of humanism in the 1946 "Letter" grotesquely coincides with the period in which the truth concerning Hitler's death-camps had become public knowledge.

48. Levinas, *Totality and Infinity.* Many commentators have erroneously accused Levinas of merely seeking to reverse the terms on Heidegger by supplanting ontology with ethics as the "true" first philosophy. But this claim is mistaken insofar as, for Levinas, ethics and ontology are "equiprimordial" phenomena, which relate to one another as communicating vessels, neither of which can be thought without the other. For an account of some of the fundamental philosophical differences between the two thinkers, see A. Peperzak, "Einige Thesen zur Heidegger-Kritik Emmanuel Levinas." In "Metaphysics and Violence," Derrida has formulated an important and much discussed rejoinder to Levinas' position on Heidegger.

49. Heidegger, *Basic Writings*, p. 199.

50. Cited in Ott, *Martin Heidegger*, pp. 316–317.

51. Löwith, *Heidegger: Denker in dürftiger Zeit*, pp. 145–146.

52. Karl-Heinz Haag, *Kritik der neueren Ontologie*, p. 8.

53. Habermas, *The Philosophical Discourse of Modernity*, p. 140.

54. Hans Blumenberg, *The Legitimacy of the Modern Age*, p. 192; emphasis added.

55. Heidegger, *The Question Concerning Technology*, p. 112.

56. For an excellent discussion of the inherent deficiencies of these later Heideggerian categories, see A. Schwan, "Martin Heidegger, Politik und praktische Philosophie," especially pp. 166ff.

57. For two recent attempts to refute the notion of Heidegger as an "antihumanist thinker," see F. Dallmayr, "Ontology of Freedom: Heidegger and Political Philosophy," and J. Caputo, *Radical Hermeneutics*, especially pp. 209ff. For a sophisticated rejoinder to this attempt to redeem a "metahumanist" dimension in Heidegger, see Richard Bernstein, "Heidegger on Humanism," especially pp. 104ff. For another important critique of Heidegger's antihumanism, see Luc Ferry and Alain Renaut, *Heidegger et Les Modernes.*

58. The literature on the subject of freedom, practical philosophy, and personal identity is of course vast. For some representative sources, see, A. Melden, *Free Action;* Charles Taylor, *The Explanation of Behavior* and "What is Human Agency?"; Harry Frankfurter, "Freedom of the Will and the Concept of the Person," *Journal of Philosophy*, 67:1(Jan. 1971):5–20.

To be sure, the notion of "free agency" as well as the conception of the "self" I have just described has come under attack in recent years in works such as Alisdair MacIntyre's *After Virtue* (Notre Dame: Notre Dame University Press, 1981) and Michael Sandel's *Liberalism and the Limits of Justice* (Cambridge: Cambridge University Press, 1982). And not infrequently, the philosophy of Heidegger has been invoked in the debate in support of the communitarian critique of the liberal, Kantian conception of self-legislating subjectivity. Despite its manifest importance, to enter into the terms of this debate with the requisite depth and sensitivity would in the (Heideggerian) context at hand lead us too far afield. But I wish to point out—and I consider this qualification essential—that I do not intend the foregoing, quasi-Kantian portrayal of the ideal of "free agency" to stand as a self-evident, unqualified endorsement of the concept. Rather, I have employed it primarily for the sake of an instructive contrast, i.e., to demonstrate the dangers and risks that are run by a philosophy such as Heidegger's in which the self-evidences of the inherited conceptions of subjectivity are so thoroughly disregarded. This having been said, it should nevertheless be added that however much this Kantian ideal of the "self" may be in need of modification, supplementation, and revision (a point I would concede to the "communitarians"), many of the arguments made against the Heideggerian devaluation of subjectivity might hold, *mutatis mutandis*, against the communitarian critique itself.

59. Heidegger, *Basic Writings*, p. 194.

60. Cf. Bernstein, "Heidegger on Humanism," p. 102: "If we think of humanism as identical with metaphysics and *Gestell* [enframing], which is itself the manifestation of the oblivion and forgetfulness of Being, then Heidegger is opposing such humanism in the strongest possible manner."

61. Heidegger, *Schellings Abhandlung über des Wesen der menschlichen Freiheit*, p. 232; emphasis added.

62. *Gesamtausgabe* 31, p. 135.

63. Heidegger, *Basic Writings*, p. 1?7.

64. Charles Taylor, "What is Human Agency?" p. 33; emphasis added.

65. Heidegger, "Only a God Can Save Us," p. 57.

66. Derrida, "Heidegger: l'enfer des philosophes," p. 172; emphasis added.

67. See Derrida, *De l'esprit*, p. 55: "Every word of the title, *The Self-Affirmation of the German University*, is traversed, steeped, illuminated, determined—I would say both defined and destined—called for by spirit."

68. Ibid. p. 64–65: "By taking the risk of spiritualizing Nazism, he might have been trying to absolve or save it by marking it with this affirmation (spirituality, science, questioning, and so on). By the same token, this sets apart Heidegger's commitment and breaks an affiliation. This [rectoral] address *seems* no longer to belong simply to the 'ideological' camp in which one appeals to dark forces—forces that would not be spiritual, but natural, biological, racial, according to an anything but spiritual interpretation of 'earth and blood.' "

Of course, what Derrida gives with one hand he quickly takes away with the other: the entire analysis is rendered problematic as a result of the italicization of *"seems."*

69. Heidegger, "Declaration of Support for Adolf Hitler and the National Socialist State," in "Political Texts: 1933–1934," pp. 104ff.

70. See Fest, *Hitler*, p. 439.

71. Derrida, "Heidegger: l'enfer des philosophes," p. 173.

72. Pöggeler, "Heidegger und die politische Philosophie" (unpublished MS), p. 21. Moreover, as Pöggeler shows in the same essay, it is likely that Derrida underestimates both Heidegger's lasting attachments to the concept of *Geist*, as well as the lasting power and influence of this concept in the German philosophical tradition, where it is traditionally counterposed to the merely calculative and pragmatic capacities of *Intelligenz*. Thus, Heidegger's apparent rehabilitation of *Geist* in his 1933–1935 writings, rather than being an

unconscionable relapse into "metaphysics" that makes his Nazism comprehensible, may have well functioned as a *critique of totalitarianism*. For totalitarianism, as an absolutization of "technique," is merely a form of universalized *Intelligenz* in Heidegger's eyes. Thus the recourse to *Geist* may have been his way of protesting—of offering "spiritual" resistance—against the vulgar, nihilistic tendencies of Nazism; i.e., against those forces that push toward a consummation of "planetary domination."

73. Lacoue-Labarthe, *La fiction du politique*, pp. 22, 18, 23; emphasis added. On pages 24–25, Lacoue-Labarthe sets forth the following vulgar apologia for Heidegger: "who in this century, confronted with the unprecedented world-historical transformations . . . has not been deceived, whether on the 'right' or the 'left'? And in the name of what could one have avoided being deceived? In the name of 'democracy'? Let us leave that to Raymond Aron, that is, to the official thought of Capital [*la pensée officielle du Capital*] (of nihilism achieved), for whom in effect everything is *valid*." Here, Lacoue-Labarthe not only pursues the dubious strategy of trivializing Heidegger's misdeeds by relativizing them (as if to say that since so many others, on both the right and left, fell victim to totalitarian ideologies, Heidegger's error is excusable; yet, there is an important difference between being an "intellectual sympathizer" of such ideologies, and—as is true in Heidegger's case—holding *political office* in an actual movement and engaging in *political crimes*, such as those in consequence of which Heidegger was stripped of his *venia legendi* in 1945). Moreover, he falls victim to the same error as Derrida—one, moreover, that is of vintage Heideggerian provenance—of failing to comprehend the crucial difference in basic normative structures (separation of powers, civil liberties, due process, etc.) that exist between democracy and totalitarianism. Finally, the jibe at Raymond Aron is, by any standard, wholly gratuitous.

Lacoue-Labarthe runs the risk of a similar mystification with reference to the Holocaust, which he attempts to explain as a natural outcome of the "spiritual logic" of the West: "In the apocalypse of Auschwitz nothing more nor less is revealed than the Occident in its essence—and which has not since ceased to reveal itself" (ibid., p. 36). Here, too, he falls victim to the same faulty method of "explanation through metaphysical abstraction" practiced by Heidegger. Although one can certainly debate the philosophical implications of Auschwitz for the West, it must in the first instance be explained as an *historical* phenomenon; and in the end, it is rather doubtful whether, in the overall logic of historical causality, one could maintain "metaphysical thinking" as even a remotely contributing factor.

74. Although I have elected to follow the customary practice of rendering the Heideggerian category of *Technik* as "technology," it is important to recognize that the implications of the German term are considerably broader than that of the English equivalent. Whereas as we tend to view technology predominantly as an efficient network of means for obtaining desired practical ends, Heidegger employs this term to refer to a metaphysical frame of reference in terms of which all objects in the modern world must be thought. In this respect, what Heidegger means by *Technik* is perhaps best captured by his category of "enframing" (*das Gestell*), discussed below.

75. See, for example, Oswald Spengler, *Man and Technics: A Contribution*

to a Philosophy of Life. Gehlen's philosophical anthropology was of course directly influenced by Heidegger's doctrines. Cf. his *Man in the Age of Technology*, trans. P. Berger (New York: Columbia University Press, 1980).

76. See Heidegger, *Identität und Differenz*, p. 72.

77. Heidegger, *The End of Philosophy*, p. 93.

78. In ibid., p. 91, Heidegger discusses this problem in the following terms: as the unique "fate of the West," metaphysics, "which is to be thought in the manner of the history of Being, is, however, necessary, because Being itself can open out in its truth the difference of Being and beings preserved in itself only when the difference explicitly takes place. *But how can it do this if beings have not first entered the most extreme oblivion of Being, and if at the same time Being has not taken over its unconditional dominance, metaphysically incomprehensible, as the will to will which asserts itself at first and uniquely through the sole precedence of beings (of what is objectively real) over Being?"* Emphasis added.

79. Heidegger, *The Question Concerning Technology*, p. 18.

80. Cf. the discussion of this theory as it relates to Heidegger's thought in note 19 above.

81. In *One-Dimensional Man*, Herbert Marcuse seems to believe that aspects of Heidegger's critique of technology remain serviceable for the ends of social criticism. Thus, as he remarks at one point, "The science of nature develops under the *technological a priori* which projects nature as potential instrumentality, stuff of control and organization. And the apprehension of nature as (hypothetical) instrumentality *precedes* the development of all particular technical organization." In these remarks, Marcuse echoes Heidegger's conviction that technology is not applied science, but modern science itself presupposes technology. There follows a citation from Heidegger's "The Question Concerning Technology" in support of this claim.

82. Heidegger, *The Question Concerning Technology*, p. 33; emphasis added.

83. Ibid., p. 19.

84. Heidegger, *Holzwege*, p. 343.

85. For the most thoroughgoing treatment of this problem in Heidegger's thought, see Guenther Stern (Anders), "On the Pseudo-Concreteness of Heidegger's Philosophy."

86. See Heidegger, *Being and Time*, pp. 449ff. (397ff.).

87. Alfred Schmidt, "Existential Ontology and Historical Materialism in the work of Herbert Marcuse," p. 54 (translation slightly altered).

88. See his interview with R. Wisser in *Antwort*, pp. 21ff.; as well as "The Question Concerning Technology," p. 26, where Heidegger warns against those who are inclined "to rebel helplessly against [technology] and curse it as the work of the devil." "Quite the contrary," he continues, "when we open ourselves to the essence of technology, we find ourselves unexpectedly taken into a freeing claim."

89. Heidegger, *Discourse on Thinking*, p. 51; emphasis added.

90. Bernstein, "Heidegger on Humanism," p. 102.

91. Heidegger, *The Question Concerning Technology*, pp. 62–63.

92. Ibid., p. 34–35.

93. Heidegger, "Only a God Can Save Us," p. 57.

94. Heidegger, *Existence and Being*, p. 282.

95. Ibid., p. 289.

96. Heidegger, "Poetically Man Dwells," in *Poetry, Language, Thought*, pp. 211–229.

97. Or as Alexander Schwan has remarked concerning the distortive influence of this category on Heidegger's thinking: "Heidegger himself levels and blends together divergent and variegated tendencies in the machinations of the will to will and, in consequence, the latter is confirmed and strengthened. Where any and every differentiation falls out of account, the moral and political responsibility of every decision has become obsolete." Schwan, "Zeitkritik und Politik in Heideggers Spätphilosophie," p. 96.

98. Cited in Wolfgang Schirmacher, *Technik und Gelassenheit*, p. 25.

99. See Löwith, *Heidegger: Denker in dürftiger Zeit*, p. 126: "It is the method of common sense, which Heidegger, invoking Hegel, attacks at every opportunity." But as Löwith goes on to show, "common sense" was not merely an object of philosophical ridicule for Hegel. Instead, it often served—as with Aristotle—as a type of external verification of the truth of philosophical speculation.

100. Habermas, *Theory and Practice* (Boston: Beacon, 1973), p. 32.

BIBLIOGRAPHY

Works By Heidegger

German

Aus der Erfahrung des Denkens. Pfullingen: G. Neske, 1954.
Beiträge zur Philosophie. Gesamtausgabe 65. Frankfurt: V. Klostermann, 1989.
Einführung in die Metaphysik. Tübingen: M. Niemeyer, 1953.
Erläuterungen zu Hölderlins Dichtung. Frankfurt: V. Klostermann, 1951.
Gelassenheit. Pfullingen: G. Neske, 1959.
Die Grundbegriffe der Metaphysik: Welt-Endlichkeit-Einsamkeit. Gesamtausgabe
    29–30. Frankfurt: V. Klostermann, 1983.
Heraklit. Gesamtausgabe 55. Frankfurt: V. Klostermann, 1979.
Hölderlins Hymnen "Germanien" und "Der Rhein."Gesamtausgabe 39. Frankfurt:
    V. Klostermann, 1980.
Hölderlins Hymne "Der Ister." Gesamtausgabe 53. Frankfurt: V. Klostermann,
    1984.
Holzwege. Frankfurt: V. Klostermann, 1980.
Identität und Differenz. Pfullingen: G. Neske, 1957.
Kant und das Problem der Metaphysik. Frankfurt: V. Klostermann, 1973.
Letter to Carl Schmitt. August 22, 1933. In *Telos* 72 (1987): 132.
"Martin Heidegger im Gespräch" (with R. Wisser). In *Antwort: Martin Heidegger
    im Gespräch.* Edited by Günther Neske and Emil Kettering. Pfullingen: G.
    Neske, 1988.
Nietzsche. 2 vols. Pfullingen: G. Neske, 1961.
"Nur noch ein Gott kann uns retten." In *Antwort: Martin Heidegger im Gespräch.*
    Edited by Günther Neske and Emil Kettering. Pfullingen: G. Neske, 1988.

Bibliography

Parmenides. Gesamtausgabe 54. Frankfurt: V. Klostermann, 1982.
Der Satz vom Grund. Pfullingen: G. Neske, 1957.
Schellings Abhandlung über das Wesen der menschlichen Freiheit. Tübingen: M. Niemeyer, 1971.
Sein und Zeit. Tübingen: M. Niemeyer, 1972.
Die Selbstbehauptung der deutschen Universität/Das Rektorat, 1933/34: Tatsachen und Gedanken. Frankfurt: V. Klostermann, 1983.
Unterwegs zur Sprache. Pfullingen: G. Neske, 1959.
Vorträge und Aufsätze. Pfullingen: G. Neske, 1954.
Was heisst Denken? Tübingen: M. Niemeyer, 1954.
Wegmarken. Frankfurt: V. Klostermann, 1967.

English Translation

Basic Problems of Phenomenology. Translated by Albert Hofstadter. Bloomington: Indiana University Press, 1982.
Basic Writings. Edited by David F. Krell. New York: Harper & Row, 1977.
Being and Time. Translated by J. Macquarrie and E. Robinson. New York: Harper & Row, 1962.
Discourse on Thinking. Translated by J. M. Anderson and E. H. Freund. New York: Harper & Row, 1966.
"A Discussion between Ernst Cassirer and Martin Heidegger." Translated by Francis Slade. In *The Existentialist Tradition: Selected Writings*. Edited by Nino Lagiulli. Garden City: Doubleday-Anchor, 1971.
Early Greek Thinking. Translated by David Farrell Krell and Frank Capuzzi. New York: Harper & Row, 1975.
The End of Philosophy. Translated by Joan Stambaugh. New York: Harper & Row, 1973.
The Essence of Reasons. Translated by Terrence Malick. Evanston: Northwestern University Press, 1969.
Existence and Being. Edited by Werner Brock. Chicago: Regnery-Gateway, 1949.
Identity and Difference. Translated by Joan Stambaugh. New York: Harper & Row, 1969.
An Introduction to Metaphysics. Translated by Ralph Manheim. New Haven: Yale University Press, 1959.
Kant and the Problem of Metaphysics. Translated by James S. Churchill. Bloomington: Indiana University Press, 1962.
"Martin Heidegger: An Interview" (with R. Wisser). Translated by V. Guagliardo and R. Pambrun. *Listening* 6 (1971): 34–40.
Nietzsche I. The Will to Power as Art. Edited and translated by David F. Krell. New York: Harper & Row, 1982.
Nietzsche II. The Eternal Recurrence of the Same. Edited and translated by David F. Krell. New York: Harper & Row, 1984.
Nietzsche III. The Will to Power as Knowledge and Metaphysics. Edited by David F. Krell; translated by Joan Stambaugh. New York: Harper & Row, 1987.
Nietzsche IV. Nihilism. Edited by David F. Krell; translated by Frank A. Capuzzi. New York: Harper & Row, 1982.
On Time and Being. Translated by Joan Stambaugh. New York: Harper & Row, 1972.

On the Way to Language. Translated by Peter D. Hertz and Joan Stambaugh. New York: Harper & Row, 1971.

"Only a God Can Save Us." In *Heidegger: The Man and the Thinker.* Chicago: Precedent Publishing, 1981.

"Plato's Doctrine of Truth." Translated by John Barlow. In *Philosophy in The Twentieth Century,* vol. 3. Edited by William Barrett and Henry D. Aiken. New York: Random House, 1962.

Poetry, Language, Thought. Translated by Albert Hofstadter. New York: Harper & Row, 1971.

"Political Texts, 1933–1934." *New German Critique* 45 (1988): 96–114.

"Preface." In William J. Richardson, *Heidegger Through Phenomenology to Thought.* The Hague: Martinus Nijhoff, 1963.

The Question of Being. Translated by W. Kluback and J. T. Wilde. London: Vision Press, 1959.

The Question Concerning Technology and Other Essays. Translated by William Lovitt. New York: Harper & Row, 1977.

"The Self-Assertion of the German University" and "The Rectorate 1933–34: Facts and Thoughts." Translated by Karsten Harries. *Review of Metaphysics* 38 (1985): 467–502.

Schelling's Treatise on Human Freedom. Translated by Joan Stambaugh. Athens: Ohio University Press, 1985.

What is Called Thinking? Translated by F. D. Wieck and J. Glenn Gray. New York: Harper & Row, 1968.

"Why Do I Stay in the Provinces?" In *Heidegger: The Man and the Thinker.* Edited by Thomas Sheehan. Chicago: Precedent Publishing, 1981.

Additional Works

Abendroth, Wolfgang. "Das Unpolitische als Wesensmerkmal der deutschen Universität." In *Nationalsozialismus und die deutsche Universität.* Berlin: Walter de Gruyter, 1966.

Adorno, Theodor W. *The Jargon of Authenticity.* Translated by Kurt Tarnowski and Frederic Will. Evanston: Northwestern University Press, 1973.

Adorno, Theodor W. *Negative Dialectics.* Translated by E. B. Ashton. New York: Seabury Press, 1973.

Antwort: Martin Heidegger im Gespräch. Edited by Günther Neske and Emil Kettering. Pfullingen: G. Neske, 1988.

Arendt, Hannah. *The Human Condition.* Chicago: University of Chicago Press, 1958.

Arendt, Hannah. *The Origins of Totalitarianism.* New York: Harcourt, Brace, Jovanovich, 1973.

Bastian, Klaus-Frieder. *Das Politische bei Ernst Jünger: Nonkonformismus und Kompromiss der Innerlichkeit.* Freiburg: Johannes Krause, 1963.

Baudrillard, Jean. "Zu spät!" *Die Zeit.* Februrary 5, 1988.

Bernstein, Richard. "Heidegger on Humanism." *Praxis International* 5 (1985): 95–114.

Blitz, Mark. *Heidegger's Being and Time and the Possibility of Political Philosophy.* Ithaca: Cornell University Press, 1981.

Blumenberg, Hans. *The Legitimacy of the Modern Age.* Translated by Robert Wallace. Cambridge, Mass.: MIT Press, 1983.

Bohrer, Karl Heinz. *Ästhetik des Schreckens*. Munich: Hanser, 1978.

Bourdieu, Pierre. *L'Ontologie politique de Martin Heidegger*. Paris: Editions de Minuit, 1988.

Bourdieu, Pierre. "Zurück zu der Geschichte/Debatte Derrida-Bourdieu." In Jürg Altwegg. *Die Heidegger Kontroverse*. Frankfurt: Athenäum, 1988.

Broszat, Martin. *The Hitler State*. Translated by John Hiden. New York and London: Longman, 1981.

Brunkhorst, Hauke. *Der Intellektuelle im Land der Mandarine*. Frankfurt: Suhrkamp Verlag, 1987.

Caputo, John. *Radical Hermeneutics: Repetition, Deconstruction, and the Hermeneutic Project*. Bloomington: Indiana University Press, 1987.

Cassirer, Ernst. *The Myth of the State*. New Haven: Yale University Press, 1946.

Chytry, Josef. *The Aesthetic State: A Quest in Modern German Thought*. Berkeley: University of California Press, 1989.

Dahrendorff, Ralf. *Society and Democracy in Germany*. New York: Norton, 1979.

Dallmayr, Fred. "Heidegger and Marxism." *Praxis International* 7 (1987): 207–224.

Dallmayr, Fred. "Ontology of Freedom: Heidegger and Political Philosophy." *Political Theory* 12 (1984): 204–234.

Dallmayr, Fred. *Twilight of Subjectivity: Contributions to a Post-Individualist Theory of Politics*. Amherst: University of Massachusetts Press, 1981.

Derrida, Jacques. *De l'esprit: Heidegger et la question*. Paris: Editions Galilée, 1987.

Derrida, Jacques. "The Ends of Man." In *Margins of Philosophy*. Translated by Alan Bass. Chicago: University of Chicago Press, 1983.

Derrida, Jacques. "Geschlecht II: Heidegger's Hand." Translated by John P. Leavey, Jr. In John Sallis, *Deconstruction and Philosophy: The Texts of Jacques Derrida*. Chicago: University of Chicago Press, 1987.

Derrida, Jacques. "*Geschlecht*: sexual difference, ontological difference." *Research in Phenomenology* 13 (1983): 65–83.

Derrida, Jacques. "Heidegger: l'enfer des philosophes." (Interview). *Le Nouvel Observateur*, November 6–12, 1987; pp. 170–174.

Derrida, Jacques. "Violence and Metaphysics." In *Writing and Difference*. Chicago: University of Chicago Press, 1978.

Derrida, Jacques. "*Ousia* and *Grammē*." In *Margins of Philosophy*. Translated by Alan Bass. Chicago: University of Chicago Press, 1983.

Dilthey, Wilhelm. *Der Aufbau der geschichtlichen Welt in den Geisteswissenschaften*. Frankfurt: Suhrkamp, 1970.

Dudek, Peter. *Erziehung durch Arbeit: Arbeitslagerbewegung und freiwilliger Arbeitsdienst, 1920–1935*. Opladen: Westdeutscher Verlag, 1988.

Ebeling, Hans. "Die Bedeutung der praktischen Selbstbeziehung in der neueren Heidegger-Kritik." *Philosophische Rundschau* 1/2 (1979): 135–143.

Ebeling, Hans. *Selbsterhaltung und Selbstbewusstsein: Zur Analytik von Freiheit und Tod*. Freiburg: Alber, 1979.

Elias, Norbert. *The Civilizing Process*. New York: Urizen, 1978.

Farias, Victor. *Heidegger und der Nationalsozialismus*. (Expanded German edition of *Heidegger et le Nazisme*). With a Foreword by Jürgen Habermas. Frankfurt: S. Fischer, 1989.

Farias, Victor. *Heidegger et le Nazisme*. Translated by Myriam Benarroch and Jean-Baptiste Grasset. Lagrasse: Editions Verdier, 1987.

Fédier, François. *Heidegger: Anatomie d'un scandale*. Paris: Laffont, 1988.

Ferry Luc and Alain Renaut. *Heidegger et les Modernes*. Paris: Editions Grasset, 1988.

Fest, Joachim. *Hitler*. Translated by Richard and Clara Winston. New York: Random House, 1975.

Frankfurter, Harry. "Freedom of the Will and the Concept of the Person." *Journal of Philosophy* 67:1 (January 1971): 5–20.

Franzen, Winfried. "Die Sehnsucht nach Härte und Schwere." In *Heidegger und die praktische Philosophie*. Edited by Annemarie Gethmann-Siefert and Otto Pöggeler. Frankfurt: Suhrkamp, 1988.

Franzen, Winfried. *Von der Existenzialontologie zur Seinsgeschichte*. Meisenheim am Glan: Anton Hein, 1975.

Gadamer, Hans-Georg. *Philosophical Hermeneutics*. Translated by David E. Linge. Berkeley: University of California Press, 1976.

Gadamer, Hans-Georg. Review of Pierre Bourdieu, *Die politische Ontologie Martin Heideggers*. *Philosophische Rundschau* 26 (1979): 143–149.

Gadamer, Hans-Georg. *Truth and Method*. New York: Seabury, 1975.

Gethmann, Carl Friedrich. "Heideggers Konzeption des Handelns in *Sein und Zeit*." In *Heidegger und die praktische Philosophie*, Edited by Annemarie Gethmann-Siefert and Otto Pöggeler. Frankfurt: Suhrkamp, 1988.

Giddens, Anthony. *The Constitution of Society*. Berkeley: University of California Press, 1985.

Goldmann, Lucien. *Lukács and Heidegger*. Translated by William Q. Boelhower. London: Routledge and Kegan Paul, 1977.

Haag, Karl-Heinz. *Kritik der neueren Ontologie*. Stuttgart: W. Kohlhammer, 1960.

Habermas, Jürgen. "Martin Heidegger? Nazi, sicher ein Nazi!" (Interview with M. Hunyadi). In *Die Heidegger Kontroverse*. Edited by Jürg Altwegg. Frankfurt: Athenäum, 1988.

Habermas, Jürgen. "Heidegger: Werk und Weltanschauung." Foreword to Victor Farias, *Heidegger und der Nationalsozialismus*. Frankfurt: S. Fischer, 1989. English translation ("Work and Weltanschauung: the Heidegger Controversy from a German Perspective") in *Critical Inquiry* 15/2 (1989): 431–456.

Habermas, Jürgen. "Martin Heidegger." In *Philosophisch-Politische Profilen*. Frankfurt: Suhrkamp, 1971.

Habermas, Jürgen. *The Philosophical Discourse of Modernity*. Translated by Frederick Lawrence. Cambridge, Mass.: MIT Press, 1987.

Die Heidegger Kontroverse. Edited by Jürg Altwegg. Frankfurt: Athenäum, 1988.

Heidegger: the Man and the Thinker. Edited by Thomas Sheehan. Chicago: Precedent, 1981.

Heidegger and Modern Philosophy. Edited by Michael Murray. New Haven: Yale University Press, 1978.

"Heidegger et la pensée Nazie." (Contains texts by Maurice Blanchot, Hans-Georg Gadamer, Philippe Lacoue-Labarthe, François Fédier, and Emmanuel Levinas.) *Le Nouvel Observateur*. January 22–28, 1988, pp. 41–49.

"Heidegger, la philosophie, et la Nazisme." (Contains texts by Pierre Aubenque, Henri Crétella, Michel Déguy, François Fédier, Gérard Granel, Stephane Moses, and Alain Renaut.) *Le Débat* 48 (1988): 113–176.

Heidegger: Perspektiven zur Deutung seines Werkes. Edited by Otto Pöggeler. Königstein: Athenäum, 1984.

Heidegger und die praktische Philosophie. Edited by Annemarie Gethmann-Siefert and Otto Pöggeler. Frankfurt: Suhrkamp, 1988.

Herrmann, Friedrich-Wilhelm von. *Heideggers Philosophie der Kunst.* Frankfurt: V. Klostermann, 1979.

Herrmann, Friedrich-Wilhelm von. *Die Selbstinterpretation Martin Heideggers.* Königstein: Athenäum, 1964.

Herf, Jeffrey. *Reactionary Modernism: Technology, Culture, and Politics in Weimar and the Third Reich.* New York: Cambridge University Press, 1984.

Hollerbach, Alexander. "Im Schatten des Jahres 1933: Erik Wolf und Martin Heidegger." In *Freiburger Universitätsblätter* 92 (1986): 33–48.

Hühnerfeld, Paul. *In Sachen Heidegger: Versuch über ein deutsches Genie.* Hamburg: Hoffman und Campe, 1959.

Jaspers, Karl. *Notizen zu Martin Heidegger.* Edited by Hans Saner. Munich: Piper Verlag, 1988.

Jaspers, Karl. *Philosophische Autobiographie.* Munich: Piper, 1978.

Jaspers, Karl. *The Philosophy of Karl Jaspers.* Edited by P. A. Schlipp. La Salle, Ill.: Open Court, 1981.

Jay, Martin. "The Rise of Hermeneutics and the Crisis of Ocularcentrism." *Poetics Today* 9:2 (1988): 307–326.

Joll, James. *The Anarchists.* Cambridge, Mass.: Harvard University Press, 1980.

Jonas, Hans. "Heideggers Entschlossenheit und Entschluss." In *Antwort: Martin Heidegger im Gespräch.* Edited by Günther Neske and Emil Kettering. Pfullingen: G. Neske, 1988.

Jünger, Ernst. *Der Arbeiter: Herrschaft und Gestalt.* In *Werke,* vol. 6. Stuttgart: Ernst Klett, n.d.

Jünger, Ernst. *Kampf als inneres Erlebnis.* Berlin: E.S. Mittler, 1922.

Jünger, Ernst. "Die totale Mobilmachung." In *Werke,* vol. 5. Stuttgart: Ernst Klett, n.d.

Kettering, Emil. "Heidegger und die Politik: Stationen einer Diskussion." In *Antwort: Martin Heidegger im Gespräch.* Edited by Günther Neske and Emil Kettering. Pfullingen: G. Neske, 1988.

Klemperer, Klemens von. *Germany's New Conservatism: Its History and Dilemma in the Twentieth Century.* Princeton: Princeton University Press, 1957.

Krockow, Christian Graf von. *Die Entscheidung: Eine Untersuchung über Ernst Jünger, Carl Schmitt, Martin Heidegger.* Stuttgart: Ferdinand Enke, 1959.

Lacoue-Labarthe, Philippe. *La fiction du politique.* Strasbourg: Associations des Publications des Universités de Strasbourg, 1987.

Levinas, Emmanuel. *Ethics and Infinity.* Translated by Richard Cohen. Pittsburgh: Duquesne University Press, 1985.

Levinas, Emmanuel. *Totality and Infinity.* Translated by Alphonso Lingis. Pittsburgh: Duquesne University Press, 1969.

Lieber, Hans-Joachim. "Die deutsche Lebensphilosophie und ihre Folgen." In *Nationalsozialismus und die deutsche Universität.* Berlin: Walter de Gruyter, 1966.

Loose, Gerhard. *Ernst Jünger.* New York: Twayne, 1974.

Löwith, Karl. *Heidegger: Denker in dürftiger Zeit*. In *Sämtliche Schriften*, vol. 8. Stuttgart: J. B. Metzler, 1984.

Löwith, Karl. *Mein Leben in Deutschland vor und nach 1933*. Stuttgart, J. B. Metzler, 1986.

Löwith, Karl. "The Political Implications of Heidegger's Existentialism." Translated by Richard Wolin and Melissa Cox. *New German Critique* 45 (1988). (First appeared as "Les Implications politiques de la philosophie de l'existence chez Heidegger." *Les Temps Modernes* 14 [1946]: 347ff.)

Löwy, Michael. *Georg Lukács: From Romanticism to Bolshevism*. London: New Left Books, 1979.

Löwy, Michael. *Rédemption et Utopie: le judaisme libertaire en Europe centrale*. Paris: Presses Universitaires de France, 1988.

Lukács, Georg. *The Destruction of Reason*. Translated by Peter Palmer. London: Merlin Press, 1980.

Lukács, Georg. *Soul and Form*. Translated by Anna Bostock. Cambridge, Mass.: MIT Press, 1974.

Lukács, Georg. *The Theory of the Novel*. Translated by Anna Bostock. Cambridge, Mass.: MIT Press, 1971.

Lyotard, Jean-François. *Heidegger et les Juifs*. Paris: Editions Galilée, 1988.

Marcuse, Herbert. "Heidegger and Politics: An Interview with Frederick Olafson." In *Marcuse: Critical Theory and the Promise of Utopia*. Edited by R. Pippen et al. South Hadley, Mass.: Bergin and Garvey, 1987.

Marcuse, Herbert. "Der Kampf gegen Liberalismus im totaltärischen Staat." *Kultur und Gesellschaft* I. Frankfurt: Suhrkamp, 1971.

Marcuse, Herbert. Letters to Martin Heidegger (August 28, 1947 and May 13 1948). *Pflasterstrand* (Frankfurt) 279–280 (1988): 46–48. English translation forthcoming in *New German Critique*.

Marcuse, Herbert. *One-Dimensional Man: Studies in the Ideology of Advanced Industrial Society*. Boston: Beacon Press, 1964.

"Martin Heidegger: Ein Philosoph und die Politik." *Freiburger Universitätsblätter* 92 (June 1986).

Martin Heidegger: Innen- und Aussenansichten. Edited by Forum für Philosophie Bad Homburg. Frankfurt: Suhrkamp, 1989.

Marten, Rainer. "Heideggers Geist." *Allmende* 20 (1988): 82ff.

Marten, Rainer. "Ein rassistisches Konzept von Humanität." *Badische Zeitung*. December 19–20, 1987.

Marx, Karl. *The Marx-Engels Reader*. Edited by Robert C. Tucker. New York: Norton, 1978.

Marx, Werner. *Heidegger and the Tradition*. Evanston: Northwestern University Press, 1971.

Marx, Werner. *Is There a Measure on the Earth? Foundations for a Non-Metaphysical Ethics*. Translated by T. J. Nenon and R. Lilly. Chicago: University of Chicago Press, 1987.

Megill, Allan. *Prophets of Extremity: Nietzsche, Heidegger, Foucault, Derrida*. Berkeley: University of California Press, 1984.

Mohler, Armin. *Die konservative Revolution*. Stuttgart: Friedrich Vorwerk, 1950.

Mosse, George L. *The Crisis of the German Ideology: The Intellectual Origins of the Third Reich*. New York: Grosset & Dunlap, 1964.

Mosse, George L. *Germans and Jews: The Right, the Left and the Search for a "Third Force" in Pre-Nazi Germany.* New York: Howard Fertig, 1970.

Müller, Max. "Ein Gespräch mit Max Müller." *Freiburger Universitätsblätter* 92 (June 1986): 13–31.

Neumann, Franz. *Behemoth: The Structure and Practice of National Socialism.* New York: Oxford University Press 1944.

Nietzsche, Friedrich. *The Will to Power.* Translated by Walter Kaufmann and R. J. Hollingdale. New York: Vintage, 1967.

Ott, Hugo. "Der junge Martin Heidegger: Gymnasial-Konviktszeit und Studium." In *Freiburger Diözesan-Archiv* 104 (1984): 315–325.

Ott, Hugo. "Martin Heidegger als Rektor der Universität Freiburg 1933/34." Part I. *Zeitschrift für die Geschichte des Oberrheins* 132 (1984): 343–358.

Ott, Hugo. "Martin Heidegger als Rektor der Universität Freiburg i. Br. 1933/34." Part I. *Zeitschrift des Breisgau-Geschichtsvereins* 102 (1984): 121–136.

Ott, Hugo. "Martin Heidegger als Rektor der Universität Freiburg i. Br. 1933/34." Part II. *Zeitschrift des Breisgau-Geschichtsvereins* 103 (1984): 107–130.

Ott, Hugo. "Martin Heidegger und der Nationalsozialismus." In *Heidegger und die praktische Philosophie.* Edited by Annemarie Gethmann-Siefert and Otto Pöggeler. Frankfurt: Suhrkamp, 1988.

Ott, Hugo. "Martin Heidegger und die Universität Freiburg nach 1945: Ein Beispiel für die Auseinandersetzung mit der politischen Vergangenheit." *Historisches Jahrbuch* 105 (1985): 95–128.

Ott, Hugo. *Martin Heidegger: Unterwegs zu seiner Biographie.* Frankfurt: Campus, 1988.

Peperzak, Adriaan. "Einige Thesen zur Heidegger-Kritik von Emmanuel Levinas." In *Heidegger und die praktische Philosophie.* Edited by Annemarie Gethmann-Siefert and Otto Pöggeler. Frankfurt: Suhrkamp, 1988.

Petzet, Heinrich Wiegand. *Auf einen Stern zugehen: Begegnungen und Gespräche mit Martin Heidegger, 1929–1976.* Frankfurt: Societät, 1983.

Plessner, Helmut. *Die verspätete Nation.* Frankfurt: Suhrkamp, 1974.

Pöggeler, Otto. "Besinnung oder Ausflucht: Heideggers ursprünglicheres Denken." In *Zerstörung des moralischen Selbstbewusstein: Chance oder Gefährdung.* Edited by Forum für Philosophie Bad Homburg. Frankfurt: Suhrkamp, 1988.

Pöggeler, Otto. "Den Führer führen? Heidegger und kein Ende." *Philosophische Rundschau* 32 (1985): 26–67.

Pöggeler, Otto. "Heideggers politisches Selbstverständnis." In *Heidegger und die praktische Philosophie.* Edited by Annemarie Gethmann-Siefert and Otto Pöggeler. Frankfurt: Suhrkamp, 1988.

Pöggeler, Otto. *Martin Heideggers Path of Thinking.* With an Afterword to the Second Edition. Translated by Daniel Magurshak and Sigmund Barber. Atlantic Highlands, N.J.: Humanities Press, 1987.

Pöggeler, Otto. *Philosophie und Politik bei Heidegger.* Freiburg: Alber, 1972.

Rauschning, Hermann. *The Revolution of Nihilism.* New York: Alliance, 1939.

Richardson, William J. *Heidegger: Through Phenomenology to Thought.* The Hague: Martin Nijhoff, 1963.

Ringer, Fritz. *The Decline of the German Mandarins: The German Academic Community, 1890–1933.* Cambridge, Mass.: Harvard University Press, 1969.

Rorty, Richard. "Taking Philosophy Seriously." *The New Republic.* April 11, 1988; pp. 31–34.

Rosenmeyer, Leopold. "Gesellschaftsbild und Kulturkritik Martin Heideggers." *Das Archiv für Rechts- und Sozialphilosophie* 46 (1960): 1–38.

Schirmacher, Wolfgang. *Technik und Gelassenheit*. Freiburg: Alber, 1983.

Schmidt, Alfred. "Existential Ontology and Historical Materialism in the Work of Herbert Marcuse." In *Marcuse: A Critical Theory and the Promise of Utopia*. Edited by R. Pippen et al. South Hadley, Mass.: Bergin and Garvey, 1988.

Schmitt, Carl. *Der Begriff des Politischen*. Berlin: Duncker und Humblot, 1963.

Schmitt, Carl. *Political Theology*. Translated by G. Schwab. Cambridge, Mass., M.I.T. Press, 1985.

Schmitt, Carl. *Positionen und Begriffe*. Hamburg: Hanseatische Verlaganstaltung, 1940.

Schmitt, Carl. *Staat, Bewegung, Volk*. Hamburg: Hanseatische Verlaganstaltung, 1933.

Schmitt, Carl. "Totaler Feind, totaler Krieg, totaler Staat." In *Positionen und Begriffe*. Hamburg: Hanseatische Verlaganstaltung, 1940.

Schmitt, Carl. "Weiterentwicklung des totalen Staats in Deutschland." In *Positionen und Begriffe*. Hamburg: Hanseatische Verlaganstaltung, 1940.

Schmitt, Carl. "Die Wendung zum totalen Staat." In *Positionen und Begriffe*. Hamburg: Hanseatische Verlaganstaltung, 1940.

Schnädelbach, Herbert. *Philosophy in Germany from 1831 to 1933*. Translated by Eric Matthews. Cambridge: Cambridge University Press, 1984.

Schneeberger, Guido. *Ergänzungen zu einer Heidegger Bibliographie*. Bern: Suhr, 1960.

Schneeberger, Guido. *Nachlese zu Heidegger*. Bern: Suhr, 1962.

Schoenbaum, David. *Hitler's Social Revolution*. London: Weidenfeld and Nicolson, 1966.

Schwan, Alexander. "Martin Heidegger, Politik und praktische Philosophie." *Philsophisches Jahrbuch* 81 (1974): 148–171.

Schwan, Alexander. *Politische Philosophie im Denken Heideggers*. With an Afterword to the Second Edition. Opladen: Westdeutscher Verlag, 1988.

Schwan, Alexander. "Zeitkritik und Politik bei Heideggers Spätphilosophie." In *Heidegger und die praktische Philosophie*. Edited by Annemarie Gethmann-Siefert and Otto Pöggeler. Frankfurt: Suhrkamp, 1988.

Schwarz, Hans-Peter. *Der konservative Anarchist: Politik und Zeitkritik Ernst Jüngers*. Freiburg: Rombach Verlag, 1962.

Schürmann, Reiner. *Heidegger on Being and Acting: From Principles to Anarchy*. Translated by Christine-Marie Gros. Bloomington: Indiana University Press, 1987.

Schürmann, Reiner. "Political Thinking in Heidegger." *Social Research* 45 (1978).

Schürmann, Reiner. "Principles Precarious: On the Origin of the Political in Heidegger." In *Heidegger: the Man and the Thinker*. Edited by Thomas Sheehan. Chicago: Precedent, 1981.

Schweppenhäuser, Hermann. *Studien über die Heideggersche Sprachtheorie*. Munich: Edition Text und Kritik, 1988.

Sheehan, Thomas. "Heidegger and the Nazis." *The New York Review of Books*. June 15, 1988; pp. 38–47.

Sinn, Dieter. "Heideggers Spätphilosophie." In *Philosophische Rundschau* 14 (1967): 81–183.

Bibliography

Sontheimer, Kurt. *Antidemokratisches Denken in der Weimarer Republik.* Munich: Nymphenburger Verlagshandlung, 1962.

Spengler, Oswald. *The Decline of the West.* 2 vols. Translated by Charles Francis Atkinson. New York: Knopf, 1986.

Spengler, Oswald. *Der Mensch und die Technik.* Munich: Beck, 1931.

Spengler, Oswald. *Preussentum und Sozialismus.* Munich: Beck, 1924.

Steiner, Georg. *Martin Heidegger.* New York: Viking Press, 1978.

Steiner, Georg. "Heidegger, Again." *Salmagundi* 82–83 (Spring–Summer 1989): 31–56.

Stern, Fritz. *The Failure of Illiberalism: Essays on the Political Culture of Modern Germany.* New York: Knopf, 1972.

Stern, Fritz. *The Politics of Cultural Despair: A Study in the Rise of the Germanic Ideology.* New York: Doubleday, 1965.

Stern, Guenther. "On the Pseudo-Concreteness of Heidegger's Philosophy." *Philosophy and Phenomenological Research* 9 (1948): 337–370.

Stern, J. P. *Ernst Jünger: A Writer of Our Time.* Cambridge: Bowes and Bowes, 1953.

Stern, J. P. *Hitler: The Führer and the People.* London: Fontana, 1979.

Sternberger, Dolf. "Die grossen Worte des Rektors Heidegger: eine philosophische Untersuchung." *Frankfurter Allgemeine Zeitung.* March 2, 1984.

Strauss, Leo. *Studies in Platonic Political Philosophy.* Chicago: University of Chicago Press, 1983.

"A Symposium on Heidegger and Nazism." Edited and introduced by Arnold I. Davidson. *Critical Inquiry* 15:2 (1989): 407–488.

Taylor, Charles. *The Explanation of Behavior.* New York: Humanities Press, 1964.

Taylor, Charles. "What is Human Agency?" In *Philosophical Papers.* 2 vols. Cambridge: Cambridge University Press, 1985.

Tertulian, Nicholas. "Quand le discours Heideggerien se mue en prise de position politique." *La Quinzaine Littéraire* 499 (December 1987): 22–24.

Theunissen, Michael. *The Other: Studies in the Social Ontology of Husserl, Heidegger, Sartre, and Buber.* Translated by Christopher Macann. Cambridge, Mass.: MIT Press, 1986.

Tugendhat, Ernst. "Heideggers Idee von Wahrheit." In *Heidegger: Perspektiven zur Deutung seines Werkes.* Edited by Otto Pöggeler. Königstein: Athenäum, 1984.

Tugendhat, Ernst. *Der Wahrheitsbegriff bei Husserl und Heidegger.* Berlin: Walter de Gruyter, 1967.

Waterhouse, Roger. *A Heidegger Critique: A Critical Examination of the Existential Phenomenology of Martin Heidegger.* Sussex: Harvester Press, 1981.

Weber, Max. *From Max Weber: Essays in Sociology.* Translated by Hans Gerth and C. Wright Mills. New York: Oxford University Press, 1946.

Wolin, Richard. "Carl Schmitt, existentialisme politique, et l'état total." *Les Temps Modernes* 523 (1990): 50–88. English translation forthcoming in *Theory and Society,* 1990.

Wolin, Richard. "The French Heidegger Debate." *New German Critique* 45 (1988): 135–162.

Wolin, Richard. "La philosophie politique de *Sein und Zeit.*" *Les Temps Modernes* 510 (1989): 5–54.

Wolin, Richard. "Recherches récentes sûr la relation de Martin Heidegger au national socialisme." *Les Temps Modernes* 495 (1987): 56–85.

Zimmerman, Michael. "The Thorn In Heidegger's Side: The Question of National Socialism." *The Philosophical Forum* 20:4 (1989): 326–365.

INDEX

217

CPSIA information can be obtained
at www.ICGtesting.com
Printed in the USA
LVOW04s0926071016

507657LV00005B/15/P